Saint James's Catapult

SAINT JAMES'S CATAPULT

The Life and Times
of Diego Gelmírez
of
Santiago de Compostela

R. A. FLETCHER

CLARENDON PRESS · OXFORD
1984

Oxford University Press, Walton Street, Oxford OX2 6DP

London Glasgow New York Toronto
Delhi Bombay Calcutta Madras Karachi
Kuala Lumpur Singapore Hong Kong Tokyo
Nairobi Dar es Salaam Cape Town
Melbourne Auckland

and associated companies in
Beirut Berlin Ibadan Mexico City Nicosia

Oxford is a trade mark of Oxford University Press

Published in the United States
by Oxford University Press, New York

British Library Cataloguing in Publication Data
Fletcher, R. A.
Saint James's catapult: the life and times of
Diego Gelmírez of Santiago de Compostela.
1. Gelmírez, Diego   2. Christian
biography—Spain
I. Title
270.4'092'4   BR275.G/
ISBN 0-19-822581-4

Library of Congress Cataloging in Publication Data
Fletcher, R. A. (Richard A.)
Saint James's catapult.
Bibliography: p.
Includes index.
1. Gelmírez, Diego, d. 1140.   2. Catholic Church—
Spain—Santiago de Compostela—Bishops—Biography.
3. Santiago de Compostela (Spain)—Biography.
4. Galicia (Spain : Region)—History.   5. James, the
Greater, Saint—Cult.   6. Christian pilgrims and
pilgrimages—Spain—Santiago de Compostela.   I. Title.
BX4705.G417F56 1984   282'.092'4 [B]   83-24019
ISBN 0-19-822581-4

Typeset by Joshua Associates, Oxford
Printed in Great Britain
at the University Press, Oxford

To the memory of
Denis Bethell
1934–1981

'Any idea how many times round the deck make a mile?'

'None, I'm afraid,' said Tony. 'But I should think you must have walked a great distance.'

'Twenty-two times. One soon gets out of sorts at sea if you're used to an active life. She's not much of a boat. Travel with this line often?'

'Never before.'

'Ah. Thought you might have been in business in the islands. Not many tourists going out this time of year. Just the other way about. All coming home, if you see what I mean. Going far?'

'Demerara.'

'Ah. Looking for minerals perhaps?'

'No, to tell you the truth I am looking for a city.'

The genial passenger was surprised and then laughed. 'Sounded just like you said you were looking for a city.'

'Yes.'

'That *was* what you said?'

'Yes.'

'I thought it sounded like that . . . well, so long. I must do another few rounds before dinner.'

Evelyn Waugh, A Handful of Dust

Preface

This book is related to my earlier study of *The Episcopate in the kingdom of León in the twelfth century* published in 1978: it has grown out of the same concerns; it has at once a narrower focus and a longer reach; it is intended for a different readership. I have written it at home, in odd moments of leisure, over a period of four years and more. This desultory mode of composition will have made a book always intended to have something of a discursive character even more rambling than it might otherwise have been. For this and other shortcomings arising from the circumstances of composition the reader's indulgence is asked.

That the book was completed at all is owing more than I can express to my wife Rachel. She has fed me, left me alone, shielded me from interruption, and in the most selfless way simply put up with me during the hard slog, the bouts of depression, the moments of elation, which attend on authorship. I thank her from the bottom of my heart.

To compose a work of this kind in an isolated farmhouse in the depths of the North Riding of Yorkshire, far from a good academic library, is to ask for trouble. It is also to contract many debts. The final stages of my preliminary research were made possible by a generous grant by the British Academy from the Small Grants Research Fund in the Humanities: I am most grateful for this assistance. In the course of writing the book I have incurred many debts to scholars who have kindly sent me copies of their books or articles. These I have acknowledged at the appropriate place in my footnotes. There remain many friends who have with great generosity helped me by answering questions, checking references, procuring photocopies, buying books for me, and (not least) by giving me hospitality on my journeys southward. I wish in particular to thank the following: in Spain, Don Antonio García y García, Professor of Canon Law at the Universidad Pontificia of Salamanca; in Cambridge, Peter Linehan; in London, George and Avril

Hardie, Philip Mansel and Michael Weinstein; in Oxford, James Campbell, Jeremy Catto, Eric Christiansen, Joe and Rosalind Pennybacker, and Christopher Tyerman.

The dedication of this book is the expression of a debt which is less easy to particularize. I met Denis Bethell in Oxford in the early months of 1966, at a time when I was reading the *Historia Compostellana* for the first time. He was unusual, then, quite possibly unique, among English medievalists, in knowing well that puzzling and tantalizing text. (I believe that he had been drawn to it initially by the information it provides about the circumstances of the disputed papal election of 1130.) It was a period when I needed encouragement: this he gave me unstintingly. Our meeting ripened into a friendship which was sunned by far more than a shared concern with the ecclesiastical history of the twelfth century. The rhythms of our lives sundered us; he to Dublin, I back to Yorkshire: an intermittent though lively correspondence and some occasional meetings linked us. (His letters, infrequent, entertaining, a shade poignant, were shot through with agreeable misunderstandings. For some reason he was convinced—despite my denials—that I was a breeder of springer spaniels, and would enquire solicitously about the state of my kennels.) It so fell out that I saw much of him during the last year of his life. And it was while he was staying with me, only a few weeks before his death, that I showed him some chapters of this book in draft. The comments that he made on that occasion, kindly, acute and learned (as his criticisms always were) I have borne in mind in revising the work for publication. In dedicating it to his memory I remember a fine scholar, a selfless friend and a good man.

Nunnington,
York
December 1982

Contents

List of Abbreviations

AC	Archivo de la Catedral
AD	Arquivo Distrital
AHN	Madrid, Archivo Histórico Nacional, sección de clero
AHN cód.	Madrid, Archivo Histórico Nacional, sección de códices
AHRG	Archivo Histórico del Reino de Galicia
BN	Madrid, Biblioteca Nacional
BRAH	*Boletín de la Real Academia de la Historia*
CAI	*Chronica Adefonsi Imperatoris*, ed. L. Sánchez Belda (Madrid, 1950)
Carboeiro Cart.	'La colección diplomática del monasterio de San Lorenzo de Carboeiro', ed. M. Lucas Alvarez, *Compostellanum* II–III (1958-9)
DMP	*Documentos Medievais Portugueses: Documentos Régios*, vol. I (Lisbon, 1958)
Episcopate	R. A. Fletcher, *The Episcopate in the kingdom of León in the twelfth century* (Oxford, 1978)
ES	*España Sagrada*, ed. E. Flórez, M. Risco, and others (Madrid, 1747-1879)
GRF	J. González, *Regesta de Fernando II* (Madrid, 1943)
HC	*Historia Compostellana*, ed. E. Flórez (Madrid, 1765) (= *ES* vol. XX)
IVDJ	Madrid, Instituto de Valencia de Don Juan
JL	*Regesta Pontificum Romanorum*, ed. P. Jaffé, revised by S. Löwenfeld and others (Leipzig, 1885)
Jubia Cart.	'La colección diplomática de San Martín de Jubia', ed. S. Montero Díaz, *Boletín de la Universidad de Santiago de Compostela* VII (1935)
LFH	A. López Ferreiro, *Historia de la S.A.M. Iglesia de Santiago de Compostela* (Santiago de Compostela, 1898-1911)
LSJ	*Liber Sancti Iacobi, Codex Calixtinus*, ed. W. M. Whitehill (Santiago de Compostela, 1944), vol. I
PUP	*Papsturkunden in Portugal*, ed. C. Erdmann (Göttingen, 1927)
R	Royal charter. See further below, Appendix B

Reilly, *Urraca*	B. F. Reilly, *The Kingdom of León-Castilla under queen Urraca 1109–1126* (Princeton, 1982)
Sobrado Cart.	*Tumbos del monasterio de Sobrado de los Monjes,* ed. P. Loscertales de G. de Valdeavellano (Madrid, 1976)
Vones, *Kirchenpolitik*	L. Vones, *Die 'Historia Compostellana' und die Kirchenpolitik des nordwestspanischen Raumes 1070–1130. Ein Beitrag zur Geschichte der Beziehungen zwischen Spanien und dem Papsttum zu Beginn des 12.Jahrhunderts* (Cologne, 1980)

I

Galicia

Cape Finisterre is a mighty spur of granite which juts out from the mainland into the Atlantic in the extreme north-westerly quarter of the Iberian peninsula. What the earliest inhabitants of that area called it we do not know. As so often elsewhere within the territories which once were part of the Roman empire, it is the Latin name that has stuck: *Finis Terrae*, the end of the world. Even though we have long known that it is not accurate, the name remains fitting. The visitor to Cape Finisterre will find it so, as he contemplates, usually between the mists which sweep in on the western wind, the awful vastness of the waters which extend before him. At Cape Finisterre you are a long way from anywhere else. This is where the world stops. Out there the sea and the sky, earth and heaven, meet.

Santiago de Compostela lies a little inland, about forty miles due east of Finisterre. It too bears a Latin name, though not one which dates from imperial times: *Sanctus Iacobus*, Sant' Iago, Saint James. For over a thousand years devotion has drawn men and women to the apostle's shrine, to a tomb beneath a church in a holy city. Here miracles have been worked, the supernatural order has intermingled with the merely human. Here too, then, earth and heaven meet. Here at the margin of Christendom may be apprehended 'the point of intersection of the timeless with time'.

Galicia is cut off from the central tableland, or *meseta*, of the Iberian peninsula by a chain of mountains. The range known as the Cordillera Cantábrica, which runs along the north coast of Spain westwards from the fringes of the Basque country, inclines to the south shortly after passing the region of Oviedo and continues in a south-westerly direction towards the present northern frontier of Portugal. This south-westerly spur—the Montes de León and the Sierra de la Culebra—rarely drops below 4,000 feet, and

some of its peaks approach 7,000 feet in height. Its line continues through the mountainous provinces of northern
Portugal, Tras os Montes, Alto Douro and Beira Alta, throw-
ing up a last bastion in the Serra da Estrêla to the east of
Coimbra, before dying into the coastal plain that leads down
to Santarem and Lisbon. It is with the region on the Atlantic
side of this formidable barrier that this chapter will be concerned, an area which now embraces the four Galician
provinces of Spain—Lugo, La Coruña, Pontevedra and
Orense.

'Hard going, wearisome mountains.' In these words did
a writer of the early twelfth century describe a journey made
by the royal court of queen Urraca from Galicia to the
meseta.[1] Communication between Galicia and the central
tableland has always been difficult. In the north the foothills
of the Cordillera Cantábrica run down close to the sea, no
Roman road was driven along the coast, and we have little
evidence of the use of the narrow coastal strip as a means of
communication during the early medieval period. There is
only one possible crossing-point of the mountains further
south, on the line drawn between the towns of Astorga and
Lugo. The road crosses two high passes, the Puerto de
Manzanal between Astorga and Ponferrada, and the Puerto
de Piedrafita del Cebrero between Ponferrada and Lugo.
Ponferrada itself is set in the fertile depression known as
El Bierzo. From here a route following the upper waters
of the river Sil leads towards Orense. Further to the south
again, the road from Zamora skirts the fringes of the Sierra
de la Culebra, passes through Puebla de Sanabria and over
the Padornela pass, forming the principal means of access
to southern Galicia. Yet further to the south the valley of
the Duero (*Port.* Douro) forms a corridor from the *meseta*
into northern Portugal.

It is much easier to travel from Galicia southwards into
Portugal than it is to cross the mountains on to the *meseta*.
In the west the flood-plain of the lower reaches of the river
Miño (*Port.* Minho) opens an easy access to Braga, Coimbra
and the coastal plain of Portugal. The river valleys of the

[1] *HC*, p. 128.

Limia and the Tamega, draining in a south-westerly direction from the highlands of southern Galicia, form natural routes respectively from Orense through Celanova to Braga and from Verín through Chaves towards Viseu and Coimbra. Further east the upper waters of the river-system which drains into the Sabor provide means of access only a little more difficult from Sanabria to Bragança.

The mountain barrier between Galicia and the *meseta* sharply differentiates the climates of the two regions. On the *meseta* winters are long and harsh, summers fiercely hot; rainfall is slight; woodland is little more than scrub. The aspect of the country is monotonous. Galicia's climate is temperate, Atlantic. Winters are generally mild, summers agreeably warm; rain is frequent, usually in the form of light showers; woodland is dense and lush. The countryside is easy on the eye, broken up and varied by outcrops of granite, rolling hills, abundance of rivers and streams. The scale of things is somehow comforting, manageable, human. There is not the desolation of the *meseta*, induced by an awareness of that brown, baked land stretching unchanging for miles and miles in every direction. These differences have not been without their effect on the inhabitants. The Galicians are friendly and cheerful; the people of the *meseta* are dour, sullen and charmless.

The *meseta* is the land of the classic staples of the Spanish economy: corn and sheep, the olive and the vine. The economy of Galicia is more varied. The Galician coastline is deeply indented with estuarine inlets known as *rías*. These provide some superlative natural harbours, as at Vigo and Corunna, and we shall see that a lively trade was developing along these coasts during the twelfth century. For much of the earlier middle ages the opportunities presented by the long, serrated, island-studded Atlantic littoral were exploited by seaborne enemies—pirates from the Muslim south and the Anglo-Scandinavian north. This never deterred the fishermen of Galicia from following a calling which has always been one of the mainstays of the Galician economy. When Diego Gelmírez issued an edict fixing prices in the market of Santiago de Compostela he listed octopus, lobster, oysters, cod, sea-bream, conger eel, pilchards and lampreys among

the fish for sale there. Fishermen returning up the Ría de
Arosa paid toll on their catch at Torres del Oeste.[2] There
were freshwater fish to be had in abundance too. When the
bishopric of Tuy was re-established in 1071, for example,
it was endowed with fisheries in the river Miño.[3]

The wild produce of the mainland was as varied as that of
the sea and the rivers which fed it. Its gathering might be
hazardous, for wolves were common—the inhabitants of
the district round Compostela were bound to turn out every
Saturday to hunt them—and even the occasional bear might
be seen.[4] Some at least of the wax and honey of which we
hear would have been made by wild ·bees.[5] Hares and partridges could be bought in the market at Compostela, rabbit-
skin cloaks in that of Guimarães. It was for the pursuit of
bigger game, wild boar or deer, that two Galician noblemen
gave their king a hound called Ulgar and a hunting-spear,
together worth 500 *solidi*, in 1118.[6] Our sources frequently
refer to nuts, and it is no surprise that this is often in association with pigs. When Pedro Gundesíndez, canon of Compostela, granted a property to the monastery of Caabeiro
he asked the monks to grant it in life-tenancy to his brother-
in-law, and suggested that the rent should consist of suitable
quantities of nuts, corn, beans, *segunda* and a pig.[7] The
masons who worked to build Lugo cathedral about the year
1130 were supplied with hams, along with chickens, sheep,
butter and bread from one of the bishop and chapter's
estates.[8]

Innumerable charters refer to other domesticated livestock
—cows, sheep and goats, chickens, ducks and geese. The
Galician economy was never a 'pastoral economy' plain and
simple, but there can be no doubt that grazing played a very

---

[2] *HC*, p. 534; AHN 1749/21.   [3] R. 13 June 1071.

[4] *HC*, pp. 179–80; *DMP*, no. 27. Cold winter weather sometimes brings
reports of sightings of wolves into the Galician local press even today.

[5] AHN 491/13; *Sobrado Cart.* I, no. 131.

[6] ·*HC*, p. 534; *DMP*, no. 1; R. 29 July 1118. Might the dog Ulgar have been
English? English dogs were much sought after abroad, and Ulgar is a possible
rendering of some such name as Wulfgar. We shall have something to say of
Anglo-Galician trade in a later chapter.

[7] AHN 491/5. *Segunda* may have been inferior grain not good enough for milling or seed, but suitable as animal-fodder.

[8] AHN 1325C/19 (2,3).

significant part in it. Oxen were presumably the principal draught animals, as they still are in Galicia. The carts they drew a thousand years ago probably looked much like the carts they draw today; narrow and boat-shaped, the sides that run towards the 'prow' not meeting but leaving a gap of a few inches between them, the solid wooden wheels giving off a high-pitched squealing when in motion. We hear much of horses and of mules, the latter often more valuable than the former.[9] It is unlikely that these were draught animals, more probable that they were the mounts and pack-animals of warriors, merchants and the higher clergy. It is in such social contexts that we hear most of them. When the lady Ermesenda Núñez disposed of her dead brother's possessions in 1073 there were numbered among them three horses, a mule, two coats of mail and two swords; and it was horses, mules, coats of mail and helmets that Osorio Bermúdez seized from his nephew Bermudo Pérez in a family quarrel.[10] It is likely that many of the greater religious communities, such as the Compostelan monastery of San Martín Pinario, kept stud-farms.[11]

Vineyards are of common occurrence in our sources, but we hear much of orchards too, and it would seem that a good deal of cider was drunk. The French author of the guidebook for pilgrims which forms a part of the so-called *Liber Sancti Iacobi* commented that it was more often to be encountered in Galicia than wine. Cider as well as wine was drunk at a king's coronation in 1111, and a render of cider was stipulated as part of the rent in a lease of 1116.[12] The same author noted that wheaten bread was rare, rye bread being more commonly consumed. Wheat was certainly grown, though references to it are infrequent. We hear much more often of barley and rye, and very occasionally of millet.[13] The drying and storage of grain and hay, always difficult in the damp climate of Galicia, many then as now have been done in the

---

[9] e.g. AHN 1325D/8 *bis.*

[10] AHN 1067/2; A. López Ferreiro, *Don Alfonso rey de Galicia y su ayo el conde de Trava* (Santiago de Compostela, 1885), apéndice x.

[11] AHN 512/10.

[12] *LSJ*, p. 359; *HC*, p. 121; *Jubia Cart.*, no. xxiv.

[13] AHN 512/6; 1325C/13; *Sobrado Cart.* II, nos. 101, 132; *Carboeiro Cart.*, no. xxii; AHN cód. 986B, fo. 132ᵛ-133ʳ.

structures known locally as *cabazos*, which are one of the most striking features of the Galician countryside: narrow, gabled sheds of stone raised on piers to some three feet above the ground to keep them out of the reach of vermin; but no certain reference to them in these early documents has yet been found, and it may be that they were developed for the storage of maize only after its introduction in the sixteenth century.

The Romans had mined gold, tin and iron in the north-west of Spain. Only the last of these, it would seem, was still an active industry during our period. Place-names such as *Ferreira* furnish one indication of it, charters another: a charter from the monastery of Celanova, for example, refers to 'the mine where men make iron'.[14] The extraction of salt was another essential mineral industry. All our references are to coastal salt-pans. Ardiu Vimáraz, for instance, left to her son by her will in 1116 'the saltworks (*salinas*) which I constructed with him' on one of the islands off the Atlantic coast. Salt transported up the Ría de Arosa towards Padrón was liable to toll at Torres del Oeste.[15] There must have been a local ceramic industry, though the archaeologists have yet to reveal its products to us. Although foreign textiles did reach Galicia, as we shall see, there was doubtless some domestic production of cloth. The measures of cloth (*pannos*) which were exchanged in 1042, at a lowly social level, for a small plot of land near Sobrado, sound like local woollens. Some flax was grown—we meet it in a Lugo charter of 1030, for instance—and this helps to explain the fine bed- and table-linen to which some of our documents refer.[16] Leather must have been worked too. Footwear was a commodity perennially in demand among the pilgrims to Santiago, to say nothing of native users; and waterproof capes were an essential item of daily equipment in Galicia before the coming of the umbrella.

Tools and techniques were rudimentary. In the market of Compostela in the 1130s you might buy axes, mattocks,

---

[14] A. Rodríguez Colmenero, *Galicia meridional romana* (Bilbao, 1977), pp. 197–214; AHN cód. 986B, fo. 151^v; compare also R. 28 March 959.

[15] AHN 512/6, 1749/21.

[16] *Sobrado Cart.*, I, no. 198; AHN cód. 1043B, fo. 55^v.

ploughshares, billhooks, sickles—all of iron—and imple-
ments of uncertain function set with stone cutting-edges
(perhaps threshing-sledges).[17] This is simple equipment, but
adequate for working the light, rich soil of Galicia. The
visitor will not see anything more complicated today. Ploughs
are still light scratch-ploughs, an iron share fastened to a
wooden beam; harrows are wooden frames with iron spikes
protruding beneath, pressed to the surface of the soil by the
weight of rocks or children, drawn by oxen. Water-mills
there were, and their use was spreading: the 'new mill' makes
a frequent appearance in our charters.[18]

The latest—and indeed almost the only—historian to
have studied the demography of early medieval Galicia
has estimated her population about the year 1000 at the
audaciously precise figure of 232,400. Dr García Alvarez's
calculations, though ingenious, are highly speculative.[19] It is
notoriously difficult, as every historian knows, to estimate
the size of the population in any given area of medieval
Europe. While it would be injudicious for one who can lay
claim to no demographic expertise whatsoever to offer any
but the most tentative of opinions on this topic, my own
impression is that this figure is a good deal too low. I would
guess that we should multiply it by at least five, conceivably
by eight, to approximate to the demographic realities of the
eleventh century. Be this as it may, it is more important for
our purposes to estimate rather the density and distribution
of the population than its aggregate size. The conformation
of the terrain has always dictated that in Galicia the spread
of the population is uneven. Much of the region is unsuitable
for tillage, some of it even for grazing: the bleak moorland
round Lugo for example, or the highlands in the province
of Orense, or the rocky coastal areas of the province of La
Coruña. In districts such as these settlement must have been
extremely sparse. As against this, it can be demonstrated

[17] *HC*, pp. 534–5. Wooden sledges set with flints and drawn by mules were
used for this purpose in Spain until recently. I have seen them for sale in the
market of León, and in use on the *meseta*, though not in Galicia—but I have
never been in Galicia at harvest-time.

[18] e.g. AHN 1325D/7 (of 1152).

[19] M. R. García Alvarez, *Galicia y los gallegos en la alta edad media* (Santiago
de Compostela, 1975), I, ch. v, especially pp. 180–2.

that other areas were densely settled. Let one example stand for many. There survives in the cartulary of the Benedictine monastery of Celanova a series of charters and inventories, thirty-four documents in all, relating to the village of Bobadela, a little to the north of Celanova itself, between the years 988 and 1040. With the aid of these it can be shown that during this period the population of the village numbered at least 186, distributed in thirty-nine different properties. (In 1753 the population was 240 in sixty properties, in 1950 was 176 in thirty-eight properties.) Assuming that the present parish boundaries correspond roughly with the village territory of *c*.1000, there is no escaping the conclusion that the density of the population was then something higher than the present-day density in the province of Orense, in which Bobadela lies, namely fifty-six persons per square kilometre.[20] Bobadela may have been a special case—not least in the survival of abundant documentation relating to it—but it can be shown that many other villages at least approached it in the density of their populations. Such figures are startling, even alarming, especially when set against the figure of eighteen persons per square kilometre postulated for the most densely settled parts of the populous county of Catalonia at the same date.[21] There can be no doubt that parts of Galicia were experiencing demographic saturation in the tenth and eleventh centuries.

On the central Spanish *meseta* the unit of settlement was and is the *pueblo*; that is to say, the large nucleated village surrounded by its own fields, with no outlying farms, separated from its neighbours by some considerable distance, sometimes as much as ten miles or so. The demands of agrarian routine and the need for defence, the simple desire for human society in the vast solitude of the plains, together dictated that it should be so. Nowadays the *pueblo* might have a population running into thousands. Doubtless they were smaller in the early middle ages, but we should probably not be far wrong if we think of them as having had populations

---

[20] García Alvarez, op. cit., pp. 88, 237–57.
[21] P. Bonnassie, *La Catalogne du milieu du Xe à la fin du XIe siècle* (Toulouse, 1975), I. 86–91. Professor Bonnassie describes the figure of 18/km² as 'presque effarante'.

of some hundreds. In Galicia the word most commonly used to describe a unit of settlement is *logar*. (This is the rendering in Gallego. The Castilian term is *lugar*. The words are of course derived from Latin *locus*.) The *logar* is a smallish village; it might today have a population of anything between fifty and three hundred people. The homesteads are normally scattered; there is not the tight bunching together that one finds in the typical *pueblo*. Each of them is surrounded by a complex of little yards, middens, orchards, vineyards and diminutive fields. Haphazardly strung out along a stream or road, on either side of a valley or near a suitable anchorage for fishing boats, the settlement may be distributed over a surprisingly large area. The *logar* does not have a centre, a focal point—again in contrast to the *pueblo*, which invariably has a central *plaza*, or square. It is characteristic that the road leading to such a settlement, which the visitor might expect to form a principal artery, dissolves within the *logar* into a confusing network of narrow lanes, with sharp twists and turns, unexpected dead-ends, and a disconcerting way of suddenly turning into a farmyard or of simply petering out on the edge of woodland or marsh: a maze where only the livestock appear to know their way about. All the evidence at our disposal suggests that the morphology of the Galician *logar* was much the same a millennium ago as it is today. That evidence is furnished by hundreds of charters recording donations, sales and leases of tiny parcels of land. The terms in which and the detail with which the bounds are described in these documents instantly call to mind the layout of the modern Galician *logar*.[22]

Larger units of settlement were almost entirely lacking. Lugo presents us with the most instructive example. Lucus Augusti had been the most important town in Galicia during the Roman period, though not a big one; her third-century walls, exceptionally well preserved, describe a circuit of only about 2,300 yards. The seat of a bishopric by (at latest) the latter part of the fifth century, Lugo was an administrative centre of some significance throughout the Suevic and Visigothic periods. Thereafter she went into a

[22] García Alvarez, op. cit., pp. 114-20, is good on this.

long decline. In the middle of the eighth century bishop Odoario found the town deserted and set about reviving it. Yet in 910 a number of Galician aristocrats promised their king, Ordoño II, that they would rebuild the 'abandoned tenements' of Lugo (*casas destructas*) and themselves take up residence in them with their families. That this second resettlement had only limited success is suggested by a document of some sixty years later which reveals contemporary anxiety to repopulate the town so that it might serve as a defensive point against Viking attack.[23] This is not to suggest that the town was literally deserted. It remained the seat of a bishopric, royal charters were issued there, and it was administered by a count from at least the middle of the ninth century. But the documents do suggest that Lugo was not attracting and holding any considerable urban population. Its commercial and industrial role was insignificant.

The shrine of St. James attracted settlers to serve the needs of clergy and pilgrims. These may have included some immigrants from outside Spain from an early date: Bertenandus *francus* was a property-owner in Compostela about the middle of the tenth century.[24] The town was walled about a century later. But the smallness of the area enclosed, and the rarity of references to trade or merchants before the latter part of the eleventh century alike suggest that the town was a modest affair. The same may be said of Tuy, Braga, Orense and Chaves. This almost non-urban state of affairs in tenth- and eleventh-century Galicia contrasts with the situation on the *meseta*. León was not only a focus for government, the seat of a bishopric and of several other religious establishments, but also a centre of trade and industry which was attracting immigration and sustaining a growing population, many of whose members probably owed their livelihood exclusively to commerce or industry.[25]

The lack of a native merchant class in Galicia may have been supplied by Jewish traders. Surviving references to them,

[23] L. Vázquez de Parga, 'Los documentos sobre las presuras del obispo Odoario', *Hispania* 10 (1950), 635–80, doc. no. I; R. 7 June 910; AHN cód. 1043B, fo. 38ᵛ (pd. *ES* XL, ap. xxiii, pp. 403–4).

[24] *Sobrado Cart.* I, no. 2.

[25] C. Sánchez Albornoz, *Una ciudad de la España cristiana hace mil años. Estampas de la vida en León* (5th edn., Madrid, 1966), *passim*.

though tantalizingly few, are suggestive. In 1044, for example, a certain Menendo González 'was entertaining Jews in his house who were transacting business there' (*tenebat suos hebreos in sua casa qui faciebant suo mercatum*); Arias Oduárez attacked them and despoiled them of 700 lengths of silk, 30 serges and 40 linens together valued at a thousand pounds—an amazing haul.[26] The incident suggests one explanation of the presence of luxury goods in aristocratic wills and church inventories, to which we shall return. It occurred in southern Galicia, not far from Celanova; perhaps the merchants who suffered had travelled up from Portugal, in whose Muslim cities we know that there existed Jewish communities. But how frequent their journeys into Christian Galicia may have been, and what merchandise they carried back with them, we have no means of telling.

Texts such as this raise questions also about the presence of coinage and the means of exchange in Galicia. Remarkable as it may seem, it is tolerably clear that no coin was minted in Galicia after the end of the Visigothic period in the early eighth century for a very long time. The earliest reference to a royal mint which we possess seems to have occurred in a lost charter of Alfonso VI which we know only through a charter of his great-grandson Fernando II dated 19 February 1158. Alfonso's charter had granted one-third of the profits of the royal mint at Lugo to the bishop and chapter of that see; it was probably issued between 1088 and 1109. What did the Galicians do for money before the existence of a native currency? Suevic and Visigothic coins remained in circulation long after the Visigothic state had perished. Some of the gold coins of Muslim Spain found their way to the north-west, but one might guess that the intrinsic value of these coins was too high to articulate a brisk exchange in Galicia's agrarian economy.[27] It is evident that there was much barter. Land was sold in 1078 for 'a mare and an excellent cloak and a cow', exchanged in 1093 for the life tenancy of a church; a share in a church was sold in about

---

[26] F. Fita, 'Los judíos gallegos en el siglo XI', *BRAH* 22 (1893), 172-7.

[27] Many references are collected in M. R. García Alvarez, 'Moneda y precios del ganado en la Galicia altomedieval', *Cuadernos de Estudios Gallegos* 24 (1969), 363-94.

1087 for 'a splendid roan stallion and a good cloak'.[28] We should beware of assuming that the prevalence of barter indicates a sluggish economy of exchange. Scores of documents from the tenth and eleventh centuries suggest rather that at a local level exchange was lively. It seems to have been articulated by the widespread acceptance of the equivalence of one *solidus* to either a measure (*modius*) of corn or a sheep. Thus we hear, for instance, of a sow worth two *modii*, and of an ox worth seven.[29]

Generally speaking, however, it appears that while a local trade based on barter was thriving, long-distance trade was rare and the regular use of coin unknown. In these respects the economy of Galicia stood in marked contrast to the regional economies of other parts of the peninsula which were in Christian hands. León and Castile, and even the Pyrenean economies of Navarre and Aragon, were accustomed to the traffic of merchants who used coin: while the economy of Catalonia in the tenth and eleventh centuries was among the most advanced in Latin Christendom.

Notable by its absence from our documentation is any reference to the buying and selling of slaves. Yet slaves certainly existed in Galicia, just as they did in other parts of Christian Spain. The principal source of Moorish slaves was capture in war. This probably meant that they were in short supply in tenth- and eleventh-century Galicia, a period when it was generally true that the Muslims of Al-Andalus held the military and naval initiatives in Spain. Those who could find a use for slaves depended, probably, on occasional windfalls. Diego Gelmírez was presented with some captured Moorish pirates in 1115, and set them to work on the rebuilding of the cathedral of Santiago.[30] Later, with new Christian initiatives under Alfonso VII (1126–57), this source of supply may have quickened. The lady Guntroda Suárez included six Moorish slaves, three men and three women, among the endowments of her church of San Pedro de Villanova in about 1145.[31]

---

[28] AHN 1081/17; *Jubia Cart.*, nos. x, xii.

[29] The use of this equivalence was first established by L. G. de Valdeavellano, 'Economía natural y monetaria en León y Castilla durante los siglos IX, X y XI', *Moneda y Crédito* 10 (1944), 28–46.

[30] *HC*, p. 199.   [31] AHN 1509/14.

Slaves were not used only for menial tasks. Two references indicate that great men particularly valued their culinary skills. (Arab cooking has no great gastronomic reputation: but those acquainted with the cuisine of Galicia will need no telling that any change could only be for the better.) St. Rosendo, the founder of Celanova, installed there as chef one Fez, described as 'a Moor from Córdoba'; and nearly two centuries later count Pedro Froílaz de Traba, the greatest lay magnate of Galicia in the early twelfth century, presented his son Fernando with a Moorish cook.[32]

Pedro Froílaz's cook was called Martín, and this Christian name presumably indicates that he had been baptized. This occurrence, if not uncommon, must make it well-nigh impossible to detect Moorish slaves in any list of names. When Rodrigo Gutiérrez married in 1037 he settled on his wife seventy-eight separate properties, eighty-one male and forty-three female slaves (*mancipios et mancipias*), flocks of sheep, a stud of mares and twenty stallions, two hundred head of other livestock, furniture, clothes and jewellery.[33] The names of some of the slaves were rather odd. Amicus is a curious name for a man, Nomenbonus a still more curious name for a woman. Were these perhaps baptismal names given to slaves who had been converted? If so, one may wonder how many other converted Moors lurk behind the impeccably Christian names—Pedro, María, García, Guntroda, etc.—of this slave list and others similar to it.

Slaves may have been integrated into more than the religion of their masters. A corrupt thirteenth-century copy of a document of 1110–28 from the monastery of Caabeiro seems to refer to the presence of a subject peasantry, now Christian but descended from Moors, on the monastic estates in this remote corner of Galicia.[34] Since the Islamic armies never occupied the extreme north-west it is out of the question—quite apart from being inherently improbable—that these people should have been downgraded descendants of

[32] AHN cód. 986B, fo. 57ʳ; Madrid, IVDJ, C.9/25.
[33] *Sobrado Cart.* I, no. 127.
[34] AHN 491/4. The crucial words refer to peasants *de maladia sive christianos quomodo progenie de paganos*. An emendation from *maladia* to *muladia* helps a little, and is justified by the consideration that copyists of the thirteenth and later centuries frequently misread Visigothic *a* for *u* and vice versa.

eighth-century Berber settlers; more likely that they were the
descendants of slaves captured in battle or acquired by other
means who had been settled on the land and had accepted
Christianity. Our Caabeiro charter might therefore be said
to bear out the contention of a distinguished historian of
medieval slavery in the Iberian peninsula that in Galicia
Moorish slaves were somehow assumed into the ranks of the
serfs.[35] Perhaps the *mancipios* of Rodrigo Gutiérrez's marriage
settlement should be termed not 'slaves' but 'serfs'.

We waver on the brink of a terminological morass into
which historians are often sucked, there to flounder help-
lessly, when they try to find modern equivalents for words
used in early medieval documents to describe social group-
ings. Who were the people whom I have described as 'serfs',
and what do we know of them? The key word is *criatio*.[36]
The *criatio*-people occupied the lowest social rung on the
ladder of the free. They were bound to the land in service
to a lord. They could be sold, exchanged, or given away.
Thus in 1087 a vendor disposed of 'my estates and my
criazone' to a purchaser. The see of Tuy was endowed in
1071 with the church of Paderne 'and all its *criazone*'. In
1102 the abbot of Jubia and Pelayo Vélaz came to an agreement over three *criatio*-men, probably brothers, disputed
between them; two of them went to the abbot and Pelayo
got the third. Diego Gelmírez acquired an estate 'with all
its *creatione*' by exchange in 1124.[37] However, such people
could own property. Three *criatos* were left a house in
Compostela by a testator in 1116.[38] As property-owners
they must have had access to the public courts of the land;
and as law-worthy men they were free men.

For many years it was believed that Galician rural society
below the élite levels consisted entirely of such *criatio*-
people. Recent research has established that there existed an
intermediate and very sizeable class of free property-owners
—allodialists they would be called elsewhere—who unlike

---

[35] This was the suggestion of C. Verlinden, *L'esclavage dans l'Europe médiévale*:
I. *Péninsule ibérique* (Bruges, 1955).

[36] Spelt variously *creatio, criacio, criazio*, etc.

[37] AHN 1508/8; R. 13 June 1071; *Jubia Cart.*, no. v; *HC*, p. 419.

[38] AHN 512/6.

the *criatio*-men acknowledged no lord below the king.[39] This rural middle class was densely distributed over the whole face of Galicia. The evidence for its existence is furnished by innumerable charters recording sales and donations of land which survive in the cartularies of monastic houses such as Celanova and Sobrado. These alienations were invariably made without the sanction of any lord. Such restraints on alienation as existed were exerted by the kinsfolk of the contracting parties whose names may be found in countless witness-lists. Relatives therefore exercised what might be called a horizontal pull upon the desire of a landowner to do what he pleased with his own; but of the vertical pressure of a superior lordship there is not a sign.

It would be rash to hazard any generalizations about these people. Doubtless they included, then as at any other time, both the fortunate and the unlucky, the contented and the ambitious, the careful and the improvident. It was an amorphous social group, as middle classes tend to be, within which it was possible both to rise and to fall. We have already seen evidence that parts of Galicia were densely populated. We know too that by Visigothic legal custom, which was still observed (as we shall see) in Galicia during this period, inheritances were divided equally among heirs at each generation. Under a customary system of partible inheritance there is a tendency for holdings to become ever smaller—offset though this may be by other factors such as a high rate of both infant and adult mortality. 'There occurred a famine and great loss of life' we read in a charter of 1001.[40] In a society thus constituted crop-failure and cattle disease bring immediate distress for which borrowing is the initial remedy. Two very interesting charters, of 1023 and 1042, record surrenders of land to creditors by debtors who could not pay the interest (*renovo*) on their loans.[41] We shall never know how widespread indebtedness was among the lesser rural allodialists, but it may have been an important factor in

[39] C. Sánchez Albornoz, 'Pequeños proprietarios libres en el reino asturleonés', in his *Investigaciones y documentos sobre las instituciones hispanas* (Santiago de Chile, 1970), pp. 178–201; M. R. García Alvarez, *Galicia y los gallegos en la alta edad media* (Santiago de Compostela, 1975), I. 72–111.
[40] *Sobrado Cart.* I, no. 132.　　　　　[41] *Sobrado Cart.* I, nos. 39, 40.

making possible the concentration of property in the hands of some of their neighbours. Take the case of Cresconio of Bobadela.[42] We know about him because in later life he entered the monastery of Celanova, bringing with him his considerable landed wealth—and his title-deeds, preserved for us in the Celanova cartulary. Between 989 and 1010 he had assembled his estate by means of numerous separate transactions, most of them involving tiny parcels of land. Fortunately for us his charters usually tell us how it was done. We hear of debtors who defaulted on interest payments; of loans for the payment of compensation to other parties which could not then be repaid; of bribes to Cresconio, a prominent man locally, to secure his advocacy in lawsuits; and, of course, of straightforward purchase. Others could prosper by hitching their fortunes to men yet higher in the social scale: allodialists formed, in Galicia as elsewhere, a ministerial class. The fortunes of one Suero Pérez, for instance, seem to have been founded upon his services to Rodrigo Ovéquiz, count of Lugo, who rewarded him with a grant of land in 1084. By ingenuity or good fortune he survived the eclipse of count Rodrigo after his unsuccessful rebellion against Alfonso VI in 1085, and during the remainder of his life—we lose sight of him after 1103—we can trace his acquisitions of land and men in a block of territory in southern Galicia which eventually came into the possession of the Cistercian abbey of Osera.[43] Some rose even higher. Diego Gelmírez himself was one of these, and he rose highest of all.

The topmost rung on the social ladder was occupied by the Galician aristocracy. Throughout the tenth century this was a very small group. To say that its members were drawn from a dozen or so families is a somewhat desperate attempt to give a rough indication of its size, but in itself a concession to twentieth-century understanding which may mislead: these aristocratic clans were all interconnected, and they had different ideas about what constituted a 'family' from ourselves. Its quality is perhaps better indicated by saying that in any one generation in tenth-century Galicia

[42] Discussed by Sánchez Albornoz, art. cit.
[43] AHN 1508/6, 8, 10, 16, 17.

there were perhaps a couple of hundred people, men and women, who *mattered*. They were linked by ties of blood and marriage both amongst themselves and with the royal house of León; they possessed enormous landed wealth; and they monopolized all the important positions in royal and ecclesiastical government. The inmates of the monastic houses which they founded and governed were keenly interested in genealogy—probably reflecting in this the taste of patrons to whom, indeed, they were often related. This, and the abundant charters of the tenth century, enable us to discover a good deal about them.

The most prominent figure in the religious life of Galicia in the tenth century was Rosendo, leader of a monastic revival, founder of the abbey of Celanova, bishop successively of Mondoñedo and Compostela. Rosendo was to Galicia what Abbo of Fleury, Dunstan of Glastonbury or Oliba of Ripoll were to central France, southern England or Catalonia respectively. If we look to his nearer relatives we may hope to catch some flavour of the *potentes* of Galicia.[44] Rosendo was descended from the royal family, for his great-grandfather Gatón, count of Astorga in the 850s, was probably a younger brother of king Ordoño I. Rosendo's aunt Elvira married Ordoño II, his niece Gotona married Sancho Ordóñez king of Galicia, his cousin Adosinda married Ramiro II, another cousin Teresa married Sancho I, another niece Velasquita married Bermudo II, and his great-niece Elvira married Alfonso V. His male relatives occupied important positions in the royal government. His grandfather Hermenegild, hero of the conquest of Coimbra at the head of a royal army in 878, had been count of Tuy and Porto and the *mayordomo* of king Alfonso III. His father Gutierre and his uncle Arias were prominent at the courts of Ordoño II (their brother-in-law) and Sancho Ordóñez (their nephew). The bishopric of Mondoñedo was occupied successively by his great-uncle Savarico (907-25), by himself (925-47) and by his nephew Arias (947-58). The see of Compostela was held by three of

[44] In what follows I am indebted to the remarkable researches of Dr Emilio Sáez, especially his 'Notas al episcopologio minduniense del siglo X', *Hispania* 6 (1946), 1-79, and 'Los ascendientes de San Rosendo', ibid., 8 (1948), 3-76, 179-233.

his relatives in the course of the century—Gundesindo (920-4), Sisnando (952-68) and Pelayo (971-85)—as well as by himself. The greatest monastic houses of Galicia were founded or restored by his family. Samos was restored by his uncle Arias in about 922; Rosendo himself founded Celanova in 934; Hermenegild, founder of Sobrado in 952, was the son of his great-uncle Aloito; Osorio Gutiérrez, the founder of Lorenzana in 969, was a first cousin.

These religious houses were lavishly endowed. Let us take the last-named, Lorenzana, by way of example.[45] Osorio Gutiérrez founded it on a central nucleus of land to which he added a number of other estates. He gave to the monks he established there no less than eighteen proprietary churches. In addition to the stock already on the land he provided them with 90 mares and 2 stallions, 150 cows and 3 bulls, 150 yoke of oxen, 1,000 sheep, 500 pigs and 300 geese. He gave them church furnishings in abundance: four big bells and four small, three crosses, four chalices and patens, three crowns, three bronze thuribles, eight altar frontals, twenty-five priestly vestments and ten harps; the three *capsas* might have been caskets suitable for use as reliquaries. He also passed on to the monks a collection of liturgical and devotional books: that he had managed to assemble a large library is indicated by the fact that prayer-books alone ran to seven volumes. For domestic use in the monastery he provided thirty-nine beds and sets of bedclothes (of differing degrees of comfort—twelve were 'beds for the poor', presumably for use in the guest-house or for the monastic servants); seven benches with their cushions; mugs, dishes, bowls and jugs of silver; 6 candlesticks, 14 spoons and 184 table-napkins. Count Osorio himself entered his new foundation; we may suppose that his declining years were spent in some comfort.

[45] The Lorenzana foundation charter is printed in *ES* XVIII, ap. xvii, pp. 332-40. This and other foundation charters of the period cry out for critical editing. The process might reveal the charter to be not altogether trustworthy, but I believe it to be sufficiently reliable to sustain the general point made here. Count Osorio's charter for Lorenzana survives in two different versions, AHN cód. 1044B, fo. 1^r-8^v (a separate quire bound into the cartulary) and 9^r-14^v. A future editor will need to take account also of a further single-sheet copy in AC Mondoñedo.

This is about as close as the surviving sources permit us to get to these noblemen. We have no Thietmar of Merseburg, no Orderic Vitalis, to illumine the aristocracy of Galicia as their writings so vividly light up the Saxon aristocracy of the tenth century and the Norman of the eleventh. But we may guess that the Galician nobility shared certain common features with their Saxon and Norman counterparts. It is reasonable to suppose that partition of inheritances between co-heirs and heiresses gave rise to frequent dissension among kinsfolk. The expanding kingships of Ordoño I and Alfonso III in the ninth century had offered new rewards— in land, booty, lordships, military command, ecclesiastical office—to enterprising and reliable king's friends. This would have driven a wedge of status and power between the new king's men and the rest. The forebears of St. Rosendo and count Osorio may have been 'made' by the ninth-century Asturian kings as consciously as the aristocracy which conquered England was 'made' by duke William of Normandy. New opportunities would have increased competition for rewards within the artistocratic group and threatened such fragile harmony as existed. The halt to expansion imposed upon the Christians of the north by the caliph Abd al-Rahman III in the early tenth century would have laid such tensions under further stress by stemming any increase in rewards and thus making more intense the competition for what remained. It is not unlikely that it was factors such as this which lay behind the internal strife which afflicted León, Galicia and Castile in the middle and later years of the tenth century. It is not impossible that such factors had something to do with the widespread foundation of monasteries during the same period.

We may be confident that this aristocratic society was frequently disrupted by feud. This would have been one of a number of reasons for the influential position occupied by its women. Feuds could be calmed by marriage-alliances; Galician like Anglo-Saxon brides could be 'weavers of peace'. Women could inherit land. If they survived the hazards of child-bearing and if their menfolk predeceased them, they might assemble under their control spectacular concentrations of property. This, for example, was the good fortune (and the dilemma) of Ermesenda Núñez, herself a descendant of count Osorio Gutiérrez, who died at an advanced age in about 1084.[46] One might have expected that monastic foundations for women would have been frequent, as in tenth-century Saxony and to a lesser degree in Anglo-Saxon England. Women were certainly influential in monastic foundation; and, as we shall see in a later chapter, double houses for men and women did exist in Galicia: but no nunnery was established in the course of the Galician monastic revival of the tenth century. This was a lack which Diego Gelmírez's patronage was to supply in the twelfth century.

Rich, well-connected, powerful though these men and women were, their horizons were circumscribed. Tenth-century Galicia was not entirely isolated, but it is not going too far to say that her contact with the rest of Latin Christendom was fitful. It had not always been so. Late antique Galicia had been very much a part of the Roman and Mediterranean world. The Galician lady Egeria had made a pilgrimage to the Holy Places in the years 381–4, and has left us her account of it.[47] The chronicler Hydatius, a bishop in Galicia from 427 until his death in about 470, conscious though he was of living his life 'at the uttermost limit of the world', was yet a travelled man whose horizons were far from modest. He had journeyed to the east as a young man and met its learned men, including the great Jerome. In later life he was interested in the affairs of the lands bordering the eastern Mediterranean, and his references to travellers from the east coming to Galicia show us something of the means by which his curiosity was satisfied. As a bishop he travelled to Gaul on an embassy to Aetius in the years 431–2. We have to wait for over six centuries before we meet another native of Galicia whose vision ranged so far.[48] The barbarian period whose beginnings were chronicled by Hydatius, little

[46] AHN 1067/1, 2.

[47] For the context of Egeria's pilgrimage see now E. D. Hunt, *Holy Land pilgrimage in the later Roman empire AD 312–460* (Oxford, 1982). The reader should bear in mind that the Roman province of Gallaecia was larger than the Galicia of today: to the east it included Astorga on the *meseta* and to the south stretched as far as the river Duero.

[48] For Hydatius see most recently E. A. Thompson, 'The end of Roman Spain, I', *Nottingham Medieval Studies* 20 (1976), 4–18 (who to my mind

though we know of it, does not seriously impair our sense that Galicia continued to be a part of some larger cultural whole. Miro, king of the Suevi who settled in Galicia, had diplomatic relations not only with fellow barbarian kings in Neustria and Burgundy but also with the emperors in Constantinople. It was perhaps he who offered to the shrine of St. Martin of Tours the weight of his son in gold as the price for a miraculous cure. The most distinguished churchman of Galicia in the sixth century, Martin of Braga, was a native of Pannonia. The Visigothic king Leovigild could impound the ships of Gaulish merchants in Galicia. The fine sarcophagus at Lorenzana—reputed to have received at a later date the mortal remains of count Osorio Gutiérrez—was probably an import from southern Gaul in the seventh century. One of the coins in the Bordeaux hoard deposited about 700 was struck at a Galician mint; it may have made its way to Aquitaine through trade. British, possibly Breton, monks settled at Bretoña, near Mondoñedo, in the sixth century. Direct connections between western Spain and Ireland may have existed in the seventh. Certain of Isidore's works appear to have reached Irish centres of learning with remarkable speed, and it is possible that the monastic customs of Fructuosus of Braga owed something to Celtic usages.[49]

It was from the eighth century onward that Galicia slipped out of the mainstream of western Christian culture. It is not easy to determine why this should have happened. The Islamic invasion and conquest of Spain is only a partial explanation. True, it made communication by land through

exaggerates the remoteness of late antique Galicia from Roman culture). Hydatius has most recently been edited by A. Tranoy in the series *Sources Chrétiennes* (Paris, 1974).

[49] For the foregoing see J. N. Hillgarth, 'Visigothic Spain and early Christian Ireland', *Proceedings of the Royal Irish Academy* 62 (1962), section C, pp. 167-94; E. A. Thompson, *The Goths in Spain* (Oxford, 1969), pp. 23-4, 68, 87-8; X. Barral i Altet, *La Circulation des monnaies suèves et visigotiques* (Munich, 1976), pp. 125-30; E. James, *The Merovingian archaeology of south-west Gaul* (British Archaeological Reports, Supplementary Series, no. 25: Oxford, 1977), pp. 221-5; M. Herren, 'On the earliest Irish acquaintance with Isidore of Seville', in *Visigothic Spain. New Approaches*, ed. E. James (Oxford, 1980), pp. 243-50; E. James, 'Ireland and western Gaul in the Merovingian period', in *Ireland in early medieval Europe*, ed. D. Whitelock, D. Dumville, and R. McKitterick (Cambridge, 1982), pp. 362-86, at pp. 373-4.

the Pyrenees to Gaul far more difficult. A Muslim presence in north-central Spain, about the upper waters of the Ebro, endured for three centuries. The traveller from Galicia into Francia overland had to run the gauntlet of passing either through Islamic territory or—perhaps still more alarming—through the territory of pagan Vasconia; the latter a larger region now after the expansion of the Gascon tribesmen in the seventh century, people on whom Christian missionaries such as Amandus had made little, if any, impression. Yet the sixth- and seventh-century evidence suggests that Galician communication with the outside world had been made largely by sea. If traffic on the western seaways faltered and died, we may ask why and look in vain for an answer. Galicia is very vulnerable to attack from the sea. Hydatius tells of Vandal raids from Africa in 445, of Herul raids from the North Sea in 455 and 459.[50] But the Arabs and Berbers who invaded Spain in the eighth century were not great sea-goers at that early date—though they were later on—and it has been shown that the Vikings did not attack Galicia before the middle of the ninth century.[51] Our sources from Galicia, Aquitaine, western Francia and the British Isles are desperately meagre for the eighth century, and this should caution us to be wary in our search for any explanation. Perhaps the truth is that as the focuses of economic life, political power and intellectual activity moved gradually eastwards—from Neustria to Austrasia, from Aquitaine to Lombardy, from Ireland to Anglo-Saxon England—so Galicia was left out in the cold.

The Asturian kingdom, it is true, had relations with the court of Charlemagne and, perhaps, his successors. Alfonso III (866-910), in particular, was a ruler whose kingship may fruitfully be interpreted as having been cast in a sub-Carolingian mould—not unlike that of his contemporary Alfred of Wessex. As we shall later see, he was in direct communication with the clergy of Tours, albeit anxiously and uncertainly. But it was in Oviedo and León and the

---

[50] Ed. Tranoy, cc. 131, 171, 194.

[51] C. Sánchez Albornoz, '¿Normandos en España durante el siglo VIII?,' in his *Orígenes de la nación española. Estudios críticos sobre la historia del reino de Asturias*, II (Oviedo, 1974), pp. 309-21.

monasteries of the northern *meseta*, not in Galicia, that the heart of the *imperium* of the Leonese kings pulsed most vigorously; such at least is suggested by the works of art, the buildings and the texts which have come down to us. By Alfonso III's day we do seem to be in an age when the Vikings were stifling such sea-borne communications as still existed. We know of raids on the Galician coast in 844 and 858; there may have been others of which we know nothing. Alfonso III was sufficiently worried by the threat of Viking attack to establish fortified strong points near his coastline, as other rulers were doing elsewhere. Perhaps the 'heathen men' against whom he fought (as his charters proudly tell us) were not always Muslims. The next big raid that we hear of occurred in 968: bishop Sisnando of Compostela was killed, the monastery of Curtis was sacked, and panicky measures were ordered for the defence of the inland town of Lugo.[52] At some point early in the eleventh century Tuy was sacked; its bishopric remained vacant for the next half-century. A pathetic piece of family history recorded in a Portuguese charter of 1018 lifts for a moment the curtain which normally obscures the more humble human consequences of the Viking raids. Amarelo Mestáliz was forced to raise money on the security of his land in order to ransom his daughters who had been captured by the Vikings in 1015.[53] Bishop Cresconio of Compostela (*c*.1036–66) repulsed a Viking descent and built the fortress intended to protect the approach to the town of Compostela from the Atlantic which may still be seen by the water's edge at Torres del Oeste. A charter of 1086 refers to this or another raid in the Nendos district.[54]

Enemies were also coming by sea from the south. The Andalusian navy was called into being after the humiliating

---

[52] Sampiro, *Cronica*, in J. Pérez de Urbel, *Sampiro, su crónica y la monarquía leonesa en el siglo X* (Madrid, 1952), at pp. 340–1; *Cronicon Iriense*, ed. M. R. García Alvarez, *Memorial Histórico Español* 50 (1963), pp. 1–240, c. 11; *Sobrado Cart.* I, no. 137; AHN cód. 1043B, fo. 38ᵛ.

[53] Printed and discussed by R. Pinto de Azevedo, 'A expedição de Almanzor a Santiago de Compostela em 997, e a de piratas normandos a Galiza em 1015-16', *Revista Portuguesa da História* 14 (1974), 73–93. It may have been in the course of this raid, which lasted nine months, that Tuy was sacked.

[54] *HC*, p. 15; *Jubia Cart.*, no. ix.

Viking descent on the Guadalquivir valley in 844. It proved itself for the first time in the repulse of the Vikings in 859. Greatly enlarged, and its dockyards at Seville extended, it was employed to patrol the Iberian coastline under the caliphs Abd al-Rahman III (912–61) and Al-Hakam (961–76). Piracy by freebooting Saracens up and down the long Galician coastline became endemic. Those who lived by the sea from Seville to Coimbra, according to the *Historia Compostellana*, were accustomed to take to the ocean and raid the Christian coasts from the mouth of the Duero right round to the Pyrenees.[55] Later on we shall see what measures Diego Gelmírez took against them.

The Saracens also held the military initiative by land. The heady days of Christian expansion under Alfonso III were soon over. The roughly even balance of power in the first half of the tenth century was tipped decisively in Córdoba's favour by the massive growth in the caliphate's resources under Abd al-Rahman III. The Leonese *rois fainéants* of the third quarter of the century were the caliph's clients. And then, towards the end of the century there fell upon all of Christian Spain the scourge of Almanzor, *vizir* of Al-Andalus and its ruler in all but name from 981. After fifty-seven victorious campaigns against the Christians Almanzor died in 1002, 'and was buried in Hell' as an eleventh-century chronicler noted with satisfaction; but not before he had, in 997, penetrated to the heart of Galicia, sacked the town of Compostela and carried off in triumph to Córdoba the bells from St. James's church. It was a calculated affront to one of Christian Spain's most holy places, and a demonstration of the vulnerability of Galicia.

Sporadic attack by land and sea, from the south and from the north, was powerful inducement to the Galicians to stay at home. This reinforced the tendency of a naturally conservative agricultural people to look backward to a reassuring past, to be content with what they knew rather than to reach out to embrace a world beyond their own. The law which they observed, the *Lex Visigothorum*, was an old law. It was the code of king Reccaswinth, enlarged by the Novels of Wamba, Erwig and Egica, that still governed the

[55] *HC*, p. 197.

vital transactions of family and therefore of political life—
the marrying and the giving in marriage, the transmission of
property to heirs, the safeguarding of the rights of widows
and orphans.[56] The names they gave their children were old
names, drawn from a distant Suevic and Visigothic past:
names such as Miro and Leovigild, Fromaric and Fagildo,
Tudemir and Attila, abound in the charters of the tenth and
eleventh centuries. The books which they copied and read
have the same sort of story to tell. Ambrose, Augustine,
Benedict, Cassiodorus, Eusebius, Fructuosus, Gregory the
Great, Jerome, Ildefonsus, Isidore, John Cassian, Julian,
Pachomius, Prosper: this is a roll-call of the learning available in about the year 700—but these are the authors
recorded in Galician documents of the ninth, tenth and
eleventh centuries.[57] Only two authors of a later date found
a place. Beatus of Liébana's commentary on the Apocalypse,
always a popular work in Christian Spain, was presented to
the monastery of Guimarães by its founder in 959, and
a copy of Smaragdus on the Rule of St. Benedict was given
by no less a person than Rosendo of Celanova to the monastery of Caabeiro in 936. The presence of this Smaragdus
is the only evidence we possess for knowledge of the Carolingian literary renaissance in western Spain.[58] The canon
law which Galician churchmen observed was likewise the
product of seventh-century codification. Pseudo-Isidore and
the collections edited by Regino of Prüm, Abbo of Fleury
and Burchard of Worms are conspicuous by their absence.[59]
The liturgy used in Spain was the so-called Mozarabic liturgy,
unwashed by the Franco-Roman liturgical currents which
had flowed over the remainder of the Christian west. Their
books were copied in the 'Visigothic' script peculiar to

[56] Many citations of *Lex Visigothorum* occur in charters of this period: see
for example AHN cód. 986B, fo. 26^v-27^r (of 1052), and *Sobrado Cart*. II, no.
392 (of 1086).

[57] M. R. García Alvarez, 'Los libros en la documentación gallega de la alta
edad media', *Cuadernos de Estudios Gallegos* 20 (1965), 292-329.

[58] On the diffusion of Smaragdus in the Peninsula see now A. Linage Conde,
Los orígenes del monacato benedictino en la península ibérica (León, 1973),
II. 794-801. All surviving MSS from Spanish scriptoria before *c.*1100 come from
Castile or further east.

[59] A. García y García, *Historia del derecho canónico*: I. *El primer milenio*
(Salamanca, 1967), pp. 176-84.

Spain, its forms betraying no influence of the Carolingian minuscule. The very few churches which survive, such as Rosendo's chapel at Celanova, are markedly conservative in style, recalling the architecture of the Visigothic age. The clergy of Galicia were not travellers. They had no dealings with the popes, and we hear of no pilgrimages to Rome or further afield.

The organization of the Galician church was also an old one. As was the case elsewhere in Christendom, the structure of ecclesiastical administration had been grafted on to the administrative framework of the later Roman empire. The earliest bishoprics in Galicia were probably situated in the towns which gave their names to the three *conventus juridici* of the Roman province of Gallaecia—Braga, Lugo and Astorga. The surviving correspondence generated by the Priscillianist controversy and the chronicle of Hydatius make it clear that there were bishops of these places by the middle years of the fifth century at the latest. Three precious documents from about a century later cast a shaft of light upon upon the ecclesiastical organisation of Galicia in the last days of the Suevic kingdom.[60] These are the records of the first (561) and second (572) councils of Braga, and the exceptionally interesting document known as the Suevic *Parochiale*, a list of the principal churches of each diocese in the metropolitanate of Braga drawn up about 580. Their testimony shows that there were by then thirteen episcopal sees in north-western Spain: Braga, Coimbra, Idanha, Viseu, Lamego, Porto, Dume, Lugo, Tuy, Orense, Astorga, Iria and the *ecclesia Britonensis*.[61] Two of these sees were of an unusual type. Dume, or Dumio, just outside the city of

[60] See the important study of P. David, 'L'organisation ecclésiastique du royaume suève au temps de Saint Martin de Braga', in his *Études historiques sur la Galice et le Portugal du VIᵉ au XIIᵉ siècle* (Lisbon–Paris, 1947), pp. 1–82.

[61] Coimbra, Idanha, Viseu and Lamego were situated in the civil province not of Gallaecia but of Lusitania, whose administrative capital was at Mérida (Emerita). Because these areas were politically subject to the Suevic kings until the conquest of their kingdom by the Visigoths in the 580s, so their bishops had become ecclesiastically subject to the metropolitan see of Braga. At some point between 653 and 666 they were returned to the province of Lusitania at the instance of the metropolitan of Mérida. Disputes between the metropolitans of Galicia and Lusitania over their respective suffragan sees were to persist for many centuries.

Braga, was the site of a monastery founded by St. Martin of Braga. The *Parochiale* says of it simply, *Ad Dumio familia servorum*. This is probably to be interpreted, as Pierre David argued, as indicating that its abbot enjoyed the dignity of a bishop and exercised jurisdiction over the monks and the tenantry (*familia*) of the monastic estates. The *ecclesia Britonensis*, now Bretoña, was the seat of a bishop who ministered to the spiritual needs of the British immigrants to north-western Spain: in 572 its bishop, Mailoc, had a Celtic name.

The sixth-century evidence conjures up before us an active church, engaged in the foundation of rural churches and the slow christianization of the countryside. So much is suggested by the *Parochiale*, by the evidence for the foundation of proprietary churches, by Martin of Braga's tract *De correctione rusticorum* and by conciliar concern for the pastoral duties of a bishop. It is also clear that monasticism was spreading in Galicia during the Suevic and Visigothic periods. Hydatius referred to a community of nuns (*virgines Dei*) at Braga, there was at least one monastery among the British settlements, Martin of Braga founded more than one, nearly all the houses in the monastic 'connection' of St. Fructuosus were in Galicia, and a seventh-century inscription attests a monastic establishment at Samos.

The structure of the Visigothic church was disrupted by the Islamic conquest and short-lived occupation of Galicia. But its memory survived. The restoration of ecclesiastical life in lands reconquered during the ninth, tenth and eleventh centuries was powered by the desire to resurrect the arrangements of the Visigothic period. In Galicia at least—for matters took a somewhat different course elsewhere in Spain —this desire was fulfilled. The diocesan structure with which the young Diego Gelmírez grew up in the 1070s and 1080s was that of the seventh century. (There is one important qualification to be made. After the Islamic conquest the bishop of Dume resided at Mondoñedo (Mindunietum), near Bretoña, and the *ecclesia Britonensis* ceased to exist as a separate see. The bishopric of Mondoñedo emerged in impenetrably obscure circumstances from a fusion of the two authorities. It was for this reason that its bishops styled themselves variously *Minduniensis, Dumiensis* or *Britoniensis* during the tenth and eleventh centuries.)

Monastic life also was disrupted, and probably disappeared altogether from Galicia in the eighth century. A convincing case for continuity of regular religious life at any site has yet to be made. The ninth century saw several refoundations, notably at Samos, and some new foundations, often under the influence of clergy who had migrated from the Muslim south of Spain; and the tenth century, as we have seen, was the great age of monastic expansion in Galicia. Here again the emphasis was on restoration, on return to a revered and cherished past. The tenth-century revival had little if any contact with similar contemporary movements elsewhere in Latin Christendom. Despite Rosendo's copy of Smaragdus, the degree to which the revival diffused observance of the Benedictine Rule in north-western Spain seems to have been small. Foreign influences on Galician monastic life were barely felt before the arrival of the Cluniacs towards the end of the eleventh century.

The evidence, sparse though it is, is all of a piece. From the eighth century until the eleventh Galicia was effectively cut off from the community of western Christendom. Poised on the margin of the Christian world, hers was a world apart. Matters were not to remain thus for much longer.

II

The eleventh century:
currents of change

In Galicia in the tenth century power was the preserve of a small clique of noble families, themselves closely linked to the royal family. So firmly entrenched was their power, and so intimate these links, that we may fairly say that it would have taken a change of dynasty to shift them. As it happened, this is precisely what did occur in the eleventh century. To understand how this came about we must shift our gaze away from Galicia and fasten it instead upon the Pyrenean kingdom of Navarre.

The origins of Navarre are desperately obscure. As a distinct political entity it is first discernible in the early ninth century, by the early tenth it was a well-established territorial principality, and a century later its royal family threw up a great ruler, Sancho *el Mayor* (1004-35).[1] Two features of Sancho's rule are particularly important for us. He absorbed under his dominion nearly all the Christian principalities of Spain: Aragon, Sobrarbe and Ribagorza to his east; to his west the county of Castile and, at the very end of his life, the kingdom of León. Sancho established himself in León, Astorga and Zamora in 1034, and drove the Leonese king Bermudo III back into Galicia. On Sancho's death in the following year his dominions were divided among his four sons, Castile falling to Fernando. Bermudo III quickly regained dominion over León, but two years later in 1037 Fernando defeated him in battle and displaced him. Fernando was to rule as king over Castile, León and Galicia until his death in 1065.

In a longer perspective it was to prove more important that Sancho should have looked outside the Iberian peninsula for ideas about the duties of kingship and for techniques

[1] For what follows, see J. Pérez de Urbel, *Sancho el Mayor de Navarra* (Madrid, 1950).

to give them effect. He organized his household on Frankish
lines. He was the first Christian Spanish king since the Visigothic age to issue coinage. He had diplomatic relations
with the princes of southern France and sometimes travelled
outside the peninsula—we find him at Saint Jean d'Angély
in 1010. Above all he entered into relations with foreign
churchmen.[2] Oliba of Ripoll in Catalonia, culturally if no
longer politically a part of Francia, became his correspondent
and adviser. It was Oliba who supplied Sancho with one of
his monks, Ponce, who seems to have become the king's
domestic counsellor on ecclesiastical affairs, and who was
rewarded with the rich bishopric of Oviedo. It was Oliba
and Ponce who prevailed upon Sancho to re-establish the
see of Palencia in 1034 and to install as its first bishop
another Catalan, Bernardo. It was again Oliba and Ponce
who persuaded Sancho to seek monks from Cluny in about
1025 and to establish them at the monastery of San Juan
de la Peña on the borders of Navarre and Aragon. These
early Cluniacs in Spain were few in number and negligible
in their influence on monastic life. What was significant was
that Sancho himself became an associate of Cluny (*socius,
familiaris*) and was thus assured of the intercession of its
monks. Though he established no permanent relations
between his family and Cluny, the personal compact into
which he had entered was not forgotten by the successors of
either party to it: for the Cluniacs were expert at prayer for
the souls of sin-laden kings, and Sancho's dynasty was to
become very rich.

Thus León and Galicia received a new master in 1037,
member of a new Navarro-Castilian dynasty. The effects of
this change upon the Galician élite were probably far more
serious than historians have allowed. Fernando I rarely went
to Galicia. It is noteworthy that the number of royal grants
to Galician monasteries and cathedral churches dropped
sharply during his reign. His gaze was fixed upon the Leonese
and Castilian *meseta* and the Muslim principalities of the

---

[2] C. J. Bishko, 'Fernando I y los orígenes de la alianza castellano-leonesa con
Cluny', *Cuadernos de Historia de España* 47-8 (1968), 31-135, contains the best
account of Sancho's ecclesiastical policies and corrects Pérez de Urbel, op. cit.,
on a number of points.

centre and south of the peninsula. The beneficiaries of his acts of piety were such houses as Sahagún, Carrión, Arlanza, Cardeña, Covarrubias, Silos, and above all the churches of the *urbs regia* of León. Galicia was, by and large, excluded from the sweep of his benevolence. But there may have been more to it than this. It is likely that Galicia was positively disaffected towards Fernando I, and suffered for it. The memory of the last king of the native dynasty, whom he had dethroned, was kept green there. In a short series of annals dating from Fernando's reign Bermudo III was remembered as 'a fighter valiant in battle'; of Fernando the annalist merely made a laconic note of the date of his coronation.[3] There was a rebellion against the king by count Munio Rodríguez; defeated, Munio was imprisoned and stripped of his lands.[4] Was he the only man to meet such a fate? Some answer to this question is suggested by a royal charter of quite exceptional interest. When Fernando I died in 1065 he divided his realms, like his father before him, among his sons. To Sancho (II) went Castile, to Alfonso (VI) León, and to García Galicia. The earliest surviving document of king García's reign records an oath which he swore to the bishop of Lugo and two Galician counts.[5] García swore to be a good lord to them and promised that he would not deprive them of the lands (*honores*) which they held then or might acquire in the future, nor send them into exile, nor molest them by encouraging their ill-wishers. We know nothing of the background to king García's oath. However, it was sworn within a mere seven weeks of Fernando's death, it shows that the Galician notables distrusted their sovereign, and it raises the suspicion that the constraints laid on the son were a response to policies pursued by the father. We also know that García later experienced at least one Galician revolt, in 1071, and that the rebels suffered confiscation of their lands.[6]

King García did not last long. He was dethroned by his brother Sancho II of Castile in the early summer of 1071. Sancho in his turn was dethroned by the third brother,

---

[3] *LFH* II, ap. xcii, pp. 225. [4] R. 19 August 1061.
[5] R. 17 February 1066.
[6] A. de J. da Costa, *O bispo D. Pedro e a organização da diocese de Braga* (Coimbra, 1959), pp. 30-1, 380-7.

Alfonso, in October 1072, and it was thus the latter who reunited all the dominions of his father and as Alfonso VI ruled over a kingdom of León, Castile and Galicia from then until his death in 1109. Galician disaffection continued. A rebellion broke out in 1085 based on the Lugo area and led by count Rodrigo Ovéquiz. The king hastened back from newly conquered Toledo and besieged the rebels in Lugo, within whose Roman walls the count had fortified himself. The town was taken, count Rodrigo and his supporters captured, deprived of their lands and scattered in exile or imprisonment. This revolt was a serious affair. Rodrigo was supported by 'followers from the whole of the province of Galicia'. Among them was the bishop of Compostela, Diego Peláez. A generation later it was believed that Diego had plotted with William I of England to betray Galicia to him. Whether or not there was any truth in this accusation— and there is some reason to believe it less fantastic than it appears—the bishop's complicity in the rebellion is indicated by the actions of the king. Alfonso arrested Diego and flung him into prison. In 1088 he was prevailed upon to resign his see at the ecclesiastical council of Husillos in the presence of the king and a papal legate. The remainder of his life was spent in exile at the court of the king's enemy Pedro I of Aragon.[7]

This steady record of Galician resentment of the new dynasty was probably the impulse behind a surprising appointment made by Alfonso VI shortly after Rodrigo Ovéquiz's revolt. In the spring of 1087 he entrusted Galicia to a French nobleman, Raymond of Burgundy, who had recently come to his court. Shortly afterwards a marriage was arranged between Raymond and the king's young daughter Urraca.[8] Raymond was to remain count of Galicia until his death twenty years later. We know very little of the

[7] R. 18 June 1088, 21 July 1088, 17 June 1089; *HC*, pp. 16–17, 254; A. Ubieto Arteta, *Colección diplomática de Pedro I de Aragón y Navarra* (Zaragoza, 1951), nos. 24, 25, 48, 68, 83, 140. Rodrigo Ovéquiz's revolt has hitherto been dated to 1087, but the royal charters make it clear that word of it was brought to Alfonso VI shortly after his conquest of Toledo in May 1085.

[8] The difficult chronological problems connected with these events are discussed by B. F. Reilly, 'Santiago and Saint Denis: the French presence in eleventh-century Spain', *Catholic Historical Review* 54 (1968), 467–83.

background to this extraordinary decision. Alfonso VI was connected to the comital family of Burgundy through his marriage in 1078 or 1079 to Constance of Burgundy: her brother was married to Raymond's aunt. It may be that abbot Hugh of Cluny had a hand in Raymond's coming to Spain; he was influential with Alfonso VI and had close ties with Raymond's family. We do not know exactly when Raymond came to Spain, though it was probably in 1086. There is some evidence to suggest that he was planning a permanent settlement there. If so, he must have been confident both that the right strings had been pulled for him and that he would make a favourable impression on the king. Alfonso's thinking presumably sprang from exasperation with his troublesome province. Galicia should be given to an outsider who should yet be linked to the new royal family, and who should be richly endowed with land and quasi-regal powers for his task. Such was Raymond.

It is at first sight curious that such a man should have gone down so well as Raymond evidently did in Galicia. One possible explanation for this might be that he did not have to contend with the entrenched opposition of a powerful nobility. For the great families of the tenth century were no longer there. It is literally the case that we lose sight of them in the second quarter of the eleventh; for the unfortunate fact is that there is something of a hiatus in our documentary sources. The copious stream of charters dries up to a mere trickle about the year 1040 and does not swell again for half a century. The uncomfortable suspicion makes itself felt that the old aristocratic families do not so much die out as simply become invisible to us. On the other hand, there are some considerations which help to allay these fears. First, as we have seen, there were revolts against the new dynasty and punishment of rebels by exile or confiscation of property. We should do well to remember that in the eleventh century the imposition of a new dynasty usually had these effects—seen at their most drastic in the destruction of the Anglo-Saxon nobility by the Normans in and after 1066. Secondly, the families of Galicia which meet our gaze at the end of the eleventh century and in the first half of the twelfth had no demonstrable links with the great houses of the tenth; and this despite the fact that they were as keenly interested in genealogy as their predecessors. Third, these new men were closely associated with the new dynasty, which gives force to the supposition that the new rulers had taken steps to raise up a new aristocracy of service on whose loyalty to themselves they could rely.

It will be profitable to examine one of the families of new men. The house of Traba cannot be described as typical, for it rose rapidly to a position of pre-eminence in Galicia. Yet in many of its features it is not unrepresentative. Furthermore, its close connections with the church of Santiago de Compostela give it a special interest for us.

The first member of the family of whom we know anything was Froila Bermúdez. His descendants were later to claim that he was a grandson of count Menendo González (d. 1008), regent during the minority of Alfonso V and himself a great-nephew of Rosendo of Celanova. The claim can be neither substantiated nor disproved, but the balance of such evidence as we possess is against it. It was probably the fruit of twelfth-century anxiety to provide the family with a distinguished ancestry. The truth may be that Froila's forebears had been among count Menendo's clients. By the 1060s Froila Bermúdez was a man of some consequence. His deputy (*vicarius*) could sit alongside count Rodrigo Ovéquiz to hear a lawsuit, and Froila himself may be found presiding over a lawsuit in which one of the parties was the monastic community of Jubia.[9] The monastery of San Martín de Jubia was the religious house with which he had the closest links, and his own lands lay close to it, in the extreme north-west of Galicia. To the monks he was 'our patron' (*dominus noster*); he made them a lavish benefaction in 1086; and when he died in 1091 he was buried there after a splendid funeral attended by two bishops.[10] But he was a man who looked beyond the confines of the foggy coasts from which he came. His charter for Jubia in 1086

[9] *Sobrado Cart.* II, no. 391; *Jubia Cart.*, no. iv.
[10] *Jubia Cart.*, pp. 45–6 and nos. iv, ix. Froila Bermúdez's grandson Menendo Rodríguez stated in a charter of 1137 that his *avi et bisavi* had founded the house. Yet it had been in existence as early as 977. Possibly Froila had been involved in a refoundation: not all the Galician houses which were founded in the tenth-century monastic revival had a continuous history through to the twelfth.

reveals that he had fought against the 'heathen men in the land of the Saracens', and its dating-clause observes that king Alfonso VI was 'ruling in the city of Toledo'——a small but significant indication of awareness of the outside world and of pride in the king's most famous conquest. Froila may have been loyal to his king, but there is no sign that he rose to any height in his service. He subscribed no surviving royal charter, he never held office as a count. It was to be otherwise with his children.

Froila Bermúdez left three daughters and at least three sons. Ermesenda married a certain Cresconio Núñez; apart from a grant she made to Jubia in 1083 we know nothing of her.[11] Visclavara seems never to have married. She was a notable benefactress of religious houses. The family house at Jubia felt her generosity, so too did nearby Cines and the more distant house of Carboeiro; so also the cathedral church of Compostela.[12] She described herself in 1114 as the 'handmaid of the handmaids of God' (*ancillarum Dei ancilla*), which suggests that she had entered religion herself. If so, she did so fairly late in life: it is unlikely that a nun would have presided over a court of law as she is known to have done in 1097.[13] The third daughter, Munia, certainly entered religion for she is nearly always referred to in our sources as 'vowed to God' (*Deo vota*) throughout her very long life—she was still alive in 1145. She too was a benefactress of Jubia.[14]

Where these ladies exercised their vocation is not clear. We are told on good authority that there were no nunneries in Galicia at this period.[15] This was a matter which was to exercise their brother Pedro. He, together with Suero and Rodrigo, are the three sons of Froila Bermúdez about whom we can be sure. The fourth candidate is no less a man than Gonzalo, bishop of Mondoñedo from c.1071 to c.1108. It has been asserted that Gonzalo was a son of Froila Bermúdez but this cannot be demonstrated from the surviving

---

[11] *Jubia Cart.*, no. vii.
[12] *Jubia Cart.*, no. xxii; Santiago de Compostela, Archivo de la Universidad, Pergaminos sueltos, no. 10; *Carboeiro Cart.*, no. 62; *HC*, p. 88.
[13] *Sobrado Cart.*, I, no. 139.
[14] *Jubia Cart.*, nos. xxi, xlvi.   [15] *HC*, p. 58; see also below, ch. IX.

documents. Chronological considerations render it unlikely. If Gonzalo became a bishop in about 1071 at the earliest possible moment, i.e. at the canonical age of thirty, he must have been born about 1040-1: this accords well with the observation that he was worn down by old age in 1104-5.[16] So far as we know, his father Froila married only once. But Gonzalo's brother Pedro was fathering children after a second marriage in 1113 and lived until 1128. It is difficult to believe that bishop Gonzalo was a son of Froila Bermúdez. Possibly he had some less close connection with the family.

Rodrigo and Suero, like their sisters, were benefactors of the family monastery at Jubia and other religious establishments.[17] They were men of sufficient standing to subscribe royal charters. Rodrigo subscribed eight such documents between 1095 and 1112, Suero six during the same period. However, it was their brother Pedro who made the biggest mark. His first appearance in our sources is in the year 1086 when he subscribed his father's grant to Jubia. By 1088 he had married Urraca, the daughter of one of the Galician supporters of the new dynasty, count Froila Arias. Pedro first subscribed a royal charter in 1090, in which he was referred to as 'lord of Ferreira' (*dominator Ferrarie*).[18] By 1096 he held the office of count.[19] Thereafter he subscribed regularly as such—sometimes with a territorial designation, *comes de Ferraria* (21 August 1096), *comes de Traba* (28 March 1098), but usually simply as *comes*—until that glorious moment in 1109 when his name could be subscribed for the first time, in a royal diploma of 22 July, *Petrus Froilaz Gallecie comes*. He kept this imposing title of count of Galicia until his death in 1128.[20]

Pedro Froílaz was connected with the royal family. He had been brought up at the court of Alfonso VI.[21] His

[16] *HC*, p. 77.
[17] *Jubia Cart.*, no. vi, xxiii; AHN 491/3; AHN cód. 1044B, fo. 44ᵛ; *HC*, p. 186.
[18] R. 28 January 1090 (a document not without some suspicious features). The Ferreira in question is a little to the south-west of Carballo in the district of Bergantiños. Traba is midway between Ferreira and Carballo.
[19] R. 11 January 1096.
[20] For the extent of Pedro's comital authority see the discussion in Reilly, *Urraca*, pp. 288-92.
[21] R. May 1112.

association with count Raymond, to which his subscriptions
to Raymond's charters testify, was rewarded when Raymond
and Urraca entrusted to him the upbringing of their son
Alfonso, the future Alfonso VII, born in 1105. Alfonso could
refer to himself as count Pedro's 'little dependant' (*clientulus*)
in one of his earliest charters.[22] As we shall see in a later
chapter, count Pedro exercised very great power during
the troubled reign of queen Urraca between 1109 and 1126.
The authors of the *Historia Compostellana* had no doubts
about his greatness. In their eyes count Pedro was 'spirited
. . . warlike . . .', a man 'of great power', yet withal 'a man
who feared God and hated iniquity', for had not Diego
Gelmírez himself 'fed him, like a spiritual son, with the
nutriment of holy teaching'?[23] Diego and he were firm
friends and political allies for most of the time, and the count
showed himself gratefully generous towards Santiago. Some
of his benefactions were of a fairly predictable type, but not
all. Two are especially interesting. He attempted to restore
the regular religious life for women at Cines. This proved
awkward, for the house had recently been revived as a
monastery for male religious. Pedro expelled the abbot and
monks, and substituted nuns. (Did they include his sisters?)
Of course, there was a row, and the matter was carried—
another sign of the times—to the papal curia. The count
himself went to Rome armed with the monastic archives and
persuaded pope Paschal II that he was in the right.[24] Still
more interesting was another venture, the grant of the family
monastery of Jubia to the monks of Cluny, effected in
1113; we shall return to this episode presently.

There was, then, a certain cosmospolitan largeness about
the way in which Pedro Froílaz bestrode his world. He was
well-travelled within Spain. His upbringing at the peripatetic
court of Alfonso VI must have familiarized him with most
corners of the kingdom of León-Castile. He had spent some
time in captivity in Aragon; he numbered among his acquain-
tances the princes of southern France.[25] We have already
seen evidence of his taste for Moorish cooking. But Galicia
was always the centre of his world and it was there that he

[22] R. 5 July 1118.
[24] *HC*, pp. 91-3 (= JL 5944, 6001, 6027).
[23] *HC*, pp. 116, 122, 174, 205.
[25] *HC*, pp. 122, 319.

most sought to be remembered. His deathbed grants to the cathedral church of Santiago were so enormous that the compilers of the *Historia Compostellana* did not wish to weary their readers by listing them, and it was in the square at Compostela that he had an iron statue of himself erected.[26]

Count Pedro had many children (It is not always possible to determine of which of his two wives each was the issue.) We know of six sons and perhaps as many as eight daughters. The four younger sons—Froila, Rodrigo, Velasco and García—need not concern us here. The two eldest, however, were men of note at whose careers it will be profitable to look more closely. Pedro Froílaz's eldest son was named Bermudo Pérez. His name first meets us among the subscriptions to a royal charter of 17 March 1107, and he lived to what must have been a great age, for he was still alive in September 1161. His brother Fernando Pérez makes his first appearance as Diego Gelmírez's constable (*municeps*) in 1116, and lived until at least the summer of 1155. Two features of their careers are specially noteworthy; the part they played in Portuguese as well as Galician affairs, and their religious patronage. To understand the first of these we must retrace our steps a little.

Count Raymond was not the only Burgundian nobleman to make a career for himself in western Spain. Shortly after his own coming to the court of Alfonso VI he was followed by his first cousin Henry, the younger brother of count Hugh of Burgundy (d. 1078) and nephew of Alfonso's queen Constance. Exactly when Henry went to Spain is not clear: 1092 looks the most likely date. About three years later the king divided the vast Luso-Galician-Extremaduran honour of count Raymond and established a separate county of Portugal for Henry, to whom he gave in marriage Teresa, one of his illegitimate daughters.[27] The son of this marriage,

---

[26] *HC*, p. 478; *LFH* IV, ap. xxi, pp. 57–9.

[27] The precise sequence of events and their interpretation remain unclear: for discussion of the chronological and other problems see D. Peres, *Como nasceu Portugal* (6th edn., Porto, 1967), pp. 55–74; B. F. Reilly, 'Santiago and Saint Denis: the French presence in eleventh-century Spain', *Catholic Historical Review* 54 (1968), 467–83; P. Feige, 'Die Anfänge des portugiesischen Königtums und seiner Landeskirche', *Spanische Forschungen der Görresgesellschaft* 29 (1978), 85–436, at pp. 110–22.

Afonso Henriques (d. 1185) was much later to become the first king of an independent Portugal. Henry died at Astorga on 30 April 1112, and his widow the countess Teresa governed the county of Portugal until she was expelled by her son in 1128.

The Traba brothers were prominent among the supporters of countess Teresa during the latter years of her rule. Fernando, indeed, became her lover—the couple were publicly rebuked by St. Theotonio for their illicit union— and the (unnamed) daughter born to them was later associated with her father in a grant to Jubia in 1132.[28] Throughout the period 1121-8 Fernando was a regular and prominent witness of Teresa's charters and it is fairly clear that he was the effective ruler of the county of Portugal. It was doubtless through Fernando's agency that a splendid marriage was arranged for his elder brother Bermudo in 1122, to Urraca, the daughter of Henry and Teresa.[29] Alongside Fernando, Bermudo played a prominent part in the government of Portugal during the ensuing six years. The power of the Traba brothers came to an abrupt end in 1128 when they were defeated near Guimarães by Afonso Henriques and forced to return to Galicia. It will be seen, however, that throughout the years 1121-8 they, with their father Pedro, dominated the whole of western Iberia from the Biscayan coast of Galicia down to the uncertain frontier between Christian and Muslim to the south of Coimbra.

The hard feelings caused by the rupture of 1128 softened fairly quickly. Subscriptions to Portuguese charters suggest that Bermudo and Fernando were soon on reasonably good terms with Afonso Henriques. In any case, they had plenty on their hands in Galicia after their father Pedro's death in 1128. Here, as in Portugal, it was Fernando who stood out. He succeeded ultimately to his father's title as count of Galicia. He stood high in the counsels of Alfonso VII of León-Castile, on several of whose Andalusian campaigns he served, notably those which resulted in the taking of Córdoba in 1146 and Almería in 1147. Alfonso VII entrusted

[28] *HC*, pp. 517-18; *Jubia Cart.*, no. xxxv; *Vita Theotonii*, in *Portugalliae Monumenta Historica, Scriptores*, ed. A. Herculano (Lisbon, 1856), pp. 79-88, at p. 81.   [29] AHN 526/5.

the upbringing of his younger son Fernando to him, and in the thirteenth century it was believed that the count had been responsible for shaping Alfonso's decision to divide his dominions, on his death in 1157, between his two surviving sons, to Fernando II going León and to Sancho III Castile. Like his father Pedro before him, Fernando was a man who travelled to foreign parts: twice he made the pilgrimage to Jerusalem.[30]

It need hardly be pointed out that the Traba brothers were very rich. Bermudo, for example, could purchase land from queen Urraca in 1113 for 3,000 *solidi*.[31] Some of the benefactions to the church which this wealth made possible were as predictable as their father's. But, like him, they experimented with new forms of patronage. Their most novel venture was the refoundation of a religious house at Sobrado. A *monasterium* at Sobrado had been granted—this may have been a concealed sale—to the brothers by queen Urraca in 1118. (In view of earlier remarks it is interesting to note that they claimed that Sobrado had been confiscated from their ancestors by Fernando I. If the truth of the claim cannot be established, the fact that it was made is an indication of the posthumous reputation of Fernando I in Galician aristocratic circles.) Urraca's grant was confirmed by Alfonso VII in 1135. There is as yet no hint that the brothers intended to install a regular religious community there. A further charter was granted in 1142 to 'all the holy men of God and St. Benedict, living according to the custom of the Cistercians'. The house had been refounded as a Cistercian monastery, a daughter-house of Clairvaux.[32] It was among the earliest Cistercian foundations in the Iberian peninsula. Bermudo himself, in his old age, between 1157 and 1161, entered Sobrado and died as a monk there.[33]

Count Pedro Froílaz was able to marry off his daughters well. Toda Pérez married count Gutierre Bermúdez, whose family came from the north-eastern parts of Galicia. His

[30] AHN 527/6, 1126/6.

[31] R. 17 June 1113. Fernando owned urban property in Lugo as well as Compostela: AHN 1325D/8 *bis*.

[32] R. 29 July 1118, 29 May 1135; AHN 526/10 (= *Sobrado Cart.*, II, no. 11).

[33] AHRG, Particulares, no. 261; AHN 556/4.

brother Suero was the most powerful nobleman in the
Asturias during the reign of Urraca and in the early years
of Alfonso VII's. Gutierre's landholdings were for the most
part near Lugo, of whose cathedral church he was a generous
benefactor, though he was buried further west, in Traba
country, at the monastery of Lorenzana. From 1109 onwards
he was a frequent witness of royal charters. He and his wife
were benefactors of Caabeiro, Carboeiro and Lorenzana.
After his death in 1130 his widow was among the early benefactors of her brothers' Cistercian foundation at Sobrado.[34]
Her sister Lupa Pérez married count Munio Peláez of Monterroso, near Lugo. The pattern will by now be familiar. Count
Munio's name was prominent among the witness-lists of
royal charters over many years from 1111 onwards. He and
his wife were benefactors of the cathedral churches of Lugo
and Santiago de Compostela. They were associated with
a Cistercian foundation at Monfero, established about 1147.
After her husband's death (*c.*1150?) Lupa founded a house
for Benedictine nuns at Dormeán.[35] So the list could be
continued. Elvira married Fernando Yáñez, the greatest
nobleman of southern Galicia. A second Toda married count
Gutierre Osorio, an important aristocrat of the León region.
Eva married García Garcés de Aza, a Castilian grandee
renowned for his wealth and dullness. Estefania married
Ruy Fernández, a member of the Castro clan, who together
with their rivals the Lara family were the most powerful of
the nobility of Castile. The even level of eminence among
the husbands whom Pedro Froílaz de Traba secured for his
girls—with one significant exception, which we shall notice
in a later chapter—is a further indication of his standing in
the first quarter of the twelfth century.

It would be intriguing to follow the family into the next
generation, in which one of its members married a reigning
monarch of León, but we have followed it far enough already.
The house of Traba and the families with which it was

---

[34] *HC*, p. 246; AHN 491/13, 526/11, 1325C/21; AHN cód. 1044B, fo. 26ᵛ-
27ᵛ, 50ᵛ-51ʳ; *Carboeiro Cart.*, no. 76; R. 10 September 1109, May 1112,
12 October 1113, etc. For Suero Bermúdez see *CAI*, pp. 255-6.
[35] *HC*, pp. 121, 188; AHRG, Particulares, no. 58; AHN 497/4, 1325C/11, 22;
R. 8 December 1111, 2 March 1112, 8 December 1113, etc.

connected formed a new Galician aristocracy. As far as we can see, this new aristocracy was raised up by Alfonso VI and his son-in-law Raymond, and sustained by his daughter Urraca and her son Alfonso VII. Entrusted with the administration of Galicia, its members had ample scope for self-enrichment and the exercise of power. And they were loyal: after Rodrigo Ovéquiz's revolt in 1085–7 there were no more dangerous Galician rebellions. Yet this new aristocracy was not quite like the one which it replaced. However close its association with the royal family, the house of Traba was never, during our period, bound to it by ties of blood as the tenth-century Galician nobility had been tied to the royal dynasty of León. Alfonso VI, Urraca and Alfonso VII married into the royal or noble dynasties of other parts of Spain, of France, of Germany; they maintained a distance between themselves and their new aristocracy of service. Secondly, we are left with the impression—for given the nature of the evidence it can be no more than this—that although the Trabas and their connections were very rich, they were not possessed of wealth on the princely scale of St. Rosendo and his relations. Their benefactions to the church, lavish though they were, did not have quite the breath-taking amplitude of the endowments granted by the monastic founders of the tenth century. Perhaps this helped to keep them loyal to the monarchs from whom further wealth might flow: if they worked hard they could always hope for more. In the third place they were less circumscribed in their interests. Political intrigue took them to Portugal, marriage removed daughters to Castile, duty took their menfolk to the peripatetic court of the king-emperors of León-Castile and to far-flung campaigning in Andalusia, litigation urged Pedro Froílaz to Rome and devotion his son Fernando to Jerusalem. They moved on a wider stage than their predecessors, and we have seen how their religious benefactions mirror awareness of a Christendom beyond Galicia. One last feature of the new aristocracy is most surprising to the enquirer familiar with tenth-century conditions. Although the new men had a firm grip on nearly all the most important positions in the secular administration of Galicia, they did not monopolize the higher ranks of the ecclesiastical hierarchy.

The Galician church of the tenth century furnishes a fine example of what German historians term an *Adelskirche*. The greater noble families shared out among themselves the plums of ecclesiastical preferment. The church was run by them and for them. If they sometimes squabbled over who should get what, there was never any question of outsiders knuckling in to take from them what they would probably have regarded as their birthright. But when we shift our gaze forward to the twelfth century, what a contrast meets the eye. Appointments to bishoprics are in the hands of the king. Many bishops have served the crown in some capacity, often in the royal chancery, before their promotion. Bishops drawn from noble families are conspicuous by their absence.[36] Bishops who were natives of France or of other parts of Spain are not uncommon. How had this come about? It is tempting to associate this shift with the change of dynasty. No medieval king needed telling that a bench of loyal bishops could assist him in containing the disaffection of a restive province. We need think only, for example, of the rapid Normanization of the English episcopate under the rule of William the Conqueror. With this instance in mind, let us examine the Galician appointments which occurred during the reigns of the sons of Fernando I.

Three bishops were appointed to Galician sees in the reign of García (1065–71). Gudesteo became bishop of Iria-Compostela probably in 1066. He was the nephew of his predecessor Cresconio, who had been 'sprung from a very noble stock' (*nobilissimo genere ortus*).[37] Cresconio had been appointed before the old Leonese dynasty came to an end, for he subscribed a charter of Bermudo III dated 9 June 1037. It is reasonable to see in Gudesteo a member of the older nobility. Relations between him and king García may have been guarded. It is significant that García made no grants to the church of Santiago de Compostela. (The argument from silence, hazardously resorted to by the

---

[36] The single possible exception is Gonzalo of Mondoñedo. As will be apparent from earlier remarks in this chapter, I am now more doubtful about his aristocratic connections than I was a few years ago: cf. *Episcopate*, pp. 61, 84.

[37] *HC*, p. 15.

historian of the early middle ages, has force here because the early charters of Compostela have been preserved in copies made, as we shall see in chapter X, a mere sixty years later than king García's reign.) No change of bishop occurred at Lugo where bishop Vistruario, first traceable in 1062, outlasted García and his brother Sancho and lived well into the reign of Alfonso VI. The only indication of his attitude to the king is furnished by the oath which he and the two Galician counts exacted from García in 1066. The bishopric of Tuy, vacant for about half a century, was restored during García's reign with his active support, if not actually at his instance; on 1 February 1071 he granted endowments to the see and its first bishop, Jorge (Georgius). Nothing is known of this man (who survived for only a short time, dying in 1074 at the latest), but it is difficult to suppose that the king's part in the re-establishment of the see did not involve some say in the choice of the bishop who was to have charge of it. King García also undertook the restoration of the metropolitan see of Braga, though its first bishop-elect, Pedro, did not receive consecration until after the king's dethronement. We may say the same of him as of bishop Jorge of Tuy.

In 1071 García was defeated, dethroned and imprisoned by his brothers Sancho II of Castile and Alfonso VI of León, who jointly ruled the kingdom of Galicia until Sancho's murder in 1072, after which Alfonso ruled it alone. Four episcopal appointments may belong to the period of joint rule in 1071–2. At Compostela bishop Diego Peláez was the choice of king Sancho, as the *Historia Compostellana* bluntly tells us.[38] Since the *Historia* fails to say anything about his ancestry, contrary to its authors' habitual practice, we may take it as likely that he was of undistinguished birth, and perhaps not a local man at all. At the neighbouring see of Mondoñedo bishop Gonzalo first appears to us in a royal charter of 13 June 1071. As we have seen, the claims of noble birth that have been made on his behalf cannot be substantiated; and even supposing that he were a member of the house of Traba, we should remember that that family

[38] *HC*, p. 16.

was itself new and that its upward social progress owed
much to the impulsion of the royal hand. Two bishoprics in
southern Galicia and northern Portugal, Orense and Lamego,
seem to have been re-established in 1071. The restoration-
charter for Orense, dated 31 July 1071, is a suspicious document which has almost certainly been tampered with. For
what it is worth, it records that Sancho II brought about
the restoration of the two sees, appointing Ederonio to
Orense and Pedro to Lamego. Nothing is known of the
antecedents of these two men.

The first Galician bishopric to fall vacant in the reign of
Alfonso VI after 1072 was Tuy, to which a new bishop had
been appointed by May 1074. His name is recorded variously
as Adericus (1075, 1088) and Audericus (1087, 1095). The
name is not Spanish but French, its bearer presumably one
of the earliest clerical immigrants to León-Castile who
secured a bishopric there. It is unlikely that the interest
exerted in his favour could have been any other than royal.
Vistruario of Lugo is last referred to in February 1086;
his successor Amor makes his first appearance in July 1088.
We know nothing of his background, but it is difficult to
believe that in the aftermath of Rodrigo Ovéquiz's rebellion
the king did not ensure that the new bishop should be a man
without local aristocratic connections, on whose loyalty
he could depend. This supposition is strengthened in the
light of what occurred at Santiago de Compostela. After
Alfonso VI had rid himself of bishop Diego Peláez in 1088
his choice fell upon Pedro, abbot of the distant Castilian
monastery of Cardeña. At Orense a bishop Juan Alfonso
appears to have held the see briefly in 1087, to be succeeded
shortly afterwards by a certain Pedro: but these are no more
than names to us. Dalmatius, who became bishop of Compostela in 1094, was a monk of Cluny: Alfonso VI and count
Raymond were instrumental in his appointment.[39] Gerald,
who received the see of Braga probably in 1095, was another
Frenchman, formerly a monk of Moissac and a protégé of the
archbishop of Toledo, in whose promotion it is again very
probable that the king and his son-in-law were concerned.

[39] *HC*, p. 20.

This brief survey of Galician episcopal appointments in the generation following the death of Fernando I in 1065 suggests, first, that kings were playing a more forceful part in them than they had been accustomed to do in the past; second, that men with distinguished family connections in Galicia were becoming more rare among the bishops; and third, as a corollary, that preferment was going to men who were outsiders either socially or geographically. It is all of a piece with this trend that the same period should have witnessed new and vigorous attempts to supervise the Galician church on the part of an ecclesiastical authority which was closely connected with the crown. Archbishop Bernardo of Toledo was the most commanding figure in the life of the Spanish church in the late eleventh and early twelfth century. We shall encounter him frequently in the pages which follow, for Diego Gelmírez was to find him the ablest and most implacable of his opponents.[40] Bernardo was a Frenchman from the Agenais, a monk successively at Auch and at Cluny. He came to Spain in 1080 at the bidding of his abbot, Hugh of Cluny, and was shortly afterwards given the abbacy of the important royal monastery of Sahagún. In 1086 Alfonso VI promoted him to the metropolitan see of newly conquered Toledo, the ancient capital of the Visigothic kingdom. Bernardo was determined that Toledo should be once again a capital—but of the Spanish church. He visited the papal curia in 1088. An old friend from his days at Cluny, Eudes of Chatillon, had recently become pope as Urban II. Of the privileges which then were lavished, with so unsparing a hand, upon the church of Toledo the most important was the bull *Cunctis sanctorum.*[41] The pope ruled that Bernardo as archbishop of Toledo should be the primate of Spain, enjoying the dignity and rights—prudently undefined—of a primate. Furthermore, in addition to his own rights as metropolitan over dioceses within the province of Toledo he was to exercise authority over those bishoprics whose own metropolitan see was for the present in Islamic hands. A few years later,

---

[40] The best treatment of Bernardo's career is to be found in J. F. Rivera Recio, *La iglesia de Toledo en el siglo XII (1086-1208)*, vol. I (Rome, 1966), especially ch. III.   [41] JL 5366.

probably in 1093, Bernardo was appointed papal legate throughout all the ecclesiastical provinces of the Spains, that is those of the Iberian peninsula together with the province of Narbonne.[42] As Bernardo interpreted it, he had been given an almost unbounded liberty of interfering in the ecclesiastical life of any part of Christian Spain.

Among his first actions after his return to Spain was a journey into Galicia to consecrate the new cathedral church of Braga on 28 August 1089.[43] This was not simply a case of a distinguished churchman performing a ceremonial function on a great occasion. It was a considered statement about who mattered most in the Galician church, a claim of the most public kind for the rights of the church of Toledo. It had not been Bernardo's first visit to Galicia. In the summer of 1087 he had visited Lugo—whose bishopric was probably vacant at the time; we cannot discount the possibility that he had some share in the election of bishop Amor—where he had presided over a suit between bishop Gonzalo of Mondoñedo and the monks of Lorenzana, and had come down strongly in favour of the latter.[44] He had also interested himself in the affairs of the church of Santiago de Compostela after the resignation—in effect, the deposition—of bishop Diego Peláez in 1088. This is a difficult matter to elucidate. The canonicity of the proceedings at Husillos, where Diego had been removed from his see, was impugned by the pope. Bernardo seems to have been caught between two fires: Urban II wished to have Diego restored, but to this Alfonso VI was irreconcilably hostile. Diego's release from captivity may have been effected at Bernardo's instance. What is certain is that the pope consulted the archbishop of Toledo in 1089 about the choice of a legate to Spain, part of whose brief was to sort out the Compostela business. The man chosen, cardinal Rainerio, later to succeed to the papacy as Paschal II, held a council at León in 1090 at which Pedro de Cardeña, Alfonso VI's bishop of Compostela, was deposed. But he could not bring about Diego

[42] On the date of this appointment see Rivera, op. cit., pp. 141-3.

[43] J. A. Ferreira, *Fastos episcopães da igreja primacial de Braga* (Famalição, 1928), I. 198.

[44] AHN cód. 1044B, fo. 30^r-31^v.

Peláez's reinstatement, and the bishopric of Compostela remained vacant. On a rather different front, we may surmise that Toledan pressure was being exerted throughout these years to enforce Galician conformity in the matter of the adoption of the Roman liturgy, decreed in 1080 but, it would seem, only reluctantly accepted by conservative Galician churchmen. And we can detect Bernardo's hand as well as the royal family's in some of the appointments to north-western sees in the 1090s; in Gerald's to Braga in 1095, for example, and in Maurice's to Coimbra in 1099.

The dispute between the bishop of Mondoñedo and the abbey of Lorenzana had concerned the monastic endowments. Bernardo's willingness to uphold the monks might have owed something to the fact that he was himself by training a monk. As we have seen, Lorenzana had been founded in 969. It had been one of the last houses established during Galicia's tenth-century monastic reformation. It was not until after the change of dynasty that new developments took place in the monastic history of Galicia. The first of these was the foundation by king García in 1067 of a monastery at Toques, about three miles north of Mellid. The new royal family had few connections with Galician monasticism. Fernando I had been a generous benefactor of Celanova but he had made no new religious foundation of his own in Galicia. What mattered about Toques was that it was a royal foundation, a little island of commitment to the new dynasty in a sea of indifference or hostility. Its church was dedicated to St. Antoninus (San Antolín), a patron in whose cult the royal family had lately been interesting itself. The foundation charter tells us that García had established the house in remembrance of his parents Fernando I and queen Sancha 'of divine memory'—which was not how many of their Galician subjects looked back at them. Though its material endowments were modest, Toques was given a generous privilege of immunity. García's charter was subscribed by men and women who included some of the staunchest supporters of the new order like, for example, Oveco Sánchez whose subscriptions to royal charters may be traced down to 1112 and whose lands lay near the vital Piedrafita pass from the Leonese *meseta* into

Galicia.[45] It is a pity that we know nothing of Tanoy, the first abbot of Toques. The new monastery continued to be the recipient of royal patronage; charters were granted by Alfonso VI in 1077 and by Raymond and Urraca in 1099.[46] Thereafter we have practically no information about it. Toques never grew into a house of any significance. To that degree it stands for a royal initiative which bore little or no fruit. But that does not mean that we should underestimate the interest of the Toques episode as one means chosen by the new dynasty of making its presence felt in Galicia.

A further new direction in monastic life was struck out in 1075 when, for the first time, a Galician monastery was placed under the patronage of Cluny. The house in question was San Salvador de Villafrio, near Lugo, the donor was Iñigo Bermúdez and the occasion of the gift his entry to Cluny as a monk. Iñigo's family connections cannot be established with certainty but there is some likelihood that he was the brother of count Fernando Bermúdez, a prominent figure at the court of Alfonso VI and also a friend to Cluny. It is probable that the Cluniac leanings displayed in the brothers' monastic patronage owed something to the example set by the royal family.[47] Sancho *el Mayor's* initiative had been taken further by his son Fernando I, who at some date between 1053 and his death in 1065 had bound himself to pay an annual *census* to the monks of Cluny, set at the very considerable sum of 1,000 gold pieces, in return for their intercession. From 1072 onwards, the year of his succession to the undivided kingdom of León-Castile, Alfonso VI's relations with Cluny were extremely close. Between 1073 and 1077 he granted four Spanish monastic houses to the monks of Cluny and in 1077 not only re-established the

[45] R. 23 February 1067.

[46] R. 17 October 1077, 23 January 1099.

[47] The Cluniac connection has attracted much attention: see, most recently, C. J. Bishko, 'The Cluniac priories of Galicia and Portugal: their acquisition and administration', *Studia Monastica* 7 (1965), 305–56; *idem*, 'Fernando I y los orígenes de la alianza castellano-leonesa con Cluny', *Cuadernos de Historia de España* 47–8 (1968), 31–135 (now reprinted in an English translation in his *Studies in Medieval Spanish Frontier History* (London, 1980), no. ii); P. Segl, *Königtum und Klosterreform in Spanien. Untersuchungen über die Cluniacenser-klöster in Kastilien-León vom Beginn des 11. bis zur Mitte des 12. Jahrhunderts* (Kallmünz, 1974).

Fernandine *census* but doubled the rate at which it was paid.
Thenceforward the colossal sum of 2,000 gold pieces made its
way from León-Castile to Cluny every year. It was the biggest
donation that the monks of Cluny ever received. Further
monastic houses were made over by the king in 1079 and
1081. Abbot Hugh of Cluny visited his court in 1077. In
1080 the Cluniac monk Robert was given the abbacy of
Sahagún, where he was shortly afterwards succeeded by
another Cluniac, Bernardo, who, as we have seen, went on
to become archbishop of Toledo in 1086.

It is into such a context of specially close links between
the royal house of León-Castile and the Cluny of St. Hugh
that we must set the eager patronage of the lay and ecclesiastical magnates of Galicia. If count Raymond made no
grants to Cluny that we know of, his widow Urraca made
over the monastery of San Vicente de Pombeiro to Cluny
in 1109. Count Henry of Portugal had close connections
with Cluny: his grandmother Hélie of Semur was the sister
of St. Hugh, and his elder brother had resigned the duchy
of Burgundy in 1078 in order to enter Cluny as a monk
(thereby occasioning a famous letter to its abbot from pope
Gregory VII). Henry was a benefactor of Sahagún; and
together with his wife Teresa he granted the church of Rates
to the Cluniac house of La-Charité-sur-Loire in 1100. Two
years later bishop Maurice of Coimbra—another Frenchman,
another Cluniac, and a protégé of the archbishop of Toledo
—granted the church of Sta. Justa in Coimbra to the same
house. Somewhat later, in 1113, as we have seen, Pedro
Froílaz de Traba granted the monastery of Jubia to Cluny.
He prudently, if uncanonically, stipulated that if the Cluniacs
should wish to depart from Jubia they should give the house
back to the Traba family. A still more interesting stipulation
was that the prior appointed from among the monks of
Cluny should be a man learned in scripture (*in divina pagina
doctus*): this is a provision without parallel in Spanish charters
of this type and date which perhaps sheds further light
upon the tastes of Pedro Froílaz and his relatives.

Cluniac monks were not the only foreign ecclesiastics who
made their way to Galicia. From the 1060s onwards we have
also to reckon with the emissaries of the reformed papacy.

Cardinal Hugo Candidus may have visited Santiago de Compostela in the course of his legation to Spain in the years
1065-7. It was a papal legate, Richard of Marseilles, who
presided over the council of Husillos in 1088 at which
bishop Diego Peláez was prevailed upon to resign his see.
It was another legate who deposed his successor and attempted
to reinstate the exiled Diego in 1090. Another visitor on papal
business was Jarenton, abbot of St. Benigne at Dijon, who
can be traced at Coimbra in 1084. Unfortunately we know
nothing of the affairs which brought Jarenton to Spain:
it is intriguing to speculate on what (if any) connection
there might have been between Alfonso VI's appointment
of Raymond to the county of Galicia in 1087 and the visit
to his dominions three years previously of the distinguished
head of a famous monastery with which Raymond's family
enjoyed close connections.

We also have the beginnings of traffic in the other direction, which probably owed its impulse at least in part to
the encouragement of the papal legates. In 1095 bishop
Dalmatius of Compostela, himself as we have seen a Frenchman and a Cluniac, travelled to France to attend Urban II's
council of Clermont. He was accompanied by 'certain bishops
from the same ecclesiastical province' (*quibusdam com-
provincialium episcoporum*).[48] Who were they? A papal
letter of 28 November 1095 concerning the affairs of the
church of Lugo was directed from Clermont to the bishops
of León, Oviedo and Mondoñedo.[49] The text makes it clear
that the three addressees had not attended the council, but
that bishop Amor of Lugo had. It also mentions the bishops
of Braga and Orense in such a way as to imply that neither of
these prelates had been at Clermont. That leaves us with the
bishops of Tuy or Astorga, or both, as the companions of
Dalmatius and Amor. Both, as it happens, were Frenchmen.
Audericus of Tuy we have already encountered. Osmundus of
Astorga (1082-96) had a northern French name and may
perhaps have come from the region of Boulogne, with whose
countess, Ida, he corresponded.[50]

There will be more to be said of these contacts between

---

[48] *HC*, p. 20.   [49] AHN cód. 1043B, fo. 38ᵛ.

[50] *ES*, XVI, ap. xxii, pp. 473-4.

the churchmen of Galicia and the papal court, for they were to be of very great importance in the career of Diego Gelmírez. Suffice it to say for the present that this early traffic in the 1080s and 1090s must be reckoned as yet another factor tending to break down the barriers between Galicia and the rest of Latin Christendom. We have seen how the sons of Fernando I, representatives of a new royal dynasty, attempted to bring their remote and rebellious province to heel. We have witnessed the emergence of new aristocratic families, watched the character of the episcopate changing, looked at the ambitions of the church of Toledo and glanced at new developments in the regular religious life. By the last decade of the eleventh century it must have been evident to the intelligent contemporary observer— such as the young Diego Gelmírez—that the ecclesiastical life of Galicia would never be quite the same again.

But there was another force more potent than any of these in reducing Galician isolation—the coming of pilgrims to the shrine of St. James. To that shrine, those pilgrims, we must now turn.

III

The early history of
the cult of Saint James

By the middle years of the eleventh century pilgrims on their way to Compostela were a common sight on the roads of western Europe. To take an example at random, a donor to the monastery of Savigny, near Lyons, in 1046 could refer casually to the number of 'foreigners making their way to the shrines of the saints, whether to St. Mary or St. Peter, St. James or St. Gil'; that is, to Vézelay, Rome, Santiago de Compostela and Saint-Gilles-de-Provence.[1] Would Compostela have been included in this quartet of famous shrines if the Savigny charter had been drawn up a hundred, or even fifty years before 1046? Probably not. As we shall see, there was a surge in the popularity of pilgrimages as such, and of the pilgrimage to Compostela in particular, during the eleventh century. We shall examine in due course what sorts and conditions of people went on these journeys, why they undertook them, and how they thought that they profited from them. But before we turn to the men and women who made the journey we must look to the end to which their journeying tended.

The *Historia Compostellana* provides us with a summary of the legend of St. James the Greater as it was believed at Compostela in the lifetime of Diego Gelmírez. Two propositions are central to it: first, that St. James preached the gospel in Spain as well as in the Holy Land; second, that after his martyrdom at the hands of Herod Agrippa I his disciples carried his body by sea to Spain, where they landed at Padrón on the coast of Galicia, and took it thence inland for burial at Santiago de Compostela.[2] Other embellishments were added later, but they need not concern us. Neither are we here concerned with the question of whether or not the

[1] *Cartulaire de l'Abbaye de Savigny*, ed. A. Bernard (Paris, 1853), I, no. 731.
[2] *HC*, pp. 5-7.

legend contains any grain of scientific historical truth. It
need hardly be said that the story is in the highest degree
unlikely. But our concern is not with what St. James and
his disciples may or may not have done, but only with what
later generations of Christians chose to believe.

Any enquiry into the early history of the cult of St. James
in Spain must still take as its point of departure a masterly
study by Louis Duchesne published nearly a century ago.[3]
Gleefully bellowing gales of rational air about the dusty
obfuscations of cherished Spanish mythology, Duchesne
established once and for all that there is no sign whatsoever
that during the first six centuries of the Christian era anyone
believed that St. James had either preached or been buried
in Spain. Research conducted since his day has unreservedly
endorsed Duchesne's findings. So far, so good. But when we
advance beyond the sixth century we enter at once a thicket
of highly problematical texts. Their origins are often obscure,
their testimony not easy to interpret, and their historical
value debatable. However, they are important for us. No
enquirer may shirk the task of trying to thread a path through
them.

The earliest, probably, is a short tract known as the
Breviarium Apostolorum.[4] It is a list of the apostles, giving
details about where they preached, how they met their
deaths, where they were buried and when their feasts were
celebrated. The version which circulated in western Europe
was a Latin translation and amplification of a Greek original.
The editor of the Latin version seems to have been a western
divine who wanted to show that not all the apostles had
restricted their labours to Italy, the eastern Mediterranean
provinces of the Roman empire and the lands beyond the

[3] L. Duchesne, 'Saint Jacques en Galice', *Annales du Midi* 12 (1900), 145-79.
[4] B. de Gaiffier, 'Le *Breviarium Apostolorum* (B.H.L. 652). Tradition manu-
scrite et œuvres apparentées', *Analecta Bollandiana* 81 (1963), 89-116. The
passage relating to St. James is best edited by M. C. Díaz y Díaz, 'Die spanische
Jakobus-Legende bei Isidor von Seville', *Historisches Jahrbuch* 77 (1958), 467-72.
The *Breviarium* and other early texts have recently been subjected to close
scrutiny by J. van Herwaarden, 'The origins of the cult of St. James of Compostela', *Journal of Medieval History* 6 (1980), 1-35. I had completed the first
draft of this chapter in 1979, before Dr van Herwaarden's article (of which he
kindly sent me a copy) was published. I was comforted to find that we had
independently reached broadly similar conclusions on all essential matters.

eastern imperial frontiers. To this end he brought Philip to Gaul and James to Spain. For him, James the son of Zebedee preached the gospel in Spain but was not, be it noted, buried there. When and where the Latin *Breviarium* originated we cannot say. It would seem to have been a seventh-century production. In England it was known to Aldhelm (d. 709); in Spain it was cited by Julian of Toledo in about 686, though he chose, most interestingly, to disregard the connection it postulated between St. James and Spain (a point on which Duchesne laid great stress).

It may have been as early as Julian's day that a writer who knew the entry in the *Breviarium* concerning St. James interpolated a short passage about the apostle into the treatise known as *De ortu et obitu patrum*, attributed, probably incorrectly, to Isidore of Seville. He too believed that St. James had preached the gospel 'to the peoples of Spain and the western places, at the world's edge'; but he too was emphatic that James had not been buried in Spain.[5] Spanish symptoms in the earliest manuscript tradition (which is south German) have led the foremost modern authority to suggest that the interpolated passage was composed in Spain or Septimania at some point before *c.*750.[6]

Our next two witnesses may be located with certainty in the Iberian peninsula; furthermore, we can satisfactorily date their testimony. A hymn in honour of St. James was composed somewhere in the Asturian kingdom of northern Spain, and an acrostic formed from the first letters of its sixty lines dates it to the reign of king Mauregato (783-8).[7] The author clearly believed that St. James had preached in Spain, though he had nothing to say about the apostle's place of burial. Noteworthy too, and a theme to which we shall return, is that for the first time the cult of the saint is

---

[5] *Patrologia Latina*, LXXXIII, col. 151.

[6] B. Bischoff, 'Die europäische Verbreitung der Werke Isidors von Seville', in his *Mittelalterliche Studien* (Stuttgart, 1966), I. 171-94. See also M. Herren, 'On the earliest Irish acquaintance with Isidore of Seville', in *Visigothic Spain. New Approaches*, ed. E. James (Oxford, 1980), pp. 243-50.

[7] Critical edition and excellent discussion in M. C. Díaz y Díaz, 'Los himnos en honor de Santiago de la liturgia hispánica', *Compostellanum* II (1966), 457-502; reprinted in his collection of essays, *De Isidoro al siglo XI* (Barcelona, 1976), pp. 237-88.

associated with a king. At about the same time the monk Beatus of Liébana composed a celebrated commentary on the Book of Revelation. Beatus is remembered for the stand he took on the orthodox side in the controversy over the heresy of Adoptianism. His commentary was in part a by-product of that dispute. It is a work well-known to art-historians owing to the survival of a large number of manu-scripts dating from the tenth, eleventh and twelfth centuries furnished with illustrations of startling beauty.[8] In the prologue to Book II Beatus listed the apostles and the regions where they preached in a passage which depends upon either the *Breviarium* or the interpolated *De ortu et obitu patrum*. Moreover, he referred to the illustration which accompanied this passage in his autograph manuscript. The illustrative scheme which survives with remarkable consistency in the extant, later manuscripts descends therefore from the scriptorium of Beatus himself. One family of manuscripts, that classified by Neuss as IIb, contains at this point in the text an illustration of the twelve apostles with captions to tell the reader where they preached. Thus, in the manu-script now at Gerona, which was copied in 975 perhaps in or near León, we find the apostles depicted at fo. 52^v-53^r; the fourth figure from the left is captioned *Iacobus, Spania*.[9]

It is from the following century that we have our first evidence for the belief that the apostle's tomb was in Spain. It is contained in the *Martyrology* of Usuard of Saint-Germain-des-Prés, which was completed about 865.[10] Usuard had travelled in Spain, and it is likely that he had picked up his information about St. James while he was there. He listed St. James's feast-day on 25 July, noted the circumstances

---

[8] The best edition of the text is that of H. A. Sanders, *Beati in Apocalipsin libri XII* (Papers and Monographs of the American Academy in Rome, no. 7: Rome, 1930). For the illustrations W. Neuss, *Die Apokalypse des Hl. Johannes in der altspanischen und altchristlichen Bibel-Illustration* (Münster, 1931) is fundamental. See also C. Cid, 'Santiago el Mayor en el texto y en las miniaturas de los códices del Beato', *Compostellanum* 10 (1965), 231-73, and for the general art-historical context J. Fontaine, *L'Art pré-roman hispanique* (Paris, 1973-7).

[9] This MS has been published in facsimile: *Sancti Beati a Liebana in Apocalypsin codex Gerundensis* (Lausanne, 1962).

[10] But not, it seems, in the slightly earlier martyrologies of Florus of Lyons and Ado: see van Herwaarden, art. cit., at pp. 18-22.

of his martyrdom, and continued thus: 'his most holy remains were translated from Jerusalem to Spain and deposited in its uttermost region (*in ultimis finibus*); they are revered with the most devout veneration (*celeberrima veneratione*) by the people of those parts'. Thus we now have trustworthy evidence for the presence of what were believed to be the relics of the saint in the extreme north-west of Spain, and for the existence of a cult there. It is time to turn our attention to Santiago de Compostela.

Remains which were believed to be those of St. James were discovered at Compostela in the first half of the ninth century. Of this we may be certain, but of little else besides. Compostelan tradition placed the discovery of the saint in the time of king Alfonso II (791–842) and of bishop Theodemir of Iria. Theodemir's predecessor Quendulfus was still alive in 818.[11] Bishop Theodemir died on 20 October 847. The discovery therefore occurred between 818 and 842: we cannot date it more precisely than this.[12] The bishop's death can be dated with a precision all too rare in the history of ninth-century Spain because it was inscribed on his sarcophagus, which was discovered in the course of excavations some years ago. What is particularly interesting about the bishop's tomb is its whereabouts. The sarcophagus was found during excavations beneath the nave of the existing cathedral of Santiago de Compostela. The bishop had chosen to be buried not in or near his own episcopal church of Iria but rather at the site where the resting-place of St. James had been revealed. Even had we no other evidence to go on, the site of Theodemir's tomb would alone permit us to infer that the place which was to become known as Santiago de Compostela was already, in his day, a specially venerated holy place; as Usuard's testimony of some twenty years later confirms.

It is possible that the site had been venerated at, or from, a considerably earlier date. So much is suggested by the results of archaeological excavations which were conducted beneath the cathedral of Compostela in 1878–9 and again

---

[11] *Sobrado Cart.* I, no. 43.

[12] R. 4 September 829 might be thought to provide an earlier *terminus ante quem*, but (as we shall see) it is a forgery.

between 1946 and 1959. These excavations were ill-conducted, ill-recorded and ill-published. Any conclusions drawn from them must be tentative. Yet their results are, at the least, suggestive.[13] The more recent series of excavations took place beneath the nave and transepts of the cathedral. A large number of human burials was revealed. They lacked grave-goods and were aligned on an east–west orientation. Some of the burials, probably the later ones in the series, were covered by grave-slabs of local granite. These slabs could be roughly dated by association with similar slabs from early Christian sites in Galicia, some of which bear dated inscriptions, to the period between *c*.400 and *c*.650. The nineteenth-century excavations took place further to the east, under the sanctuary of the existing cathedral. Unhappily these were unscientifically conducted and far from adequately recorded. Antonio López Ferreiro, canon of Compostela and later her incomparable historian, himself took part in them and has left us a usable account of what was found. López Ferreiro described the discovery of the remains of a structure which irresistibly recalls an early Christian *cella memoriae* or *martyrium*. The foundations of a rectangular stone enclosure or building were disclosed, whose overall measurements were 6.4 metres (East–West) by 4.7 metres (North–South). It had been divided internally into two parts of unequal size by a partition wall running North–South. This wall was interrupted in the middle by an aperture giving access from the smaller western chamber into the larger eastern one. The eastern chamber was paved in mosaic, the western in brick tiles (? *opus signinum*): it would seem therefore that the western chamber was of lesser importance than the eastern, as it were an atrium leading to a place of special significance. At the centre of the eastern chamber was a rectangular pit, lined with stucco and covered with

---

[13] For the nineteenth-century excavations see *LFH* I, ch. 6, and F. Fita and M. Fernández Guerra, *Recuerdos de un viaje a Santiago* (Madrid, 1880); for those of the twentieth century see M. Chamoso Lamas, 'Noticia de las excavaciones arqueológicas que se realizan en la catedral de Santiago', *Compostellanum* 1 (1956), 5–48, 275–328, and 2 (1957), 225–330. In the absence of any adequate archaeological report the best general account of all the excavations and their significance is to be found in J. Guerra Campos, 'Excavaciones en la catedral de Santiago', *La Ciencia Tomista* 88 (1960), 97–168, 269–324.

slabs of marble. It contained no human remains. (There is some reason for supposing that the mortal remains of the patron saint were abstracted from an earlier resting-place in the sixteenth century and re-buried beneath the apse of the cathedral.) The emplacement for some fixture, conceivably an altar, was discovered beside the pit. Here then we seem to have a shrine of some kind which attracted the devout to be buried near it. The constructional details, in particular the use of mosaic, permit it to be dated in the Roman or immediately post-Roman period. Its Christian character cannot be established with absolute certainty, but the series of apparently Christian burials near by which seems to start about, very approximately, the year 400 at latest, renders it very likely that the shrine was a Christian one.

We seem to be confronted by a phenomenon not uncommon in the early Christian archaeology of Europe: the grave of some holy man or men which attracted adherents of the cult to be buried near by; a *cella memoriae* or *martyrium*, with burials *ad tumbas*. There are plenty of analogies scattered from Syria to Ireland. It is worth noting in this context that most scholars are now agreed that the place-name Compostela is derived from late Latin *componere*, 'to bury', *compositum* > *compostum*, 'burial', with diminutive suffix *-illa* > *-ela*, 'little cemetery'.

In the light of the foregoing (if light it may be called), a recent suggestion deserves serious consideration. At the end of his fine study of Priscillian, Dr Henry Chadwick cautiously raised the possibility that the heretic Priscillian might himself have been the holy man whose tomb was venerated at Compostela.[14] Priscillian may have been a native of Roman Gallaecia. After his execution at Trier in 385 his disciples brought his body back to Spain for burial, where it was reverenced as the relic of a martyr. Oaths were sworn at his tomb, miracles sought and perhaps claimed. The centre of his cult appears to have been somewhere in Galicia, and it was certainly in Galicia that Priscillianism survived to trouble orthodox churchmen such as Hydatius, Turibius of Astorga and Martin of Braga throughout the

[14] H. Chadwick, *Priscillian of Avila* (Oxford, 1976), p. 233; cf. also pp. 150, 224-30.

fifth and sixth centuries, even possibly into the seventh. It would be ironic indeed if the shrine of St. James did and does in reality shelter the mortal remains of the first schismatic and heretic ever to be executed by the secular authorities at the instance of orthodox Christian churchmen. This piquant—and of course highly speculative—possibility aside, what is tolerably clear is that an early Christian holy place existed at Compostela and that it was attracting devotion until at least the early seventh century. From there to the time of bishop Theodemir is a mere two hundred years. It is not impossible that the memory of such a cult, or even manifestations of it that have left no archaeological trace, should have persisted through this intervening period.

Of the circumstances in which the early cult site was rediscovered by bishop Theodemir in the ninth century we know next to nothing. The two surviving accounts of the discovery date, in the form in which we have them, from the latter part of the eleventh and the early part of the twelfth century.[15] It is doubtful whether much trust may be reposed in these late and meagre narratives. What we should like most of all to know is why Theodemir was convinced that the relics discovered were those of St. James. We have already seen that the Christians of northern Spain were interesting themselves in St. James in the latter part of the eighth century. Is there any trace at all of a cult of St. James in Spain before then—and in particular before the Islamic conquest? For long it was thought that none existed, until, about a generation ago, an archaeological discovery at Mérida brought about a reversal of accepted views. An inscribed stone was found which recorded the dedication of a church in honour of St. Mary and stated that the relics of a number of other saints had been deposited beneath the principal altar: these saints included St. John the Baptist, St. Stephen, St. Paul, St. John the Evangelist, St. James, St. Julian, Sta Eulalia, St. Tirsus, St. Genesus and Sta Marcella.[16]

---

[15] *LFH* III, ap. i, pp. 3-7; *HC*, pp. 8-9.

[16] J. M. Navascués, 'La dedicación de la iglesia de Sta María de Mérida', *Archivo Española de Arqueología* 21 (1948), 309-59, and the emendations to Navascués's reading proposed by J. Vives in an article of the same title in *Analecta Sacra Tarraconesia* 22 (1949), 67-73.

Although that part of the inscription which bore the dating clause had been damaged, there is some likelihood that the date had read *ERA DCLXV*, that is AD 627. Whether or not this is so, what is quite plain is that the dedication stone dates from the Visigothic period. Here then are relics of one of the saints named James present in seventh-century Spain, and where there are relics there is a cult.[17]

It has long been recognized that certain cults moved northwards in the eighth and ninth centuries, as their adherents fled from Islamic domination towards the security of northern Spain or Francia, taking their relics with them. We should bear in mind that Islamic rule in the Asturias and Galicia was short-lived: it lasted for only about a generation. Arab chroniclers furnish an account of the siege and conquest of Mérida in 712-13, probably based on a document which recorded the terms of surrender, which tells us that some of the Christian inhabitants had fled to the north, leaving their churches in Mérida deserted. Sta Eulalia was of course Mérida's own saint, and a very powerful patron she was in the sixth and seventh centuries, as the *Vitas sanctorum patrum emeretensium* vividly shows us.[18] Her body is now held to repose not in Mérida but in Oviedo, so a translation must have occurred at some point. Oviedan tradition, represented by bishop Pelayo in the early twelfth century, held that the translation took place during the reign of king Silo (774-83). Pelayo's reputation for historical veracity is at best a tarnished one, but we have no means of showing that he was wrong; and there are indeed some independent indications that, even if he got the date wrong, a translation of Eulalia's relics to Oviedo did occur late in the eighth or early in the ninth century. Or take a different saint from a different city. The Visigothic kings of the seventh century had vigorously promoted the cult of

---

[17] We have no means of determining *which* James: whether James the son of Zebedee ('the Greater'), or James the son of Alphaeus, or James 'the brother of the Lord'. For the suggestion that the liturgical evidence (which I am altogether unqualified to assess) might point in the direction of St. James the Greater, see J. Pérez de Urbel, 'El culto de Santiago en el siglo X', *Compostellanum* 16 (1971), 11-36.

[18] R. Collins, 'Mérida and Toledo: 550-585', in *Visigothic Spain. New Approaches*, ed. E. James (Oxford, 1980), pp. 189-219.

Sta Leocadia whose relics rested in Toledo. In the early ninth century Alfonso II built an elaborate church in her honour in his royal city of Oviedo. Comparable early medieval practice elsewhere suggests that it would be very unlikely indeed for a royal foundation of this scale to have been unfurnished with relics of the saint in whose honour it was built. It is likely that the relics of Sta Leocadia had made their way northwards from Toledo to Oviedo.[19] One last example will drive the point home. The Galician monastery of Samos was refounded and dedicated to St. Julian— whose name features on the Mérida dedication stone—by abbot Argericus between 842 and 850: Argericus was an immigrant from the Muslim south.[20]

The principal line of communication from south to north on the Atlantic side of the peninsula was the great Roman road which ran from Mérida by way of Salamanca and Astorga to Lugo. If we are prepared to trust some notoriously controversial evidence, we may discern by its fitful light a group of travellers who made their way (in all probability) up that road during the first half of the eighth century. Their concerns are not without interest to our enquiry. The evidence is contained in a group of charters associated with the name of Odoario, bishop of Lugo from *c.*740 until *c.*760. These charters present formidable problems. None of them survives in its original form: they are copies, variously of the tenth, eleventh and thirteenth centuries. The lands with which they deal are in or near Lugo: all were the subject of litigation in the eleventh or later centuries. We should expect to find that their texts have been tampered with, and all historians who have examined them are agreed that this has occurred. Disagreement arises over the extent of the tampering. Are these documents, at one extreme, outright forgeries of a much later period? or are they, at the other, fundamentally authentic eighth-century texts which have undergone only minor touchings-up later on? These questions,

---

[19] For Eulalia's translation see *ES* XXXVII, ap. xv, pp. 354–5; Alfonso II's building operations have been most recently discussed by J. Fontaine, *L'Art pré-roman hispanique* (Paris, 1973), I, ch. 17 and 18.

[20] *Diplomática española del período astur*, ed. A. C. Floriano (Oviedo, 1949–51), I, no. 57.

all too familiar to the student of early diplomatic, cannot
be answered with confidence. This is not the place to attempt
a thorough examination of the charters. Let us simply agree
to look on them with a kindly eye while tracing the story
told by the two most important for our purposes, which
I shall call the Odoario charter and the Meilán charter.[21]

The Odoario charter, which happens by a stroke of good
fortune to be the least unreliable of the series, purports to
have been issued by the bishop himself. It opens with a
narratio cast in the form of an autobiographical fragment.
I was consecrated a bishop in Africa, he tells us. There came
a time of Muslim persecution of Christians: they were deprived
of their property and reduced to slavery and their churches
were destroyed; some, including myself, were expelled
from their native land. We (for at this point he shifts into the
first person plural) remained in exile for a long time, during
(?) the time of Pelayo until (?) the reign of king Alfonso.
(The very corrupt text is unfortunately well-nigh incom-
prehensible in its references to time at this point.) Then we
went to Lugo, which we found uninhabited. Now we are
working to rebuild the city, to construct the church of
St. Mary there and to restore agricultural life near by. There
seems to be a kernel of historical truth, or at least plausibility, in the bishop's story. The Christian communities
of north Africa did experience persecution in the second
decade of the eighth century. Pelayo, first ruler of the
Asturian principality, is said to have exercised power between
718 and 737; Alfonso I ruled from 737 until 757. The
Berbers who had been settled at and near Lugo abandoned
the region in about 740 at the time of their revolt against the
Arab and Syrian Muslims of the south. It is unlikely that
all these facts would have been known to whoever at Lugo
put together the Odoario charter in the form in which we
have it, at some point in the tenth century. It is a pity that
the bishop does not tell us where he spent his exile. The
implication is that it was in southern Spain.

---

[21] L. Vázquez de Parga, 'Los documentos sobre las presuras del obispo
Oduario de Lugo', *Hispania* 10 (1950), 635–80, where all the charters are printed
in an appendix to the study: the Odoario charter is no. i and the Meilán charter
no. iii.

Bishop Odoario went on to record the arrangements he had made for the resettlement of a number of places near Lugo. At three of them he had caused churches to be built, and had dedicated them. At Bocamaos the church was dedicated to St. Julian, at Mazoy to Sta Eulalia and at Meilán to St. James: three saints, it will be noticed, whose names feature in the Mérida inscription. At this point the Meilán charter takes up the story. It runs in the name of a certain Avezano, already identified in the Odoario charter as one of the bishop's followers. Avezano tells us that, with his wife and sons, he came from Africa and settled in Galicia. Under the authority of Alfonso I he resettled various places in the neighbourhood of Lugo. At one of these places, which he calls by his own name (*villa Avezani*) but which may be identified as Meilán, he built a church in honour of St. James. He provided it with endowments in land and livestock, and gave its clergy vestments, plate and books. It was consecrated by bishop Odoario.

At this point we may pause. It is regrettable, but inevitable given the nature of the evidence, that a discussion so laborious should have issued, thus far, in findings so frail and so ambiguous. However, if we cannot establish certainties, we can state plausibilities. Before we proceed further some sort of summary of suggestions is in order. There was evidently a Christian cult-site of early type at what is now Santiago de Compostela. The archaeological evidence suggests that the cult was focused upon the shrine of some unknown holy man and that it was active from the late or sub-Roman period down to the early seventh century. At about the time that the archaeological evidence at Compostela appears to peter out we have our first secure indication of a cult of one of the saints named James at Mérida in southern Spain. At about the same time, again, some western churchmen were beginning to claim that the apostle St. James the Greater had preached in Spain. The claim, apparently unknown to Isidore, seems to have been rejected by Julian of Toledo. Then came the Islamic invasion and conquest of Spain. From the ensuing wreckage of Visigothic Christian culture, certain saints' cults (among other things) were salvaged. The movement of these cults from south to north, and sometimes the physical translation of relics, is reasonably well documented. We can even discern a little, albeit through a glass darkly, of the travels and tribulations of one party of refugees. We have a plausible context—and it would be rash to pitch it more strongly than this—in which to place a northward drift of devotion to St. James. Towards the end of the eighth century, courtly and monastic circles in northern Spain were displaying interest in St. James. And then the miraculous intervenes. The early Christian site is rediscovered: a tomb is revealed at the ends of the earth. Men believe it to be, *know* it to be, the tomb of St. James. A bishop chooses to be buried there, and not long afterwards a writer in distant northern Francia can refer to a *celeberrima veneratio*. In the present state of our knowledge this is as far as we may go.

We must now return to the hymn in honour of St. James composed in northern Spain between 783 and 788. We do not know why it was composed, let alone by whom. Could it possibly have been written for the occasion of the dedication of a church to St. James? Be that as it may, it is in this hymn that we encounter for the first time the association of a king, Mauregato, with the cult of St. James. But it does not seem to have been a specially close association. St. James is 'the shining golden head of Spain' (*caput refulgens aureum Ispanie*); he is 'possessed of Spain' (*potitus Ispania*). He is the guardian and patron (*tutor, patronus*) 'to us' (*nobis*), that is to Christian Spaniards in general, not simply to king Mauregato. Similarly, St. James is a 'mild shepherd' (*mitis pastor*) not merely to the king but also to the clergy and the people. The acrostic which enables us to date the hymn is a prayer on Mauregato's behalf addressed not to St. James but to God. The king's relationship with the saint was not a particularly intimate one and certainly not an exclusive one.

The same may be said of Alfonso II, in whose reign the resting-place of St. James was revealed. A royal charter of 4 September 829 has survived in a twelfth-century copy, purporting to be a grant of privileges to the apostle's church: but it is manifestly spurious. Later Compostelan tradition held that Alfonso II built there not only a church in honour of St. James but two further churches, two monastic houses and a wall to surround the whole complex.[22] This report must be treated with the greatest caution. The church of St. James is all that we may be sure about. Our only indication of what it was like is contained in a document of 899 drawn up at the time of the consecration of the church which replaced it, that is the church known as Compostela II built by Alfonso III. We learn from this that Alfonso II's church had been small and poorly built, of rubble puddled in clay.[23] Perhaps we should make some allowance for the understandable desire to magnify the splendour of Alfonso III's church by stressing the simplicity of its predecessor. But there is no good reason for rejecting the report out of hand. Alfonso II's church seems then to have been a modest little affair. It would therefore have been in marked constrast, in both size and quality of construction, with the buildings with which the king had embellished his *urbs regia* of Oviedo—an architectural ensemble which in conception if not in scale may be compared with the works undertaken by Charlemagne at Aachen.[24] The same contrast greets us when we consider the endowments of the church of Compostela. The forged charter of 829 apart, we can trace only one grant of property by Alfonso II to the church of St. James, referred to in an undated precept of Alfonso III.[25] Of course, there may have been other grants of which record has been lost. But the care with which the early charters of Compostela were preserved—of which we shall have something to say in a later chapter—renders this unlikely. The church of Oviedo on the other hand—though here too the early charters present extremely knotty problems—was magnificently endowed by Alfonso II.

The record of Alfonso II's two successors was no more striking. Ramiro I (842-50) continued and extended the

[22] Discussed fully but uncritically in *LFH* II, ch. 2: I doubt whether much reliance can be placed on the eleventh- and twelfth-century charters as a guide to the architectural arrangements of the ninth. K. J. Conant, *The early architectural history of the cathedral of Santiago de Compostela* (Cambridge, Mass., 1926) is disappointingly thin on this early period.

[23] R. 6 May 899: *ex petra et luto opere parvo.*

[24] It is noteworthy that one of Alfonso II's architects at Oviedo had a Frankish name, Tioda.   [25] R. 866 × 910.

building programme of Alfonso II in the Asturias. Oviedo and Naranco were the royal centres from which he ruled. A very late source, from Muslim Andalusia in the thirteenth century, tells a story of the poet al-Ghazal's embassy to the Vikings (of Ireland?) in about 845, on the way back from which he called at Santiago 'with a letter from the king of the Vikings to the ruler of that city'.[26] This might, just possibly, indicate that Ramiro I sometimes used Compostela as a royal residence; but it would be most unwise to repose much trust in such evidence as this. At a much later date it was believed that Ramiro I had been assisted by St. James to win a victory over the Moors at Clavijo in 844, in gratitude for which the king was supposed to have lavished upon the church of Santiago de Compostela the right to certain categories of annual tribute paid by all the dwellers within Christian Spain. But the story is without historical foundation. The battle of Clavijo was fought not in 844 but in 859, and its victor was Ordoño I, not Ramiro I; the diploma of Ramiro I by which the privilege was granted is a forgery of the mid-twelfth century; and the legend of the apostle's assistance, however interesting the light it may cast on what the men of the twelfth century wished to believe, tells us nothing at all of the ninth.[27] As for Ordoño I (850-66), he showed no more interest in St. James than had his father Ramiro. The charter for Compostela that bears his name and purports to be a confirmation and amplification of Alfonso II's charter of 829, is, like the earlier one, a later forgery.[28]

The ninth-century evidence suggests that the Asturian kings down to and including Ordoño I were not greatly interested in St. James. A small church, meanly built, with modest endowments: it is an unimpressive record. All this was to change very suddenly in the latter part of the century.

[26] The episode has been discussed with spirit and ingenuity by W. E. D. Allen, *The poet and the spae-wife* (Dublin, 1960): not all will be convinced.

[27] Clavijo and the events allegedly associated with it have provoked a considerable controversial literature. C. Sánchez Albornoz disentangled history from Legend in 'La auténtica batalla de Clavijo', *Cuadernos de Historia de España* 9 (1948), 94-139, reprinted in his *Orígenes de la nación española*, III (Oviedo, 1975), pp. 281-311. For the history of the controversy see T. D. Kendrick, *Saint James in Spain* (London, 1960). See also below, ch. XI.

[28] R. 858.

It is an easy matter to identify the agents of change. They were Alfonso III, who reigned from 866 to 910, and Sisnando, bishop of Iria from 880 (at latest) until 920.

In early medieval Europe saints' cults did not simply happen: they were made. Perhaps that statement is too sweeping. It would a little refine and qualify it if we were to say that small-scale, local and popular cults might be transformed if influential people were persuaded that it was in their interests to show devotion to one, or several, saints' shrines. In western Francia the shrines of St. Martin at Tours, St. Denys near Paris, and St. Remigius at Rheims *mattered* to the Merovingians and the Carolingians in ways that the shrines of other saints did not. This was partly because the clergy who were the guardians of these shrines had taught their rulers that certain directions and forms of devotion were expected of kings who hoped to live long, father children, defeat their enemies, win land and booty, attract followers and perhaps above all be remembered; partly because kings looked to holy protectors, saintly companions, the more readily when these saints were, in a sense, theirs—and no one else's. The cult of a saint could, thus, be influential in moulding a kingdom. When in the sixth century king Leovigild made Toledo his capital city it was under royal influence that a new cult was promoted. It is clear that the cult of Sta Leocadia mattered to the later Visigothic kings, though it is hard to find words in which to say why it did so which will carry meaning and conviction to a twentieth-century understanding. Being protected by Leocadia, showing reciprocal devotion for Leocadia—more jealous protection than she showed for anyone else, more lavish devotion than anyone else could show for her—were two sorts of activity which were inseparable from other sorts of kingly activity which took place in Toledo: legislating, striking coin, presiding over church councils, commissioning sculptors and goldsmiths to fashion wonderful works of art—to name just some of the things we happen to know about. Like many rulers of Spain before and since, Leovigild wanted to persuade his nominal subjects that Spain was one country, ruled by one king, from one place, under one law. Leocadia's was a royal cult in a royal city. She could make a king more imposing, perhaps more powerful.

The Asturian kingdom in the ninth century was different in several obvious and important ways from its Visigothic precursor. But its kings wanted it to look as Gothic as possible. If when we try to imagine what ninth-century Oviedo was like it is with such places as Aachen or Pavia or Winchester that we most readily compare it, we must remember always that it is of Visigothic Toledo that we are meant to be thinking. 'He established at Oviedo, both at court and in the church, all the ceremonial (*ordinem*) of the Goths, just as it had existed in Toledo.' The words are those of a chronicler writing in the 880s about Alfonso II.[29] Unlike their contemporaries in western Francia or Wessex, the Asturian kings issued no legislation. They did not need to, because they had made their own the great Visigothic codifications of the seventh century. Like the Gothic kings, too, they wanted a saint of their own. Their choice fell on St. James. His cult was deliberately fostered and promoted by Alfonso III and bishop Sisnando. We know just enough about them to be able to see how they did it.

Alfonso III was a very generous benefactor of the church of St. James. Among his earliest gifts was a processional cross of gold, elaborately worked and studded with precious stones, a copy of the famous 'Angel Cross' (*Cruz de los Angeles*) presented by his ancestor Alfonso II to the church of Oviedo. This Compostela cross was stolen in 1906 and has never been recovered, but photographs of it survive and it was described by López Ferreiro.[30] It bore an inscription recording that it had been given to Santiago by Alfonso III and queen Jimena in 874, and continuing: *Hoc signo vincitur inimicus. Hoc signo tuetur pius.* These words recall, as they were surely intended to do, the vision of Constantine and his victory at the Milvian Bridge. They may have had a special relevance in the 870s. On the death of Ordoño I a certain

---

[29] *Cronica Albeldense*, in M. Gómez Moreno, 'Las primeras crónicas de la Reconquista: el ciclo de Alfonso III', *BRAH* 100 (1932), 562-628, at p. 602.

[30] *LFH* II, pp. 169-73. See also H. Schlunk, 'The crosses of Oviedo', *Art Bulletin* 33 (1950), 93-114; P. E. Schramm, *Herrschaftszeichen und Staatsymbolik*, II (Stuttgart, 1955), pp. 480-4.

Froila, count of Galicia, had claimed the throne in opposition
to Alfonso III. Froila did not last long but for a short time
he had been very dangerous. His bid had started in Galicia,
but he had evidently taken possession of Oviedo, for it was
by 'the senate of Oviedo' (*a senatu Ovetensi*)—whatever
these words may mean—that he was slain. Alfonso, meanwhile, had fled eastwards into Alava. Now we also happen to
know that count Froila had deprived the church of Santiago
de Compostela of some landed property, for it was restored
by Alfonso III in January 867, which must have been very
soon after Froila's death.[31] In other words, St. James had
been on the side of the rightful, or at least the victorious,
claimant. He was a patron worth having. The cross was a
mark of gratitude.

Alfonso III vastly increased the landed endowments of
the church of St. James. The extent of his generosity may
be most vividly apprehended in a diploma dated 6 May 899,
a sort of *pancarte* confirming all the properties of the apostle
on the occasion of the consecration of his new church.[32] Two
points about these grants are significant. First, that certain
of them were conveyances of estates which had been forfeited by men who had rebelled against the king;[33] and
second, that others were grants of land in territories recently
conquered by the king from the Moors.[34] The preambles to
these charters, which deserve attentive scrutiny, testify to the
intimacy of relationship between king and saint. St. James's
intercession protects Alfonso III from rebels and helps him
to enlarge his kingdom. St. James is the king's *patronus*; he
promises 'an ample recompense' (*remuneratio copiosa*) to
the king his servant; he is the giver of victory over the king's
enemies.[35]

It is well to bear in mind that St. James was not the only
saint whom Alfonso III could regard as his patron. Facundus
and Primitivus, the saints of his new monastic foundation

[31] Sampiro, *Chronica*, in J. Pérez de Urbel, *Sampiro: su crónica y la monarquía
leonesa en el siglo X* (Madrid, 1952), pp. 275–346, c.1; R. 20 January 867.
[32] I am with Floriano and Sánchez Albornoz in believing, against Barrau-
Dihigo, that R. 6 May 899 is fundamentally authentic.
[33] e.g. R. 885, 24 June 886, 11 July 895, 25 November 895.
[34] e.g. R. 17 August 883, 30 December 899.
[35] e.g. R. 30 June 880, 17 August 883, 25 July 893.

at Sahagún on the plain of León, were also for him 'very powerful patrons' (*fortissimi patroni*).[36] Due allowance being made for this, however, the links forged between king and apostle to which the royal charters testify were formidable. It was Alfonso III, again, who together with bishop Sisnando rebuilt St. James's church at Compostela. Not only was this, as we have seen, a bigger and better church than that erected by Alfonso II: it was also bigger than any other of the several surviving buildings which may be attributed to the patronage of Alfonso III.[37] Basilican in form, its nave about eighty feet long, with arcades giving on to side-aisles, and a rectangular apse, it was decorated with marble and sculpture (*petras marmoreas, columnas sculptas, columnelis marmoreis*) brought by sea from sites in Portugal of (presumably) the Roman or Visigothic periods: thus in yet another way St. James profited from Alfonso III's wars of conquest.[38] The consecration in 899 was attended by no less than seventeen bishops, one of them from far-off Zaragoza. The relics of numerous saints were deposited there: these included, we note with interest, relics of Sta Eulalia and Sta Leocadia.[39]

We possess one further testimony to Alfonso III's promotion of the cult of St. James which, if genuine, is a document of the utmost importance for its early history. It takes the form of a letter addressed by the king to the clergy of Tours in 906. If genuine: for it has generally been regarded with scepticism by modern historical scholarship. I believe it to be authentic. However, lest a chapter already bearing a heavy freight of technicality be overloaded with anxious hesitations, I have relegated discussion of it to an appendix, and shall proceed here on the assumption that it is indeed what it purports to be.[40] The letter concerns Alfonso III's

[36] R. 30 November 904.

[37] See the plan in P. de Palol and M. Hirmer, *Early medieval art in Spain* (London, 1967), p. 40.

[38] Some of this re-used material is now displayed in the cathedral museum at Compostela.

[39] It is just within the bounds of possibility that Alfonso III sought and received from pope John IX, in 898, recognition of the presence of St. James's body at Compostela: the matter is discussed by C. Sánchez Albornoz, *Orígenes de la nación española*, III (Oviedo, 1975), pp. 803–15.

[40] See below, Appendix C.

negotiations with the clergy of Tours for the purchase of what he refers to as an imperial crown (*corona imperialis*). He proposes that the transaction be mediated through the offices of the count of Bordeaux in the coming month of May 906. He goes on to request a copy of any book available at Tours relating the posthumous miracles of St. Martin. In return he can provide the community there with a copy of a work little known (he believes) outside Spain, devoted to the bishops of Mérida. (That is, the *Vitas sanctorum patrum Emeretensium*, which we have already met; and we should note in passing the interest of the passage of this hagiographical text from Mérida to the north-west.) They have asked him, he continues, who the apostle is whose tomb is venerated in Galicia; let them know that it is James the son of Zebedee. This is attested by many reliable texts (*multae veridicae historiae*); and miracles are worked at his shrine. He closes by indicating exactly where the centre of the cult is to be found; at the place we know today, though the king gives it no name, as Santiago de Compostela.

Alfonso III's letter to the clergy of Tours furnishes us with an account of what influential people in northern Spain believed about St. James in the early years of the tenth century. It shows us how closely the king was associated with the cult. Its reference to miracles worked at the tomb suggests that the resting-place of St. James was already the goal of pilgrims; in the following chapter we shall encounter evidence which demonstrates that this was indeed so. It refers, rather vaguely, to the existence of a literature bearing on the martyrdom of St. James and the translation of his remains to Galicia. It provides evidence that the cult was not widely celebrated, or even known, outside Spain. Perhaps most interestingly of all, the letter implies that the king and his circle would like to know more about the workings of the cult of St. Martin. The power of St. Martin is made manifest in his miracles—of course it is; so too the power of St. James. Martin's miracles have been recorded in writing (so the king has heard rumour); there is no evidence in the letter to suggest that James's have been similarly given permanent memorial. The king would like to know more. His is the letter of a man who is still something of

a beginner in this business of shrine-promotion; who is eager
to learn from experts. What better mentors could he have
picked on? The king's letter reinforces the argument deployed
in this chapter, that the growth of the cult of St. James at
Compostela was tended, principally, by Alfonso III and his
bishop Sisnando.

This is one way of making the growth of the cult of
St. James intelligible to us. But this line of approach carries
in its train a difficult question; which may best be stated
thus: the Asturian kings had chosen Oviedo as their *urbs
regia*, their seat of royal power and majesty; besides embellish-
ing it with palaces and churches they had made it into 'a
veritable spiritual fortress' by packing it with relics of the
saints assembled from all over Spain.[41] Why did Alfonso III
not take the body of St. James to add to his relic-collection
at Oviedo? In the light of all we know about kings and their
patronage of saints' cults during this period, this is something
that should have happened—but didn't. Why not?

The answer to such a question can be neither simple nor
confident. By way of approach it might be useful to direct
our attention for a few moments to the contemporaries of
the Asturian kings in a different corner of Christendom,
the Anglo-Saxon rulers of Wessex. Two features of West
Saxon kingship during the period between, roughly, the
mid-ninth century and the mid-tenth are germane to our
enquiry. In the first place, this was an expanding kingship,
in the sense that it was during this period that the 'small
Wessex' created by the princes who were Bede's contemporaries was enlarged into a 'greater Wessex' embracing first
the whole of southern England, then the midlands and
finally much of the north as well—most, in short, of the
area of what we now call England. Second, this movement
of expansion was accompanied by manifestations of royal
munificence, royal patronage and piety, directed towards
the shrines of local saints in the areas which were undergoing
aggregation to a West Saxon system of royal authority. The
two processes were related.

Take Alfonso III's younger contemporary, king Athelstan

[41] The phrase is that of Dr Collins in the paper already referred to, 'Mérida
and Toledo', at p. 214.

(924–39). His reign saw the almost definitive subjugation of a hitherto independent Viking Northumbria to West Saxon rule. It also witnessed some spectacular royal generosity towards the great shrines of Northumbria, of St. Wilfrid at Ripon, of St. John at Beverley and of St. Cuthbert at Chester-le-Street. It is about the king's relations with the last of these that we are best informed. When Athelstan visited Chester-le-Street in 934 he offered 'royal gifts' (*regia munera*) at the saint's shrine. The author of the *Historia de Sancto Cuthberto* listed them: three gospel-books, a missal, a very sumptuous copy of the *Vita Sancti Cuthberti*; a number of ecclesiastical vestments including the magnificent stole and maniple which still survive among the relics of St. Cuthbert at Durham; church plate in gold and silver, candelabra, bells, drinking-horns, standards, an enormous quantity of cash, and a huge landed estate at Wearmouth. 'Royal gifts' indeed. It has been well said recently that the West Saxon kings of the tenth century 'would have to earn Saint Cuthbert's favour if they were to rule the north'.[42] Here we can see one of them doing it. And it worked. No wonder St. Cuthbert's intercession made Athelstan victorious in his wars. No wonder St. Cuthbert's clergy offered grateful and loyal prayers for the West Saxon kings. No wonder they inserted Athelstan's name prominently in their *Liber Vitae*.

Now suppose that we were to read, for Wessex, the Asturias; for Northumbria, Galicia; for Athelstan, Alfonso III; and for St. Cuthbert, St. James: would our understanding be advanced? Misgivings might cluster about the implied suggestion that the relationship between the Asturias and Galicia was akin to that between Wessex and Northumbria. Had not Galicia been a part of the Asturian kingdom from at least the time of the departure of the Berbers in about 740? But this is precisely the point. Had it?

All that we know of the Asturian rulers in the century and a half which separates Pelayo from Ordoño I—and, notoriously, it's precious little—suggests that these princes were

---

[42] By Dr P. Wormald, in *The Anglo-Saxons*, ed. J. Campbell (Oxford, 1982), p. 155. Athelstan's gifts to St. Cuthbert are listed in the *Historia de Sancto Cuthberto*, in *Symeonis monachi opera omnia*, ed. T. Arnold (Rolls Series, London, 1882), I. 196–214, at pp. 211–12.

small-scale operators whose effective authority, whatever the claims and traditions to which they considered themselves the heirs, was confined to a restricted zone of territory between the Cordillera Cantábrica and the Bay of Biscay. This was where the 'royal places' from which they exercised their rule were situated: Cangas de Onís, Pravia, Oviedo, Naranco. This was where, on the evidence of the charters, their demesne lands lay. This was where they concentrated their relic-collection, built churches, founded monasteries. This was where they were buried and remembered. If they looked further afield for their wives, they tended to look eastwards, towards Alava. And it was often eastwards that they fled when they were in trouble; Alfonso II in 783, for example, or Alfonso III in 866. This in itself suggests that trouble was something that tended to come from the west, that is from Galicia. Now these indices of a firm royal presence just cited are conspicuously lacking in Galicia: no royal places, very little demesne land, no royal monasteries, scarcely any church-building, no known marriage-connections, not a single royal burial.

We hear of Galician rebellions: against Fruela I, against Silo, perhaps against Alfonso II, against Alfonso III. Rebellions imply an authority to rebel against. But we cannot be absolutely certain that in these instances they do. Our only sources for these revolts are the chronicles of the reign of Alfonso III, and we need to ask ourselves when, where, by whom and for whom these were composed. These questions have not yet satisfactorily been answered, but it is commonly agreed that these works were 'court' productions. It was as rebellions that the king and his circle wanted these goings-on to be interpreted; but they may have looked rather different at the time they happened. There is a related difficulty about the word *comes*. We all know that it means a count, and that a count is an officer appointed by the king to exercise certain powers in his name. A count is a royal functionary. But not all counts were. There were men in western Francia in Alfonso III's lifetime who were self-styled counts and owed nothing to their king; Gerald of Aurillac is one example. But we do not need to look beyond the Pyrenees. Count Diego of Castile and count Vela of

Alava, who lived in the days of Alfonso III, do not look like royal officers. Neither does count Froila of Galicia.

What influence the Asturian kings of the mid-ninth century may have exercised in Galicia was probably beginning to be mediated through the bishops. Bishop Sisnando of Iria, the collaborator with Alfonso III in the promotion of the cult of St. James, was the nephew of his predecessor bishop Adaulfo (who seems to have held the see about the late 850s and early 860s). It is of great interest that this prominent ecclesiastical dynasty was not Galician. The family came from the Asturias. Furthermore, it enjoyed close relations with the royal house. Bishop Adaulfo is a very obscure figure, but what seems to glimmer through later legend about him is that he was not well liked in Galician aristocratic circles and looked to the king to uphold him. Let us not forget that in the course of his movement against Alfonso III count Froila had seized some of the temporalities of the church of St. James; nor that one of Alfonso's earliest actions as king was to restore this property. The surge of royal generosity to Santiago occurred from the early 880s onwards—shortly after Sisnando's succession to the bishopric. This may not have been coincidental. Perhaps it was Sisnando who persuaded Alfonso III that if the royal authority were ever to make any headway in Galicia some new initiative was needed. Certainly Sisnando would have had every interest in so doing. Moreover, there were important ways in which he could help. It was Sisnando, for instance, who handled the earlier stages of the negotiations with the clergy of Tours which are alluded to in the king's letter of 906.[43]

The new initiative was going to be costly. Precisely how costly we can see very clearly in Alfonso III's charters. If the king had ever entertained anxieties on this score, the passage of time would have allayed them. Alfonso III could afford it. He could afford it because he was both the creator and the beneficiary of an expanding kingship—comparable in many ways, which deserves exploration, to West Saxon kingship or, a more imposing parallel, Ottonian. At the end

[43] On Adaulfo and Sisnando see the full if uncritical account in *LFH* II, chs. 6–13.

of Alfonso's long reign the Asturian monarchy was something different from what it had been at its beginning. Alfonso conquered and started to settle vast new tracts of land in northern Portugal and on the plains of León. (The Galician nobility did well out of this, as we may see from the abundant charters of the tenth century. It helped to attach them much more firmly to the royal dynasty.) The king's propagandists, whose work survives in the chronicles composed during his reign, were confecting a new image of kingship. The king was predestined with God's help to unite all Spain under his rule. Imperial claims and pretensions were taking shape, shortly after Alfonso's death (if not indeed before it) to become visible in the imperial title. Here again there are comparisons with England and Germany to be investigated; and here of course is the explanation for the king's desire to acquire an imperial crown from Tours.

Our knowledge of the early Asturian monarchy is so fragmentary that these remarks, at the end of a chapter in itself somewhat discursive, are bound to be hesitant, exploratory, speculative. Alfonso III believed, as he tells us in his charters, that St. James had helped to make him a great king. The reciprocal process, it may be suggested, was equally interesting and important. Alfonso III made James a great saint. He put him (so to say) on the map. They rose to prominence together. The king advertised and diffused a cult even as he consolidated a tenuous hold over Galicia and defeated his enemies and enlarged his kingdom. Alfonso III and bishop Sisnando could not know, as we know, that something far bigger was being launched than ever they could have anticipated. How and why that happened, how and why the shrine of St. James became a great international attraction, is quite another story. It will be examined in the following chapter.

IV

Pilgrimage and pilgrims,
to Compostela and elsewhere

In 1032 Bermudo III of León, the last ruler of the dynasty of Alfonso III, made a grant of land to the church of Santiago de Compostela. The estates thus transferred had been forfeited by one Sisnando Galiárez, whose recent revolt against the king was described at some length in the royal charter. Sisnando's crime was that the had rebelled, in the king's words, 'against me and against the lord bishop Vistruario of the apostolic place'.[1] It is a small but significant reminder to us that the links between the kings of León and the church of St. James had remained exceptionally close since the time of Alfonso III. To trace these links in detail would take us far from our immediate concerns. The testimony of the royal charters shows clearly that the kings of León had continued to regard St. James as their patron. The phrase *patronus noster* (with variants) occurs again and again in the charters of the tenth and eleventh centuries.[2] For Ordoño II the saint is 'the hauberk of justice' and 'the helmet of safety'.[3] For Bermudo II the *sors regni*, the 'luck' or fortune of the kingdom, is assured by the intercession of St. James.[4] He helps these kings to rule their kingdom well; he gives them victory over their enemies.[5]

Royal courts set fashions, in religious devotion as in much else besides. It was doubtless through the direct or indirect encouragement of the royal family that the cult of St. James began to spread within Christian Spain. Alfonso III's collaborator in promoting the cult, bishop Sisnando, had received a grant of land from the king as early as 883 for the

---

[1] R. 25 August 1032.
[2] e.g. R. 30 January 915, 21 November 927, 5 March 951, 29 September 985, 5 March 1011.
[3] R. 29 January 915.   [4] R. 24 May 991.
[5] R. 8 August 929, 2 March 958.

foundation of a church in honour of St. James in the region
of the Asturias, the area of which Sisnando was a native.[6]
A charter of 914 reveals that Egila, the grandmother of
Ordoño II's wife, herself married to one of the greatest men
of the kingdom, count Gaton of Astorga, had granted land
in El Bierzo, between Astorga and Lugo, to the shrine of
St. James.[7] Aristocratic patronage in its turn set a fashion
which was followed at more lowly social levels. Alfonso III
granted land near Alcoba de la Rivera, not far from León,
to St. James in 885, and in his charter referred to the nearby
'road which the merchants (*cives*) of Galicia are accustomed
to use in their comings and goings'. Might it have been
through the devotion of such travelling *cives* that a church
dedicated to St. James had been founded at Viñayo, not far
away, before 918?[8]

Evidence of this kind, the records of grants of land and
church-dedications, shows us, albeit in an imperfect way,
how the new cult seeped through the mountain barriers of
Galicia on to the central plateau of the Spanish peninsula.
As the renown of the apostle spread, so his shrine became
in its turn a magnet drawing devout suppliants to it. In this
fashion the pilgrimage to Santiago de Compostela was born.
Who the earliest pilgrims were, and whence they came, we
have no means of telling. It is not surprising to discover
that our first references to their coming date from the time
of Alfonso III and bishop Sisnando. When the king granted
salt-pans in Salnés to the church of St. James in 886 he
stipulated that these were for the use 'of the monks, the
poor and also the pilgrims'.[9] Phrases of this sort become
very common in royal charters after this date.[10] They confirm the evidence of Usuard's *Martyrology* of *c.* 865 and
of the Tours letter of 906 which were cited in the preceding
chapter.

An incident in the middle years of the tenth century
shows us how far the renown of the shrine of St. James had
spread. The evidence is furnished by a letter from a Catalan

---

[6] R. 25 September 883.   [7] R. 6 December 914.
[8] R. 885, 8 January 918.   [9] R. 24 June 886.
[10] e.g. R. 25 July 893, 25 November 899, 20 April 911, 30 January 915,
18 May 920, 28 June 924, and many others.

prelate, Cesarius, to pope John XIII.[11] Cesarius was one
of the most distinguished Catalan churchmen of his generation. In 945 he had founded the monastery of Montserrat,
near Barcelona. About ten years later he became bishop of
Tarragona, and it was this that brought him into contact
with the clergy of Santiago de Compostela. In his letter he
told the pope how he had gone 'to the church (*domum*)
of the apostolic see of St. James, who is buried in Galicia,
the region of his apostolate'. There he had requested 'the
blessing of the province of Tarragona'. After examination
of his claims, which the bishops of Galicia found to be good,
he was consecrated by bishop Sisnando II of Iria-Compostela
in the presence of king Sancho I of León and nine Galician
and Leonese bishops, probably on 29 November 956. On his
return to Catalonia his claims were contested by the bishops
of Barcelona, Gerona, Vich and Urgel, and the archbishop
of Narbonne, on the grounds that 'the said apostolate,
alleged to have been in the west of Spain, was not the apostolate of St. James, because that apostle was brought here
only after his death'. Cesarius cited the text of the *Breviarium
Apostolorum* in support of St. James's—and his own—
claims and appealed to the pope. The latest editor of the
letter, by plausible emendation of a desperately corrupt text,
has interpreted it as a request for an archbishop's pallium.

The ecclesiastical politics that lie behind this extraordinary
document are hardly our concern. Cesarius seems to have
wanted to reconstitute the ecclesiastical province of Tarragona under himself as metropolitan, and to have run up
against the opposition of the Catalan bishops whose loyalties
lay with Narbonne. What is interesting is that in his bid for
recognition Cesarius should have turned to the bishop of
Iria-Compostela as the authority who might adjudicate in
such matters and might command such spiritual prestige
as would enable him to override domestic opposition. No
less interesting is the revelation that some of the Catalan
clergy were not convinced of the claims that were being
made on behalf of St. James. They admitted the translation

[11] For what follows, see R. d'Abadal i de Vinyals, 'L'abat Cesari, fundador
de Santa Cecilia de Montserrat i pretès arquebispe de Tarragona', in his collected
essays *Dels Visigots als Catalans* (Barcelona, 1970), II. 25–55.

of the saint's corpse; they did not recognize his Spanish apostolate during his lifetime.

These Catalan bishops were not alone in their scepticism. The Leonese scribe Florentius who copied a Bible in 953—now lost, but described by a seventeenth-century antiquary —referred only to St. James's preaching in Judaea. In another Bible, now preserved at León, copied by the scribe Sancho under the direction of the same Florentius in 960, we are roundly informed of St. James that 'he is buried in Jerusalem'. Another doubter may have been the Andalusian Recemund, bishop of Elvira. He was a learned and well-travelled man—he was sent by the caliph of Córdoba on an embassy to the court of Otto I in 956: yet in his famous *Calendar*, while noting St. James's feast-day, he had nothing to say of the saint's burial in Galicia.[12]

But the doubters were fighting a losing battle. It is during these same years of the mid-tenth century that there occur the first records of distinguished visitors coming from distant parts of Christendom to the shrine of St. James. The earliest whom we can trace was Godescalc or Gottschalk, bishop of Le Puy, who visited Compostela as a pilgrim in the year 951.[13] Some years afterwards came Raymond II, count of Rouergue.[14] A still more distant and distinguished visitor is recorded in 961. *Vgo Remensis episcopus*—that is, Hugh of Vermandois, archbishop of Rheims, was at Compostela on 27 February 961, when he set his name thus to a document issued there.[15] A few years later, when in 970 the Viking band which had killed bishop Sisnando II in 968 was finally expelled from Galicia, they met their defeat at the hands of a certain count *Guillelmus Sancionis*: might this have been William-Sancho, count of Gascony, on his way to or from Santiago de Compostela?[16] It is at about the same time, too,

[12] J. Pérez de Urbel, 'El culto de Santiago en el siglo X', *Compostellanum* 16 (1971), 11-36.

[13] J. M. Lacarra, L. Vázquez de Parga and J. Uría Ríu, *Las peregrinaciones a Santiago de Compostela* (Madrid, 1948-9), I. 42, note 6.

[14] *Liber miraculorum sancte Fidis*, ed. A. Bouillet (Paris, 1897), I, c. 12, pp. 41-2.

[15] AC Santiago de Compostela, Tumbo A, fo. 13: printed in *España Sagrada* 19, 367-70.

[16] Sampiro, *Cronica*, in J. Pérez de Urbel, *Sampiro, su crónica y la monarquía leonesa en el siglo X* (Madrid, 1952), pp. 341, 432.

that we should locate a probable, though unproven, visit from Abbo of Fleury.[17]

These are stray references in the few sources that happen to have survived from the third quarter of the tenth century. They present us with a remarkable clutch of men—the most famous monastic reformer of his day, an Auvergnat and a Neustrian bishop, two Languedocien lords who were survivors in the wreckage of the sub-Carolingian world; not forgetting an ambitious cleric from the Spanish March. What they had in common was their social or ecclesiastical distinction; that is why we know about them. We can be certain that there were others of less distinguished rank or office, perhaps many others, of whom individually we know nothing. The concern of the royal charters with pilgrims who were 'poor' is significant; and we have already met a Frenchman, apparently of no very exalted rank, in the town of Compostela in 955—though of course we cannot demonstrate that it was devotion to St. James that had brought him there in the first place.[18] Further evidence comes from a surprising source, an Arabic panegyric poem celebrating Almanzor's exploits in 997 when he led an army into Galicia, sacked and burnt the town of Compostela and led off the bells of the apostle's church in triumph to Córdoba. The poem tells us that Santiago de Compostela was the goal of pilgrims coming from all over the place.[19] Though the occasion of Almanzor's expedition remains somewhat mysterious, we can at the least safely deduce that Compostela was a town worth sacking. Booming cult-sites usually were, as the Vikings could have told him. Perhaps we have here the explanation for *their* descent on Compostela a generation earlier in 968.

It is a simple matter enough to compile a list of names; all that is required is a certain dogged industry. It is more difficult to discover why these people went on pilgrimage: why any people have done so in the past; why they still do.

[17] M. Défourneaux, *Les Français en Espagne aux XIe et XIIe siècles* (Paris, 1949), p. 66.

[18] *Sobrado Cart.* I, no. 2.

[19] J. Pérez de Urbel, 'El culto de Santiago en el siglo X', *Compostellanum* 16 (1971), 11–36.

'I have found that which my soul was seeking; I shall hold fast to it and shall not let it go.' It was in these words that one of the earliest pilgrims to the Holy Places, Jerome, attempted to sum up the spiritual renewal that lay at the heart of his journey.[20] A secular age such as our own will seek to 'explain' religious experience, but too often succeeds only in explaining it away, and thereby necessarily missing the point. It is with the thirsty soul (an unfashionable and uncomfortable concept) that we must start if we are to understand pilgrimages. For a pilgrimage marks, or should mark, a decisive stage in the religious development of the individual who undertakes it.[21] It is not for nothing that in Christian tradition the idea of journeying is associated with conversion: all pilgrimage-roads lead, at least potentially, to Damascus. Ritual immersion in the Jordan at the place where it was believed that Jesus had been baptized by John the Baptist impressed upon the pilgrim to the Holy Land that he was beginning a new life. The pilgrim is stained with sin in his everyday life, but his pilgrimage is designed to take him away from the daily round. The dislocation which a journey entailed, the rupture with accustomed people and routines, were part of a process of spiritual therapy. Returned with new and contrite heart, the pilgrim should experience spiritual renewal, a closer walk with God. Prayers for the returning pilgrim will ask that 'he should not again wander from the paths of the Lord'.[22] Pilgrimage is a time for amend-ment of life. It is a form of initiation.

The notion of *anachoresis*—withdrawal, disengagement from the secular world—was at the heart of the ascetic movement which took so firm a hold of Christians in late

[20] Jerome, *Ep.* 46 (ed. J. Labourt (Budé: Paris, 1951), II. 114). The letter runs in the name of Paula and Eustochium, but scholars are agreed that it was the composition of their friend Jerome. For Jerome and other early pilgrims see now the masterly study by E. D. Hunt, *Holy Land pilgrimage in the later Roman Empire* (Oxford, 1982).

[21] Of the many works devoted to pilgrimage I have found particularly stimu-lating the essay by A. Dupront, 'Pèlerinage et lieux sacrés', in *Mélanges en l'honneur de Fernand Braudel*, vol. II, *Méthodologie de l'histoire et des sciences humaines* (Toulouse, 1973), pp. 189–206. I am grateful to Professor J. A. Bossy for drawing my attention to this article.

[22] 'Ne ultra deviet a viis tuis', from a twelfth-century German pontifical quoted by A. Franz, *Die kirchlichen Benedictionen im Mittelalter* (Freiburg-im-Bresgau, 1909), II. 278.

antiquity and the early middle ages.[23] It is no coincidence
that pilgrimage and ascetic monasticism should have emerged
at about the same time as means of living a purer Christian
life. Both sprang from an act of *anachoresis*. The pilgrim and
the monk alike renounced the *saeculum*. And pilgrimage, like
monasticism, drew on biblical roots. The type of the pilgrim
was prefigured in Abraham: 'Get thee out of thy country,
and from thy kindred, and from thy father's house.' (Genesis
12:1.) The example of Abraham was quoted approvingly by
the unknown author of the Epistle to the Hebrews, in
chapter 11, which is a key passage for the understanding of
our subject. Abraham and others like him 'confessed that
they were strangers and pilgrims on the earth'. The word
rendered 'pilgrim' in the Authorized Version appeared in
the Vulgate as *peregrinus*. This became the normal term in
medieval Latin for 'a pilgrim'. But we should bear in mind
that it had originally been a technical term in Roman law.
A *peregrinus* was an alien, a stranger to the community;
a man without kin, without friends, without sureties, without patrons; a man alone. In late antiquity it was Augustine
who swooped upon the possibilities latent in this term and
exploited them more vigorously, more movingly and more
influentially than any other Christian thinker. The true
Christian is a *peregrinus* in this world. He has renounced his
worldly *patria*. The city that he seeks is a heavenly one, and
its houses are not made with hands.

Ascetic renunciation of the homeland—to become literally an expatriate—gave rise to the most characteristic
manifestation of *peregrinatio*, pilgrimage, in the early middle
ages: the wanderings of the saints. This was a form of
religious exercise especially associated with the Irish, though
by no means their exclusive possession. For those who
practised it, life became a pilgrimage conducted in self-
imposed exile. Columba 'sailed away from Ireland to Britain,
wishing to be a pilgrim for Christ' (*pro Christo peregrinari
volens*); Egbert, who travelled in the opposite direction,
vowed to live in Ireland as a pilgrim and never to return to

[23] In what follows I am much indebted to the writings of Peter Brown: for
some reflections upon *anachoresis* see his *The making of late antiquity* (Cambridge, Mass., 1978), chapter 4, especially pp. 85–6.

his homeland.[24] Hundreds of similar examples might be cited. As an ideal it was at its most influential between the sixth and ninth centuries, though it was not dead—— a point which is worth stressing because it is often over-looked——in the period which is my main concern.[25]

Many though these peregrine holy men were, it could in the nature of things never have been more than a tiny proportion of the population of Christendom who undertook a lifelong pilgrimage in this fashion. Others might renounce the world to live as a pilgrim only towards the end of a secular career; king Ine of Wessex, for example, only after a reign of nearly forty years. For the vast majority, however, the experience of pilgrimage would come in the form of a journey, long or short as the case might be, *to a place*, and then back home again. In western Christendom——for we must leave on one side the obviously very special case of the Holy Places themselves——the place was one made sacred by its association with a holy man or woman; normally the resting-place of his (or her) body. It is important to grasp that the shrine of a saint was a potentially active source of spiritual energy. Though dead in the flesh, the saint was *there*; a formidably powerful being who, if approached properly, could bring help to the suppliant. That is to say, the saint could work miracles. 'All sites of pilgrimage have this in common; they are believed to be places where miracles once happened, still happen, and may happen again.'[26] This is the essence of the shrine: it is 'a place where earth and heaven meet in the person of the dead, made plain by some manifestation of supernatural power, some wonderful happening'.[27] The supplication of faith——expectant faith—— is answered in the form of a miracle. As an Irish cleric of

[24] *Adomnan's Life of Columba*, ed. and trans. A. O. and M. O. Anderson (Edinburgh, 1961), c. 4a, p. 186; Bede, *Historia Ecclesiastica*, ed. C. Plummer (Oxford, 1896), III, c. 27, p. 193.

[25] Consider, for example, the case of Anastasius of Cluny (d. *c.*1085?): *Vita sancti Anastasii auctore Galtero*, in *Patrologia Latina* CXLIX, cols. 425-34.

[26] V. and E. Turner, *Image and Pilgrimage in Christian culture* (Oxford, 1978), p. 7. It is a pity that this valuable work is disfigured by the repellent jargon of the social scientist.

[27] P. Brown, 'Relics and social status in the age of Gregory of Tours', in his *Society and the holy in late antiquity* (London, 1982), pp. 222-50, quoted from p. 225.

the ninth century put it, 'You will not find the King whom
you seek unless you bring him with you.'[28] If miracles
revealed God's power in and through his saints, they also
plumbed the wells of faith within the individual suppliant;
and that *self*-knowledge lay at the heart of the pilgrim's
spiritual renewal.

So much for general considerations. The mistake we must
not make, however, is to suppose that the subject of pilgrimage may safely be left in the hands of the anthropologist
or the sociologist of religion or of others who claim to traffic
in the larger generalities relating to the workings of human
beings. And this for one simple reason: it is an observable
fact that the impulse to undertake pilgrimages is stronger
at some periods than at others. Historians of the middle
ages are agreed that between, roughly, 950 and 1150 the
practice of pilgrimage in the second sense—a journey to
a miracle-working shrine—experienced a surge of popularity.
Contemporaries, indeed, commented on it, such as the
chronicler Raoul Glaber in the middle years of the eleventh
century. We must try to explain this, for the fortunes of
Compostela (in the most literal sense) in the days of Diego
Gelmírez were very largely founded on it.

Two lines of approach are promising. The first of them
concerns changes in the penitential discipline administered
by the ecclesiastical authorities.[29] The penitential system in
vogue during the early middle ages had been developed
largely, though not exclusively, under the influence of Irish
and Anglo-Saxon moral theologians between the sixth and
the eighth centuries. (We are not here concerned with the
penitential system of the early church which these new
developments displaced.) The controlling notion was that
penance was a form of heavenly medicine. Rigorous demands
upon the penitent sinner not only induced a mood of proper
contrition but also (it was hoped) served to bridle the passions
which might give rise to future sin. The sinner confessed his

[28] K. H. Jackson, *A Celtic Miscellany* (revised edn., Harmondsworth, 1971),
no. 121, p. 136.
[29] For a clear exposition see C. Vogel, 'Le pèlerinage pénitentiel', in *Pelle-
grinaggi e culto dei santi in Europa fino alla prima Crociata* (Convegni del Centro
di studi sulla spiritualità medievale, IV, Todi, 1963), pp. 39–92.

sin to a confessor, who laid down an appropriate penance in accordance with the tariffs of penitential books such as those associated with the names of Columbanus, Theodore or Egbert of York. When the penance had been completed— but only then—absolution was granted. Now an important change was coming over this system during our period. It was heralded by no act of policy such as might have been recorded in, for example, the decrees of ecclesiastical councils, but arose (it seems) from the spontaneous and therefore largely unrecorded practice of individual confessors. Hence it is peculiarly difficult to date. It is evident that the change was very gradual: the first signs of its appear in the ninth century; it seems to have become widespread by the second half of the eleventh. During this time it became the practice for confessors to grant absolution to sinners not on the completion of penance but rather at the moment of confession itself. This change served to underscore and to widen the distinction between sin and its punishment. The sinner had confessed his sin and received absolution; but he would still have to suffer in the next world the punishment for his sin. However, the discipline of penance in this world could serve to wipe out the punishment that awaited the sinner in the next. Penance as 'satisfaction' for sin came to receive more emphasis than the older idea of penance as spiritual 'medicine'. Thus this modification of the practice of the church, while laying more stress on the individual act of contrition and the saving grace mediated through absolution, paradoxically resulted in more fervent and more literal fulfilment of the actual course of penance itself.

This development helps to explain much that is not otherwise easily explicable in the culture of Europe between *c.*950 and *c.*1150: for instance, the prodigious number of monastic foundations, the extraordinary appeal of the crusading movement, and the great surge in the popularity of pilgrimages. A period of time spent *in peregrinatione*, i.e. as an exile, makes its appearance among the tariffs laid down in the penitential books of the seventh and eighth centuries. But the practice of confessors reflected social realities, and as the practice of temporary pilgrimage to a shrine gained upon the practice of lifelong pilgrimage, so

we find them beginning to send the penitent sinner to one
(or more) named shrines. It was thus that the practice of
penitential pilgrimage was born.

A famous story which occurs in three miracle-collections
of this period, including those of Santiago, expresses neatly
how efficacious such pilgrimages were believed to be.[30]
A sinner confessed a grave sin to his priest, who sent him on
a penitential pilgrimage to Santiago de Compostela (or to
Saint-Gilles, or to Vézelay, depending on our source). He
carried with him a written account of his sin which he was
told to place upon the altar in the church of his destination.
When he did so, the sheet of parchment was found to be
blank. The writing had miraculously disappeared. The act of
pilgrimage had, literally, erased the sin. We have plenty
of examples of the same idea at work in the practice of the
churchmen of this period. Abbo of Fleury sent the abbot
of Beaulieu on pilgrimage to Rome and Monte Gargano as
a penance for simony.[31] Peter Damian sent an Italian nobleman to Jerusalem, 'so that you may abate the rigour of
God's justice by the satisfaction of a distant pilgrimage'.[32]
Adhémar III, viscount of Limoges, 'setting out for Santiago
on pilgrimage, instructed (*ammonitus*) by abbot Gerald of
Uzerche, gave one of his properties' to the monastery before
his departure.[33] Shortly before his death in 1031 king Robert
of France visited several shrines 'to evade the awful sentence
of the day of judgement'.[34] A few years later, in 1035,
Robert the Magnificent, duke of Normandy, set out for
Jerusalem 'making satisfaction to God' (*Deo satisfaciens*)
for the death of the brother whom years before he had
poisoned.[35]

---

[30] *LSJ* pp. 262-3.

[31] Aimon, *Vita sancti Abbonis*, in *Patrologia Latina* CXXXIX, coll. 398-9:
note that Aimon thought that Abbo was doing something novel.

[32] Peter Damian, Ep. VII, xvii (*Patrologia Latina* CXLIV coll. 455-8): cf. also
his *Opuscula* V and LVI (ibid. CXLV, coll. 89-98, 807-20).

[33] *Cartulaire de l'Abbaye d'Uzerche*, ed. J.-B. Champeval (Paris–Tulle, 1901),
no. 543. The date was between 1068 and 1090. It is not clear whether the
admonition was to undertake the pilgrimage or to make the gift or both.

[34] Helgaud of Fleury, *Epitoma vitae regis Rotberti pii*, ed. R.-H. Bautier and
G. Labory (Paris, 1965), c. 27, pp. 124-8.

[35] *Gesta consulum Andegavorum*, in *Chroniques des comtes d'Anjou*, ed.
L. Halphen and R. Poupardin (Paris, 1913), p. 50.

The appearance of liturgical provision for pilgrims is one testimony to the importance of the penitential pilgrimage in the central middle ages. Rituals were devised, prayers composed, for the blessing of pilgrims and their accoutrements. These accoutrements, the pouch or scrip and the staff—the hat was to follow later—are themselves of interest: for the appearance of what was in effect a kind of pilgrim 'uniform' testifies to a new self-consciousness on the part of the pilgrim, a feeling that he should be set apart, distinguished, from other men and women. The nexus of ritual and equipment reinforces what was said earlier about the solemnity of the pilgrim's undertaking in the context of his religious life. Charters could be dated by it: 'on the day in which he took up his scrip (*sportam*) for his pilgrimage to Santiago'.[36] It was a never-to-be-forgotten moment in a man's earthly career.

In an oft-quoted passage Eckhard of Aura referred in about 1100 to the priestly blessing of scrip and staff as a 'new ritual'.[37] It has for long been known, in a general way, that he was correct. In earlier ages the ecclesiastical authorities had required simply that pilgrims should confess before they set out; there had been no special ceremony of blessing. We can now see much more clearly how new the 'new ritual' was. The so-called *Romano-German Pontifical* is the first collection to contain it.[38] A pontifical is a liturgical book containing prayers and ceremonies for all the rites conducted by a bishop—confirmation, ordination, the consecration of churches, exorcism, the blessing of an abbot, prayers in time of war, plague, drought, flood, dearth, cattle-murrain, and so forth. The *Romano-German Pontifical* was compiled at Mainz about the year 960. Comprehensive, orderly and dignified, it rapidly became authoritative and was

[36] *Cartulaire de l'Église cathédrale de Grenoble*, ed. J. Marion (Paris, 1869), no. cxvi.

[37] Eckhard of Aura, *Chronicon universale*, in *Monumenta Germaniae Historica, Scriptores*, VI. 214.

[38] *Le Pontifical romano-germanique du dixième siècle*, ed. C. Vogel and R. Elze (Studi e Testi vols. 226–7 (text), 266 (introduction and indices), 3 vols., Rome, 1963–72). See also C. Vogel, 'Les rites de la pénitence publique aux Xe et XIe siècles', in *Mélanges offerts à René Crozet*, ed. P. Gallais and Y.-J. Riou (Poitiers, 1966), I. 137–44.

diffused among the churches of Latin Christendom with astonishing speed. (It is a small indication of the isolation of western Spain that the *Pontifical* did not penetrate there until very much later.) The earliest recension contained no provision for the blessing of pilgrims and their accoutrements. However, in one eleventh-century manuscript (Vienna 701) there features a 'Blessing on scrips and staves (*capsellas et fustes*) and those who are about to set out with them to seek the shrines and intercession of the holy apostles'.[39] The most recent editor of the *Pontifical*, Mgr. Vogel, is prudently hesitant to date this manuscript precisely. At different points in his apparatus he offers us 'avant 1070', '1021/ 1031?', and 'dans la première moitié du XIe siècle'.[40] But the crucial point is that the benediction in question was itself an addition to the manuscript in which it occurs: the text of the pontifical begins on folio 4^r; the benediction is a later addition on folio 3^v. It could have been inserted at about the very time that Eckhard was writing; a new ritual indeed.

At much the same time one of the earliest surviving representations of a pilgrim in the new 'uniform' was executed. It is an outstandingly fine piece of sculpture in stone carved for the decoration of the cloister of Sto. Domingo de Silos, itself a house on the pilgrimage-road to Compostela. It portrays Christ on the road to Emmaus—and we should note the context of a *journey*—but accoutred as a pilgrim to Santiago, carrying a scrip decorated with the scallop-shell which was the distinctive mark of the pilgrim to the shrine of St. James.[41]

If Christ could be portrayed as a pilgrim, it may be said that pilgrimage was a Christ-like undertaking: an *imitatio Christi*. Men and women famous in the world's history could be portrayed as pilgrims too; Helena the mother of Constantine, for example, or Charlemagne. The latter is a particularly interesting case, for it was one of the manifestations of the myth of Charlemagne which was being

[39] Ed. cit., II, no. ccxii, p. 362: note the reference to Abraham.
[40] Ed. cit., III, pp. 34, 56, 67.
[41] The date of the Emmaus at Silos has been much debated: I understand that it is now thought unlikely that the work was carried out before c.1090.

elaborated during precisely this period. The rendering of Charlemagne as a pilgrim must have commended the idea of pilgrimage to those who revered his memory, looked back to him, listened to poems and songs about him: that is, not only kings, but the secular nobility and gentry generally—let us simply say, adopting a favourite medieval classification, the *bellatores* as against the *oratores* and the *laboratores*. This brings us to our second line of approach in trying to explain the phenomenon of pilgrimages in the central middle ages.

We may start by asking ourselves this: what do influential churchmen present as the ideal pattern of Christian observance for the layman, and to whom do they present it? It is obvious enough that both the content of the moral pattern preached by the authorities and the social groups at which it is directed will change from time to time. In the early middle ages before (let us say) the tenth century the target of ecclesiastical attention was principally composed of barbarian kings and their warrior aristocracies.[42] In the twelfth and thirteenth centuries the target was, increasingly, the urban bourgeoisie and the urban poor. The moral teaching of the friars reflected, either in approval or rejection, the mores of the town-dweller.[43] These changing concerns were the expression of ecclesiastical adaptation to social change.

During the intervening period the more thoughtful churchmen were concerned to deepen the Christian observance of those whom our sources refer to by such terms as *bellatores, potentes*, and the like: the directing secular élites of the feudal age.[44] There was plenty of scope for such deepening. An aristocracy which listened for recreation to *Beowulf* or the *Chanson de Roland* or the *Siete Infantes de Lara* was one

[42] J. M. Wallace-Hadrill, *Early Germanic kingship in England and on the Continent* (Oxford, 1971); P. Wormald, 'Bede, *Beowulf* and the conversion of the Anglo-Saxon aristocracy', in *Bede and Anglo-Saxon England*, ed. R. T. Farrell (*British Archaeological Reports* 46, 1978), pp. 32-95.

[43] B. H. Rosenwein and L. K. Little, 'Social meaning in the monastic and mendicant spiritualities', *Past and Present* 63 (1974), 4-32.

[44] See the interesting remarks of I. S. Robinson, *Authority and resistance in the Investiture Contest. The polemical literature of the late eleventh century* (Manchester, 1978), pp. 101-2.

into which Christian moral teaching had not penetrated very
deeply. The traditional teaching of the clergy had been that
for the layman who remained in the secular world there
was very little hope of salvation. The only sure road to
heaven lay in renunciation of the *saeculum* by entry to a
monastery; in short by an act of *anachoresis*. However, from
the tenth century onwards some churchmen could be found
who were prepared to encourage devout layman to remain
in the world and to claim that their prospects of salvation
were no worse than the chances of those who had renounced
it. This was a change in sensibilities which was to have far-
reaching consequences for European civilization.

The key text is the *Vita* of St. Gerald of Aurillac composed by Odo, abbot of Cluny, in about 940.[45] Gerald,
self-styled count of Aurillac, was another survivor among
the drifting flotsam of Carolingian west Francia. He carved
out for himself a principality in the Auvergne in the second
half of the ninth century which he ruled in effective independence until his death in about 909. Odo was concerned
to present Gerald as a man in some sense holy—a *sanctus*
—despite the fact that he did not become a monk, because
of the manner in which he exercised his worldly responsibilities. For Odo the office of a count, no less than that
of a king, was a Christian one. The virtues which Gerald
displayed were of a fairly rudimentary sort, and Odo's
reporting of them sheds a lurid light on social conditions in
the Auvergne in the ninth and tenth centuries. Gerald was
never drunk when presiding over a court of law. He always
insisted on paying for goods requisitioned by his vassals
from the peasantry. His personal life was virtuous; he would
read and meditate on the scriptures; he was chaste; he was
charitable; he was moderate in food and drink, unostentatious
in his dress—he wore no gold jewellery and could make
a sword-belt last twenty years. He founded a monastery at
Aurillac. And he went on pilgrimages. Odo laid special
stress on this last. There were several shrines which Gerald
was accustomed to visit, such as those at Tours, Limoges and

---

[45] Odo of Cluny, *Vita sancti Geraldi Auriliacensis comitis*, in *Patrologia
Latina* CXXXIII, coll. 639–704; there is an English translation in G. Sitwell,
St. Odo of Cluny (London, 1958), pp. 90–180.

elsewhere, but above all he used to go to Rome: at least seven times he visited the tombs of the apostles Peter and Paul. Odo emphasized the regularity of his pilgrimages: as a matter of routine Gerald went to Rome every other year. Odo wanted to show that pilgrimage was one of the foremost religious exercises of the Christian gentleman.

Odo of Cluny's biography of Gerald of Aurillac had a didactic purpose, and it can be shown to have been influential. About a century after his day a monk of Limoges named Adhémar of Chabannes composed a chronicle which is our principal source of information about the affairs of south-western France in the late tenth and early eleventh centuries. Adhémar included in his work a well-known pen-portrait of William II, count of Poitou and duke of Aquitaine (d. 1029). His sketch was not original but was copied almost word for word from Einhard's celebrated description of Charlemagne. But Adhémar added one new touch to his portrait of William which was not to be found in his source. 'From his youth it was his custom to visit the shrines of the apostles in Rome once every year; and if he found that he could not go to Rome he would make up by undertaking a devout pilgrimage to St. James of Galicia.'[46] We note with interest that by Adhémar's day Compostela, never mentioned by Odo of Cluny, is on the same sort of footing as Rome for pilgrims from southern France. The more general point needs stressing that Odo's teaching was bearing fruit. Going on pilgrimage was something that prominent territorial lords were expected to do, irrespective of whether or not they were being urged to it as penitents by their confessors.

Here is an example which instructively brings together both pilgrimages and monastic foundations. It is the foundation-charter for a small religious house, Notre Dame de la Ferté-Avrain, established by Hervé, archdeacon of Orléans, in about 1035.[47] Hervé's charter tells us that he had gone on pilgrimage to Jerusalem, 'desiring to wash away my sins by

[46] Adhémar of Chabannes, *Chronicon*, ed. J. Chavanon (Paris, 1897), III, c. 41, p. 163.
[47] J. Doinel, 'Un pèlerinage à Jérusalem dans la première moitié du XIᵉ siècle', *Bibliothèque de l'École des Chartes* 51 (1890), 204-6.

my tears at those most holy shrines'. He brought back with him relics from the Lord's Sepulchre which he determined to deposit in the church of a religious house, 'not only for the remission of my own sins, but also for the salvation of the souls of my parents Havranus and Adela, my late brother Peter and my living brothers Alberic and Thedwin'. The act of pilgrimage and the act of founding a monastery are brought together here. What unites them is the emotion of guilt experienced by the pilgrim-donor. (Notable too is the sentiment of family solidarity.) Guilt, anxiety, dread—these are emotions which meet us time after time in accounts of pilgrimages and pious benefactions from this period. Who was encouraging these feelings? in what sort of people? and why?

These are large questions, and ones to which satisfactory answers have not yet been proposed. The tenth and eleventh centuries saw very far-reaching changes in the economic, social, political and intellectual arrangements of western Europe. New wealth, new opportunities, new social mobility, new relationships; moral disorder; the assertion of certain disciplines to guide the perplexed beneficiaries of these processes.[48] It was so often the 'new men' who experienced, or were brought to experience, the emotion of guilt. Gerald of Aurillac himself was a 'new man'. But there were many more of them in the eleventh countury than there had been in the ninth. Take, for example, the Catalan adventurer Arnal Mir de Tost.[49] Of modest origins—his father had been castellan of Tost, not far from Urgel in the eastern Pyrenees—he amassed through successful soldiering for a variety of paymasters both Christian and Muslim in the middle years of the eleventh century a prodigious fortune in land, no less than thirty castles, and vast quantities of movable goods. Inventories of the latter have survived, so that we are permitted a rare glimpse of the material trappings of an upstart feudal lord. Arnal Mir and his wife possessed clothes of silk and a Bukhara carpet; in the winter they

[48] For a stimulating dicussion see A. Murray, _Reason and society in the middle ages_ (Oxford, 1978), especially chs. 2-4.

[49] For Arnal Mir see P. Bonnassie, _La Catalogne du milieu du Xe à la fin du XIe siècle_ (Toulouse, 1975), II. 789-97.

could wrap themselves in cloaks of ermine. Frisian hatters
and glovers in Lucca and Le Puy had contributed to their
ample wardrobe. Arnal Mir had 'plenty' (*plurimos*)—he did
not trouble to number them—of gold rings set with precious
stones; his wife Arsendis could deck herself in a gold tiara
for grand occasions. The silver cutlery on their dinner table
must have glinted agreeably in the light shed by the candles
in their silver candlesticks; while the variety and quantity
of their *baterie de cuisine* suggests that their repasts were
generous. In their leisure moments they could divert themselves with one of their three ivory chess-sets. When Arnal went
to war his charger was caparisoned with saddle and harness
chased with silver; he could take his pick of thirteen tents;
he did not bother to enumerate his swords and coats of mail.
And there was masses more besides. We know enough about
how Arnal Mir had made his pile to be confident that a confessor would have found plenty of guilt, and anxiety about the
destination of his soul, on which to play. He went on pilgrimage to Compostela in 1071. Was it guilt and contrition which
sent him there? Was it a fulfilling of what was expected of
a man in his now exalted station? Was it both?

Arnal Mir, like his near-contemporary Rodrigo Díaz,
el Cid, rose from undistinguished beginnings to become
a very great man indeed; one of Catalonia's *potentes*. His was
one of the most remarkable 'success-stories' of the eleventh
century. There were many men of modest background who
prospered, though less sensationally, during this period.
If churchmen were holding up the ideal of pilgrimage to
society's *potentes* as a means of assuaging guilt, demonstrat-
ing virtue and averting the wrath to come, they were presenting it too to men of lower station. Many of these men were
such as could be described as *milites*; men who followed
the profession of arms. As a result of the work of several
scholars, and especially of Professor Georges Duby, it is
now a commonplace that *milites* occupied a more important
niche in European society by 1100 than they had done in,
say, 900.[50] It is fairly clear that, at least from the mid-eleventh
century onward, churchmen were concerned to civilize these

---

[50] See his collected essays *Hommes et structures du moyen âge* (Paris–The
Hague, 1973), especially 'Les origines de la chevalerie', pp. 325–41.

unruly thugs whose main claim to consideration lay in their skills in combat. The clergy were presenting them with a social role over which some sort of Christian veneer had been daubed. Some of the signs of this process are familiar. For instance, certain thinkers—Guibert of Nogent, Stephen of Muret, Bernard of Clairvaux and others—were coming to urge that there was a holiness in certain types of war which the Christian *miles* should wage. Or again, the very procedure, the ceremonial, of becoming a *miles* was gradually invested with a religious significance. Knighthood, as we may begin to call it, was turning into a Christian vocation. Another sign lay in the encouragement of *milites* to undertake pilgrimages.

The earliest recorded pilgrim from England to Santiago de Compostela was such a man. His name was Richard Mauleverer, the village where he held some property still bears the family name—Allerton Mauleverer, about ten miles west of York—and he made his pilgrimage shortly before 1105.[51] That is all we know of him. It is all too sadly characteristic of the sources for this period that we can, when dealing with people of his social rank, so very rarely penetrate beyond a name and an approximate date to the personality and the motive behind the bleak reference in charter or chronicle. The miracle-collections that survive deserve more attention than they have yet received.[52] Casual soundings among those of the eleventh century, such as the miracles of Ste. Foi and St. Benedict, reveal that many of the beneficiaries of the miracles recorded therein were *milites* who had come on pilgrimage to the shrine. Another indication, however imprecise, that eleventh-century pilgrims were people of fairly modest wealth and station, might be found in the spate of foundations of hospitals and guest-houses from *c.*1050 onwards.[53] Great people might travel in style and expect to be put up in comfort at the smartest

[51] *Early Yorkshire Charters*, ed. W. Farrer (Edinburgh, 1914–16), II, no. 729.

[52] For a rather later period, good use of some English miracle-collections has been made by R. C. Finucane, *Miracles and pilgrims: Popular beliefs in medieval England* (London, 1977). Benedicta Ward, *Miracles and the medieval mind* (London, 1982) was published only after the final version of this chapter had been drafted.

[53] Much information about such establishments in Spain is to be found

monasteries: in 951 bishop Gottschalk of Le Puy had travelled 'with a great following' (*magno comitatu*) and had success- fully sought hospitality at the monastery of Albelda. But humbler travellers would need different treatment.

This brings us to the last feature of eleventh-century pilgrimages. Many participants were even humbler than the *milites* (itself a term that could embrace men of extremely modest rank). We meet these men and women, once again, in the miracle collections where they tend to occur as indivi- duals or small family groups. One of the most interesting features of the eleventh century, however, is the appearance of large parties of pilgrims composed of what contemporary chroniclers vaguely called 'the poor', organized by local bishops and abbots. In 1026 the abbot of Verdun led a party of 700 to the Holy Land: this was the size of a respectable army in early eleventh-century France.[54] In 1056 a party under the leadership of abbot Albert of Liège made the journey to Compostela. We do not know how many men and women it numbered, but our source assures us that the band of pilgrims was a large one.[55] In 1064 a gigantic expedition led by four bishops travelled from Germany to the Holy Land. One contemporary estimated its size at 12,000 persons. Even if we regard this as surely an exaggeration and—shall we say?—halve it, we still are left with a body of about the same size as the army with which William of Normandy conquered England two years later.[56] These military com- parisons are not made unadvisedly. The biggest of all pilgrim expeditions were those which set off at the bidding of pope Urban II in 1096. We call them the armies of the First Crusade, but the participants did not. They thought of themselves as undertaking a special and unusual sort of pilgrimage.

scattered in J. M. Lacarra, L. Vázquez de Parga and J. Uría Ríu, *Las pere- grinaciones a Santiago de Compostela* (Madrid, 1948-9): see especially the docu- ments printed in vol. III, nos. 36-54, pp. 44-60.

[54] Hugh of Flavigny, *Chronicon*, in *Monumenta Germaniae Historica, Scrip- tores*, VIII, p. 393.

[55] J. Stiennon, 'Le voyage des Liégeois à St. Jacques de Compostelle', *Mélanges offerts à F. Rousseau* (Brussels, 1958), pp. 553-81.

[56] E. Joranson, 'The great German pilgrimage of 1064-1065', in *The Crusades and other historical essays presented to Dana C. Munro*, ed. L. J. Paetow (New York, 1928), pp. 3-43.

Here again, as with other social groups, we are witnessing the presentation of certain patterns of Christian behaviour to the laity by the clergy. These were patterns which were long to endure. Consider this: 'I am a good Christian, catholic and faithful. I pay tithes and first-fruits, I give alms to Christ's poor, I go on pilgrimage like a good Christian; last year I went with my wife to the Virgin of Montserrat, and this year to St. James of Compostela.' The speaker was Pierre Sabatier, weaver, of Varilhes, near Foix, in about 1320.[57] Marxist historians have claimed to discern in this mobilization of the masses by the clergy simply a vast exploitative system articulated by the cult of relics. Relics are the focus of cults and attract pilgrims; pilgrims bring offerings and the churches become rich; the masses are drawn in and kept in a submissive posture both morally and economically. Such an interpretation—which has of course a respectable ancestry in Protestant polemic during the Reformation—is not lightly to be dismissed, but it is too one-sided to be wholly convincing. What it fails to allow for is the fact that *all* ranks of society experienced this clerical influence. It was not simply a question of an ecclesiastical hierarchy, by implication closely tied to a feudal nobility, preying upon a subject peasantry. What is really striking is that the whole of lay society was being encouraged to submit to a common Christian discipline. Some will interpret this as a rather late stage in the Christianization of Europe; some as an element in that very complex process called for short 'the Gregorian Reform'; some as a pragmatic response by churchmen to economic and social trends. Perhaps, in any case, these are no more than three different ways of saying the same thing.

In trying to say something about the phenomenon of medieval pilgrimage one runs the risk of losing sight of the individual pilgrim himself. The solemn notes which have been sounded here—contrition, amendment of life, deepening of Christian observance—may not have sounded for him at all. Most pilgrims (we may suspect) were perfectly ordinary people with only the humdrum problems of daily life to contend with; provided always that we bear in mind that that

[57] E. le Roy Ladurie, *Montaillou* (English trans, London, 1978), p. 300.

little word 'only' can mask whole worlds of tempestuous and ghastly experience. In the miracles of Santiago we meet a family from Poitou who went to Compostela to escape a plague that was ravaging their homeland; a barren couple who sought the intercession of St. James to assist them in conceiving a child; a paralytic seeking a cure; a man who had been cured of cancer of the throat (?) by contact with a shell of St. James brought back from pilgrimage by a neighbour and who then went to Compostela in gratitude for his cure.[58] Naturally, the miracle stories record only the successes. There must have been many sufferers, like St. Gerald the founder of La Sauve-Majeure in Gascony, who were dragged from shrine to shrine in vain.[59] There were too those whose afflictions were less tangible, less easily avowed, less open to inspection. The most harrowing story in the miracles of St. James concerns a young man from near Lyons, also named Gerald, who with his widowed mother followed the trade of a skinner. He was devoted to St. James and was accustomed to go on pilgrimage to Compostela every year. He was unmarried, but chaste. But one day, shortly before setting out on his annual pilgrimage, he committed the sin of fornication. In the course of his journey the Devil appeared to him in the guise of St. James and told him that the only way in which he could purge himself of his sin was by amputation of the offending member. Accordingly he cut off his genitals, immediately afterwards stabbing himself in the stomach and thereby dying a lingering and horrible death. The story continues with an account of his miraculous resuscitation through the intercession of St. James, but we need follow it no further.[60]

[58] *LSJ*, pp. 263-4, 268-9, 273-4, 286.

[59] *Vita sancti Geraldi fundatoris Silvae-Majoris in Aquitania, Acta Sanctorum, Aprilis* I (Brussels, 1865), c. 2, pp. 408-9. He was taken to Rome, Montecassino and Monte Gargano; ironically, he was cured on his return to his native Corbie by the intercession of St. Adalard.

[60] *LSJ*, pp. 278-82, where the gruesome story is attributed to Anselm of Bec and Canterbury, who appears to have had it from Hugh of Cluny. The same story, with variations, is told by Guibert of Nogent, who claimed to have got it from Geoffrey of Saumur, nephew of Hugh of Cluny. An earlier version of it, lacking the theme of sexual mutilation, occurs in a poem composed at Montecassino, where the miracle is said to have taken place near Cluny in the time of abbot Hugh. I am grateful to Dr P. P. A. Biller for drawing my attention to this complex literary web, which might repay further attempts to disentangle.

There is some reason for supposing that Gerald was not the only sufferer from the torments of sexual guilt whom one might have encountered on the road to Compostela at this period.[61]

People went on pilgrimages for every sort of reason. Some churchmen were worried by the fact that not all reasons were good.[62] There was little that they could do about it. In the early summer of 1151 earl Ronald (or Rognvald) of Orkney set off with a large party of his fellow Orkneymen on a pilgrimage to the Holy Places.[63] They had a cracking good time. Round the coast of Muslim Spain 'they ravaged far and wide and got much booty'. They wintered near Narbonne, where the elderly Ronald enjoyed a flirtation with Ermengarde, the daughter of count Aymeric of Narbonne. They repaid his generosity, which had proved so unexpectedly agreeable, by capturing the stronghold of a nearby brigand. After resuming their journey in the spring of 1152 they attacked, captured and burnt a Saracen galley somewhere off Sardinia. Arrived at their goal they landed at Acre, visited Jerusalem and on 10 August—note the precision of dating—they bathed in the Jordan. On their way back they put into port somewhere in the Aegean where they got very drunk; one of them was killed in a brawl. The winter of 1152-3 was spent in Constantinople where the emperor Manuel Comnenus, tactful and long-suffering as always in his dealings with barbarians from the west, received them in audience: or so they later claimed. In 1153 they went overland to the Adriatic, crossed to Italy, travelled by way of Rome through Lombardy and Germany back to Denmark, and thence homewards across the North Sea. Earl Ronald was hardly the model pilgrim as conceived by high-minded churchmen. The pilgrim was not meant to carry arms; Ronald and his men not only carried them but used them. The pilgrim was meant to abstain from fleshly pleasures; this did

---

[61] See the curious passage on the stream called *Lavamentula* in *LSJ*, p. 354.

[62] G. Constable, 'Opposition to pilgrimages in the middle ages', *Studia Gratiana* 19 (1976), 125-46.

[63] For what follows, see *The Orkneyinga Saga*, trans. A. B. Taylor (Edinburgh, 1938), pp. 275-303. The pilgrims 'stayed a short time' in Galicia, but we are not told that they visited the shrine of St. James.

not deter Ronald from his dalliance with Ermengarde. The pilgrim was meant to travel with only the bare necessities for the journey; the Orkneymen enriched themselves with plunder. The *Orkneyinga Saga* is engagingly frank about such matters—far more so than the accounts composed by ecclesiastics. It is also wonderfully revealing about what the pilgrims got out of it. Here is no solemn piety. Instead, the author's comment is far more robust. After they had crossed the sea for the last time, berthed their longships at Kirkwall, stepped out again on to their native Orkney soil, this is what he tells us. 'They all passed for men of more importance after the journey they had made.'

V

The making of a bishop

We do not know when Diego Gelmírez was born. He was entrusted with important administrative responsibilities as early as 1093, was ordained priest and elected a bishop in 1100, and died at an advanced age in 1140. These indications, such as they are, would suggest that he was born about the middle of the 1060s. This is imprecise, but as near as we are ever likely to get. The *Historia Compostellana* contains two passages which shed a little light on his family background.[1] Diego was a native of Galicia and came of a respectable family (*natus probis secundum seculum parentibus*). His father Gelmirio could best be described as a *miles* —a word whose connotations at this period it is not easy to grasp with any confidence, but which, from the pen of a Frenchman writing in Compostela in the 1120s, probably implied not simply the profession of arms but a certain social rank guaranteed by the possession of property and a certain code of behaviour appropriate to it. Gelmirio had been in the service of bishop Diego Peláez, from whom he had held the castle of Torres del Oeste, and on whose behalf had administered for many years the districts of Iria, La Mahía and Postmarcos; the land bounded on the south side by the river Ulla and the Ría de Arosa, and on the north side by the river Tambre and the Ría de Muros y Noya, between the town of Compostela and the Atlantic. Gelmirio —the name was derived from the Germanic Hildemir[2]— was evidently a man of complete trustworthiness in the bishop's service. The area he governed was the heartland of

[1] *HC*, pp. 19–20, 254.

[2] Holders of the name may be traced from the Suevic and Visigothic period onwards: an archpriest of Orense of this name attended the Third council of Toledo in 589; a ring inscribed ILDIMER, apparently of the sixth century, is preserved in Pontevedra Museum; Gildimirius subscribed a charter of *c*.690; Ildemirus the priest subscribed another of 818; and the name is not infrequent in documents of the tenth and eleventh centuries.

the *honor*, or temporalities, of Santiago and the castle of Torres del Oeste was of great strategic importance. He was probably of no very exalted social rank. Diego's panegyrists would have been unable to resist drawing attention to his parents' *nobilitas*, had they possessed it. As it was they could describe them only as *probi*—'respectable'. Gelmirio, then, was a man of the middling sort, in all probability a native of the area near Compostela, conscientious and competent in his ministerial role; a rising man, who might hope to do better by his children than his father had done by him. If they could be confident of a good start in life, they knew that they would still have to work hard to go far. It was perhaps from his family that Diego got his self-confidence, his ambition and his energy.

Diego had four brothers, Munio (or Nuño), Gundesindo, Pedro and Juan. Another brother, also named Pedro, is mentioned in the *Historia*: possibly he was a half-brother, the issue of a second marriage by Gelmirio. We do not know of any sisters, though it is possible that Diego's nephew, yet another Pedro, was a sister's son. Diego must early on have been destined for an ecclesiastical career. He received his education in the cathedral school of Compostela.[3] Our ignorance about the Compostela school in the middle years of the eleventh century should not lead us to underestimate the quality of the education it could provide. Bishop Pelayo of León (1065-86) could boast of the education he had received there.[4] Diego never became a man of very wide or deep intellectual cultivation, but he had been given a good grounding in the scriptures and in law, he became a patron of learning in a modest way, and by the time he reached middle age he had assembled a private library of at least fifteen volumes—not a negligible collection.[5] After his schooling at Compostela Diego spent some time at the royal court of Alfonso VI. The king's daughter Urraca referred to this many years later when she reminded Diego in 1116 that her father 'brought you up from your adolescence' (*te ab ipsa educavit adolescentia*).[6] We can rarely be sure precisely what writers of this period intended by the term

---

[3] *HC*, p. 254.   [4] R. 10 November 1073.
[5] See below, Appendix D.   [6] *HC*, p. 212.

adolescentia: here I think the implication is that Diego was attached to the royal household while he was in his teens. It would have been a time to watch and to learn, to make himself useful and agreeable to those whose interest might be enlisted in his favour. The sequel permits us to assume that he acquitted himself well. By the time he was 'grown-up' —*adultus*, another vague term—he was back in Galicia in the household (*curia*) of his patron bishop Diego Peláez.[7] This must have been before the year 1085, when the Galician rebellion in which the bishop was implicated broke out. It was perhaps at this time that the young man was rewarded with a canonry in the church of Santiago.[8]

How Diego managed to survive the wreckage of his patron's fortunes we shall never know. We have no materials relating to his life between 1085 and 1090. One can think of more than one reason why he should have been reluctant, later on, to talk about this period or to let his biographers write about it. Speculation is fruitless, but it is fair to surmise that the young Diego saw his career at stake and fought hard to save it. In fighting hard he may not have been able to keep his hands clean. His extreme reluctance in later years to travel through the kingdom of Aragon, where Diego Peláez lived out his exile, might just possibly indicate that his anxiety not to see the man who had given him his first leg-up in his career was not untinged by guilt.

His great opportunity came after the appointment of Raymond of Burgundy to the county of Galicia. Apparently on the advice of the cathedral community of Compostela, he chose Diego as his chancellor and confidential adviser (*cancellarius et secretarius*).[9] We cannot date this appointment accurately: it must have occurred between the time of Raymond's nomination as count of Galicia in the spring of 1087 and Diego's first spell as administrator of the diocese in 1093-4. There survive five charters given in Raymond's name which were drawn up under Diego's

[7] *HC*, p. 254.
[8] *HC*, p. 20.
[9] *HC*, p. 20. Diego claimed later on that he had been Raymond's confessor as well (*HC*, p. 458), but this could have been at any time before Raymond's death in 1107.

direction.[10] In these documents he described himself variously as the count's scribe or notary (*scriptor, notarius*). His service in the peripatetic household of count Raymond during these years broadened his experience to embrace activities beyond the confines of the merely secretarial. In 1094–5, for example, he accompanied the count's army on its campaign to Coimbra and Lisbon, in the course of which he had a narrow escape from the Saracens.[11] In later years he would refer to his travels as a young man: his attendance at the courts of Alfonso VI and then count Raymond would certainly have kept him on the move.[12] As to his duties, we know so little of the count's chancery that nothing may be said beyond that they were concerned with the drafting and production of official documents. One generalization, however, may safely be made. During this period such service to the crown (or, as in Diego's case, to a prominent member of the royal family) was normally rewarded with ecclesiastical preferment. We can see this exemplified in Germany, France and England, and it is probably only because no serious work has yet been devoted to the chanceries of Fernando I and Alfonso VI that we cannot yet see it in Spain.[13]

Diego's first substantial reward came in 1093 when Raymond appointed him administrator of the temporalities of the church of Santiago. We should remember that the bishopric had been vacant since the deposition of Pedro de Cardeña in 1090. By long-established custom the kings of León-Castile exercised what in England would have been called regalian right during such vacancies.[14] That is to say,

---

[10] R. 13 November 1094, 25 February 1095, 24 September 1095, 1 May 1096 and 21 August 1096. The penultimate of these is incorrectly dated 1106: Reilly, *Urraca*, p. 23, n. 42, has proposed the emendation to 1096.

[11] *HC*, p. 360. R. 13 November 1094 and 25 February 1095, both drawn up by Diego for Portuguese beneficiaries, were granted during this campaign, probably in or near Coimbra.   [12] *HC*, p. 474.

[13] But see the study of the career of Sampiro, royal notary and finally bishop of Astorga (d. 1042) in J. Pérez de Urbel, *Sampiro: su crónica y la monarquía leonesa en el siglo X* (Madrid, 1952), pp. 11–125. For some slightly later examples from León, see *Episcopate*, pp. 80–3.

[14] R. A. Fletcher, 'Regalian right in twelfth-century Spain: the case of archbishop Martín of Santiago de Compostela', *Journal of Ecclesiastical History* 27 (1977), 337–60.

they took the temporalities of the vacant see into their own hands and diverted the revenues therefrom into their treasury. Alfonso VI had first appointed Pedro Vimara to administer the temporalities—the *honor*—of Santiago. His steward-ship proved so rapacious that he was deprived of office and replaced by Arias Díaz. According to the *Historia Com-postellana* his administration proved no less oppressive than that of his predecessor: every rank of society groaned under his yoke, and so harsh lay his hand upon the canons of the cathedral church that they even went short of food and clothing. The death of Arias Díaz was a merciful release. It was at this point that count Raymond, having sought advice from the bishops of Lugo, Mondoñedo, Orense and Tuy, directed the elders (*quosdam seniorum*) and the people (*populum*) of the church of Santiago to submit a nominee whom he might appoint to the vacant post. At a meeting held under Raymond's aegis, which was also attended by members of the Galician nobility (*principes*) the unanimous choice was Diego Gelmírez. We may make what we will of this. We are told that the electors recalled how just and moderate had been the administration of Diego's father Gelmirio in a similar charge. While we need not doubt this, we may also suggest that count Raymond played a rather larger part in the appointment of Diego than the *Historia*'s account implies.

Diego administered the *honor* of Santiago for a year.[15] At the end of it a new bishop was found for the see in the person of Dalmatius, a monk of Cluny who was at that time exercising supervision over the Cluniac houses of Spain.[16] He was appointed, we are told, by Alfonso VI, count Ray-mond and the infanta Urraca; but they acted on the advice (*consilio*) of the clergy and people of Compostela, with the permission of abbot Hugh of Cluny, and with the approval of the Roman church. This last provision was most important:

[15] R. 28 January 1090 was subscribed by Diego Gelmírez as *maiorinus et dominator Compostelle honoris*. This has suggested to some authorities that he had been entrusted with the administration of the temporalities already at that much earlier date. This is possible but to my mind not very probable. The charter itself is not entirely above suspicion.

[16] *HC*, p. 20. R. 13 November 1094 was subscribed by Dalmatius, thus pro-viding us with a *terminus ante quem* for his promotion.

Urban II had ceased attempting to bring about the restoration of Diego Peláez; Dalmatius was *persona grata* to both king and pope. But he did not last long. Towards the end of 1095 he attended the council of Clermont, and shortly after it acquired from the pope an important privilege exempting his see from the jurisdiction of any metropolitan and placing it directly under the authority of the church of Rome.[17] But he died soon after his return to Compostela in March 1096.[18] Once again, at the request of the clergy and people of Santiago. Diego Gelmírez was appointed by king, count and infanta to administer the diocese; by the summer he was describing himself as the *vicarius* of St. James.[19] Meanwhile, the death of Dalmatius had been the signal for the ex-bishop Diego Peláez to make another bid to recover his see. He went to Rome to lay his case again before the papal court. No ruling was forthcoming, and hence no new episcopal appointment could be made. It was for this reason that Diego Gelmírez's second administration of the *honor* lasted for so long, about four years (1096–1100). Towards the end of this period Alfonso VI sent an embassy to Rome in an attempt to hasten a decision in the long-drawn-out suit. His messengers found Urban II dead (29 July 1099) and Paschal II elected pope in his place (13 August). The new pope swiftly brought matters to a conclusion. He ruled that Diego Peláez had been justly deposed and in a letter of 29 December 1099 ordered a new election to be held.[20] The tribulations of the see of Compostela were nearly at an end.

For the greater part, therefore, of the last decade of the eleventh century Diego Gelmírez had had charge of the temporalities of the see of Santiago de Compostela. He sometimes referred to himself as *vicarius* of the see;[21] once

[17] *HC*, pp. 21–3 (= JL 5601): for further discussion of this privilege see below, ch. VIII.

[18] The date of his death was probably 16 March 1096: see Vones, *Kirchenpolitik*, p. 100, n. 2. It is likely that he travelled from France back to Galicia by sea, since he can be traced at Saintes in the early weeks of 1096: *Cartulaire de Saint-Jean d'Angély*, ed. G. Musset (Paris–Saintes, 1901), I, no. clxxxiii.

[19] R. 21 August 1096.

[20] *HC*, pp. 25–6 (= JL 5810, 5811). Diego Peláez had already given up hope of reinstatement before the death of Urban II, for he was back in Aragon by July 1099 when he subscribed one of the charters of Pedro I of Aragon.

[21] R. 21 August 1096, 19 May 1097.

as *honores sancti Iacobi dijudicans;*[22] once—possibly—as
maiorinus et dominator Compostelle honoris.[23] The *Historia
Compostellana* called him *protector et defensor,* elsewhere
gubernator et dominus; and to his predecessors Pedro Vimara
and Arias Díaz it referred respectively *regius villicus* and
maiorinus.[24] Most of these terms, 'lord', 'governor', 'protector'
and the like, are imprecise. Only two of them may be regarded
as technical terms denoting administrative office. In Spanish
documents of this period *villicus* usually meant the steward
of an estate. *Maiorinus* was the Latin form of the title rendered in the Romance vernacular as *merino.* At this period it
was the task of the *merino* to administer justice and to
enforce royal rights within a given area; he was, below the
level of count, the principal royal official in local administration. Diego's vicariate of the lands of St. James would have
involved him not only in the supervision of estate-management
but also in the administration of justice, in providing for
defence and peace-keeping, and in the collection of the king's
public revenues. When we recall that in addition to these
responsibilities Diego was, between 1093 and 1096 (at the
least), a prominent member of count Raymond's secretarial
staff, and that in the winter of 1094–5 he had gained experience of military action we can gauge the extent of his energies
and talents and judge how well fitted he was to assume, as a
bishop, responsibilities still wider.

The *Historia Compostellana* furnishes us with an elaborate
account of Diego's election to the bishopric of Santiago,
which yet contains some dark corners. We may suspect
that this is deliberate. The general course of events is clear
enough, their interpretation less so. It is fairly obvious that
strings were being pulled behind the scenes, but we cannot be
sure who was doing the pulling, nor in which direction.
Narratives of episcopal elections in eleventh- and twelfth-
century Spain are exceedingly rare: this is one of the fullest
we possess.[25] We must see what we can do with it.[26]

[22] R. 28 March 1098.
[23] R. 28 January 1090—though this charter (as we have seen) presents
problems.   [24] *HC,* pp. 18, 19, 23.
[25] For others, see *Episcopate,* pp. 77.
[26] Vones, *Kirchenpolitik,* pp. 100–48, provides what is now the fullest

When Paschal II's letter of 29 December 1099 reached the clergy of Compostela, Diego had already left—for Rome. He had gone there on pilgrimage (*orationis gratia*), we are told, but it is difficult to believe that his journey had no other motive.[27] This suspicion deepens when we learn that at the papal curia he very probably met Guy, the archbishop of Vienne. Now Guy was the brother of count Raymond of Galicia. What more natural than that Raymond's client should have solicited the interest wielded by his patron's brother, a churchman of outstanding renown who was later to become pope as Calixtus II, on his own behalf at the curia?[28] We should bear in mind too that as a result of the papal privilege acquired by Dalmatius in 1095 the pope's concern with the Compostela election was an intimate one; for thenceforward the bishops of Compostela were to be 'subject to none except the metropolitan bishop of Rome . . . as special suffragans of the Roman see'. Certainly Diego succeeded in impressing the pope. Paschal ordained him subdeacon and sent him back with a letter to the canons of Compostela (18 March 1100) telling them with a characteristically scrupulous regard for the rights of electors that he regarded Diego as a fit person to be promoted to holy orders (*ad sacros ordines*).[29] Perhaps Diego would have liked the pope to have gone further. Nevertheless, the letter of

investigation of Diego's election and consecration. The work reached me after this chapter had been drafted. Dr Vones displays great ingenuity in his handling of the sources for these mysterious episodes, but in the last resort I find him not quite persuasive. However, certain of his emphases are valuable, and I have introduced changes into my text in deference to them. Our final positions remain a certain way apart. The focus and scale of his book permitted treatment at considerable length, and the reader who seeks a thorough airing of these questions should turn to it.

[27] *HC*, p. 26. There is no mention of him in R. 16 January 1100, an important grant by Alfonso VI to the church of Santiago, which suggests that he had by then already departed. The main purport of Dr Vones's argument is that Diego had *already* been elected and consecrated a bishop: this I cannot accept.

[28] We cannot be absolutely certain that this meeting took place, but it looks likely. On one of his two visits to Rome (1100, 1104) Diego met Guy: *HC*, p. 272. Guy is not known to have been in Rome in 1104. Further, Guy had been appointed papal legate to England in 1100 and it is fair to assume that he visited the pope to be briefed for his (in the event, abortive) legation.

[29] *HC*, p. 27 (= JL 5822). The letter hints interestingly but obscurely at some domestic opposition to Diego among his cathedral colleagues. Dr Vones is sceptical of its authenticity.

18 March came pretty close to being a directive to the electors.

Meanwhile, at Compostela, the canons had prudently put off acting upon Paschal's letter of 29 December 1099 until Diego should have returned. He for his part hastened back armed with the papal letter of 18 March, and on 1 July 1100 he was—though unwilling (!)—elected bishop of Santiago de Compostela. Where was he elected, and by whom? The *Historia* implies that the election was held at Compostela, but never states it clearly—which is a little odd, but not necessarily suspicious. Who precisely the electors were is hard to determine. The *Historia* offers us two separate and in some respects divergent accounts. The author of Book I, chapter 8—Nuño Alfonso, canon of Compostela and later bishop of Mondoñedo—writing as a member of the cathedral chapter, states:[30]

visis domini papae istis subsequentibus literis [i.e. the letter of 18 March 1100] eum nolentem, atque renitentem cum nobilioribus totius Gallaetiae, et assensu regis Adefonsi, et comitis Raimundi qui nobiscum laudantes aderant, in episcopum elegimus.

But the same author states unequivocally, and only a few lines later (Book I, chapter 9), that after his election Diego set out for Toledo 'where the lord king Alfonso was'. These passages can be reconciled if we assume that in the first of them *assensu* governs both king Alfonso and count Raymond, while *aderant* refers not to the king but only to Raymond and the *nobiliores* (or even simply to the latter). On this interpretation, what Nuño—who took part in the election —is trying to tell us is that the chapter did the electing, having previously sought the consent of the secular authorities. The Galician nobility were present, as was also (probably) the immediate secular lord, count Raymond; but they took no active part.

A rather different slant is given by the author of Book II, chapter 2.[31] This was Gerald of Beauvais, a Frenchman who became a canon of Compostela about the year 1112 and who was writing his account about ten years later: his testimony

[30] *HC*, pp. 26-7.   [31] *HC*, p. 255.

is therefore not that of an eyewitness or participant. He wrote as follows:

Cumque postea clerus et populus ecclesiae beati Jacobi eligeret sibi episcopum, consilio eiusdem regis A. et comitis Raymundi atque Gallaeciae principum praedictus Didacus electus est in episcopum. Prius tamen quam a laicali manu acceperat ecclesiam et honorem ecclesiae beati Jacobi, reddidit B. Toletano archiepiscopo et Romanae ecclesiae legato coram episcopis Gallaeciae qui interfuerunt electioni eius, videlicet D. Auriensi, P. Lucensi, A. Tudensi, G. Minduniensi, et principibus Gallaeciae, clero, atque populo Compostellae.

Gerald of Beauvais was a more up-to-date cleric than Nuño Alfonso, and his concern in this rather odd passage seems to have been to show that Diego's election took place in conformity with the norms adumbrated by the ecclesiastical reformers of recent years. (Whom did he need to convince?) The clergy and people of Compostela do the initial electing, though the electoral procedure seems not to be complete until king, count and *principes* have done their part. That part, however—and this is crucial—is confined to providing *consilium*, and not, as in Nuño's account, *assensum*. Four Galician bishops are present at the election, though what they do is left vague. Finally, to avoid any suspicion of the taint of lay investiture Diego surrenders his church and its temporalities into the hands of a papal legate, presumably then (though we are not told this) to receive them back from him.

This is very tendentious stuff. It would be preposterous to believe that so skilled a political operator as Diego would ever have given so easy a handle as this to his arch-opponent of Toledo. The great interest of Gerald's account, however, lies in what it has to reveal about the movement of ideas at Compostela between the first decade of the century, when Nuño wrote, and the third, when Gerald was writing.[32]

[32] This takes us to the kernel of my unease about Dr Vones's interpretation of these events. Where he sees Diego's election and consecration as having been highly irregular, and the authors of the *Historia Compostellana* as trying artfully to conceal this, I would see an electoral procedure of a type fairly common in the kingdom of León-Castile at the turn of the century but which churchmen of a reforming temper might later find it embarrassing to contemplate in retrospect. Ironically, it was Diego who was more responsible than any other agent for encouraging this movement of ideas. As for the authors of the *Historia*, I have

Does the second passage shed any more light upon Diego's election? It confirms that the king, count and nobility were consulted before the election was completed. It gives us the additional and credible information that the Galician bishops were present too.

To sum up the foregoing, it looks as though Diego was the candidate favoured by the royal family. Given his previous career, this is hardly a matter for surprise. There might have been one or more rival candidates among the Compostelan clergy. Possibly there was a faction at Compostela which wanted Diego Peláez back. By a remarkable burst of initiative he succeeded in mobilizing papal interest in his favour. Every possible precaution was taken over the election, which in itself suggests that it might have been more of a touch-and-go affair than our reports of it (from the winning side only, we should remember) permit us to see. No doubt there were awkward moments for Diego on 1 July 1100. But, taken all in all, it was a triumph of shrewd management. The bishop-elect of one of the most famous and wealthy sees in Christendom must have retired to bed a happy man that night.

Diego was not consecrated as bishop until the following Easter Day, 21 April 1101.[33] Why was his consecration delayed for nearly ten months? By the terms of the privilege of 1095, reinforced by the papal letters of 1099, future bishops-elect of Compostela were to be consecrated by the pope alone.[34] However, Diego did not wish to travel through the kingdom of Aragon for fear of the ex-bishop Diego Peláez and his supporters (*propinqui*). He therefore besought the king to write to the pope with the request that Diego might be consecrated in the kingdom of León-Castile (*apud nos*). The king's letter was conveyed to the papal curia by two canons of Compostela, Hugo (later bishop of Porto) and

elsewhere described them as 'more muddled than cunning'; and would hold to that opinion. See my review of Dr. Vones's book in the *American Historical Review* 86 (1981), 1084-5.

[33] *HC*, pp. 27-31 (= JL 5839, 5840, 5860, 5861).

[34] The clergy of Compostela's previous metropolitan, Braga, may have put up a fight against this. Vones, *Kirchenpolitik*, pp. 135-47 has some useful observations on this subject, though I would not go so far as he does in drawing conclusions from the very meagre evidence available.

Vincent. It was evidently supported by a letter from three Galician bishops—Pedro of Lugo, Alfonso of Tuy, and Gonzalo of Mondoñedo—and the clergy of Compostela. Paschal II proved agreeable. In letters of 14 October 1100 he announced to the Galician clergy and the king that he had instructed bishop Godfrey of Maguelonne, in southern France, to go to Spain to consecrate Diego; or, if he could not do it, the ceremony was to be performed by bishop García of Burgos.[35] Having received these letters the two canons set out on the return journey. But then disaster struck. They fell seriously ill. Vincent died, and Hugo was laid up sick for a long time. When no word came back to Compostela, further letters from king and clergy were sent to the pope, carried on this occasion by Nuño Alfonso (the author, as we have seen, of this section of the *Historia*) and Munio Gelmírez, the bishop-elect's brother. Paschal II's replies, renewing his permission, were issued on 25 March 1101. The envoys retraced their steps. In the meantime Hugo had recovered and made his way back to Spain, presumably picking up the bishop of Maguelonne on the way. It was at Godfrey's hands, doubtless assisted by the Galician bishops, that Diego Gelmírez received his consecration on 21 April 1101.[36] His long episcopate had begun.

The cathedral community at whose head Diego now found himself was probably a somewhat demoralized one. The see had been without sustained episcopal guidance for about fifteen years. It was committed to a very expensive building programme at a time when its two principal sources

[35] For the bishopric of Maguelonne's connections with the papal see, JL 5375, 5377 (of 1088). By the terms of JL 5653 the see of Burgos had been granted the privilege of exemption in 1096.

[36] We are not told who consecrated Diego. I assume that it was Godfrey of Maguelonne (1) because the letter instructing him to do so (14 Oct. 1100) does not survive among the records of Compostela, i.e. it was presumably kept by its addressee; and (2) because the second letter sent to him (25 Mar. 1101) *was* preserved at Compostela, i.e. the second group of envoys presumably found that Godfrey had already set out on his mission when they reached Maguelonne and went on their way with the letter. It is impossible to believe that the second group could have travelled from Rome to Compostela via Maguelonne and that the arrangements for an episcopal consecration could have been made in the short space of time between 25 March and 21 April. The only possible conclusion is that Hugo had recovered from his illness and completed his mission, as suggested in the text.

of revenue were threatened: the king's agents had encroached upon its landed endowments, and we may assume (though we cannot prove it) that political disturbance within Spain —of which more presently—had discouraged pilgrims and thus reduced income from that quarter.[37] A clique of reformers had recently replaced an ancient and cherished liturgy with a new and strange one of which conservative Galician church- men were suspicious. An assertive archbishop of Toledo who enjoyed the support of the pope was hostile to a Galician tradition of *de facto* autonomy in ecclesiastical affairs.

A less self-confident man than Diego might have been daunted. As it was, his boisterous energy and self-assurance sustained him. But more was needed than these qualities alone. To breathe new life into his church he had to make plain to friends and enemies alike what manner of man he was and what attitudes he would take up on the large ques- tions of his day. He had to raise as it were a standard round which supporters might rally. He had to show men 'where he stood'. The key to an understanding of his career lies in his intense ambition for the glory of St. James. This would endear him to the community which clustered about St. James's shrine. But devotion alone, however single-minded, however lacking in conventional scruple, was not enough. By temperament and early experience Diego was a man of the world. He had the wit to see that his world was changing and the intuition to grasp how change might be made to serve his apostle's—his own—purposes. He would have to persuade, cajole or browbeat his colleagues into seeing it too, grasping it for themselves. He had to reconcile conservatives to change. He had to show his chapter that moderate reform need not alarm. These things will become clearer as we proceed. For the present, let two episodes from early in his episcopate stand as portents.

In the autumn of 1102 Diego carried out a visitation of the properties held by the see of Compostela to the south of the river Miño, in the county of Portugal and the diocese of Braga.[38] There were many of these, but we need concern

---

[37] Building operations had been temporarily suspended (as we shall see in Chapter VII) but the programme itself had not been abandoned.

[38] For what follows see *HC*, pp. 36–42. For the literary genre to which this

ourselves only with one—the church of St. Fructuosus (now São Fructuoso de Montelios) on the outskirts of Braga, built by the saint in the seventh century, harbouring his relics after his death, and granted to the church of Santiago in 883. The body of Fructuosus was especially dear to the people of Braga. The saint was their 'defender and patron' (*defensor et patronus*). Fructuosus was to Braga what James was to Compostela. Diego formed the plan of carrying off the body to Compostela—and did so. It was a bold manœuvre, conducted so swiftly and secretly that there was not time for any serious opposition to it to take shape. Diego had anticipated opposition; not surprisingly, for though legally he may have been acting within his rights, morally speaking he was perpetrating an outrage.[39] The episode typifies his lack of scruple. It may have other lessons for us, but to these we shall return in a later chapter.

Two years later Diego paid his second (and last) visit to Rome. It was almost certainly during the course of this journey that he met an archdeacon of Lucca named Gregory distinguished for his legal interests. Some years later, probably in 1110, pope Paschal II promoted Gregory to the college of cardinals. It was as cardinal-priest of S. Crisogono, at some point before his death in 1113, that Gregory published a canon-law collection known to scholars as the *Polycarpus*, which he dedicated to Diego Gelmírez.[40] No doubt Gregory had been collecting and sifting his materials for years: but it needed, as he politely explained in the dedicatory letter, the urging of Diego to get him to sit down and knock them into shape. Diego had realized the need for an up-to-date manual of canon law in Spain. This was a characteristic concern of ecclesiastical modernizers:

account belongs see P. J. Geary, *Furta Sacra: Thefts of relics in the central middle ages* (Princeton, 1978). The legal background to the episode is investigated thoroughly in Vones, *Kirchenpolitik*, pp. 219–59.

[39] It still arouses strong feelings. 'Diogo Gelmires, para roubar o corpo do santo, que os fiéis veneravam como patrono, foi o primeiro a violar-lhe o túmulo que os próprios Arabes haviam respeitado': A. de J. da Costa, *O bispo D. Pedro e a organização da diocese de Braga* (Coimbra, 1959), p. 19.

[40] All previous work on the *Polycarpus* has been superseded by U. Horst, *Die Kanonessammlung Polycarpus des Gregor von S. Grisogono. Quellen und Tendenzen* (Munich, 1980), to which invaluable work, a copy of which Dr Horst most kindly sent me, I am indebted for what follows.

we might compare the introduction of a new corpus of canon law into England by archbishop Lanfranc and his circle a generation earlier. Up-to-date the *Polycarpus* certainly was. Gregory drew heavily upon the compilation of Anselm of Lucca and the *Collection in 74 Titles*, the two most authoritative collections of the recent past, and he included pronouncements of Gregory VII, Urban II and Paschal II, and conciliar material from as late as Piacenza (1095). The scope of his book was comprehensive and its orderly arrangement made for ease of reference. While seven of the eight books into which the work was divided were generally conservative in tone—they owed much to the *Decretum* of Burchard of Worms—the first book, which was devoted to the primacy and special rights of the see of Rome, was strongly papalist. Diego's request for this law-book is one of several indications that he was firmly on the side of change, of ecclesiastical reform.

For Diego, therefore, the management of the church of Santiago de Compostela presented challenges and opportunities. These must be set against a background composed from the public events which were preoccupying the peoples of León-Castile during the first decade of the twelfth century. This was one of the grimmest periods in the kingdom's history. There can have been few among the subjects of Alfonso VI who could, without deceiving themselves, have looked to the future with any optimism. To understand this state of affairs we must retrace our steps a little.[41]

On 6 May 1085 Toledo had surrendered to Alfonso VI, and on 25 May he made his formal triumphal entry into the city. Coincidentally, 25 May was also the date of the death, in exile, of pope Gregory VII whose thinking may have

[41] Some narrative of political and military events is unavoidable here if Diego's later doings are to be rendered intelligible, but I have kept it to a minimum. By opening the following account in the year 1085 I start in the *middle* of the story, with all the attendant risks that this entails. It is no part of my purpose, neither can I spare the space, to survey, however briefly, the complex sequence of events. which had occupied the previous half-century or so since the extinction of the caliphate of Córdoba in 1031. The essential background may be found—to name only recent works in English—in J. F. O'Callaghan, *A history of medieval Spain* (Ithaca/London, 1975), chs. 5 and 8; A. MacKay, *Spain in the middle ages, from frontier to empire, 1000–1500* (London, 1977), chs. 1 and 2; D. W. Lomax, *The reconquest of Spain* (London, 1978), chs. 2 and 3.

influenced Alfonso's decision to lay siege to Toledo in 1081. The ancient capital of the Visigothic kings was Alfonso VI's most famous conquest. To characterize it in this way is well enough, provided we do not fall into the error of supposing that it crowned a career devoted to conquest since his accession in 1065. Toledo marked a new departure. The city was the nucleus of a principality, the kingdom of Toledo, which was one of several successor-states to the defunct caliphate of Córdoba. These small Muslim principalities are known to historians as the *reinos de taifa*, the 'party' or 'faction' kingdoms. The most important of the remaining *taifa* kingdoms were Zaragoza, Albarracín, Valencia, Badajoz, Seville, Granada and Almería. Rich, factious and vulnerable, the *taifas* had fallen prey to the diplomacy of the Christian rulers of northern Spain during the mid-century years. Their subjection had been expressed in the annual payment of very large sums of gold by way of tribute. These tributes were known as *parias*. The influx of gold into León-Castile and Catalonia—for Aragon and Navarre never profited to such an extent as these two—had far-reaching effects. It made the kings of León-Castile very rich. The income from *parias* was probably the most important source of their public revenues in the second half of the eleventh century. Some of this wealth was passed on to the churches within their kingdoms, for example to Fernando I's foundation of San Isidoro de León. Some of it found its way into the coffers of their aristocracy. The *paria* regime made possible the spectacular careers of adventurers such as Rodrigo Díaz, *el Cid*. Some of the riches of the Islamic south found their way across the Pyrenees to more distant beneficiaries, notably to the abbey of Cluny, as we saw in chapter II.

Why it was that Alfonso VI decided to kill one of the geese that laid these golden eggs by conquering Toledo has never yet been satisfactorily explained. But if the reasons for this shift in policy remain unclear, its consequences are plain. Alarmed, the rulers of the *taifas* of Seville, Granada and Badajoz determined to seek help from across the Straits of Gibraltar against the Christian king. After some hestitation and with misgivings which, as events turned out, were to be only too well-founded, they entered into negotiations with Yusuf ibn-Tashufin the Almoravide ruler of Morocco. The Almoravides were adherents of an Islamic sect which had originated in the basin of the Senegal in the 1040s, had spread like wildfire among the Berber tribes of north-west Africa known as the Sanhaja (the ancestors of the Tuareg), and had thrown up a precarious state which was to dominate the area for a couple of generations. The growth of Almoravide power was itself an indirect result of the collapse of the Spanish caliphate. One of the main aims of Córdoba's foreign policy in the previous century had been to prevent, by careful distribution of subsidies, the emergence of any strong political unit in north-west Africa. In fact, the bases of Almoravide power were ill-founded. But this was not apparent in 1085. The rulers of the *taifas* knew the fame of the Almoravide armies. They also knew that the Almoravides were uncouth, uncultured fanatics. They did not like the sound of them, but they needed their help.

Yusuf accepted their invitation. He crossed the Straits with a large army in June 1086 and marched by way of Seville towards Badajoz. Alfonso VI was at the time engaged in besieging distant Zaragoza. He hastened across Spain and offered battle at Sagrajas, a little to the north of Badajoz. There, on 23 October 1086, Yusuf inflicted a resounding defeat upon him. Then, obedient to his agreement with his employers, Yusuf took his army back to Morocco. We must beware of exaggerating the impact of Sagrajas. For Alfonso VI it was humiliating, but not disastrous; it inspired anxiety, but not panic. One of the expressions of that anxiety was the king's appeal to France—specifically to Burgundy, his wife's homeland—for military aid. One of the results of this appeal was the coming to Spain in 1087 of duke Eudes of Burgundy and his cousin Raymond. But the campaign anticipated never took place, for there was no enemy to fight. The Almoravides remained in Morocco throughout the year. Alfonso VI and his French reinforcements frittered away their time in an abortive siege of Tudela in southern Navarre. In the following year, 1088, the Almoravides did come back, but they did not repeat their success of two years before. They besieged the castle of Aledo, between Murcia and Lorca, one of the most southerly of Alfonso's outposts, for four months, but the king managed to relieve it and Yusuf returned to Africa. Alfonso's trusted lieutenant Alvar Fáñez was collecting *parias* as usual from Seville and Granada in the autumn. The year 1089 was quiet, but in 1090 Yusuf returned to Spain and laid siege to Toledo itself for about a month during the summer. It was successfully defended by Alfonso VI with the aid of king Sancho Ramírez of Aragon.

On this occasion Yusuf did not go back to Morocco. His dealings with the *taifa* kings had shown him how great was the gap between his religious ideals and theirs; had taught him too how precarious was their power. He claimed furthermore that they were not playing fair by him, but negotiating behind his back with the very man against whom they had engaged him to fight, the king-emperor of León-Castile. He did not dally. On his return from Toledo he occupied Granada and Malaga. In March 1091 his troops took possession of Córdoba, in May it was the turn of Carmona, then Seville was laid under siege. Alfonso VI sent an army under Alvar Fáñez to relieve the city, but it was defeated at Almodóvar del Rio, and Seville fell to the Almoravides in September. Almería went the same way, then Murcia. In 1092 Aledo was lost. Valencia would have followed had it not been for the prompt action of the Cid who hastened over to frighten away an Almoravide force and lay siege to the city himself. Of the three rulers who had summoned Yusuf to their aid in 1086 the only one now remaining in power was al-Mutawwakil of Badajoz. In desperation he turned to Alfonso VI, ceding to him the cities and associated territories of Santarem, Lisbon and Cintra in the spring of 1093. But when in the following year the Almoravides attacked Badajoz they conquered it so quickly that Alfonso VI had no time to gather an army to go to its relief. They went on to overrun the lands ceded to him in the preceding year. Raymond's Portuguese campaign in the winter of 1094–5, referred to earlier in this chapter, was an abortive attempt to recover them.

The only bright spot in 1094 was the Cid's conquest of Valencia in June and his defeat of an Almoravide army sent against him at Cuarte in October. The next two years were a little more cheerful. Alfonso VI regained Santarem in 1095, and Pedro I of Aragon took Huesca in 1096. But in 1097 Yusuf, who had been absent from Spain for some years, returned to take command of his armies. He made for Toledo, but was intercepted by Alfonso VI at Consuegra where he defeated the Christian forces. Discouraged, however, from persevering against Toledo he sheered off to the north-east where he encountered another army under Alvar Fáñez near Cuenca: this too he defeated. In 1099 Toledo was once more attacked, and its surrounding territory ravaged. In the same year the Cid died (10 July) and the Almoravides laid siege to Valencia. Alfonso VI was diverted in 1100 from its relief by yet another attack on Toledo; later in the same year his son-in-law Henry of Portugal was defeated by the Almoravides. In the spring of 1102 the king supervised the evacuation of Valencia: Jimena, the Cid's widow, retired to end her days at the monastery of Cardeña, and Jerónimo, his bishop of Valencia, was translated to the Leonese diocese of Salamanca. The city was occupied by Yusuf's armies in May. Later in the year (or possibly in 1103) they took over the *taifa* kingdom of Albarracín. The only *taifa* state now remaining was Zaragoza.

In 1104 Alfonso VI captured Medinaceli. Perhaps heartened by this the Castilians dispatched a raid into Andalusia in the spring of 1105; but their troops met defeat at Almoravide hands on their way home. In September 1106 Yusuf died and was succeeded by his son Ali (1106–43). After suppressing a revolt in Morocco he crossed to Spain early in 1107, eager to continue the war. The heaviest blow fell in 1108. In May Ali's brother Tamim captured the town of Uclés and laid siege to its castle. A Castilian relief force went to its aid. Tamim inflicted a decisive defeat upon this force. As a result of the battle a number of strong points near Toledo fell into Almoravide hands, including Alcalá de Henares. In the following summer the old king died (30 June 1109). During the period of political turbulence which followed his death Ali launched a further attack on Toledo. Talavera and Madrid were sacked; so was the monastery of San Servando outside the walls of Toledo; the city itself was closely invested for two weeks and heroically defended by

Alvar Fáñez and archbishop Bernardo. In May 1110 Zaragoza finally passed into Almoravide hands.

The period between 1091 and 1109 was one of grave peril for the kingdom of León-Castile. It was not simply that Alfonso VI's conquests between the Duero and the Tagus were threatened. The Almoravides had re-united Islamic Spain as in the days of the caliphate. They were fanatics who believed that it was their mission to extend the reach of the faith by means of holy war. They were persecutors of the Christian communities which came under their rule. Alfonso for his part was so harassed by the constant necessity to look to his southern frontier that he had little time to devote to the pressing need for the resettlement (*repoblación*) of the conquered territories. In consequence his most imposing conquest, Toledo, remained a vulnerable outpost in a virtual desert. He was short of manpower not only for resettlement but also for his armies. The papal letters of October 1100 and March 1101 contained orders that Spanish soldiers and clergy were not to go to the Holy Land—presumably the reference was to the crusade of 1101—but to defend their own land against the Almoravides: we may take it that the pope's prohibition was prompted by the king.[42] Finally, of course, the absorption of all the *taifa* kingdoms by the Almoravides had cut off the supply of *parias*. A savage blow was thereby struck at the health of Castilian public finance, whose consequences were to dog the crown throughout the last years of Alfonso's reign and for the whole of his daughter's.

Who was to succeed Alfonso VI on the throne of León-Castile? This question dominated the internal political life of the kingdom during Diego Gelmírez's early years as bishop of Santiago de Compostela. The brother, García, whom Alfonso had long before dethroned died in prison in 1090: there were no other close male relatives. Although Alfonso VI was much married he never succeeded in fathering a legitimate male heir. When Raymond of Burgundy came to his court in 1086–7 the king had three daughters. The only legitimate one was Urraca, the offspring of queen

[42] See especially *HC*, pp. 88–9 (= JL 5863).

Constance of Burgundy: as we have already seen, she was betrothed to Raymond in 1087 (and possibly married to him in the same year—we do not know the exact date of their marriage). By a mistress named Jimena Múñoz he had already had two other daughters, Elvira and Teresa. The former married Raymond IV of St. Gilles, count of Toulouse, before July 1094. Teresa, as we know, married Henry of Burgundy, count of Portugal, perhaps in 1095 (again, we have no sure chronology). If we can believe the evidence of a set of annals transmitted in the earliest manuscript of the *Historia Compostellana*, the relevant part of which seems to have been composed in or soon after 1126, Raymond was permitted to entertain great expectations. 'King Alfonso had caused him to come from Burgundy to Spain and had promised him all his kingdom with a sworn oath.'[43]

In 1091, however, an event occurred whose consequences were to unsettle Raymond's hopes. When in March the city of Córdoba fell to Yusuf its previous governor Fath al-Mamun was killed in the fighting. He left a young widow, Zaida, who took refuge with her father-in-law al-Mutamid, ruler of the *taifa* of Seville. The Almoravides invested Seville in June and took it in September. At some point in the year, perhaps when Alvar Fáñez was in Andalusia vainly trying to relieve the city, Zaida made her way as a refugee to the court of Alfonso VI. Later legend has been at work on this encounter. We hear how her plight moved and her beauty bewitched the elderly king-emperor. A more prosaic version has it that her liaison with the king brought him a string of fortresses on his southern frontier; but this story too has difficult features. All that matters for us is that, probably in 1093, she bore the king a son, who was christened Sancho. The existence of Sancho profoundly altered the situation. Alfonso doted upon the son of his old age, and we may take it that as he grew up he showed signs of promise. By 1102 his name featured among the subscriptions to royal diplomas. In 1105 and 1106 his name headed the witness-lists, coming

---

[43] *HC*, p. 611, a statement which like others relating to the succession must be regarded as highly tendentious. The question of the succession to Alfonso VI has attracted much attention. The most recent treatment is that of Reilly, *Urraca*, chs. 1 and 2, with references to all earlier literature.

immediately after the royal subscription, above those of Raymond and Urraca. By 1107 it was clear that he was the heir apparent. We also know that he was given charge of Toledo, the new *urbs regia* of Alfonso VI (as of his Visigothic predecessors), the site of the principal royal treasury and, threatened as it was, the symbol of Alfonso's Christian *imperium*.

What was the king's design? We cannot be sure. But he may, like his father Fernando I before him, have been thinking in terms of partition. The *regnum* which Raymond had (perhaps) been promised could have been Galicia, with the attached territories of Salamanca, Zamora and Avila which he was busily trying to resettle during these years. If the *regnum* of Toledo was to go to Sancho, perhaps Castile was to go with it. Who then was to get León? Perhaps Henry of Portugal. He certainly had designs on León at a later date (in 1110–12), and a recently discovered charter of 1105 has been interpreted as indicating the existence of such designs as early as that date. Should this have been so, Henry's lands would have been awkwardly cut into two, a county of Portugal and a kingdom of León separated by Raymond's Galician and Extremaduran territories.

Where so much remains uncertain one thing is clear. Count Raymond resented Sancho's claims and was apprehensive of Henry's ambitions. The question of the Spanish succession began to involve other interested parties outside the Peninsula. Raymond turned for assistance to abbot Hugh of Cluny, who sent as his envoy to Spain one Dalmatius Geret, a native of Burgundy whose family was well known to the count. Cluniac interests could not but be involved in the succession question. In simple material terms Cluny depended on the rulers of León-Castile for a large proportion of her annual income. With the supply of money now diminished, if not cut off entirely, owing to the expansion of the Almoravides at the expense of the *taifas*, the chill winds of economic stringency were blowing about the vast and as yet unfinished building programme initiated by abbot Hugh largely on the strength of the Alfonsine subsidy. (Urban II had consecrated the new abbey church of Cluny in 1095, but the works were still far from complete.) Cluniac finance was bound up with political stability in León-Castile, the essential pre-condition for Christian initiatives against the Muslims. What exactly the abbot commissioned Dalmatius Geret to do we cannot tell. All we have is a document recording the results of his mission. This takes the form of a letter addressed by Raymond and Henry to abbot Hugh, carried to him by Dalmatius. The letter is undated, and none of the several attempts to date it has been altogether convincing: my own view is that it belongs to the years between 1105 and 1107.[44] It records a secret agreement between the cousins relating to the disposal of the kingdom after Alfonso VI's death. With its details we need not concern ourselves. Its most important provisions were, first, that Henry would assist Raymond to succeed to the throne of León-Castile against all other claimants; second, that they were to share the contents of the royal treasury at Toledo between them in the proportion of one-third to Henry and two-thirds to Raymond; and third, that Henry was to hold certain territories (either Toledo or Galicia) from Raymond as vassal from king. Although the infante Sancho was not named in the letter its provisions were clearly directed against him. In short, Raymond sought to buy off Henry in order to ensure his own succession to the undivided kingship of León-Castile. It is important to note that Raymond now had a male heir. His wife Urraca had given birth to a boy on 1 March 1105. The child was christened Alfonso. This was Alfonso Raimúndez, later to be the emperor Alfonso VII (d. 1157). Henry and Teresa had as yet no son.

This was the position in the summer of 1107. (We know that Dalmatius Geret was back in Burgundy by 13 August, which provides a *terminus ante quem*.) Quite suddenly, all was changed. Raymond, who seems not to have been a healthy man, was taken ill and died, probably on 20 September. The immediate result of Raymond's death was the holding of a council at León in December to review the question of the succession. This was attended not only by

---

[44] This was the dating favoured by Pierre David, 'Le pacte successoral entre Raymond de Galice et Henri de Portugal', *Bulletin Hispanique* 50 (1948), 275–90: though it is not without its difficulties it seems to me the most plausible of the various possibilities.

the lay and ecclesiastical notabilities of Alfonso's realm but also by archbishop Guy of Vienne, the late count's brother and the friend, as we have seen, of Diego Gelmírez. The *Historia Compostellana* supplies us with an account of what took place at León, but confines itself to the provisions that were agreed upon *in the event that Urraca should marry again*. After her second marriage in 1109 these provisions became of critical importance. But unless the marriage that finally took place was already being discussed at León in December 1107—which is unlikely—it is clear that the arrangements reported by the *Historia* were only a small part of the deliberations which occurred there. In the absence of other narrative sources it is tempting to use the evidence of the *Historia* as a guide to what transpired at León. This temptation should be resisted. Instead we should look to the strictly contemporary and less controversial evidence of the royal charters. If we can discover how Raymond's widow styled herself in official documents we may have some clue as to the decisions reached that winter. Three charters granted by Urraca, to different beneficiaries, have survived from the period between Raymond's death and Alfonso VI's. (None is an original.) The earliest is dated 13 December 1107 and may pre-date the León meeting. In it Urraca styled herself *totius Gallecie domina*; in other words, she assumed that she had succeeded her husband as lord—or lady—of Galicia. The next was issued on 21 January 1108, after the council. Urraca styled herself *tocius Gallecie imperatrix*. (It would be imprudent to read too much into the more exalted title. Raymond had styled himself *imperator* of Galicia in a charter of 17 March 1107.) The conclusion I would draw is that Urraca's rule in Galicia had been confirmed by the king at the assembly in León. Finally, in a charter of 22 February 1109 she styled herself once more *totius Galletie domina*. But this is not all. The charter of 21 January 1108, a grant to the cathedral church of Lugo, was made

for the soul of my husband the lord duke [*sic*] Raymond who lived but a short time with me and departed from this frail world before me, and for me for whom a like fate awaits, and for my son Alfonso that he may live [reading *vivere* for *iure*] and rule in happiness.

This reference to the future reign of Alfonso Raimúndez indicates that some dispositions about his rights in the succession had recently been made, presumably at León.

This is little enough to go on. Still, it looks as though such changes as were necessitated by Raymond's death were kept to a minimum. Sancho, presumably, remained the king's heir apparent. Urraca was to keep Galicia and her son Alfonso was to exercise rule over some—unspecified —territories after her. Henry of Portugal had lost his ally but not, we may suppose, put aside his hopes.

At about the same time as the León council the king-emperor was stricken with the illness which was to prove his last. He was bedridden for the remaining seventeen months of his life. To what extent Alfonso was mentally as well as physically incapacitated is an important question to which we do not know the answer. If he had had a stroke he may well have been. His Jewish physician Joseph Ferrizuel, nicknamed Cidellus ('little boss'), seems to have played an important role as an intermediary between the king and his advisers during Alfonso's last illness.[45] It is not beyond the bounds of possibility that he played a major part in the decision-making of those last frantic months.

Frantic they certainly were. In the summer of 1108 the cruellest blow of all was struck. The Castilian army which was defeated by Tamim at Uclés in May was led by the young infante Sancho; and in the fighting he was killed. Alfonso VI, old and mortally ill, had lost his son and heir. The whole matter of the succession had to be reconsidered. The Almoravide enemy was at the gates. Time was short. Our sources remain meagre, allusive and untrustworthy. Valiant attempts to unravel a coherent story have been made, but they carry conviction only when the reader is lulled into suspending his very proper belief that bricks cannot be made without straw. It is clear enough that there was panic, intrigue and divided counsel. It is also clear that a plan, attributed to the king, finally emerged. Daring in its simplicity, it was also daring in its recklessness. León-Castile needed

[45] Y. Baer, *A history of the Jews in Christian Spain* (Philadelphia, 1961), pp. 50-1, 68 and references there cited. But note the cautions of Reilly, *Urraca*, p. 52, n. 25.

a king of proven military experience. The man chosen was
the ruling monarch of neighbouring Aragon, Alfonso I,
known to later generations as *el Batallador*, 'the Battler'.
He had succeeded his half-brother Pedro I in 1104, and was
by now a man of about thirty-six. He was unmarried and
therefore available as a husband for the widowed Urraca.
He enjoyed a great and deserved reputation as a soldier. In
these respects, he was exactly the man to be the saviour of
León-Castile. As against this, he was not well liked among
the aristocratic circles of León and, especially, Castile;
and in the eyes of churchmen he was barred from marrying
Urraca by consanguinity, for the pair shared a great-
grandfather in Sancho *el Mayor* of Navarre. But Alfonso VI,
or the faction which acted in his name, was undeterred.
The Aragonese marriage project went ahead. The precise
terms of the arrangement are, it need hardly be said, unclear.
Urraca claimed in 1110 that 'not long before his death my
father the emperor Alfonso handed on to me the whole
kingdom (*regnum totum tradidit*)'. In the earliest surviving
official document issued by the queen, a charter dated
22 July 1109 of which the original survives, she styles herself *totius Yspanie regina*; which would seem to bear out
her claim.[46] Did Alfonso VI design that Alfonso *el Batallador*
should be simply a king consort, his role primarily a military
one, without independent political power, though doubtless
with some territorial endowment? It is not impossible. But
we simply do not know. We do not even know for certain
when the marriage took place, though it was very probably
in the early part of October. This is soon enough after
Alfonso VI's death on 30 June for us to be confident that
it had been planned while the old man was still alive.

Conceived and rushed through by frightened men in
a hurry, the Aragonese marriage raised more problems than
it was intended to solve. What would be the attitude to it
of the bishops? What provision, if any, had been made for

[46] *HC*, p. 115, AC León, no. 1002 is I believe the original of R. 22 July
1109 (though Professor Reilly regards it as a closely contemporary copy): the
diploma is notable for its particularly impressive witness-list, which included
the archbishop of Toledo and ten other bishops, the abbots of three important
monasteries, and a bevy of high-ranking laymen such as Alvar Fáñez, Pedro
Ansúrez, Gómez González, Froila Díaz, Pedro Froílaz de Traba and others.

Henry of Portugal? Or for the young Alfonso Raimúndez?
How would Pedro Froílaz de Traba, the boy's guardian, and
the rest of the Galician nobility react to it? Diego Gelmírez's
career as bishop of Santiago de Compostela was to be intimately affected by the way in which these questions were
gradually to be answered over the next several years.

VI

'A second Jezebel':
Diego and queen Urraca

The authors of the *Historia Compostellana* did not like queen Urraca. In the first place, she was a woman, and there was widespread belief that women should not and could not exercise political power. Secondly, and as we have already seen, the political situation at the time of Alfonso VI's death was unusually menacing. The problems which Urraca faced were formidable, and though they were not of her own making she tended to be blamed for them. Her predicament had something in common with that of queen Melisende in the kingdom of Jerusalem after 1131, or of Matilda the empress in England after 1135. A comparative study of these three queens would be illuminating, but this is not the place for it. Urraca was by no means devoid of the qualities of rulership. She was loyal to the memory of her father; sensible in her choice of advisers; capable of decisive action; shrewd and hard in negotiation; brave and resourceful in facing the changed responsibilities of Spanish monarchy in the early twelfth century. Yet we have to work hard to find evidence of these qualities. The hostility of the *Historia* —and of other contemporary sources—renders it difficult to get close to the queen and to arrive at a balanced assessment of her reign. Urraca has had a bad press from nearly every historian from her own day until our own. Only very recently has an attempt been made to redress the balance.[1]

Urraca was born in about 1080, she married count Raymond in about 1092, and was widowed in 1107. There were

[1] Bernard F. Reilly, *The kingdom of León-Castilla under queen Urraca 1109–1126* (Princeton, 1982). This admirable study supersedes all previous literature devoted to Urraca's reign. I am grateful to Professor Reilly for very generously allowing me to consult parts of his book in advance of publication. The present chapter was drafted before I had seen his work. I am relieved to find that on most essential issues we are in agreement. On the rare occasion where we disagree I have ventured to record my dissent in a footnote.

two children of the marriage, Sancha, born in or before 1102,
and Alfonso, born in 1105; the latter was often referred to
by his patronymic Raimúndez before his own accession to
the throne. As we have seen, Urraca married again in 1109,
shortly after the death of her father Alfonso VI. She reigned
from 1109 until her death in 1126. The political history of
her reign is exceedingly complicated. It may be divided for
purposes of convenience into two roughly equal parts. The
first extends from 1109 until the winter of 1116–17. These
years were dominated by the failure of the Aragonese marriage
and the consequences stemming therefrom, and by the
pressure of the Almoravides upon the southern frontier of
the kingdom of León-Castile.

Urraca's marriage to Alfonso *el Batallador* of Aragon was
short-lived. Even before it took place it had aroused the
opposition of her brother-in-law count Henry of Portugal.
Soon after it had been celebrated the greatest magnate in
Galicia, count Pedro Froílaz de Traba, came out against it.
It was condemned by the bishops, led by Bernardo of Toledo,
on the grounds of consanguinity, and they were upheld by
the pope. The king of Aragon made himself unpopular in
León-Castile. The royal couple may have been temperament-
ally unsuited to one another; and they failed to produce
any children. By the autumn of 1112 king and queen had
parted. Three consequences followed from the confused
events of these years. The king of Aragon had gained control
of much of eastern Castile: the queen wished to recover
these territories, the king to retain them; the issue could
be decided only by war. In Galicia a faction grouped round
Urraca's infant son Alfonso Raimúndez had established
a quasi-independent rule: to it we shall return shortly.
Count Henry of Portugal had managed to take possession
of some of the western territories of León which he governed
in virtual independence. After his early death in 1112 his
widow Teresa, Urraca's half-sister, inherited his position and
his claims. Meanwhile, the situation on the southern frontier
was perilous. The Almoravides captured Talavera in the late
summer of 1109 and ravaged about Madrid and Guadalajara:
it was probably at this time (though it might have been in
1110) that a famous siege of Toledo occurred. In 1110 the

last of the *taifa* kingdoms, Zaragoza, fell to the Almoravides, and a Christian army was defeated near Santarem in Portugal; the town itself was lost to the Almoravides in 1111. In 1112 Guadalajara was again attacked. In 1113 the valley of the Tagus was once more the target of the Almoravides: Oreja, Coria, Zorita and Albalate were captured; the great Christian captain Alvar Fáñez was defeated while trying to relieve Oreja; the Almoravides penetrated as far north as Berlanga, only a few miles south of the Duero. In 1114 the Toledo region was raided again, probably twice. It was not until 1115 that a Christian counter-offensive produced some successes—three successive governors of Cordoba were defeated and killed by raiding parties from Toledo—but these proved only temporary checks to the tide of Almoravide success. Oriel Aznárez, the governor of Toledo, was defeated in 1116, and further strong points in Portugal fell to the Moors. In 1117 Ali ben Yusuf, the Almoravide leader, himself crossed to Spain at the head of an enormous army. He besieged Coimbra for three weeks, an episode which was to be long remembered in Portuguese tradition. Coimbra survived; but the same year saw also a further reverse for the army of Toledo.

In Galicia the first reaction to the Aragonese marriage came from Pedro Froílaz de Traba. As the guardian of the child Alfonso Raimúndez he took his stand on the decisions taken at the council of León in 1107, by which the kingdom of Galicia was to go to Alfonso Raimúndez in the event that his mother Urraca should remarry: 'when he heard for certain that the king of Aragon had married the boy's mother, he rebelled against him'.[2] Count Pedro was opposed by a faction among the Galician nobility which the *Historia Compostellana* refers to as a 'brotherhood' (*germanitas*) under the leadership of Arias Pérez. Some historians have detected here a clash of principles: 'Galician separatists' under Pedro Froílaz against 'loyalists' under Arias Pérez. But this is anachronistic. It is more likely that the divisions were drawn on regional lines. Traba country was in the extreme north-west. The members of the brotherhood

[2] So the anonymous chronicler of Sahagún, in R. Escalona, *Historia del real monasterio de Sahagún* (Madrid, 1782), p. 304.

were for the most part drawn from central and southern Galicia.

Diego Gelmírez was presented with the first of many difficult choices which were to force themselves upon him during Urraca's reign. At the council of León Diego had been associated with Pedro Froílaz in the guardianship of Alfonso Raimúndez. But he may have felt a personal loyalty to Urraca, a respect for the deathbed wishes of Alfonso VI. Here too, local interests may have played a part in shaping Diego's decision. The brotherhood included several of Diego's vassals, powerful and (as we shall soon see) dangerous men whose wishes had to be respected. There are also signs that at this time the relations between Diego and Pedro Froílaz, normally cordial, were strained. This is a very obscure matter, but it seems that the two men had recently quarrelled over the status and patronage of a religious house at Cines, and that in a recent election to the see of Mondoñedo the candidate chosen was a man of the Traba interest who was unacceptable to Diego.³ Diego's reaction was the epitome of caution. After ostentatious hesitation he aligned himself with the brotherhood in opposition to count Pedro. This must have occurred late in 1109 or early in 1110.

His position shifted in the course of the year 1110.⁴ Several factors combined to bring about a *rapprochement* between Diego and the count, with the focus of their loyalties firmly upon the young Alfonso Raimúndez. The king of Aragon made his first and only appearance in Galicia. The expedition was not a success. He made himself unpopular with churchmen and laymen alike, and the only charter he granted there, to the abbey of Samos, is notable for its short and undistinguished witness-list.⁵ Pope Paschal II, following the archbishop of Toledo, condemned the Aragonese marriage. The signs multiplied that, even without the spur of ecclesiastical censure, the marriage could not last. In the light of these developments it must have been impossible for Diego to maintain his stance of loyalty to the political

³ For Cines see *HC*, pp. 91-3 (= JL 5944, 6001, 6027); for the Mondoñedo election, R. A. Fletcher, 'Obispos olvidados del siglo XII de las diócesis de Mondoñedo y Lugo', *Cuadernos de Estudios Gallegos* 28 (1973), 318-25.
⁴ For what follows see *HC*, pp. 98-121.   ⁵ R. 13 July 1110.

arrangements which went with it. Meanwhile, the tension
in Galicia between the Traba faction and the brotherhood
increased; the tenuous peace snapped towards the end of
the year. Pedro Froílaz succeeded in acquiring the castle
of Castrelo do Miño, just to the east of Ribadabia. This
acquisition, in an area far to the south of the Traba landholdings, but conveniently close to Portugal with whose
count Henry he was in touch in the course of the year,
was presumably intended by Pedro as the beginning of
some sort of initiative against the brotherhood. Certainly
it was interpreted thus. Most unwisely, Pedro installed his
wife and Alfonso Raimúndez in this distant outpost. There
they were besieged by the forces of the brotherhood. It
was at this point that Diego Gelmírez became involved.
The besieged very naturally requested that Diego, as titular
head of the brotherhood, should come to guarantee articles
of surrender. Diego attended only with extreme reluctance.
Had he already been negotiating with the count of Traba?
Very probably. At all events, the meeting at Castrelo was
conducted in an atmosphere of the deepest suspicion between
Diego and his nominal allies of the brotherhood. They
struck after the conclusion of negotiations with the besieged
in the castle. Diego, the countess of Traba and Alfonso
Raimúndez were arrested by Arias Pérez.

The incident was unpleasant—Diego was not maltreated
but his travelling chapel was ransacked—but in the longer
term its effects may have been beneficial. Diego was given
the best possible pretext for aligning himself with count
Pedro. Released after a few days' imprisonment to negotiate
with him, Diego seems to have had no difficulty in finding
common ground. They agreed that they must treat with
Urraca on the basis of firm loyalty to Alfonso Raimúndez.
The queen was delighted. Diego threw over the brotherhood
and joined the Traba camp. In a carefully staged ceremony
at Compostela on 17 September 1111 the young prince
was crowned and anointed king by Diego. In the banquet
that followed count Pedro Froílaz acted as seneschal
(*dapifer*), his son Rodrigo was marshal (*alfericeus*), another
son, Bermudo, had charge of the royal cellars (*vinum et
siceram . . . ministrari praecepit*), and Munio Peláez, count

Pedro's son-in-law, was in charge of the food (*regalis offer-torius*). There could have been no doubt about who was to be in charge of the new king's court. In the singsong that ended the evening's carousal we may feel sure that bishop Diego and the Traba clan bellowed most lustily what the author of the *Historia Compostellana* delicately referred to as 'hymns of joy'.

The events of 1109–11 have been dwelt on at some length, mainly because, thanks to the *Historia*, we know a good deal about them. It had not been an easy time for Diego. There had been uncertainty, divided counsels, disloyalty of vassals, oath-breaking, suspicion, deception and violence. We must not suppose that Diego's experience was unique, simply because we happen to know about it. We are presented with the familiar if pitiable spectacle of confused men trying to muddle through a crisis. As in many—perhaps most—political crises, the only issue at stake was survival. Diego Gelmírez was nothing if not a survivor.

The accord with queen Urraca reached in 1111, and its gradual erosion, make up the thread which will enable us to follow the labyrinthine politics of the next six years. The immediate results of the accord are clear. It gave Urraca the opportunity of tapping Galician resources in men and money for the coming war with Aragon. It effectively forestalled any intervention in Galicia nominally on behalf of Alfonso Raimúndez by the count and countess of Portugal. It strengthened Traba power in Galicia. It provided Diego with the chance to insert Compostelan clerks into the royal chancery, with all the possibilities for exerting influence that this implied.[6] It gave Diego access to royal aid in suppressing Galician trouble-makers: one of its first fruits was the siege and capture of Arias Pérez at Lobeira in April 1112.[7]

What is less clear is the significance of the coronation ceremony of September 1111. Some have supposed that Alfonso Raimúndez was crowned king of Galicia. This seems

---

[6] R. 19 September 1111 is the first of a long series of charters drawn up by Martín Peláez, canon of Santiago de Compostela. On the royal chancery during this period see Reilly, *Urraca*, pp. 205–11 and references there cited.

[7] *HC*, pp. 126–7.

most unlikely. He is never described as such in our sources. There is no sign that he was in any sense a nominally independent ruler; for example, he did not as yet issue charters or coinage in his own name. Rather, he seems to have been elevated to the position of joint-ruler with his mother. A charter of 11 February 1111, which must have been drawn up very soon after the new accord had been reached (and well before the coronation) puts the matter thus in its dating-clause: *regnante Urraka regina et filio suo parvulo Adefonso in Legione*.[8] After the coronation Diego and count Pedro set out for León so that there the boy and his mother could jointly receive the homage of the kingdom's leading men. As it happened they never got there, being defeated by an Aragonese army at Viadangos and forced to flee back to Galicia;[9] yet the episode suggests that joint rule was envisaged. We begin to find the royal chancery, frequently though not invariably, issuing diplomas in the names of both mother and son.[10]

Harmonious co-operation was the keynote of relations between Diego and the queen in the course of the year 1112. Urraca spent most of the first half of the year in the Asturias and Galicia. From Astorga in March she went to Oviedo, and thence moved south-west to Lugo. She spent Easter (21 April) at Compostela, visited Tuy, and returned to Compostela after that. About the middle of May she moved back to Lugo, and perhaps paid a visit to the Mondoñedo area about the same time. It was a comprehensive review of her Galician provinces, and the abundant royal diplomas which have survived leave one in no doubt that her main motive was to raise men and money for the war with Aragon. At Compostela she implored the assistance of St. James, helped Diego to round up Arias Pérez and made a handsome grant of lands and privileges to the cathedral church.[11] We are not surprised to learn that this 'wonderfully fired the spirits of the clergy' to assist the queen. They gave

[8] AHN 893/5. It is noteworthy that Urraca seems to have wanted to have her son crowned in the *urbs regia* of León at some point in 1110: *HC*, p. 98.

[9] *HC*, pp. 121-3.

[10] The earliest is R. 14 April 1111, though this may lie under some suspicion since it survives only in an eighteenth-century abstract. Several diplomas from the year 1112 were joint productions.   [11] *HC*, pp. 124-7; R. 14 May 1112.

her 100 ounces of gold and 200 silver marks. The results of her efforts were eminently satisfactory. A Galician army crossed the mountains to the *meseta* and defeated the Aragonese at Astorga; Alfonso *el Batallador* fled to Carrión, pursued by the queen. Diego had accompanied the army as far as Triacastela, returning thence to Galicia to suppress a revolt which had broken out in his rear.[12]

Signs of strain appeared in 1113. Urraca's summer campaign was directed to the recovery from the Aragonese of the important town and fortress of Burgos.[13] Diego was summoned to join the queen's army, which he did rather too slowly for her liking. While they were together in July the relations between them seem to have deteriorated. Urraca doubted Diego's commitment to her cause; he resented the presence of some of his old Galician enemies at her court. An agreement which was drawn up between them on 8 July shows that one of the divisive issues was Diego's liability for military service in the royal army. There was probably more to this quarrel than the *Historia Compostellana* permits us to see.[14] In 1113 Diego made his first serious attempt to persuade the pope to raise his episcopal see to metropolitan rank. His strategy on this occasion involved reliance upon the assistance of archbishop Maurice of Braga, at a moment when the latter's relations with both the queen and archbishop Bernardo of Toledo were singularly bad. This would not have endeared Diego to Urraca. After Diego had returned to Galicia he stayed there for the rest of the year; excusing himself with an unconvincing pretext from attendance at the council of Palencia in October—a council which was an impressive display of royalist confidence and Toledan primatial power, where the Braga party took an ignominious beating. Diego, meanwhile, was stoking up his alliance with the Trabas; it seems that count Pedro too had incurred the queen's displeasure.[15] But oil was poured on these troubled waters. Urraca probaly kept her Christmas court in Galicia, and the archbishop of Toledo skilfully

[12] *HC*, pp. 128-32.   [13] *HC*, pp. 153-70.
[14] For what follows, see now Vones, *Kirchenpolitik*, pp. 289-343, where the background to the council of Palencia is minutely investigated.
[15] *HC*, pp. 174-5.

detached Diego from his flirtation with the archbishop of Braga.

The frail harmony between Diego and the queen was further threatened in 1114. After spending the early part of the year in Castile, Urraca travelled to Galicia in the summer. A private charter from León dated 26 July refers darkly to *discordia* between the queen and her son at this time.[16] It is likely that we should connect this with what the *Historia* has to tell us of a plot against Diego by Urraca in the course of the summer.[17] The queen planned to capture the bishop at Iria. He got wind of it and managed to mobilize Galician aristocratic opinion in his favour. Urraca, her bluff called, was forced to swear an oath of friendship. The most striking feature of the text of the oath was its concern with the preservation of the integrity of the *honor* of Santiago —that is to say, the complex of lands and rights which made up the temporalities of the bishopric. We must conclude from this that Urraca had intended to confiscate some or all of the *honor*, perhaps as a ransom for Diego's release from captivity. Some indications that this was the way the queen's mind was working had already been given. A little earlier, perhaps when the court was in Galicia at the end of 1113, Urraca had claimed that three brothers who were among the clergy of Compostela were *capite censos*.[18] It is not clear exactly what this claim meant, but the general sense of it was an assertion of rights over persons of servile condition. Now the three brothers in question were distinguished men, trusted members of Diego's entourage. One of them, Pelayo Bodán, had been a notary of Alfonso VI for at least ten years and had been sent on business to the papal curia. Another, Diego, had been a canon of Compostela since at least 1101 and had been sent by his bishop

[16] Quoted by Reilly, *Urraca*, p. 98, n. 34.   [17] *HC*, pp. 194-6.

[18] *HC*, pp. 186-7. On the brothers Bodán see also R. 1 April 1101, 14 May 1107; *Colección de Documentos de la Catedral de Oviedo*, ed. S. García Larragueta (Oviedo, 1962), no. 121; J. F. Rivera Recio, *La Iglesia de Toledo en el siglo XII* (Rome, 1966), p. 150; Vones, *Kirchenpolitik*, p. 123, n. 109 and references there cited; R. A. Fletcher, 'Diplomatic and the Cid revisited: the seals and mandates of Alfonso VII', *Journal of Medieval History* 2 (1976), 305-37, at pp. 307-8. Their family *monasterium* was probably at Bodaño, in Deza: we shall return to it at the end of this chapter. (*LFH* III, p. 444, identified it as Budiño, but this is less plausible than Bodaño, philologically speaking.)

to acquire an important privilege from Alfonso VI in 1107. As successful servants of church and state, they must have been men of substance; their family was in any case a landed one. Aided by Diego Gelmírez, they had no difficulty in rebutting the queen's claims. The interest of the incident lies in its revelation of the expedients to which Urraca was being forced by the pressures of insolvency.

But there were yet other currents playing about the events of the summer. Diego heard about the plot from Pedro Froílaz de Traba; he in his turn had heard it from the queen herself. The implication is surely inescapable that Urraca had tried to detach count Pedro from his alliance with Diego, and had very nearly succeeded in doing so. This circumstance probably explains the otherwise inexplicable oath of friendship sworn about this time to Diego by count Pedro, his wife, two of his sons and several of his prominent vassals.[19] A pact of friendship implies recent estrangement; and the concern of the pact with the *honor* of Santiago echoes queen Urraca's contemporaneous oath. But this was not the only concern of the Traba oath. Pedro Froílaz and his family promised 'that we shall act according to your [i.e. Diego's] counsel and command over the raising up of the *infante* the lord Alfonso [i.e. Alfonso Raimúndez] and in the providing of him with lands, while we retain him in our custody'. This is a very interesting provision, and it tells us two things. The first is that Traba guardianship of the young king was being threatened, presumably by the queen who wanted her son in her own custody. The second is that some sort of political initiative was being planned by Diego on behalf of or in the name of Alfonso Raimúndez, now in his tenth year. What this was is revealed elsewhere.[20] Diego believed that 'the kingdom of Galicia should be subject to the lordship (*dominio*) of king Alfonso the queen's son'. This is the first occurrence of the term *regnum Gallaeciae* in the *Historia Compostellana*, and a startling revelation of the drift of Diego's plans. Alfonso Raimúndez was a king without a kingdom. Diego proposed to give him one, at his mother's expense. No wonder that Urraca had been alarmed,

---

[19] *HC*, pp. 189–90.   [20] *HC*, p. 194.

nor that a Leonese notary should have referred to *discordia* between mother and son.

The sequel to these events is not known. Urraca had returned to León by October, and spent the winter in Castile. Her Christmas court may have been held at Palencia. Diego probably attended it, in itself a sign that some sort of reconciliation had taken place, and it was at Palencia on 3 January 1115 that the queen made a handsome grant of lands and churches lying a little to the south-east of Compostela to the church of St. James. (It is not impossible that the reconciliation had been lubricated by cash, that this 'grant' was in fact a concealed sale.) The words of the queen's diploma laid special stress both on her son's kingship—'with my son the lord Alfonso, now blessed and consecrated to the summit of the kingdom'—and on Diego's loyalty, 'most faithful in all things to me and to my son'. These emphases recur in another grant by the queen issued towards the end of the year, on 26 November 1115.

We must not be deceived, as we may be sure that Diego was not, by these honeyed words of friendship. In the following year a further quarrel between queen and bishop took place. It proved to be an altogether more serious business for Diego. Early in 1116 Urraca heard rumours that Diego's loyalty was weakening. She hastened to Galicia and a reconciliation between the two was arranged. After this the queen went into southern Galicia to put down a baronial rebellion near the Portuguese frontier. This accomplished, she made her way back to Lobeira where Diego's enemies urged her to imprison the bishop and confiscate the *honor* of Santiago. To this end she tried once more to engage the help of Pedro Froílaz de Traba, and once more he managed to reveal the plot to Diego. The bishop returned to Compostela and surrounded himself with troops. A meeting was arranged between the two parties and a new peace was made. To guarantee it, Diego was to choose twenty prominent aristocrats (*potentiores*), ten from Galicia and ten from the rest of the kingdom, who should swear as Urraca's oath-helpers to maintain it.[21]

[21] *HC*, pp. 204–8. The only pointers to the chonology of these events are two diplomas for the southern Galician monastery of Poyo: R. 29 February and

The peace very rapidly broke down. Urraca made her way to Lugo and thence to León, but though constantly badgered by Diego's emissaries she failed to assemble the oath-helpers as she had promised to do. It had been stipulated that in the event of her failure to fulfil the terms Diego should have the right to declare the peace void. This he now did. The sequel was startling.[22] Count Pedro Froílaz and the young king Alfonso Raimúndez were absent at this time beyond the Duero. We do not know what they were doing there: it is quite likely that the simplest explanation is the most plausible, namely that after the events of the spring the count wanted to get the boy as far away as possible from his mother. At any rate, what the *Historia* calls a 'serious quarrel' (*magna discordia*) between mother and son broke out. As soon as Alfonso Raimúndez heard of the dissolution of the recent peace between Diego and the queen he approached Diego with a proposal that he should now be proclaimed king of Galicia, as was his due. Diego, perhaps with some misgivings, agreed. Count Pedro and the young king returned to Galicia and were met by Diego at Iria.[23] Alfonso Raimúndez was then formally conducted, as king, to Santiago de Compostela.

Urraca's response was prompt and vigorous. She dashed back to Galicia by way of Triacastela and Mellid—that is, along the pilgrimage road—collecting support from the great magnates of eastern Galicia as she went, in the persons of count Rodrigo Vélaz de Sarria and count Munio Peláez de Monterroso. She made extravagant promises to Diego—

31 March 1116. I would associate the first of these with the queen's military expedition. The second, to judge by its witness-list, was almost certainly issued at Compostela: half of its ecclesiastical *confirmantes* were members of the cathedral community. I would suggest that the reconciliation here referred to had just taken place and that the royal court spent Easter (2 April) at Compostela. The reference at *HC*, p. 204 to the queen's grant of Caldas before the campaign is mistaken: as we shall see, it was made in May (though it might have been promised earlier on). I have ventured to emend the *praeterea* of *HC*, p. 204, line 18, to *postea*. It should finally be said that there is a suspicious resemblance between the events of 1114 and 1116, but after careful examination of the texts I am satisfied that we are not confronted by a doublet.

[22] *HC*, pp. 208-15.
[23] In other words they had come by sea, which might mean with Portuguese help. It is worthy of note that count Pedro was acting in alliance with countess Teresa of Portugal later in the year: *HC*, p. 216.

Lobeira, Ferreira and Montaos—in a bid for his loyalty to her. She encouraged disaffection in the town of Compostela, where Alfonso Raimúndez and the countess of Traba had established themselves in Diego's episcopal palace. (Pedro Froílaz was away from Compostela by now, at the head of an army, in whose ranks also the queen was busy sowing discontent.) Diego saw that the game was up. With difficulty he persuaded Alfonso Raimúndez and the countess Mayor to leave the town, and awaited the queen's arrival in trepidation. She came to Compostela, negotiations took place and a settlement was arranged. We are not told its terms, but they included the grant of a church at Caldas—very much less than what the queen had promised—on 18 May, which is our only secure date in this phase of the events of 1116.

The attempted coup on behalf of Alfonso Raimúndez had obviously been the work of Pedro Froílaz de Traba. Thanks to Urraca's prompt initiative it had misfired. Morally speaking, Diego had come out of it rather badly. He had abandoned the queen for the Traba faction, and then thrown over his new allies as soon as Urraca's army had appeared on the scene; despite the fact that he was acting in accordance with the plans that he had concocted with count Pedro in 1114. We already know him as a slippery customer, but he was not usually a man to give way to panic. In 1116, however, he was threatened from yet another quarter. Hitherto he had always been safe in his own city of Compostela, but at just this time a serious challenge to his authority was breaking out precisely there. The Compostela rebellion of 1116-17 will be examined in the next chapter. Here it is sufficient to say that it was led by members both of the urban bourgeoisie and of Diego's own cathedral chapter; that at least in its early stages it had the support of the queen; and that as it developed in the summer of 1116 it constituted the gravest menace not only to Diego's authority but to his very life which he ever had to face.

Diego was isolated in the summer of 1116. Pedro Froílaz had not forgiven him for his betrayal in May, and was conducting a guerrilla war against his dependants during the months of summer. The town of Compostela was slipping from his grasp. He had to establish a firmer relationship with the queen. At some point in or after July he went and sought her out on the Tierra de Campos. To his relief, Urraca was prepared to treat. But she would insist this time on a more far-reaching settlement.[24]

The peace which was finally made at Sahagún in October 1116 between the queen and the partisans of her son is reported at length but somewhat vaguely in the pages of the *Historia Compostellana*.[25] Given the authors' habit of saying as little as possible about Diego's reverses, there is some ground for suspecting that the peace of Sahagún was a triumph for the queen. It was evidently regarded as an important settlement, the first such since the death of Alfonso VI to offer any hope of lasting concord. It was to run in the first instance for three years. Its most far-reaching provision was for the division of the kingdom between mother and son. The experiment of joint rule had not worked; Alfonso Raimúndez was to be given an independent authority. Gerald of Beauvais, the author of this part of the *Historia*, is oddly reluctant to tell us any details about the partition. Some historians[26] have supposed that it was now, in 1116, that Alfonso Raimúndez was given a kingdom of Galicia. But had this been so Gerald would certainly have told us. In any case, in the spring of that year queen Urraca had so successfully outmanœuvred the faction which wanted precisely this that it is inconceivable that she should have conceded it during the summer. Furthermore, Urraca's dealings with Galicia during the next three years leave one in no doubt as to her continuing authority there. Alfonso Raimúndez did indeed get independent authority as a result of the negotiations at Sahagún, but altogether elsewhere, in the area referred to by contemporaries as *Extrematura*, i.e. beyond the river Duero, in the Toledo region. This was a master-stroke on Urraca's part, and it explains the rueful

[24] *HC*, p. 221. I would suggest that the oaths recorded at *HC*, pp. 200-2 belong here. The main argument, though there are subsidiary ones as well, is that the queen's oath is dated 'in the eighth year after the death' of Alfonso VI, i.e. in the period of twelve months beginning on 1 July 1116. Clearly they have been displaced in the text as we have it, whether by accident or design.

[25] *HC*, pp. 224-6, and note the imposing witness-list of R. 15 October 1116. It is interesting to note in passing that a bishop of Granada was present. I am less surprised at this than Professor Reilly seems to be: Reilly, *Urraca*, p. 115, n. 96.

[26] Including myself, a few years ago: *Episcopate*, p. 16.

silence of the *Historia*. For the first time Alfonso Raimúndez was detached from his Galician supporters. His new mentor would be the archbishop of Toledo—Diego's most dangerous ecclesiastical rival—and his new entourage would be Castilian.[27] Diego Gelmírez and the Trabas had lost the contest for custody of the young king.

Almoravide pressure on the southern frontiers of Christian Spain eased after 1117. Ali's attempt on Coimbra in that year was the last big Muslim initiative, and it failed. Hesitantly at first, but with increasing confidence, the Christian princes began to push the war into the enemy camp. The first major success was Alfonso *el Batallador's* capture of Zaragoza, after a seven-months' siege, in December 1118. It was very probably because Almoravide troops had been diverted to the defence of Zaragoza that the archbishop of Toledo and Alfonso Raimúndez were able to take the strong point of Alcalá towards the end of the year, thereby helping to ensure the defence of Toledo from the Almoravide salient to its north-east. The king of Aragon followed up his success by taking Tudela in 1119. In 1120 he defeated a large Almoravide army at Cutanda, and absorbed Calatayud and Daroca.

These events were watched with interest in Galicia. If they had any direct repercussion in the north-west it was probably the falling-off of Urraca's demands for money for the expenses of frontier defence. For Diego the three years following the peace of Sahagún were dominated by his final and successful negotiations with pope Gelasius II and his successor Calixtus II to have his see raised to metropolitan status. This was an enterprise in which he badly needed royal support, so he had every reason to cultivate good relations with the queen. As far as we can see, harmony was maintained. It was with royal help that the rising in Compostela was suppressed in 1117. Diego provided the queen with troops in the autumn of the same year. She paid a visit to Galicia in the summer of 1118. Diego attended her court at Burgos in the spring of 1119, and for part of the way thither she provided him with a royal escort.[28] We hear

[27] See for example the witness-list of his first known diploma, R. 27 November 1116. [28] *HC*, pp. 249–50, 269–70; R. 29 July 1118.

of only one source of unease. Urraca is said to have forbidden Diego to attend Calixtus II's council of Rheims in October 1119.[29] But we should not make too much of this. The queen's claim that the peace of Galicia would be jeopardized by Diego's absence was no more than the truth. She may have had an eye to her half-sister Teresa, now styling herself not countess but *queen* of Portugal, to the south.[30] And though the pope had insisted that Diego attend the council in person, he may have been as reluctant to go as the queen was to permit him. The three-year peace of Sahagún was to expire in the autumn. How could Diego possibly absent himself from the kingdom at such a delicate moment? The *Historia* makes rather a song and dance about telling us that Diego had made every preparation for his journey to the papal curia.[31] Perhaps it protests too much. All the more reason for suspecting that the royal prohibition may not have been unwelcome to him.

The ending of the three-year truce must have engendered uncertainties about the future and an atmosphere of suspicion. Urraca is said to have had another reason for preventing Diego from going to Rheims. 'Certain people had persuaded the queen that [Diego] wanted to go to Gaul so that he might endeavour to confer the kingdom of Spain upon king Alfonso the queen's son.' These words form the threshold for our entry into the immensely complicated happenings of the year 1120. Before trying to unravel the story it will be useful to isolate some of the underlying strands. In the first place, Diego had at last got his archbishopric; the papal privilege conferring it had been drawn up at Valence on 26 February 1120. So he was a little less dependent on royal benevolence than he had been in the years 1118 and 1119. Second, pope Calixtus II felt keenly the responsibilities of a kinsman for his nephew Alfonso Raimúndez. Of several indications of this we need cite only one example, the papal

---

[29] *HC*, p. 279 (277). Reilly, *Urraca*, pp. 137–9, interprets the events of 1119 rather differently.

[30] On the titles of the rulers of Portugal see P. Feige, 'Die Anfänge des portugiesischen Königtums und seiner Landeskirche', *Spanische Forschungen der Görresgesellschaft* 29 (1978), 85–436, at pp. 139–47. I am most grateful to Dr Peter Linehan for furnishing me with a copy of this important study.

[31] He had intended going by sea.

bull *Egregiae memoriae* of 4 March 1120.[32] The pope insisted that the young king had been deprived of his rights by his mother and that they should be restored to him. Third, Urraca was hoping to take advantage of Aragonese pre-occupation with frontier warfare and mobilize a campaign to recover the territories in eastern Castile lost to the king of Aragon back in the years 1110–12. Finally, in order to do this she needed money. She decided to seek it in the north and west of her kingdom.

In mid-April Urraca was at Astorga. Towards the end of the month she had gone to the Asturias. Thence she moved west to Galicia. She was at Compostela in the middle of June, and may have paid a visit to Braga. On 6 August she was at Samos, heading eastwards, and by the end of the month seems to have been back on the Leonese *meseta*. The diplomas issued by the queen in the course of this journey—like those of 1112—bear witness to her pre-occupation with raising money. She sold a Roman temple to the bishop and chapter of Astorga for bullion and 2,083 solidi. Samos contributed 10 marks of silver and 700 solidi. Her grants to count Suero Bermúdez, and to the church of Oviedo, were made 'in return for service' (*propter servicium*), a formula which may well indicate an unacknowledged sale. Her particularly lavish benefaction to the cathedral church of Santiago, made 'on account of the forthcoming wars', was reciprocated in bullion from the cathedral treasury— a 'silver (covered?) table' (*mensam argenteam*)—and cash from Diego's personal fortune.[33] We should note too that a captured rebel baron was released only after payment of 'massive sums of money' (*pecunias immensas*).[34]

But there were further goings-on at Compostela. Once again there were rumours that Urraca was conspiring to arrest the archbishop (as he now was). On this occasion they were reconciled through the mediation of two French ecclesiastics, Henry, abbot of St. Jean d'Angély, and Stephen, chamberlain of Cluny. A contemporary chronicler in York recorded the vital information that in the summer of 1119 abbot Henry had been sent by the pope to escort archbishop Ralph of

---

[32] *HC*, pp. 316–17 (= JL 6828).   [33] *HC*, p. 303; R. 13 June 1120.
[34] *HC*, p. 312.

Canterbury to the papal curia.[35] Henry would therefore have returned to the curia late in 1119. It is hard to avoid the impression that his journey to Spain must have been undertaken on the orders of pope Calixtus. Now Henry was a man of very distinguished family.[36] In particular, he was connected, albeit rather remotely, to the greatest magnate in southern France, duke William IX of Aquitaine: Henry's sister-in-law had previously been married to the half-brother of William's mother. William IX himself was queen Urraca's first cousin. It is of the utmost interest to find that William too was in Spain at this time.[37] He subscribed Urraca's diploma of 21 August 1120. This was a grant to the monastery of Cluny, and it was undoubtedly negotiated by Stephen the chamberlain. It must surely have been at about the same time that Clementia, the dowager countess of Flanders, wrote a letter of anxious enquiry about Alfonso Raimúndez to Diego.[38] Clementia was the pope's sister, aunt therefore of the young king. As so often, we have tantalizing scraps of information but no coherent narrative. It looks as though the pope—an aristocrat of the most distinguished connections, accustomed to moving among the great on terms of easy familiarity—was mobilizing the most powerful force available to him, not ecclesiastical censures but the network of aristocratic kin, to bring pressure to bear upon Diego Gelmírez and queen Urraca in the interests of his nephew Alfonso Raimúndez.

The agreement that was reached between Diego and the queen through the mediation of Henry and Stephen is summarized in the *Historia Compostellana*.[39] Its terms are

[35] Hugh the Chantor, *The history of the church of York, 1066–1127* (ed. and trans. C. Johnson (Edinburgh, 1961), p. 63.

[36] Henry's exotic career has been sorted out by C. Clark, ' "This ecclesiastical adventurer": Henry of Saint-Jean d'Angély', *English Historical Review* 84 (1969), 548–60, though she was unaware of its Spanish dimension. Note that *HC*, p. 324 describes Henry as a *contribulis* of queen Urraca.

[37] He had arrived in May 1120: see J. M. Lacarra, 'Documentos para el estudio de la reconquista y repoblación del valle del Ebro (segunda serie)', *Estudios de Edad Media de la Corona de Aragón* 3 (1947–8), 499–727, no. 114 at p. 518. William IX and pope Calixtus II had met in May 1119, and only illness had prevented William from attending the council of Rheims: see F. Villard, 'Guillaume IX d'Aquitaine et le concile de Reims de 1119', *Cahiers de Civilisation Médiévale* 16 (1973), 295–302 and references there cited.

[38] *HC*, p. 321.   [39] *HC*, pp. 313–14.

extremely puzzling. Urraca promised to be a faithful friend
(*fidelis amica*) to Diego. Furthermore, she gave him the lordship of all Galicia (*totius Gallaeciae dominium*). On her
orders Arias Pérez, Fernando Yáñez, Bermudo Suárez, Juan
Díaz and other unnamed magnates (*principes*) of Galicia did
homage (*hominium*) to him, placing themselves and their
possessions beneath his lordship (*dominio*). They acknowledged him as 'their lord, their patron, their king [*sic*] and
their prince, saving their fealty to the queen'. Nothing is
reported about Alfonso Raimúndez, but that does not mean
that nothing was said. We should remember that Gerald of
Beauvais was chronicling Diego's achievements, not writing
a political history of queen Urraca's reign. Other documents
of the year 1120 show plainly that the young king continued to rule beyond the Duero.[40] Alfonso Raimúndez's
rights under the Sahagún agreement of 1116 had been
renewed if not enlarged: to that extent Henry and Stephen
had faithfully carried out the pope's commission. Another
omission is more surprising. The report in the *Historia*
makes no allusion to the Traba family. Now Urraca's diploma
for the church of Santiago dated 13 June was subscribed by
no member of the family. Among its *confirmantes* were,
however, the four magnates who did homage to Diego under
the new agreement. These were all men who had on occasions
in the past been at loggerheads with Pedro Froílaz (and also,
it is only fair to state, with Diego). Diego's new position as
'lord of Galicia', whatever it really meant, was obviously
intended as some diminution of the authority of Pedro
Froílaz who had enjoyed the dignity of count of Galicia
since 1109. Furthermore, it is only very shortly after the
1120 agreement that we find count Pedro's son, Fernando
Pérez de Traba, up in arms against Diego.[41] It appears that
in 1120—as in 1114 and 1116—the queen was trying to
separate Diego from his Traba allies. On this occasion she
succeeded.

The latter part of the year brought a development full of
menace for Diego. The projected Aragonese campaign never
took place. Instead, Urraca and Alfonso *el Batallador* made

[40] e.g. AHN 894/3: regnante rege Adefonso in Toleto, regina Urraka in
Legione.   [41] *HC*, pp. 314-15, 444.

peace. The fact is referred to in an Aragonese charter of 29 December.[42] But it had evidently occurred much earlier than that, for Diego sent news of it to the pope, and Calixtus replied to him in a letter dated 19 December, denouncing it in violent terms.[43] We have another witness to tell us something of this settlement. William IX of Aquitaine returned home towards the end of the year and wrote thence to Diego in terms of anxiety, not to say panic.[44] He reported that Urraca and Alfonso *el Batallador* were intending to deprive Alfonso Raimúndez of his inheritance. Diego must look to the young man's safety. The archbishop should seek the help of Pedro Froílaz. Together let them get custody of the young king. If they feared for his safety, let him be sent by sea to William's province of Gaul. As it happened, Diego had already acted before he received William's letter. For the pope's letter of 19 December congratulated him on bringing about a reconciliation between Urraca and her son (*quod pacem et dilectionem inter matrem et filium nepotem nostrum regem Hyspanie reformasti*). How he did it we do not know. But it is reasonable to assume that it would have involved a *rapprochement* between Diego and the Trabas; in other words the undoing of the queen's machinations of the summer.

The renewal of the old alliance between Diego and the Traba family had dangerous implications for the queen. It was at precisely this period that Fernando and Bermudo, the sons of Pedro Froílaz, were beginning to fish in the waters of Portuguese politics. As early as January 1121 Fernando Pérez could be described as 'lord of Coimbra and Portugal'. From February he was regularly subscribing Teresa's charters. He must have become her lover by then, for the daughter she bore him was old enough to be associated with her father in a grant to the Traba family monastery of Jubia in 1132.[45] His brother Bermudo married Teresa's daughter Urraca in 1122. Now at this time Teresa had designs

---

[42] J. M. Lacarra, 'Documentos para el estudio de la reconquista y repoblación del valle del Ebro (tercera serie)', *Estudios de Edad Media de la Corona de Aragón* 5 (1952), 55-668, no. 306, at p. 532.

[43] AC Toledo, cod. 42/21 fo. 66v; cod. 42/22 fo. 48r.

[44] *HC*, pp. 319-20.

[45] *Jubia Cart.* no. XXXV. For further details about the Traba involvement in

on southern Galicia; indeed, the whole area south of the Miño and the Sil may have been under her control. If an alliance between the Trabas to the north and the Portuguese to the south were to be joined by the archbishop of Compostela and the massive resources of his see, queen Urraca would have lost all control of western Galicia from the coast of Biscay to the river Mondego.

She delivered her counterstroke in the summer of 1121.[46] Acting perhaps not without a sense of irony, she requested that Diego accompany her on campaign into southern Galicia —against Teresa of Portugal. Diego was, understandably, extremely reluctant to serve. When finally compelled to do so, he tried to persuade the queen not to push the war far into Portuguese territory. From Urraca's point-of-view the campaign was a success. Teresa was chased back across the Miño near Tuy and even besieged for a time at Lanhoso. But she was in touch with Diego: it was from Teresa that he heard that Urraca planned to arrest him. Teresa's information was good. As the Galician army was returning home by way of the valley of the Limia and the monastery of Celanova, Urraca suddenly had Diego arrested at Castrelo do Miño. There were echoes of the past here, perhaps deliberately 'orchestrated' by the queen. It had been at Castrelo that Diego had been arrested in 1110, and his captor on that occasion, his old enemy Arias Pérez, was one of the queen's accomplices in 1121. Two others were Juan Díaz and Fernando Yáñez: the fact that the queen's henchmen included three of the men with whom Diego had confederated in the year before is a further indication that he had thrown them over in returning to the Traba alliance. It was in Juan Díaz's castle of Orcellón that he was held at first, and under

Portugal, see now P. Feige, 'Die Anfänge des portugiesischen Königtums und seiner Landeskirche', *Spanische Forschungen der Görresgesellschaft* 29 (1978), 85–436, at pp. 163–7, and references there cited.

[46] For what follows see *HC*, pp. 315, 322–35, 341–50; the papal letters are JL 6926–30. A very different chronology has been proposed by Dr Feige and Professor Reilly, who would place the events here allotted to 1121 in the year 1120: see in particular Reilly, *Urraca*, pp. 144–52. I am not convinced by their arguments, and prefer the traditional chronology first worked out, like so much else in Diego's career, by López Ferreiro. Vones, *Kirchenpolitik*, p. 420, also follows López Ferreiro.

Juan Díaz's escort that he was transferred from there to Cira
—in which we might detect another grim irony, for the
castle at Cira had been built not long before with Diego's
permission.

The stroke misfired, though perhaps not so completely
as the *Historia Compostellana* would have us believe. The
townspeople of Compostela vigorously supported their archbishop. It may be that we should see in this the fruits of
Diego's efforts since 1117 to cultivate their goodwill.[47] As
ill luck would have it the queen's return to Compostela took
place on 24 July, the vigil of the feast of St. James. On the
following day all festivities were cancelled and the canons
wore mourning. The town would have been full of pilgrims
from near and far, of peasants from the surrounding countryside come into town for a holiday, of hucksters hoping for
a good trade. Soon the town was in an uproar, and Urraca
had to seek safety in the cathedral. Meanwhile her son
Alfonso Raimúndez deserted her and left the town to join
Pedro Froílaz de Traba. Shortly afterwards Juan Díaz,
coming to Compostela to confer with the queen, was captured
by the archbishop's supporters. Urraca had no choice but
to release Diego. He had been in captivity for only eight days.

But Urraca had charges to lay against Diego. The *Historia
Compostellana* never tells us precisely what they were, but
they were evidently grave. Surely they were charges of
treason occasioned by his negotiations with the Portuguese.[48]
She had confiscated his castles and lands pending an accord.
As ever 'thirsty for money', as the *Historia* puts it, she
intended that any settlement should involve the payment
of a huge ransom. Diego for his part was not idle. As soon
as he had been released he made contact with his relative
Pedro, the dean of Compostela, then studying in France.
Pedro consulted the abbot of Cluny and with his assistance
made his way to the papal curia, then in southern Italy, to
apprise Calixtus II of these events. The pope's reaction was
sharp. 'Touch not mine anointed', he quoted, and threatened

---

[47] In 1120 he had secured their immunity from toll throughout the queen's
dominions: R. 13 June 1120.

[48] Not, I think, with the French, as López Ferreiro suggested: *LFH* IV,
p. 39, n. 1.

Urraca's kingdom with an interdict. The letters he sent may have hastened a settlement, though it was not reached without great difficulty and a near-outbreak of civil war. After complicated negotiations Urraca swore an oath of friendship to Diego and on the last day of the year restored his castles to him.

Calixtus II had addressed Urraca as *illustris regina*, but her son, his nephew, as *strenuus et gloriosus Hispaniarum rex*. The studied employment of this protocol suggests that the pope was continuing to press for some enlargement of Alfonso's authority at the expense of his mother's. It is probable that the Traba clan was doing likewise. When Urraca returned to Galicia early in 1123 she arrested Pedro Froílaz, his sons (we are not told which ones) and his wife.[49] It is almost impossible to reconstruct the background to this incident. We know that in January Diego presided over a council which was convened to discuss, among other things, *discordia* between the queen and her son.[50] A charter of January 1123 records that Alfonso Raimúndez was reigning as 'king in Toledo and in Galicia'.[51] Another charter refers to Pedro Froílaz in the company of 'his king'.[52] This is not much to go on, but it is just enough to suggest another initiative on count Pedro's part to establish Alfonso Raimúndez as king of Galicia (as in 1116); and to account for the queen's vigorous action against him.

To what extent Diego was implicated is not clear. We are hardly surprised to learn from the *Historia Compostellana* that there was little trust between the archbishop and the queen.[53] Events followed a not-unfamiliar pattern. There

[49] *HC*, pp. 382, 389.

[50] *HC*, p. 427: Vones, *Kirchenpolitik*, pp. 438–41, has convincingly argued that this council should be dated 1123 rather than 1125.

[51] AHN 894/5.

[52] *LFH* IV, p. 89. I have not been able to trace this charter. López Ferreiro did not give its date, but the implication is that it was of late 1122 or early 1123. There should also be mentioned a charter which in its existing form bears the impossible date 26 September 1119 by which Alfonso Raimúndez, styling himself *rex Hispaniae* and acting *una (cum) consensu domini Petri Galecie comitis*, made a grant to the religious house of Moraime: on the problems of this charter see Reilly, *Urraca*, p. 140. It is noteworthy, in this context, that when count Pedro made a grant to the monastery of Jubia in 1125 the dating clause of his charter read *regnante rege domino Adefonso*, without reference to queen Urraca: *Jubia Cart.* no. xxx.   [53] *HC*, pp. 381-2.

were accusations by the queen, the purchase of her goodwill by Diego (300 marks this time), negotiations by intermediaries, and on 27 March 1123 the swearing of new oaths of friendship.[54] Not long afterwards Urraca was approached by some men who were disaffected towards Diego: they offered to capture and murder him. The queen ostentatiously refused to have anything to do with them; she wanted the new peace to work.[55] An exchange of property between archbishop and queen in May, and the queen's instrumentality in securing the benefaction of a rich but otherwise unknown lady named Tigria Jiménez at much the same time, indicate harmonious relations.[56]

It would appear that they remained harmonious for the remainder of Urraca's reign. The joint rule of Urraca and Alfonso Raimúndez continued, with the latter persevering in the governance of an appanage based on Toledo—*apud Toletum imperante,* his own words.[57] Relations between mother and son were sometimes strained, but there were no further instances of *magna discordia.* The two sometimes issued charters jointly, and we find the son subscribing his mother's charters. They could take vigorous joint action, as when they turned upon Diego in 1124 for attempting to interfere in the affairs of the church of Toledo after the death of archbishop Bernardo.[58] If Alfonso Raimúndez was more active, especially from 1124 onwards, in granting charters in favour of Galician beneficiaries, this may reflect —in so far as it reflects anything beyond the accident of documentary survival—simply a tactful willingness on the part of the queen to allow her son a larger share of their joint authority.[59] In short, Alfonso Raimúndez never did become a 'king of Galicia' during his mother's reign: to that degree Pedro Froílaz had failed.

[54] *HC*, pp. 382-5, 388-9.

[55] *HC*, pp. 389-94. We do not know when Pedro Froílaz and his relatives were released from captivity, but they were evidently at liberty in 1124: *HC*, p. 414. I cannot agree with Professor Reilly (*Urraca*, pp. 191-2, 310, 361) that the count remained a prisoner until the queen's death in 1126.

[56] R. 18 May 1123; *HC*, p. 387.

[57] R. 6 April 1124, and the testimony of several private charters, e.g. *Sobrado Cart.* II, no. 342 (9 March 1125).

[58] R. 10 May 1125, 21 July 1125; *HC*, pp. 396, 420, 421-2.

[59] e.g. R. 8 April 1124, 31 May 1124, 1 June 1125.

Had Diego failed too? Any answer to this question will presuppose that we know what he was trying to do; and any interpretation of his actions has to be based on information provided by the *Historia Compostellana*. The *Historia* is a very full record, but for our purposes it is not full enough. We know enough of Diego's part in the politics of Urraca's reign to be certain that both those politics and the part he played in them were exceedingly complicated. The only honest course is to admit that we do not and never shall know enough to enable us satisfactorily to elucidate them.[60] There are many features of the *Historia* which render it a difficult witness to interpret. Perhaps the most trying of all is the very uniqueness of its testimony. The case may be put thus: suppose that we had a *Historia Toletana* commissioned by Bernardo of Toledo, or a *Historia Ovetensis* commissioned by Pelayo of Oviedo, would the story told by these hypothetical works have differed *in kind* from the narration of the *Compostellana*? Very probably not. To put this in a different way, the first step towards an understanding of Diego's actions may be to isolate what he had in common with his episcopal colleagues during the reign of queen Urraca.

An appreciation of queen Urraca's government must take as its starting-point the fact that she was throughout her reign short of cash. The cutting-off of the supply of *parias* in the last decade of the eleventh century had induced a state of what a distinguished Spanish historian has called 'endemic fiscal crisis' in the public finance of the kingdom of León-Castile.[61] It seems clear that Alfonso VI had rashly grasped at the easy remedy for needy rulers—debasement of the coinage.[62] Inflation necessarily followed: we are told that soldiers needed higher wages during Urraca's reign.[63] But

---

[60] My only general misgiving about Professor Reilly's otherwise excellent study of queen Urraca's reign is that he is to my mind a little too confident that the charters of the period can be made to yield a coherent political story. I find the example of king Stephen's reign a chastening one: although it is incomparably better served by the sources than Urraca's reign, there is still much that remains mysterious about the history of the period 1135-54 in England.

[61] C. Sánchez Albornoz, *Estudios sobre las instituciones medievales españolas* (Mexico City, 1965), p. 486. [62] *HC*, p. 74.

[63] *HC*, p. 175. Already count Raymond had found it hard to pay his troops: *HC*, p. 61.

she was a ruler who had great need of soldiers for the defence
of her frontiers, be it against the Almoravides or the Aragonese. Beset by such necessities, whither could she turn for
the money she so desperately needed? She did what any of
her contemporary rulers, similarly circumstanced, were
accustomed to do——an Alexius Comnenus, a Henry IV,
a William Rufus. In the words of the *Historia Compostellana*,
'she stripped the churches throughout her kingdom of their
gold and silver and their treasures'.[64] There is abundant
evidence to support this assertion. Diego Gelmírez, like his
fellow bishops and abbots, was concerned to protect the
endowments of his see against royal depredation. Viewed
from this angle, Diego's achievement was not a meagre one,
though it was hard-bought.

Bishops, however, were more than just the harassed
custodians of ecclesiastical endowments. Urraca's reign was
notable for the number of assemblies which were held in
the kingdom of León-Castile at which the principal focus
of concern was the restoration of peace and order. These
gatherings were convened on royal, episcopal or papal initiative, and they were attended largely, though rarely exclusively, by ecclesiastics. It is of great interest to discover
that at one of them, held at Compostela and presided over
by Diego, 'the peace of God which is observed among the
Romans and the Franks and other nations of the faithful'
was proclaimed.[65] These western Spanish councils of the
early twelfth century were occasioned by the same sort of
pressures as we can detect behind the peace-councils of
eleventh-century Francia and the Spanish March.[66] How
effective the decrees and menaces of the bishops were we
cannot be sure. But that the councils were held at all is
a sign that the higher clergy were taking their collective
responsibilities seriously. Diego was prominent among those
who shouldered the burden.

[64] *HC*, p. 367.　　　　　　　　　　　　　　　[65] *HC*, p. 418.
[66] H. Hoffmann, *Gottesfriede und Treuga Dei* (Stuttgart, 1964); H. E. J.
Cowdrey, 'The Peace and the Truce of God in the eleventh century', *Past and
Present* 46 (1970), 42–67. Much material related to this theme is also to be found
in the very acute study of T. N. Bisson, *Conservation of coinage. Monetary
exploitation and its restraint in France, Catalonia, and Aragon* (c. *A.D. 1000-
c.1225*) (Oxford, 1979).

Any assessment, however, of Diego as 'a bishop in politics' during Urraca's reign will need also to take account of what he did not have in common with his colleagues. He was a native of Galicia, bishop of a Galician see, minister to the shrine of an apostle who was in some eyes the special shepherd of the people of Galicia.[67] Contemplating his actions during Urraca's reign the historian will find it impossible to believe that for much of the time his conduct was not to some degree shaped by pressures which may loosely be described as local. So much we may sense from the record of the *Historia*; to substantiate it is a different matter.

Diego's first local loyalty was to the shrine and church of St. James. It overrode all others.[68] During the reign of queen Urraca he planned, negotiated and finally achieved the raising of the see of Santiago de Compostela from episcopal to archiepiscopal status. This was the greatest triumph of his life. It will be more fittingly examined in a discussion of his relations with the papacy: but it is important to state here that there was an intimate connection between his public conduct in the affairs of Spain during Urraca's reign and the progress of his ecclesiastical ambitions. This relationship has been very fully explored by Dr Ludwig Vones, and it is sufficient for the present to refer the reader to his work.[69]

A second source of local pressure was represented by the Traba family. The alliance between Diego Gelmírez and count Pedro Froílaz forged in the years 1110 and 1111 endured fairly consistently for the remainder of Urraca's reign; though it had its shaky moments (1114, 1116, 1120, 1123). This is not surprising, for their common interests were manifold. They shared a responsibility for the rights of Alfonso Raimúndez, imposed upon them in the most public fashion by a king whom they had every reason to revere at the council of León in 1107. Of course, they

[67] A theme enunciated several times in the so-called *Codex Calixtinus*.

[68] Cf. the characteristically penetrating comments of R. W. Southern, *Saint Anselm and his biographer* (Cambridge, 1963), p. 128: 'To speak of these loyalties as "local" immediately gives the impression that they were rather trivial: it would be a better definition of their character to say that they were personal and sacred.'

[69] Vones, *Kirchenpolitik, passim*, but especially ch. IV.

might differ as to how this responsibility should most fittingly be discharged. The count—at least as his conduct is portrayed in the *Historia*—was more willing than Diego to take political initiatives detrimental to the interests of the queen. As a corollary, it may be that Alfonso Raimúndez came to suspect that Diego was lukewarm in his cause—a theme to which we shall return in a later chapter. But the common ground between count and bishop was too solid for these issues of ways and means to be really divisive. Another area of shared concern probably had as its focus the relationship between Galicia and the remainder of the kingdom of León-Castile. To claim that Pedro Froílaz was a 'Galician separatist' is, as has already been said, anachronistic. The political turbulence in the affairs of Galicia between 1109 and 1126 —which we may in any case tend to exaggerate because we know so little of the other provinces of the kingdom— was of a less dangerous order than the rebellions of the eleventh century which were glanced at in an earlier chapter. Pedro Froílaz was not like count Rodrigo Ovéquiz: he had done too well out of the new dispensation; he had too much to lose. Neither was Diego Gelmírez like Diego Peláez. The political issue in Urraca's reign was not secession but control. Nevertheless, given the fissile nature of the kingdom of León-Castile; given the pressure on the frontier, which brought fissile tendencies into the open; given the government's demands for money, necessitated by defence of the exposed frontiers: given these things, it is not surprising that resentments should have festered. So far as we know, Pedro Froílaz never took part in the warfare on the southern frontier during Urraca's reign (except possibly in 1116). Diego's quarrel with the queen at Burgos in 1113 over his obligation to perform military service is suggestive. What had Galicia to do with the defence of eastern Castile against the Aragonese? What, indeed, did Galicia have to do with the defence of the Tagus frontier against the Almoravides?

Further common ground between Diego and count Pedro may have been defined by their dealings with other prominent Galician laymen. These dealings are extremely difficult to elucidate. It is not simply that the *Historia Compostellana* is partisan. Its record for much of Urraca's reign was composed by Gerald of Beauvais, an immigrant from northern France. He had a low opinion of Galicians and little interest in or understanding of the network of local families round Compostela; their landholdings, their connections by neighbourhood and marriage, the offices they held, the patrons they looked to, their resentments, their rivalries and their feuds. In trying to peer behind the *Historia* we are thrown back on the evidence of the charters, scant in number and resistant to easy interpretation. Furthermore, our concern is with men of a rather lower social rank than, say, the members of the Traba family; and these people are elusive. They are as elusive as Diego's own family. But that is precisely why an effort must be made to get at them.

Let us start with Arias Pérez, the most prominent among Diego's opponents (at least until 1121) and the one about whom the *Historia* has most to tell us. Indeed, he is the only one of whose character we can form some impression. Arias Pérez was active, resourceful, spirited and persuasive: 'he was so eloquent that he could turn black into white and white into black'. He was not a member of the higher ranks of the aristocracy (*non fuit tamen magnae nobilitatis*).[70] His father, Pedro Arias, could be described and could describe himself as a knight (*miles*)—like Diego's father Gelmirio.[71] Of the little that we know about the father, two things are significant. The first is that he granted his share (*portionem*) in an estate at *Villa nova* to the church of Compostela. Villanueva is a common enough place-name in Galicia, as in the rest of Spain, but it is likely that the one in question is the Villanueva in the district of Deza only a few miles to the south-east of Compostela.[72] The second is that in 1096 Pedro Arias had subscribed a charter of count Raymond in favour of the monastery of Carboeiro, which is also in Deza.[73] These items enable us to link him to a man named Luzo Arias. Although it is impossible to be sure of this, it is very probable that Luzo and Pedro Arias were

---

[70] *HC*, p. 475.

[71] He subscribed himself *miles de Deza* in a charter of 1115: *LFH* III, ap. xxxiii, at p. 102.

[72] *HC*, p. 189: for the place-name, see *Historia Compostelana, o sea Hechos de D. Diego Gelmírez*, trans. M. Suárez, ed. J. Campelo (Santiago de Compostela, 1950), p. 185, n. 2.   [73] R. 11 January 1096.

brothers.[74] Now Luzo (presumably from Lucius) was a most
unusual name in Galicia; with its aid we may trace the family
a little further. Arias Luzu, I would suggest, was the father
of Luzo and Pedro Arias. He subscribed royal charters in 1066,
1071 and 1075—the last of them a grant to Carboeiro.[75]
Furthermore he witnessed, possibly conducted, the survey
of an estate at Pastoriza, in the parish of Brandariz, also
in Deza, in 1062.[76] Pastoriza came into the possession of
Carboeiro by the grant, already referred to, of 1096. Still
using the evidence of the rare name Luzo, I would hazard
the guess that a man named Leovigild Luz mentioned in the
Historia Compostellana was the son of Luzo Arias and the
grandson of Arias Luzu.[77] A genealogical tree will make these
suggestions clearer. Pedro Arias, Arias Pérez and Leovigild
Luz were all conspirators against Diego Gelmírez in 1110.

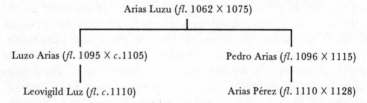

Arias Luzu (*fl.* 1062 × 1075)

Luzo Arias (*fl.* 1095 × *c.*1105)   Pedro Arias (*fl.* 1096 × 1115)

Leovigild Luz (*fl. c.*1110)   Arias Pérez (*fl.* 1110 × 1128)

We know a little more about Luzo Arias. He held office
—like Diego—under count Raymond. By the year 1095
possibly, by 1101 certainly, he was *villicus terrae* in—of all
places—Deza.[78] This enables us to make a further connection. It was to Luzo Arias, as *villicus* of Deza, that a man
named Alfonso Ramírez turned for assistance in the course
of a lawsuit against the church of Santiago de Compostela
at some point in the early years of the twelfth century.
The *Historia* describes him contemptuously as a *corbulo*,
a rather unusual word meaning 'a porter'.[79] But Alfonso
Ramírez was no menial: together with Arias Luzu he had

---

[74] The evidence is as follows: (1) they shared a patronymic; (2) Luzo Arias
gave land at Villanueva in Deza to the church of Compostela: *HC*, pp. 70-1
(where note that he is described as coming from the ranks of the *milites* as
opposed to the *consules* and *comites*); (3) he and Pedro Arias subscribed next
to one another in the Carboeiro charter of 1096 (also in R. 24 October 1102).

[75] R. 25 June 1066, 31 July 1071 (a doubtful charter) and December 1075.

[76] *Carboeiro Cart.*, no. xxiv.   [77] *HC*, p. 105.

[78] *HC*, p. 62; R. 24 September 1095, 1 April 1101.   [79] *HC*, p. 62.

subscribed the royal charter for Carboeiro in 1075. His
claim concerned the church of Sta Eulalia de Losón, a mere
three miles or so from Carboeiro; we shall return to it presently. It is possible that Juan Ramírez was the brother
of Alfonso Ramírez. This Juan Ramírez was another who
held office under count Raymond. He was described as
a *merino* in 1095; in 1101 he subscribed a charter as *villicus*
of the district of Salnés, on the south side of the Ría de
Arosa.[80] In five charters, including the grant to Carboeiro
in 1096, he subscribed alongside either Luzo Arias or Pedro
Arias or both.[81] He subscribed a further nine royal charters
between 1105 and 1123. Our only other piece of information about him is of great interest: he was one of the conspirators (alongside Arias Pérez) who arrested Diego on the
queen's orders in 1121.[82]

In the light of Juan Ramírez's connections with Salnés
as well as with Deza it is of interest to note that Luzo Arias,
whose interest Alfonso Ramírez had sought in the Losón
lawsuit, was married to a wife, Mayor, who possessed land
in Salnés.[83] Now their nephew Arias Pérez also had interests
in Salnés. An estate which he granted to the church of
Compostela at some unknown date may have lain in Salnés.[84]
Throughout Urraca's reign he showed himself particularly
eager to acquire lands and castles in Salnés.[85] And when
Diego finally managed to nobble him at the funeral of the
countess of Traba in 1128 it was a church (*monasterium*)
in Salnés, at Arcos da Condesa, that he promised to give
to Santiago.[86]

Now both Deza and Salnés were areas containing landed
endowments of the church of Santiago de Compostela; in
other words, sensitive areas. The church of Sta Eulalia de
Losón claimed by Alfonso Ramírez was said by his Compostelan opponents to belong to the endowments of the

[80] R. 11 February 1095, 1 April 1101.
[81] R. 24 September 1095, 11 January 1096, 28 March 1098, 1 April 1101,
24 October 1102.
[82] *HC*, p. 329.   [83] *HC*, p. 70.
[84] *HC*, p. 188 (though there are difficulties about this identification).
[85] *HC*, pp. 109, 131, 313, 335, 382, 443 (Lobeira); 108 (Lanzada and Torres
del Oeste). The first of these was a royal castle, the others belonged to the *honor*
of Santiago. We should bear in mind that Gelmirio, Diego's father, had been
castellan of Torres del Oeste.   [86] *HC*, p. 476.

monasterium of Piloño. Piloño in its turn had been owned
by Alfonso VI and his sister Doña Elvira; they had inherited
it from their father Fernando I. (We should very much like
to know how he had got hold of it.) Elvira had granted her
share of it to Compostela in 1087, Alfonso VI had granted
his share thirteen years later.[87] Diego's anxiety to keep hold
of it is indicated by the fact that it was named in a papal
privilege confirming the possessions of his church in 1110.[88]
As for Losón, Urraca confirmed Compostelan possession
of it ten years later.[89] Another *monasterium* near Piloño,
though a lesser one, at Brandariz, had come into the possession of Compostela in the same way. We have already seen
that Pastoriza, in the parish of Brandariz, in which Arias
Pérez's family seems to have had some interest, was granted
to the monastery of Carboeiro in 1096. How intriguing—
and how tantalizing—to find that Urraca later gave some
land there to the church of Santiago.[90] Much more might be
said about Deza. Here is one last scrap of information which
provides food for thought. Urraca's attack on the three
brothers Bodán in 1113, referred to earlier in this chapter,
occurred at a time when we are told that Arias Pérez was
stirring up trouble for Diego at the royal court: and they
came from Deza; their family *monasterium*, granted to
Compostela, was probably at Bodaño.

Similar sorts of dispute over the possessions of the church
of Santiago can be discerned in the district of Salnés. Early
in his epicopate Diego was busying himself with the enforce-
ment of Compostelan claims there. Cordeiro, for example,
had been granted to Santiago in 1028. It was alienated by
Pedro Vimara, the official who administered the *honor*
after the deposition of bishop Diego Peláez. Diego seems to
have recovered it later on, for we next hear that he had
entrusted it as a fief (*praestimonium*) to Pedro Garcés. He

---

[87] R. 25 April 1087, 16 January 1100, 13 November 1100. The church was
evidently a rich and important one: it is mentioned in a tenth-century charter
(R. 24 May 991), and Doña Elvira's charter of 1087 makes clear that Piloño
had given its name to an administrative *territorium*.

[88] *HC*, pp. 85-6 (= JL 6264). Dr Vones believes that the text of this privilege
has been tampered with: if this were so (and I am not convinced that it is so)
the present argument would only be reinforced.

[89] R. 13 June 1120.   [90] *HC*, p. 125.

later deprived Pedro of it.[91] Gogilde was another estate recovered after alienation. At some point before 1107 Diego rescued it from lay hands, and the nearby church 'from the thirsty covetousness of knights' (*a sitibunda militum cupiditate*).[92] He was also active in acquiring new endowments in Salnés by gift, purchase and exchange.[93]

It was not only landed wealth which made Salnés valuable to the church of Compostela. The Ría de Arosa is a fine anchorage. We hear of a Norman ship blown off course by storms which put in there for shelter.[94] Doubtless there were many others like it. When king Sigurd the Jerusalem-Farer of Norway wintered in 'the land of Jacob' in 1108-9 it is very likely that his sixty ships were beached beside the Ría de Arosa.[95] The river Ulla which flows into the Ría and its tributary the Sar are navigable as far as Padrón, the port for Santiago de Compostela. Pilgrims coming by sea would arrive there, and so would merchants. On their way up to Padrón they would pass Diego's castle at Torres del Oeste. There the Ría is only a bowshot wide and shipping may easily be controlled; there tolls were levied.[96] These were probably a very valuable asset to Diego. The English and Lotharingian merchants who were waylaid between Padrón and Compostela in about 1130 were robbed of goods valued at 22,000 marks.[97]

Salnés, then, like Deza, was important to the church of Compostela. It is little wonder that Diego had enemies there. In 1114, it was while in Salnés that queen Urraca plotted to capture Diego and sought collaborators. In 1123 it was Diego's disinherited vassal Pedro Garcés who conspired to murder him.[98]

The landholders and officials in Salnés and Deza and elsewhere were men of much the same social rank as Diego. Their early lives and expectations must have been very similar. Luzo Arias, Juan Ramírez and Pedro Vimara look like much the same sort of man as Diego's father Gelmirio.

[91] R. 15 November 1028, 30 December 1028; *HC*, pp. 18, 393.
[92] *HC*, p. 59.   [93] *HC*, pp. 70, 72, 174.   [94] *HC*, p. 291.
[95] *Heimskringla*, trans. E. Monsen and A. H. Smith (Cambridge, 1932), p. 607.
[96] AHN 1749/21.   [97] *HC*, pp. 505-6.
[98] *HC*, pp. 194, 389-94.

Diego and Arias Pérez had known one another from child-hood.[99] Some of the resentments felt against Diego are likely to have arisen from uncomplicated feelings of jealousy springing from the fact that, in that competitive society, he had done so well for himself. It is interesting that Arias Pérez's hostility to both Diego and Pedro Froílaz was allayed by marriage to the count's daughter Ildaria, probably in about 1121-2.[1] It must have cost the old count some pain; he had been accustomed to dispose of his girls to husbands of altogether more exalted rank. But desperate times exacted desperate courses.

The going has been somewhat hard over the last few pages, but I make no apology for that. It might be thought that the end of a chapter devoted to the relations between Diego Gelmírez and queen Urraca would be a fitting place for some rousing words on 'the conflict between church and state' in 'the age of Hildebrandine reform'. Not so. What we can sense, if neither fully comprehend nor satisfactorily demonstrate, is a scene which was in some respects homelier than such phrases imply, but none the less fractious for that: and at this I have tried to hint. Diego moved in a very exalted world peopled by kings and queens, popes and cardinals, dukes and counts. But the world from which he came was narrow. The Galician squirearchy was a force to be reckoned with. It contained some stubborn and tenacious men, with long memories and few scruples. The politics of Galicia were charged by rivalries between families, between neigh-bours, between contestants for lands and offices. We shall encounter these rivalries again in the next chapter.

---

[99] *HC*, p. 107.   [1] *HC*, pp. 389, 475-6.

VII

The cathedral community

Although this was not formally confirmed until 1095, the seat of the bishop had been transferred from Iria to Compostela at some point in the first half of the tenth century. However, it is clear that there had been some sort of religious community at the shrine of St. James under the authority of the bishop from a much earlier date—possibly from the time of bishop Theodemir himself. From the latter part of the ninth century—and presumably the initiative for this was bishop Sisnando I's—this community seems to have been a monastic one. A series of charters from 885 until the late 920s consists of grants made 'for the maintenance of the monks serving God there' (*pro victu et vestitu monachorum Dei deserviencium*), or similar phrases.[1] The community numbered at least twenty-eight persons in the year 898.[2] We do not know which rule they followed, though we may be reasonably confident that it was not the Benedictine. At some point in the tenth century the community seems to have reverted to a secular life, for we find its members referred to neutrally as 'servants of God' (*servi Dei*) or simply 'clergy' (*clerici*).[3] Although no less than three monks occupied the see during this period—Rosendo (968-74?), Pelayo Rodríguez (977-85?) and Pedro de Mesonzo (985-1003)—we have no reason to believe that any of them tried to revive the regular religious life at Compostela. In addition to the disappearance of monastic life, numbers sharply declined. We are told that there were only seven canons to serve the basilica of St. James during the episcopate of Cresconio (c.1035-66). Diego Peláez attempted to increase the number to twenty-four: but these men were, in the words of one of Diego Gelmírez's

---

[1] Quoted from R. 20 April 911.
[2] *LFH* II, ap. xxiii, pp. 42-3.
[3] e.g. R. 21 May 958, 1 June 986.

henchmen, 'utterly ignorant of the ecclesiastical office' (*ecclesiastici officii penitus ignaros*)—which may simply mean that it was very difficult in Galicia in the 1070s to find clergy who were acquainted with the Roman liturgy.[4]

In attempting to assess the state of the cathedral chapter (as we may now call it) when Diego Gelmírez became bishop, we are dependent very nearly exclusively on the *Historia Compostellana*. We should remind ourselves yet again that this is a partisan compilation. It presents the views of the reformers and it was designed to extol the achievements of Diego Gelmírez. It is not likely that its authors under-estimated the shortcomings of the unreformed chapter. Due allowance being made for this, it yet remains clear that three different kinds of shortcoming existed.[5] In the first place, the economic arrangements for the support of the chapter were haphazard. Its members evidently possessed certain revenues in common, for we hear of a refectory where, in theory, a common meal was provided. But these shared revenues were insufficient; they scarcely sufficed for six months of the year. In consequence we are told, some of the clergy 'had departed from their church', which is presumably to be interpreted as meaning that there was a fair amount of non-residence. Furthermore, individual canons had to look to their own private incomes to provide for themselves what the common revenues could not. The *Historia* tells us, doubtless with some exaggeration, that because there were inequalities of wealth some canons starved while others lived off the fat of the land. Hence, perhaps, the jealousies and tensions of which we hear, some even erupting into bloodshed. Secondly, the manner of life of the chapter was unseemly. The hints at violence apart, it is not of the grosser vices that we hear. It was simply that the canons lived as such men should not (*minus canonice*), in a fashion that ill-befitted the guardians of the shrine of St. James, the corporation in whose trusteeship reposed one of the great churches of Christendom. They were dirty and unshaven; they dressed like laymen of the knightly classes, affecting the fashionable shoes with long pointed

[4] *HC*, p. 544.
[5] For what follows, see *HC*, pp. 54-7, 144, 243, 255-6, 543-4.

toes which attracted the denunciations of ecclesiastical moralists in other parts of Europe about this time; their vestments, if they bothered to wear them at all, were too various to please men of reforming temper who wanted to see the clergy in uniform. Thirdly, the canons were intellectually undistinguished. Cathedral schools of this period were notoriously volatile: the presence of a gifted teacher could bring a school celebrity almost overnight, his departure or death effectively close it down. Diego evidently judged that the quality of the education to be had in Compostela had deteriorated since the days when he and bishop Pelayo of León had received their grounding there. It is difficult to test his judgement. The *Cronicon Iriense*, which was composed about 1090 by an author who may well have been a member of the chapter, is not the work of an ill-educated man. Perhaps Diego's main anxiety was that such learning as was to be had at Compostela was out of date. We have already seen that this was his view of the learning available in the field of canon law.[6]

There is nothing surprising about these shortcomings. We meet complaints about them frequently in the polemical literature of the day. In this connection as in others it is useful to see Diego's activities against the wider backdrop of similar episcopal concern in other parts of western Christendom. It was not that the Compostela chapter of the 1090s was composed of mountebanks whose manner of life gave cause for scandal; just as the married members of the chapter at, say, Bayeux were not reckless debauchees (a comparison which reminds us that no accusations of sexual irregularity were brought against the canons of Compostela). The rhetoric of reformers is often—and is often meant to be— misleading. The ladies of the close at Bayeux and elsewhere were as respectable as those of Barchester, but that did not prevent the zealots from referring to them crudely as 'tarts' (*meretrices*). This is why it is so hard to see exactly what it was that the reformers wanted to do away with; too often we have only a caricature. The canons of Compostela were probably an easy-going lot; a bit seedy and shabby

---

[6] See above, ch. V, and below, appendix D. The *Cronicon Iriense* has been edited by M. R. García Alvarez, *Memorial Histórico Español*, 50 (1963), 1-240.

and down-at-heel; out of the swim of things; set in their old-fashioned ways; and, as was suggested in an earlier chapter, perhaps feeling rather sorry for themselves in the 1090s. Diego wanted to smarten them up, make them distinctive, give them *esprit de corps*—in short to make something of them. He did.

'He ploughed his clergy with the share of discipline.' In these words did one of his admirers, who had himself experienced them, characterize Diego's reforms. His impact on the cathedral community was immediate and far-reaching, for the principal reforms had been completed by the spring of 1102, and they endured (with some modifications) until well beyond his own day. He vastly enlarged the size of the chapter by regrouping absentees and recruiting new members 'from various places' until he had established a body of seventy-two canons. (This number was of course suggested by the seventy-two disciples of the Lord.) This was a prodigious size, and it is some indication, however vague, of the wealth of the see of Compostela that it could afford to support so many. Toledo's chapter was only thirty strong in the 1130s, and even the big cathedral chapters of northern France and England did not approach the size of Santiago; Lincoln had forty-two prebendaries in the early twelfth century, and Rouen probably under fifty. To support his new chapter Diego overhauled the existing economic arrangements. He took steps to ensure that the canons 'should not lack for food throughout the year', tells the *Historia*. Precisely what these steps were is not quite clear, but the words used in another context, by a different author of the *Historia*, imply that Diego divided the endowments of the see between bishop and chapter.[7] We are also told that he prevented 'the usual bickering' (*consuetum schisma*) by ensuring equal shares for all the canons: this suggests the creation of individual prebends of roughly equal value.[8] The final measure attributable to the

[7] Compare *HC*, p. 55 (Pedro Anáyaz) with p. 544 (Gerald of Beauvais); but note that R. 16 January 1100 implies some division *before* Diego's episcopate. For the practice elsewhere in western Spain see *Episcopate*, pp. 148–9.

[8] *HC*, p. 256. Arrangements for sharing the offerings made at the altar of St. James are explained in *LSJ*, pp. 387–8.

years 1100-2 was his rebuilding of the canons' refectory. At the same time as the economy of the cathedral community was put on a sounder footing, Diego reformed the manner of life of the canons. In the face of opposition he insisted upon stricter rules of dress: the canons were no longer to enter the choir unless decently clad in surplices. He also made provision to better their learning. He hired a master to teach rhetoric (*magister de doctrina eloquentiae*), who taught 'us', says Pedro Anáyaz, by which he presumably meant those who were already canons in 1100. (We should much like to know where Diego found him and who he was.) The newly appointed canons were said to be 'learned in the study of letters' and 'skilled in the church's liturgy'.[9]

The capitular reforms were comprehensive and thorough, their rapid completion a tribute to Diego's energetic will and administrative talents. They would seem to have been completed to his own satisfaction by 22 April 1102, on which day he took an oath of loyalty from each member of the chapter. (The document recording the text of the oath and the names of the canons was later incorporated into the *Historia Compostellana*.[10]) One of the authors of the *Historia*, the Frenchman Gerald, commented later that Diego tried to implant 'the customs of the churches of France' at Compostela.[11] To an extent this observation was true of his capitular reforms. The broad lines of the economic organization which sustained the community— division of temporalities, individual prebends for the canons —was of French derivation. Earlier cathedral organization in Spain is a very dark matter, but it does seem to have involved certain elements of a common life, characteristic of a regular as opposed to a secular capitular framework.

---

[9] *HC*, pp. 55, 544; cf. the reference in *LSJ*, p. 379 to the door *de gramaticorum scola* on the north side of the cathedral. See also R. Wright, *Late Latin and Early Romance in Spain and Carolingian France* (Liverpool, 1982), pp. 220-7, for the educational changes at Compostela: the implications of the argument, here and elsewhere in this important study, are far-reaching. In the light of Dr Wright's work it might be more appropriate to translate *eloquentia* in this context as 'pronunciation' or 'elocution', than as 'rhetoric'.

[10] *HC*, pp. 56-7: for the correct date see the earliest extant manuscript of the *Historia*, Salamanca, Biblioteca de la Universidad, MS 2658, fo. 24^r.

[11] *HC*, p. 255.

Thus, for instance, the council of Compostela of 1056 had
stipulated that cathedral chapters should have a single
refectory and a single dormitory.[12] These usages did not
entirely disappear in the wake of Diego's reforms. We have
already seen that he rebuilt the canons' refectory. That
there was also a dormitory is revealed by the *Historia*'s
account of Diego's movements when he was in danger of
his life during the disturbances of 1117: he avoided the mob
by a moonlight escape over the roof-tops into the canons'
dormitory. On the other hand, it is clear that many of the
canons had dwellings in the town: Pedro Anáyaz, for
example, lived on the north side of the cathedral next to
the monastery of San Martín Pinario.[13] So the capitular
organization was a hybrid, owing something to Spanish
tradition and something to foreign example. This puzzled
outside observers. It may account for the curious statement
by the French author of the guidebook for pilgrims that the
canons of Compostela observed the 'Rule of St. Isidore'.[14]
Isidore composed no rule for canons but he was the fountain-
head of Spanish Christian tradition, and the writer may have
used the word *regula* in the loose sense of 'customs', rather
than 'rule' strictly so called. At all events, this hybrid form
was the product of deliberate, not of muddled thinking;
for it was reproduced at some of the newly established
cathedrals in the province of Santiago during the twelfth
century, for example at Avila and Salamanca.

Another French feature of the Compostela chapter was
the new nomenclature used to describe the cathedral digni-
taries. The head of the chapter had traditionally been entitled
abbas. This title may have come down from the time of
bishop Sisnando I when the monks who composed the community were indeed headed by an abbot—by abbot Spano-
sindo in 898, for example—though the word was widely
used in western Christendom in the early middle ages to
denote an ecclesiastic who was not necessarily the head of
a monastic community. The last of the line of *abbates* was
Gundesindo, first traceable as such in 1087, last so styled

[12] For this council, see G. Martínez Díez, 'El concilio compostelano del
reinado de Fernando I', *Anuario de Estudios Medievales* 1 (1964), 121-38.
[13] *HC*, pp. 243, 370.   [14] *LSJ*, p. 387.

at the time of the oath-takings of 1102. Five years later, in 1107, he was referred to as *prior canonice*, 'prior of the chapter'.[15] This style, an importation from southern France, was generally used for the next dozen years or so to describe the head of the chapter. Gundesindo was succeeded by Pedro, the bishop's nephew, in about 1111. He too normally referred to himself, in his subscriptions to charters, as *prior canonice*.[16] However, Gerald of Beauvais referred to him in the *Historia*, when recounting certain events of 1121, by a new title, also derived from France: *decanus*, 'dean'.[17] He in his turn was succeeded shortly after this by another Pedro—Pedro Helias, later archbishop (1143-49)—who regularly used the new title.[18] The head of the chapter was always thereafter styled dean. Likewise the title *primiclerus* or *primicerius* was replaced by its French equivalent *cantor*, 'precentor'. The last of a long line of *primicleri* was Pedro Gundesíndez, who held office from *c*.1119 until *c*.1136. His successor Pelayo styled himself *cantor* in an inscription recorded by López Ferreiro.[19] *Thesaurarius*, 'treasurer', started to replace the traditional Spanish term *sacrista* at an earlier date, before Diego's episcopate: Segeredo *tesaurarius* subscribed a charter of 1087.[20] The fourth cathedral dignitary was the *magister scolarum*, another title borrowed from southern France, traceable from *c*.1118.[21] (Despite the fact that the first holder of this dignity was a native of Beauvais, the northern French equivalent title, 'chancellor', never found favour at Compostela.)

Not all Diego's capitular innovations had a French ancestry. The institution of cardinals at Santiago de Compostela was modelled on Roman practice.[22] In seeking this distinction for certain members of his chapter Diego was following, wittingly or not, the example set by some of the more

---

[15] R. 30 May 1087, 14 May 1107.
[16] e.g. *LFH* III, ap. xxxiii, p. 102; R. 31 March 1116.
[17] *HC*, p. 346.　　　　[18] e.g. in his subscription to R. 18 March 1131.
[19] *LFH* IV, p. 171.　　　　[20] R. 30 May 1087.
[21] Gerald of Beauvais described himself as *didascalus* at *HC*, p. 265, elsewhere as *magister scolarum*.
[22] For what follows, see *HC*, pp. 33-4, 93-4 (= JL 5881, 6042, 6208); *LSJ*, p. 386; S. Kuttner, 'Cardinalis: the history of a canonical concept', *Traditio* 3 (1945), 129-215.

distinguished churches of Germany. By special papal concession, cardinals 'after the fashion of the church of Rome'
were instituted at, among other places, Aachen (in 997)
and Cologne (in 1052). By a papal bull which in the form
in which we have it is undated, but appears to come from
soon after Diego's consecration in 1101, Paschal II allowed
Diego to create cardinals at Compostela. The surprisingly
vague terms of the concession were clarified a few years
later. There were to be never more nor less than seven cardinals (as at Cologne); on solemn feast-days they were to
be permitted to wear mitres adorned with gems, like the
cardinals of the Roman church; and the only persons to be
allowed to say mass at the altar of St. James were they,
together with bishops and papal legates. This was a notable
addition to the dignity of Diego's chapter. It was only one
of several ways in which Diego tried to make the church of
Compostela look 'Roman'.

At all times during Diego's long tenure of the see, the
chapter of Compostela contained what might be called
'honorary' members. Three of Diego's episcopal colleagues
were numbered among the canons in 1102, the archbishop
of Braga and the bishops of Tuy and Orense. Two later
archbishops of Braga, Maurice and Paio, held canonries at
Compostela. A visiting papal legate, cardinal Deusdedit,
was enrolled among the canons in 1119; in 1127, no less
a person than king Alfonso VII.[23] But the great majority
of the seventy-two must always have been 'working' canons.
Their primary task was to carry out the elaborate liturgical
and ceremonial duties associated with the worship of God
and the cult of St. James. (Because our sources tend to
take this orderly routine for granted, so do we. It is only
the interruptions to routine that get remembered: as for
instance in 1110 when an Italian knight proved his exceptional devotion by riding his charger, 'than which I hold
nothing more precious', right into the cathedral to present
himself and his horse to St. James.[24]) But we must always
try to remember that the life of the community was dominated by the rhythms and demands of an annually recurrent

[23] *HC*, pp. 57, 145, 268, 340, 458.   [24] *LSJ*, pp. 275-6.

devotional cycle. Secondly, there was a network of administrative business to attend to. The bishop's assistants in the running of the diocese, notably the archdeacons, were all members of the chapter. Temporalities had to be administered. The building programme had to be supervised. Arrangements had to be made for the reception of pilgrims. The courts through which the bishop's lordship of the town was exercised had to be staffed. Finally, there was service of a more specialized type to the bishop. During this period there was still no sharp distinction between cathedral and episcopal establishments. The men who transacted business on the bishop's behalf were normally members of the chapter. They could rise to great heights in his service.

Several members of the Compostela chapter became bishops: to name only a few, Nuño Alfonso was promoted to the see of Mondoñedo in 1112, Hugo to that of Porto in 1113, Alfonso Pérez to Salamanca in 1130 and Pedro Anáyaz to León in 1135. For reasons that will become clear in due course, service to Diego could lead to service in the royal chancery; and we shall meet, among others, Bernardo, treasurer of Compostela, chancellor to Alfonso VII between 1127 and 1131. Other canons were employed as Diego's agents for negotiating delicate pieces of business. Geoffrey, canon and archdeacon, was but one of several members of the chapter who visited the papal curia for Diego more than once, in 1101, 1107 (?) and 1109–10; he also accompanied Diego thither in 1104. It is purely by chance that we hear of two canons who spent some time in Apulia and Sicily in the early 1120s to raise funds for the building operations at Compostela. When in 1130 Diego wanted to secure a grant of olive groves near Talavera from Alfonso VII, it was one of his canons who was sent to conduct the negotiations at the royal court.[25]

Diego could thus make available to the members of his chapter—at least to those among it who were the recipients of his patronage—a wide range of opportunities. They were evidently not slow to grasp them. The rewards—in terms of responsibility, command, patronage, access to the great, and

[25] For these examples see *HC*, pp. 31, 44, 79, 84–5, 401, 499.

so forth—accessible to a bishop or a royal chancellor are obvious enough. But the crude material rewards available to the canons of Compostela should not be underestimated. There were, for example, other plums of ecclesiastical preferment to be had. Take Fernando Pérez, another canon who moved into the royal chancery, where he served queen Urraca as a notary. In addition to his canonry at Compostela he picked up another at León; the León prebend seems to have been a fat one.[26] He was not the only pluralist. Munio Gelmírez enjoyed the obviously rather unusual opportunities for self-enrichment available to a brother of the bishop. To the authors of the *Historia* he was one of the 'big men' (*optimates, proceres*) of Galicia. He had a retinue of knights, in his leisure he could relax in his castle, and, engagingly, he gave his fellow canons his revenues from five proprietary churches to be employed after his death to commemorate him annually in a slap-up feast (*ut . . . canonici splendide procurentur*).[27] There was nothing mealy-mouthed about the chapter of Compostela under Diego Gelmírez.

It was said in an earlier chapter that the canons of Compostela at the time of Diego's succession to the bishopric were a demoralized bunch of men; that it was Diego's task to revive their flagging spirits. The busy, boisterous society revealed by the record of the *Historia* is our witness to the re-animation which he effected. How did he do it? Any glimmer at an answer must be tempered by the recognition that here we encounter the intangibles of mood, feeling, style and personality which by definition must elude us. But we can at least try to pick up some of the nuances. Diego's relic-stealing expedition to Braga in 1102 has already been mentioned. The passage relating to the reception of the relics at Compostela deserves quoting at length.[28]

The bishop heard that the holy bodies had already crossed the river

[26] The matter is clinched by his subscription of R. 12 October 1113 as canon of both León and Compostela. For the León prebend see *Episcopate*, p. 234. There were other pickings too: see AHN 512/13.

[27] *HC*, pp. 126, 133, 153, 169, 188. Chapter feasts were evidently an important feature of the canons' life: see *HC*, p. 471.

[28] *HC*, pp. 40-1. Gogilde (on which see also *HC*, pp. 59, 148) is a little to the north of Pontevedra; Milladoiro is about three miles south of Santiago de Compostela. The plague here referred to is not known from any other source.

Miño, which is the boundary between Portugal and Galicia, and had been deposited in a safe place. All necessary preparations having been made, he hurried to the monastery where the relics had been placed. Taking them up he began to make his way back publicly by way of the estates of St. James with great reverence and rejoicing to the city of Compostela. When he reached the village of Gogilde he sent messangers ahead to the clergy and people of Compostela to warn them of the arrival of the saints and to tell them how he wished that they should be received. The clergy and people heard with great joy what divine providence had ordained, that the bodies of the saints should be transferred from Braga to Compostela. They understood that they were to be preserved from plague and weakening fever by their merits and intercessions as well as by the protection of the most blessed apostle James (the presence of whose most holy body gives renown to the city of Compostela). The clergy went out in a seemly procession, followed by the population of the whole city, barefoot, as far as the place known as Milladoiro, to meet them. When the bishop arrived he ordered those who were with him to take off their shoes as he had done. The clergy, clad in their holy vestments and barefooted, took up the glorious bodies of the saints. The crowds of people followed them. Then, led by the bishop and clergy singing hymns and psalms, with pious devotion they bore the relics into their city and lodged them in the church of the holy apostle James.

Obviously, it was beautifully stage-managed by Diego. Bishops who had shrines to care for had to be showmen. But there was more to it than this. The translation of the relics was a collective act uniting bishop, chapter, clergy and people of the town. It was an occasion which focused, which fused together, in a ceremony which owed something to rituals of penance and also, very probably, to secular rituals in honour of royalty, an intense religious devotion, a communal pride and a warm social solidarity. It served to define the relations of the participants with the rest of the world; in particular with their neighbours and rivals, the smartly discomforted clergy and people of Braga. It topped up the charge, so to say, of the holy city of Compostela by infusing into it an additional current of holiness. It assembled energies in a renewal of self-confidence and purpose.

We can glimpse in the ceremonial which framed Diego's 'holy theft' something of his technique, and sense the optimism which succeeded the chilly desolation of the 1090s. But it would be rash to assume that all was plain sailing for Diego. The relations between a bishop and his cathedral chapter have always been a focus for certain tensions. The cathedral community at Compostela in the early twelfth century was no exception to this general rule. We have seen that there may have been some opposition to Diego's promotion to the bishopric, and that some of his capitular reforms aroused resentment. The oath-swearings of 1102 were indeed an admission on the bishop's part of his misgivings about the loyalty of some members of his chapter; misgivings which were (as we shall see) only too justified. We are also told that the destruction of the old and revered high altar of the cathedral in the course of Diego's building operations was hurtful to conservative opinion within the chapter.[29]

Straightforward conservative instincts may not have been the only reason for opposition to Diego's building programme. Our sources never tell us this, but it would be surprising if some among the chapter did not view the very ambitious scope of this programme with apprehension. Building operations at the cathedral complex of Santiago de Compostela were continuous throughout Diego's long episcopate. Just as we must try to remember the daily liturgical round, so too we must recapture its setting: dust and rubble; scaffolding, rope and pulleys; canvas and leather; the tang of pitch and timber, and the smell of wet cement; the squealing of the carts as they brought their loads of granite, and the chink of the masons' chisels as slowly, laboriously, it was cut to shape.

The church built at the end of the ninth century by Alfonso III and bishop Sisnando I—Compostela II—still stood in Diego's youth. It had been repaired early in the eleventh century after the destruction caused by Almanzor in 997. Bishop Cresconio had added towers at its western end about the mid-century. Otherwise it was unchanged. It was bishop Diego Peláez who conceived the idea of rebuilding St. James's church on a vastly bigger scale.[30] The most

[29] *HC*, p. 51.
[30] For the architectural history of the cathedral see G. E. Street, *Gothic Architecture in Spain* (2nd edn., London, 1869); *LFH* III, pp. 47–150; K. J. Conant, *The early architectural history of the cathedral of Santiago de Compostela* (Cambridge, Mass., 1926); W. M. Whitehill, *Spanish Romanesque architecture of the eleventh century* (Oxford, 1941); M. Chamoso Lamas, V. González and B. Regal, *La España Románica: Galicia* (2nd edn., Madrid, 1980).

notable feature of the plan of the new church was its east end: the choir containing the high altar was to be ringed to the east by an ambulatory furnished with five radiating absidal chapels. This feature indicates the thinking behind the rebuilding: the new basilica was designed to accommodate large numbers of pilgrims. Controversy surrounds both the date at which the work was begun and its architectural ancestry. This is not the place to attempt to resolve questions which may indeed, on the evidence to hand, be insoluble. Suffice it to say that though preliminary works may have started as early as 1074-5, in the early twelfth century it was commonly though not unanimously held that building had begun in 1078. National prejudice has clouded discussion of its architectural ancestry. However, we have no reason to disbelieve the statement that the architects were two men bearing French names, Bernard and Robert; and the stylistic analogies of Compostela III are with the big pilgrimage churches of western France (especially Tours, Limoges and Toulouse) and with the abbey church of Cluny. Before his deposition in 1088 Diego Peláez saw the east end of the new church arise—choir, ambulatory, radiating chapels and probably at least the eastern parts of the transept (also provided with protruding chapels, two to each arm of the transept). It would seem that at this point work was interrupted, during the troubled last decade of the century. Slight changes in the design of the triforium, and a break in construction indicated by the masonry, constitute the evidence for this hiatus. It is likely that the building team was dispersed for a time. So much is suggested by the presence of Stephen, *magister operis sancti Iacobi*, at Pamplona in 1101, where he was engaged on the building of a new cathedral.[31]

Building at Compostela was resumed early in the episcopate of Diego Gelmírez. As is usual with romanesque cathedrals, precision in the dating of its various phases is

[31] J. Goñi Gaztambide, *Catálogo del Archivo Catedral de Pamplona*, I (829-1500), (Pamplona, 1965), nos. 86, 87. His wife Renaldis (ibid., no. 104), like her husband, had a French name. Stephen is also traceable, in the company of the exiled bishop Diego Peláez, at Leire in the kingdom of Aragon-Navarre, in 1098: see F. Iñíguez Almech, 'El monasterio de San Salvador de Leyre', *Príncipe de Viana* 27 (1966), 189-220.

unattainable, though we have a fairly good idea of the sequence. The eastern parts of the church were evidently in use by 1105-6, for it was during Diego's fifth year as bishop that the new high altar received its silver frontal, and it was presumably at about the same time (if not earlier) that the five absidal and four transeptal chapels were consecrated.[32] The remains of Alfonso III's church were demolished in 1112, by which date we may presume that the crossing and at least the eastern parts of the nave had arisen.[33] 'A large part' (*non modica pars*) of the basilica had a roof of beams and thatch which was burnt in the disturbances of 1117. Afterwards it was repaired, and perhaps it was at this time that a solid stone roof was laid.[34] Our best-informed witness tells us that 'the greater part' (*maior pars*) of the new church was completed by 1124.[35]

The cathedral itself, however, was only a part, albeit the largest part, of Diego's building operations. We have already seen that he rebuilt the canons' refectory. He also provided them with a cloister. This fulfilled an ambition he had long cherished. In a revealing passage the *Historia* tells us that Diego was embarrassed by the gibes of pilgrims who commented unfavourably on the lack of a cloister: he wanted his church to have one, 'like the churches beyond the Pyrenees', even though 'they were poorer and less distinguished' than his own. Work on the cloister seems to have started between 1124 and 1128, but was still incomplete in 1137.[36] The conventual buildings of the canons, the cloister and related offices, all lay on the south side of the cathedral. On its north side Diego constructed an episcopal palace for himself. Existing accommodation being less than satisfactory,

[32] *HC*, pp. 51-3; *LSJ*, p. 384. The chapel of Ste Foi (reading *Fidei* for *Sedis* at *HC*, p. 53) was dedicated by bishop Pedro of Pamplona, previously a monk at Ste Foi de Conques: this is traditionally dated 1105, though there is no warrant for this date.   [33] *HC*, pp. 137-8.

[34] *HC*, pp. 229, 249. The pilgrims' guidebook (*LSJ*, p. 382) states incorrectly that the basilica was roofed in tiles. The granite of that area looks brown when freshly dressed, softening to grey only after a long period of exposure. Perhaps it was the colour which misled the author into taking the roofing material for tile.   [35] *HC*, p. 473.

[36] *HC*, pp. 371, 473-5, 545, 588. An earlier cloister is referred to at *HC*, p. 41: perhaps it had to be swept away in the course of the rebuilding of the cathedral.

he built early in his episcopate what the *Historia* describes as 'a three-chambered complex of rooms at first-floor level, with a tower' (*tricameratum solium cum turri*) to serve as his own residence. This was seriously damaged in 1117. Although it was repaired soon afterwards, Diego determined in 1120 to extend it into something more fitting to his new dignity as archbishop and papal legate. He threw out a long arm running eastwards, parallel to the nave of the cathedral, as far as the north transept (on to whose doorway one of its entrances gave). It was big enough to house large numbers of important guests, and his biographers could describe it as fit for a king. It had its own water-supply and was thereby well-placed—and with good reason—to stand a siege.[37]

Between the eastern end of the palace and the entrance to the north transept there stood in a small court one of the wonders of Compostela—an enormous fountain completed in 1122 to the designs of Bernardo, the cathedral treasurer. The pilgrims' guidebook describes it in some detail. Its bowl was big enough for fifteen people to bathe in at once. In its midst rose a bronze column surmounted by four lions from whose mouths gushed water freely available for citizens and pilgrims. You couldn't see, remarks our author, where the water came from nor where it went to. The *Historia* tells us. Bernardo had had conduits laid, sometimes above and sometimes below the level of the ground, from about a mile outside the city, to convey the water towards the cathedral where its use was shared between the fountain and the monks of the nearby monastery of San Martín Pinario. These conduits were roofed in stone to ensure that the water should be both pure and cool. It was a notable work of engineering.[38]

Cathedral, chapter buildings, cloister, palace, public works: these constituted the cathedral complex brought to fruition by Diego Gelmírez. They by no means exhaust the list of buildings attributable to his initiative and erected at his expense within or without the town of Santiago de Compostela. But they suffice for the present to give some

[37] *HC*, pp. 54, 217, 220, 249, 307–8: its garden is referred to at *HC*, p. 472.
[38] *HC*, pp. 369–72; *LSJ*, p. 379; *Episcopate*, pp. 235–6.

notion of the sweep of his architectural ambitions. They also raise uncomfortable questions about the cost of fulfilling them.

Precise figures do not exist. But we may suppose it impossible to exaggerate the demands made upon the resources of bishop and chapter by the building programme. A large labour force must have been needed throughout the year: we are told that Bernard and Robert had fifty men working under their direction in the time of Diego Peláez.[39] Occasional windfalls might provide additional labour: in 1115 Diego was able to set Moorish captives to work.[40] Some labour and materials were provided gratis by pilgrims. It was customary for each pilgrim on passing through Triacastela to take up a piece of limestone and carry it with him as far as *Castaniolla* —probably Castañeda, between Mellid and Arzúa—where it was burnt for lime which was then transported to Compostela.[41] Skilled craftsmen of various kinds were needed too. The sculpture about the Puerta de las Platerías and in the cathedral museum is still there to witness to this. Diego summoned a founder from France to cast bells. We hear of glaziers and painters.[42] Skilled carpenters must have been needed. We have already seen that there were men to hand who could work in silver and bronze.

Some of the money needed came from Diego's personal fortune. When, for example, work started on the cloister he offered 100 silver marks, and made provision for the income from a herd of a hundred cows to be devoted to the project after his death.[43] Like his contemporary abbot Suger of St. Denis, Diego was skilled at conjuring gifts from the great. In 1137 Alfonso VII promised to give 200 gold pieces annually towards the building of the cloister. Alfonso I of Aragon presented the great silver chandelier which hung before the high altar.[44] Fund-raisers were sent to distant places. The two canons sent to seek contributions in southern Italy have

[39] *LSJ*, p. 386. As the author elsewhere observed (ibid., p. 382) the local granite is 'very hard, like marble'.   [40] *HC*, p. 199.

[41] *LSJ*, p. 352. Fuel would have been hard to come by in the bare uplands round Triacastela, but the area near Castañeda is (as the name implies—'chestnut trees') well-wooded.

[42] *HC*, pp. 426–7; *LSJ*, pp. 378, 382.   [43] *HC*, p. 474.

[44] *HC*, p. 588; *LSJ*, pp. 385–6.

already been mentioned. It would be surprising indeed if
Diego sent no appeals to France, though we hear of none.
(He was capable of asking an archbishop of Canterbury to
send him troops.[45]) One of the miracles of St. James tells
a revealing story. In 1103 a ship conveying passengers from
the Holy Land to Apulia was overtaken by a storm. The
travellers called on St. James, some vowing to go as pilgrims
to Compostela, others offering money towards the building
of the cathedral. A knight who was on board, himself in
the course of a pilgrimage to Compostela, collected the
money. Immediately, St. James appeared to them and
promised that they would be saved. The storm died down
and they came safe to harbour. The knight went to Compostela and offered the money to the building fund.[46]
Evidence of this sort, which could be multiplied, gives us
some idea of how revenues that might be called extraordinary
were sought for the construction and embellishment of the
cathedral and its related buildings. We must presume, however, that the bulk of the money needed had to come from
ordinary revenues; that is to say, from the see's endowments.

Information about the endowments is patchy. Royal
diplomas by which lands, churches and privileges were
granted to the church of St. James have been preserved in
the cathedral cartulary known as Tumbo A, copied in the
years 1129-31.[47] No systematic record exists of the benefactions of other donors, though stray references in the *Historia*
and elsewhere make it plain that these were—as one would
expect—very considerable. The laborious exercise of plotting
all recorded landed possessions on a map yields little beyond
the unsurprising information that they were far-flung.
Already by the end of the ninth century they were strung
out between Coimbra in the south and Oviedo in the north,
from the Atlantic islands of Ons and Salvora in the west to
Villasabariego, near Mansilla de las Mulas, to the east of
León.[48] By Diego's day they had come to include properties
still more widely distributed: urban property in Huesca,

[45] *Sancti Anselmi Cantuariensis Archiepiscopi Opera Omnia*, ed. F. S. Schmitt
(London, 1938-61), IV, ep. 265.   [46] *LSJ*, pp. 271-2.
[47] For further discussion of this cartulary, see below, ch. X.
[48] R. 6 May 899.

estates between Auch and Toulouse in southern France, land in the valley of the Duero near Toro, olive groves at Talavera on the Tagus, the castle at Faro on the outskirts of the modern Corunna, to give only a few examples.[49]

Even did we possess complete listings of Compostelan properties, which we do not, there would still be questions we should ask in vain. How were these properties managed? What was their annual value to the church of St. James? It was considered indicative of Diego's straits during the disturbances of 1116-17 that the episcopal table could be supplied only through purchase of foodstuffs in the market of Compostela.[50] So we may assume that the bishop's household, and probably the cathedral community at large, relied upon regular revenues in kind from their estates. The men of Cacabelos owed an annual render of six *modii* of barley, three of wheat, one cow, three pigs, three measures of wine, four sheep, twenty chickens, one hundred eggs, two pounds of wax and one of pepper; all to be paid over at Martinmas to Diego's steward.[51] What proportion of Compostelan properties were managed directly in this fashion we cannot tell. It is however certain that other endowments were leased. Diego had to keep a watchful eye on these to prevent their slipping away altogether. The handsome estate at Cornelhã, for instance, in the valley of the Limia in what is now northern Portugal, had been granted to Santiago as long ago as 915.[52] Half of it was leased to archbishop Maurice of Braga in 1109; his successor Paio seized the other half in about 1118, and it was only with great difficult that Diego managed to repossess it in 1121.[53]

Diego and his chapter had other sources of revenue beyond the see's endowments. The income from spiritualities will

---

[49] For these examples see respectively R. March 1098 (Pedro I of Aragon); *HC*, p. 44; R. 30 May 1087, and cf. also R. 13 February 1147 and *LFH* IV, ap. xvi, pp. 43-5; *HC*, pp. 498-9; R. 24 May 991, and cf. also *HC*, p. 86 (= JL 6264).   [50] *HC*, p. 220.

[51] R. 22 February 1130: cf. also *HC*, p. 499 for the arrangements for the annual transport of oil from Talavera to Compostela; so bulky a commodity must surely have gone by water, i.e. down the Tagus to Lisbon and then up the Atlantic coast.

[52] R. 30 January 915; for its bounds see R. 8 January 1061.

[53] *HC*, pp. 145-6, 264-5, 327. The story was a good deal more complicated than appears from my summary in the text.

be considered in a later chapter.[54] Pilgrims obviously constituted an enormously important source of revenue, but we have no means of estimating its size.[55] Seigneurial revenues such as *fonsadera* (= scutage) and *luctuosa* (= relief) were available to Diego, also the mysterious tax called *tributum quadragesimale*; under the same heading we should count the profits of justice.[56] It was also in his capacity as the lordly sponsor of campaigns against pirates that Diego received a share, usually a fifth, of any booty taken.[57]

A further source of wealth was the town of Compostela itself, for the bishop enjoyed the lordship (*señorío*) of the town. Urban life in northern Spain was booming in Diego's lifetime, and the almost townless Galicia of an earlier period was being transformed.[58] Compostela shared in this transformation. What did the town look like in Diego's day? Our starting-point has to be the description in the pilgrims' guidebook.[59] The site on which the town is built lies between two streams, the Sar to the south-east and the Sarela to the north-west. The ground slopes gently downhill from east to west, the cathedral lying at what was in Diego's time the western edge of the city; so that the pilgrim arriving from the east would look down towards the cathedral as he entered the walls by the *Porta Francigena* (now Puerta del Camino). The city walls had been built in the time of bishop Cresconio, about the middle of the eleventh century.[60] They were pierced by seven gates and enclosed within their circuit of some 2,400 yards—about the same size as Roman Lugo— a roughly rectangular area. Within there lay, apart from

[54] See below, ch. IX.

[55] *HC*, pp. 590-5 recounts Alfonso VII's attempts to lay hold of a share of it towards the end of Diego's life.

[56] *HC*, p. 178; C. Sánchez Albornoz, 'El *tributum quadragesimale*: supervivencias fiscales romanas en Galicia', in his *Estudios sobre las instituciones medievales españoles* (Mexico City, 1965), pp. 353-68.

[57] *HC*, pp. 135, 199, 303, 527-8, 529; H. Grassotti, 'Para la historia del botín y de las parias en León y Castilla', *Cuadernos de Historia de España* 39-40 (1964), 43-132.

[58] See, in general, L. G. de Valdeavellano, *Sobre los burgos y los burgueses de la España medieval* (Madrid, 1960); J. Gautier-Dalché, *Historia urbana de León y Castilla en la edad media* (Madrid, 1979). [59] *LSJ*, pp. 376-7.

[60] This is debatable. The other contender, bishop Sisnando II (952-68), planned to build a wall but we are not told that he did so. We hear nothing of any wall at the time of Almanzor's expedition in 997.

the cathedral, two large ecclesiastical establishments, the monasteries of San Martín Pinario and San Pelayo de Ante-altares: the latter certainly had a walled precinct and the former may have done. Unlike some other towns of northern Spain—León, Oviedo, Burgos, for example—Compostela had no royal palace or castle.[61] Our sources give the impression that the walled area was fairly densely settled and built over.[62] It contained four churches in addition to those already mentioned; two further churches stood outside the walls. In 1136 a house of Augustinian canons, Sta Maria la Real del Sar, was founded outside the walls by the banks of the Sar. Some of the houses in the town had upper storeys: a charter of 1112 contrasts *kasas terrenas* with *sobrados*.[63] Since in the sixteenth century it seems that most of the dwelling houses were of wood, we may safely assume that this was also the case in the twelfth: it is suggestive that their walls were easy to break down.[64] The vast cathedral complex will have stood out all the more imposingly above the modest houses which surrounded it. The visitor could have been in no doubt about who mattered most in Compostela.

A charter of 1147 refers to a spot where 'announcements are made in the market-place'.[65] The word for announcements—*preconia*—has given its name to the street now called Preguntoiro, to the east of San Pelayo de Anteltares, and this is our only clue to the whereabouts of the market-place. It is not far from the *Porta de Macerellis*, 'through which the precious juice of Bacchus enters the town'.[66] The name of this gate, evidently something to do with butchery, also hints at commerce. The goods for sale in the market are listed in Diego's edict of prices.[67] There is nothing exotic there: food and drink, shoes and clothing, pottery and tools; these are goods one may see in the Compostela market today,

[61] But individual members of the royal family could and did own property there, for example Doña Elvira, daughter of Fernando I: R. 13 November 1100. When Alfonso VII visited Compostela in 1127 he stayed in the house of one of the citizens: *HC*, p. 452.

[62] Extra-mural settlement is implied by the reference to the *civitas et suburbium* at *HC*, p. 335. The foundation charter for Sar makes clear that there was such settlement on that side of the city in 1136: *LFH* IV, ap. viii, at p. 22.

[63] R. 14 May 1112, and cf. also *HC*, p. 125.

[64] *HC*, pp. 234-5.

[65] R. 11 July 1147.

[66] *LSJ*, p. 377, and cf. also *HC*, p. 533.

[67] *HC*, pp. 532-6.

the staples of an urban community not very far removed, in an economic sense, from its rural background. But there was more sophisticated trafficking too. The Maurinus with whom Diego found refuge while fleeing from the mob in 1117 seems to have been a cloth merchant. When king Alfonso VII wanted to dispose of a valuable gold chalice he sent it to Compostela to be sold 'because he knew of no place in the whole of Spain where it would sell better'.[68] There was money in Compostela. Some of it was struck there. The Compostela mint is first heard of towards the end of the eleventh century. By a characteristically unscrupulous piece of bullying Diego managed to wrest control of it from the reluctant hands of Alfonso VI.[69] Far more money must have been brought by pilgrims. From an economic point of view, the most important single consequence of the habit of pilgrimage was the movement and spending of what in the aggregate must have amounted to very considerable sums of money. The pilgrims spent it on footwear; on food and lodging; on souvenirs, especially the scallop-shells which pilgrims to Santiago took home with them as pilgrims to Jerusalem took home palms.[70] They spent it on being swindled by fraudulent money-changers.[71] It seems that they also spent it on prostitutes, despite Diego's attempts to run these enterprising ladies out of town.[72]

One of the miracles of St. James tells of some German pilgrims to Compostela in 1090 who were the victims of a cruel fraud in Toulouse.[73] There were wealthy people and they travelled 'with plentiful quantities of rich goods'. Were they merchants? It is hard otherwise to see why they should have encumbered themselves in this way. Sources from this period have a good deal to tell us about merchants who masqueraded as pilgrims to avoid paying tolls.[74] Irrespective of whether they behaved in this manner, foreign merchants

---

[68] *HC*, pp. 234, 488.
[69] R. 13 November 1100, 14 May 1107; *HC*, pp. 65-8, 85-6, 307-8, 495. The mint was situated near the door of the north transept of the cathedral, its site recalled by the modern street-name Rua da Antigua Casa da Moeda.
[70] *LSJ*, pp. 153, 273-4, 379-80.   [71] *LSJ*, pp. 162-3,
[72] *HC*, p. 533.   [73] *LSJ*, pp. 267-8.
[74] See for instance the tariff edited by J. M. Lacarra, *Un arancel de aduanas del siglo XI* (Zaragoza, 1950).

were coming, it seems frequently and in some numbers, to
Compostela or to its port, Padrón. We hear in the *Historia*
of English, Lotharingian and Norman merchants; and one
of the many striking revelations of the English account of
the conquest of Lisbon in 1147 is that the skippers on both
sides of the narrow seas were evidently conversant with the
lanes that led across Biscay to northern Spain.[75] Others
came overland, like the Barcelona business man who was
the beneficiary of no less than thirteen of St. James's
miracles.[76] The ecclesiastical legislation of the period displays steady concern for the protection of merchants on
their travels.[77] Some settled in Compostela. There were
certainly Frenchmen there.[78] John the Lombard, a moneyer,
was Italian, and so perhaps was his partner Tandulf. Adhémar
the moneyer perhaps came from southern France.[79] Of the
native merchant community we know nothing, but it is
impossible to believe that it did not exist.

The Compostela bourgeoisie was a force to be reckoned
with. Its members could exert pressure on their rulers to
exact valuable privileges for themselves. In 1095, for example,
count Raymond granted the merchants of Compostela
freedom from distraint except with the sanction of a tribunal
which sat in their home town.[80] In 1120 queen Urraca
exempted the citizens from the payment of toll (*portaticum,
portazgo*) throughout her kingdom.[81] The surviving evidence
conjures up a prosperous, self-confident, assertive urban
community, possessed of shrewd political sense. Ecclesiastics
who were lords of towns in other parts of Europe found
such communities hard to control. It is not surprising that
Diego should have encountered difficulties. His authority
was twice challenged, first and most seriously in 1116–17,
and again in 1136. Some historians have argued that the
unrest which occurred was the expression of a simple and
straightforward contest between a 'progressive' bourgeoisie

---

[75] *HC*, pp. 291, 505–6; *De expugnatione Lyxbonensi*, ed. C. W. David (New
York, 1936).   [76] *LSJ*, pp. 286–7.
[77] e.g. *HC*, pp. 418, 485.   [78] *HC*, p. 234.
[79] *HC*, pp. 61, 65; R. 13 November 1100.
[80] R. 24 September 1095.
[81] R. 13 June 1120. In Spain as elsewhere such tolls were much resented:
cf. *HC*, pp. 60–1 on the *portazgo* at Puente Sampayo.

and a 'reactionary' episcopal seigneur.[82] But it was a good
deal more complicated than this. For this reason, and also
because the story sheds so welcome a light upon the uncertainties and tensions inherent in Diego's relations with
crown and nobility, town and chapter, it is worth spending
a little time upon the first of these encounters.

The first series of disturbances began in the spring of 1116
and lasted until the summer of 1117.[83] Their immediate
occasion was a political manœuvre by queen Urraca. Gerald's
narrative in the *Historia*, narrow of vision as ever, sees only
a woman's irresponsibility. But in the larger context of
the political situation in Spain as a whole, the queen's actions
appear intelligible and shrewd. As we saw in the last chapter,
relations between Diego and the queen were extremely
strained in the spring and summer of 1116. Neither should
we forget that Almoravide pressure on the southern frontier
of the kingdom of León-Castile was still being maintained;
nor that Alfonso I of Aragon remained an unwelcome
presence in eastern Castile. Urraca could most effectively
embarrass the bishop of Compostela and protect her rear by
kindling the latent opposition to Diego in his own cathedral
city.

With the queen's encouragement a party among the
citizens was brought to rebel against Diego's authority. They
were successful. Diego lost all power over the town. He was
virtually imprisoned. His excommunications went unheeded.
His rents were cut off and his episcopal palace destroyed.
After about six months he gave in to the queen; the fruit
of his submission was the peace of Sahagún in October
1116. But what followed was even more alarming. Although
the queen's orders had been that Diego be restored to his
authority in Compostela; and although he had staged a

[82] See most recently R. Pastor de Togneri, 'Las primeras rebeliones burguesas
en Castilla y León (siglo XII). Análisis histórico-social de una coyuntura', in her
Conflictos sociales y estancamiento económico en la España medieval (Barcelona,
1973), pp. 13-102. The analogies with the communal movement of northern
France, which exist but should not be pressed too far, have been recently re-
stated by J. Gautier-Dalché, *Historia urbana de León y Castilla en la edad media*
(Madrid, 1979), pp. 225-30.

[83] For what follows, our only source is Gerald's vivid narrative in *HC*, pp.
211-49. The extent of his partisanship is indicated by his habit of likening Diego's
opponents to Judas Iscariot. For the political background, see ch. VI.

spectacular translation of relics given to him by the queen in order to rally support to himself (somewhat as in 1102 with St. Fructuosus); it quickly became clear that some among the opposition were in no mood to give up what they had gained. In the spring of 1117 Urraca came to Galicia. Some sort of armed confrontation was unavoidable. An attempt by the royalists to disarm the rebels was bungled and at this point the situation passed out of control. Diego and the queen with a small following were cornered in the upper storeys of the bell-tower at the west end of the cathedral (presumably one of the towers built by bishop Cresconio). Their besiegers set fire to the lower storeys, doubtless availing themselves for fuel of the abundant building materials which were to hand. The queen, leaving under what she thought was a safe conduct, was roughly handled by the mob; Diego escaped through the mediation, it seems, of the abbot of San Martín Pinario.[84] Others were less fortunate; at least four prominent people were killed. With difficulty and in some danger, Diego and Urraca escaped from the town and rallied their forces. No less than five armies converged on Compostela, and the insurgents gave in. The queen was all for retribution; but Diego, who would have had to live with the results, counselled moderation. The ringleaders were exiled, the remainder got off with an immense fine. Such, in very summary form, were the events at Santiago de Compostela in the years 1116 and 1117.

The most intriguing question is that of the nature of the opposition to Diego. The leaders initially stirred up by queen Urraca were 'certain citizens more powerful than the rest'. Diego had long suspected their loyalty and had tried to bind them to him by an oath. This is as much as we are told. In addition to these men there were certain members of the cathedral chapter among the opposition. This is implied at several points in Gerald's narrative, and once stated unambiguously. Three leaders are singled out in the *Historia*, but only one among them is named. Arias Núñez forced Diego to make him an archdeacon; at one point he took refuge in the monastery of San Martín Pinario, but emerged

---

[84] The grant made to the abbot in 1118 (AHN 512/7) looks like an expression of gratitude.

later to take part in the last days of the rebellion. We are not
told that he was a member of the chapter; we are not even
told whether or not he was a clerk. It is prudent to resist
the temptation to identify him with the canon named Arias
Núñez who was an archdeacon in the 1120s and 1130s.
(Arias and Nuño were very common names in early twelfth-
century Galicia.) Another leader, unnamed, is described in
terms which make it clear that he was not a native of the
town; it is hinted that he wanted to lay hands on some of
the landed endowments of the see; and he evidently knew
something of warfare. The third leader mentioned, again
unnamed, was a cleric and almost certainly a member of the
chapter. He was a man for whom Diego had great affection:
he had been brought up in the bishop's household, educated
in France at the bishop's expense, granted lands by the
bishop, and listened to as a trusted counsellor. All three were
natives of Galicia. Gerald, usually so prodigal of information,
is oddly reluctant to name them. Arias is not named in the
text, only in rubrics which are not to be found in all manuscripts (which is why they are missing in Flórez's edition).
The implication is that some or all of them were still about
when he composed his account.[85] The rebels as a whole were
regarded by our author as being below the social rank of
those accustomed to exercise power. They behaved 'like
serfs and peasants when they were given power to rule',
commented Gerald. (Was it at home in Beauvais at the time
of the communal uprising of 1099 that he had seen 'serfs
and peasants' ruling?) Queen Urraca's robust comment
on them is best left in the decent obscurity of a learned
language (*sterquilinium*). But the leaders were obviously
men of some social position.

What were their grievances? The only thing we may be
certain about was their dislike of Diego's administration of
the town. They seem especially to have resented that this
was so much a family affair. When the movement began,
Diego's brother was *villicus* of the town, that is to say the
official principally charged with its administration, and his
nephew Pedro was prior of the chapter. Among the earliest

[85] The reference to the antipope on *HC*, p. 221 shows that this section was
composed between 1118 and 1121.

demands of the rebels was that they should be dismissed. The brother, Gundesindo, was later murdered, and Pedro narrowly escaped the same fate. Another who was killed was Diego the Squinter, whom the bishop had appointed *villicus* when he was trying to restore his authority early in 1117. This hatred for his connections extended to Diego himself, as he well knew: 'It's me they're really after, not you', he told the queen when they were trapped together in the blazing tower. The more extreme among the ringleaders wanted him deposed. People and objects near and dear to him were treated with savage malice: his palace destroyed; his principal household officers butchered.

Behind these expressions of resentment we cannot get. We do not know precisely what it was about the running of the town that the opposition found so hateful. Perhaps it was simply that it was run by and for a clique of family and clients of which Diego was the boss. All the ringleaders were Galicians. Diego loved French ways, gave ecclesiastical preferment to French clergy, entrusted the keeping of the official record of his pontificate to a Frenchman—and was sheltered by French townspeople in the course of his escape from Compostela. Might we have here a clue to another of the underlying causes of the rising? Perhaps: but we cannot be sure. The leader who was not a native of the town sounds like a man of similar social background to Diego. His ambitions over the temporalities of the see are suggestive. Was he a landowner who considered that he had been cheated of his rights by the church of Santiago? Was he a member of a rival family—in rivalry for the same kind of jobs—to the family of Gelmirio? Again, perhaps: as we saw in the last chapter, there were plenty of people of precisely this type among the Galician squirearchy. We cannot now recover the dense tissue of family feuds in the Tierra de Santiago.

'They made an agreement which they called a brotherhood' (*conspirationem quam vocant germanitatem*), wrote Gerald. It was fortified by an oath. We know only two of its several heads. But these were evidently written down, for when the revolt was suppressed it was stipulated that 'their charter (*chirographum*) should be given to the bishop to be destroyed'. When Diego's administrators had been edged out, the rebels set up officers of their own to run the city. Daily meetings were held, at which 'they concerned themselves with laws and judgements' (*leges et iudicia pertractabant*)—whatever that may mean. 'They made new laws and decrees' (*renovant leges et plebiscita*). This is tantalizing stuff. We should much like to know more of such things. Regrettably we cannot.

This was not the end of the story. In 1118 Diego feared that the exiles would obstruct his envoys to the papal court. They had sympathizers among the remaining members of the cathedral chapter.[86] The confluence of different groups of opponents, so apparent in 1116-17, was noted again by Gerald when he recorded certain events that occurred in 1127: Diego's enemies were composed of 'noble knights who dwelt outside the city, citizens of Compostela who were bound to him by oath, and clergy, canons of our church, whom he had himself brought up in his own household'.[87] This same coalescing of groups is evident once more during the disturbances of 1136.[88] These followed much the same pattern as those of 1116-17, and we need not dwell on them at such length. Once again we witness a challenge to Diego's authority mounted by disaffected canons and citizens. Again he lost control of the town, saw his officers displaced and his regulations discarded. Again he was the target for attack. A tired old man now, he was roused from his siesta on 10 August and again had to resort to ignominious flight from a mob who stoned him at the very high altar of his own cathedral. Again, order was restored and punishment meted out.[89] One feature of the goings-on of 1136 differentiated them from those of 1116-17. At one point the rebels tried to get king Alfonso VII on their side. They offered him a huge bribe—3,000 marks—if he would deprive Diego of his temporalities and send him into exile.

---

[86] *HC*, pp. 261, 265, 291. [87] *HC*, pp. 447-8.
[88] For what follows see *HC*, pp. 567-82.
[89] R. 17 July 1137. The ringleader named in this charter, Guillermo Seguin, was named in *HC*, p. 572 as *huius proditionis maximus incentor*. Can the Juan Lombardo whose confiscated goods were its subject possibly be identical with the moneyer of this name who was active a generation earlier? Guillermo Seguin was *villicus* of Compostela after Diego's death, in 1140-1 and again in 1149-50: AD Braga, Gaveta dos Arcebispos, no. 4.

(The size of the sum they offered is one indication that they were men of substance.) The king was tempted but resisted. Instead he sent to pope Innocent II and asked him to send a papal legate to Spain to look into the dispute. Cardinal Guido was dispatched in answer to this request, and the council of Burgos over which he presided in October was concerned, among much else, with the settlement of the summer's disturbances at Compostela.

Gerald tells us that the pilgrims present at Compostela in 1117 were shocked and dismayed by what they witnessed. But pilgrims themselves could be a source of trouble. When the count of Toulouse and his brother went on pilgrimage to Compostela at some point in the 1060s they were refused access to the shrine because it was after nightfall when they got to the town. Great men were not accustomed to being treated in this manner. They went off and gathered a gang of 200 other pilgrims and returned to the cathedral. Small wonder that when the flickering light of the torches they carried revealed this menacing posse the gates of the apostle's oratory miraculously burst open.[90] The brawling of pilgrims within the cathedral could lead to bloodshed, even to homicide.[91] A man in Diego's position had to be accustomed to violence. In part he brought it on himself: it was the price he had to pay for his achievements. He transformed his chapter. He rebuilt his cathedral. He embellished his city. These were notable triumphs, but they were won only at a cost. The events of 1116-17 and 1136 were part of that cost. They shook Diego's authority to its foundations. But he rallied—showing characteristic political skill— and came through relatively unscathed.

One feature of the events of 1136 is worthy of remark. The disturbances were very quickly brought to the notice of pope Innocent II, both unofficially by a citizen of Pisa who witnessed them while in Compostela as a pilgrim,[92] and officially by Alfonso VII. The pope had harsh words for those who had presumed to molest an archbishop. There

[90] *LSJ*, pp. 282-3.
[91] *La Documentación pontificia hasta Inocencio III*, ed. D. Mansilla (Rome, 1955), no. 269 (from the year 1207).
[92] *HC*, p. 583; the papal court was at Pisa throughout 1136.

was nothing surprising about this: just so had Urban II reacted to the deposition of Diego Peláez nearly half a century earlier. But the speed with which the news reached the pope in 1136, the resolution with which he ordered certain measures in the confidence that his commands would be carried out—these features were new. What changes had been worked to make them possible?

VIII

'The Gospel according to the Mark of silver': Diego and the Papacy

'Spain knows nothing of papal decisions.' The speaker was bishop Arnulf of Orléans at the synod of Rheims in 991, and we may take it that this was the view of well-informed churchmen in northern France in the last decade of the tenth century.[1] Something over a hundred years later pope Calixtus II was held to have declared that he had loved Santiago from his childhood and had spent fourteen years wandering in foreign lands, enduring robbery, imprisonment and shipwreck in search of legends about him.[2] The first statement has been wrenched from its context. As to the second, it is doubtful whether a historian could now be found to defend the proposition that the letter given in the name of pope Calixtus which prefaces the collection usually (if incorrectly) known as the *Liber Sancti Jacobi* or *Codex Calixtinus* contains sentiments which might with any remote degree of plausibility be attributed to that pope. Nevertheless, the contrast revealed by these statements embodies an important historical truth. In the late tenth and early eleventh century the churchmen of Galicia had no dealings with the popes; but by the time of Calixtus II's pontificate (1119-24) they did. Diego Gelmírez played a significant part in bringing about this transformation. The amount of space devoted in the *Historia Compostellana* to his dealings with the papal curia is an indication of how important he thought those dealings were. They constitute the subject of the present chapter.[3]

[1] *Patrologia Latina*, vol. CXXXIX, col. 320.   [2] *LSJ*, p. 1.

[3] By far the most important work on this topic, and one that has been referred to more than once in earlier chapters, is Vones, *Kirchenpolitik*. This copious and exhaustive work contains references to all earlier literature on the subject. It is

We have already glanced in an earlier chapter at the beginnings of relations between the papal curia and the churchmen of north-western Spain. We have seen that a papal legate may have visited Compostela about the time of Diego Gelmírez's infancy; that bishop Diego Peláez was deposed at a church council presided over by another legate; that he subsequently tried and failed to be reinstated with the help of papal authority; that bishop Dalmatius and some of his colleagues attended the council of Clermont in 1095. We have also seen how it was in some sense as 'the pope's man' that Diego Gelmírez got his bishopric in 1100—remembering always that he was other men's man as well; not least, his own. The young Diego would have taken note of these developments in the 1080s and 1090s. He would also have observed other, related changes. In his childhood and youth two successive pontiffs, Alexander II and Gregory VII, had succeeded in imposing a change of liturgy upon the churches of Aragon, Navarre and León-Castile. Two monks of Cluny had successively been charged with the abbacy of the great royal monastery of Sahagún. The second of them, Bernardo, had in 1083 acquired from Gregory VII the privilege of freedom 'from the yoke of every ecclesiastical or secular power' saving only subjection to the apostolic see of Rome. The same man had soon afterwards been promoted to the archbishopric of Toledo and had received from Gregory's successor Urban II in 1088 the privilege of primacy over all the Spanish churches. Not long afterwards, probably early in 1091, bishop Pedro of Braga had sought and obtained the restoration of the metropolitan status of his see; and here we should remember that the bishoprics of Galicia were in the province of Braga. As it so happened, the pope to whom Pedro had turned was not the rightful one but the imperial antipope Clement III. However, Pedro's successor Geraldo, a protégé of the archbishop of Toledo, was only a few years later (1099 or 1100) to acquire the same concession from the rightful pope, Paschal II.

Many historians have believed that during this period the

---

marked throughout by formidable erudition and shrewd critical acumen, and is as nearly definitive as the surviving evidence permits such a study to be. It has been invaluable to me in the preparation of this chapter.

papacy pursued a deliberate policy designed to increase its influence in areas of Christendom hitherto immune from it. Politically speaking, it is held, this was the essence of the Gregorian or Hildebrandine reform. Thus the extension of the papal reach in Spain was part and parcel of one grand design whose working out may also be seen in the British Isles, in Scandinavia, in eastern Europe and in the crusading states of Outremer. This interpretation is the work of German scholars or of those who have come under the influence of German historical scholarship; many of them principally concerned with the development of canon law. It is a historians' and lawyers' gloss upon the records of a multitudinous sea of decisions and transactions of the greatest possible diversity, spread over many years, effected by many different people in many different places moved by purposes so various as to confound the understanding. Such a gloss or construct is in itself an heroic achievement. But it is bound to over-simplify, and over-simplification of so complex a set of circumstances can lead to grave misapprehension. The historians trained in the tradition alluded to have alarmingly neat notions about the processes they study. 'Qui dit découverte, dit surprise, et dissemblance', wrote Marc Bloch. But the foggy Anglo-Saxon mind can comfort itself with no such encouraging reflections. We are invited to detect in the ecclesiastical reform movement of this period clarity of vision, consistency of principle, continuity of direction, regularity of routine and the smooth functioning of sleek institutional gadgetry. Would that it were so easy. But the medieval papacy was an institution all too human, and its workings display all the muddle that we associate with human affairs. The closer you look at the papal wood, the more obstinately does it remain just a lot of trees.

It is true that certain churchmen, most notably Gregory VII himself, had a vision of a society organized on Christian lines whose divine directing power should be mediated through the bishop of Rome as successor to St. Peter and Vicar of Christ. This was impossible of realization, a fact which even Gregory was compelled to acknowledge in the course of his disastrous pontificate. Those who had a will

to it—there were never very many of them—lacked the
means; the time, the men, the skills, the resources. It was
a bold vision, and it still retains the power to move and to
excite. Yet it is unfortunate that Gregory VII's name should
have become attached to this epoch in the history of the
church. Did the clergy of north-western Spain think of themselves as living in 'the Gregorian age'? How did they look
upon the papacy? Some answer to this question will, it is
hoped, emerge in the pages that follow. It is necessary
here, however, to make one last preliminary point. Papal
government during this period was on the whole something
passive; acted upon rather than acting. There is plentiful
evidence to suggest that matters presented themselves in
this light to most of the higher clergy of western Christendom, including those of Spain. They were not given to
thinking in abstractions about 'the papacy'. The case was
rather that the popes commanded an arsenal of weapons
which they might be brought to share with those who had
need of them, who asked for them and who (not least)
could pay for them. A canny man in an unfriendly world
will avail himself of this arsenal; will grasp by fair means
or foul the weapons which might be useful in offence or
defence. For a bishop of Compostela, then, what are the
sources of unfriendliness? The unsurprising answer rings
back loud and clear from the pages of the *Historia Compostellana*: his neighbours. That meant above all others the
churchmen of Toledo and Braga. If we ask what they could
do to Diego Gelmírez, the answer takes us to the heart of
his concerns. They could dim the lustre of St. James. That
mattered very much. A bishop of Compostela who let it
happen would be betraying a sacred trust. Protection, then,
in the sense of special, privileged arrangements, was what
the churchmen of Compostela sought from the popes in the
first instance. From that impulse much was to follow.

Bishop Dalmatius was the trail-blazer. One of the fruits
of his journey to Clermont in 1095 was the papal privilege
Et decretorum synodalium.[4] This contained two important
provisions. The first was a confirmation of the transfer of

[4] *HC*, pp. 21-3 (= JL 5601), *incipit* corrected from AC Santiago de Compostela, Tumbo B, fo. 240.

the seat of the bishopric from Iria to Santiago de Compostela. The second was the concession to bishop Dalmatius

that both you and your successors hereafter shall be subject to none except the metropolitan bishop of Rome; and that all those who come after you in that see shall be consecrated by the hand of the pope, as special suffragans of the see of Rome.

The bearing of the second provision is obvious enough. It gave the church of Compostela exemption from the authority of her metropolitan, the archbishop of Braga, and indeed from any other Spanish ecclesiastic including the primate of Toledo. At that particularly vulnerable moment in the life of a bishop-elect, the occasion of his consecration when the metropolitan could insist upon a profession of obedience, the bishops of Compostela were removed entirely from the reach of a Spanish ecclesiastical jurisdiction. This was a much-coveted and very important concession.[5] One of Diego's earliest actions as bishop was to dispatch two of his canons, Nuño Alfonso (the later bishop of Mondoñedo) and the archdeacon Geoffrey to Rome to secure a confirmation of it from pope Paschal II.[6]

The privileges gained in 1095 and confirmed in 1101 were not enough for Diego. He wanted more. Above all he wanted the see of Compostela to be raised to metropolitan rank, 'so that the church of St. James might glitter with the honour it deserved', as the *Historia* put it. His argument was simply that every church in Christendom where an apostle's body was held to repose enjoyed the status of an archbishopric at the least—except the church of Santiago de Compostela.[7] We need look for no more complex reasoning than this. Precisely when this ambition took shape it is not easy to say. It may have originated with bishop Dalmatius, or even earlier in the days of bishop Diego Peláez. Diego Gelmírez certainly held it by 1104, for it was the principal motive for his second visit to Rome which he paid in that year.[8] In 1104 he drew a blank. Paschal II was sympathetic but unyielding, and

---

[5] Similar privileges of exemption were granted to the sees of Burgos (in 1096), León (1104) and Oviedo (1105).   [6] *HC*, pp. 32-3 (= JL 5880).

[7] *HC*, pp. 256-7. For all that concerns the negotiations over the archbishopric see Vones, *Kirchenpolitik*, especially ch. IV.

[8] *HC*, pp. 42, 45-6, 257. Dr Vones would place this visit in 1105: *Kirchenpolitik*,

fobbed Diego off with the grant of the right to wear a pallium on certain solemn occasions of the liturgical year.[9] Since by this date the pallium was normally worn only by metropolitans this must have been regarded by Diego as a step in the right direction, albeit a short one. Nearly six years passed before he made another attempt. A papal letter which probably belongs to the spring of 1110 refers cryptically to a request made by Diego's envoys on their master's behalf and announced they will be able to explain why it was that it could not be granted.[10] These were the opening moves in what Diego must have known would be a protracted game. His next and much more serious attempt was made in 1113, but again the pope was evasive.[11] On this occasion Diego enlisted the support of the papal chancellor John of Gaetà, and a surviving letter from him throws light on Diego's strategy. The proposal was to transfer the metropolitanate of Mérida, then of course under Muslim domination, to Santiago de Compostela. As we shall see, this was to be the solution eventually adopted. Two years later, in 1115, Diego was again in touch with Paschal II. There is no evidence that he raised the matter of the archbishopric on this occasion, but he did manage to squeeze other concessions in his favour: exemption from attending ecclesiastical councils during the present time of civil disturbance—this was a blow against Bernardo of Toledo who had been convening church councils in his capacity as papal legate—and the right to wear the tunicle and stole for every-day, non-ceremonial occasions.[12]

Diego was nothing if not tenacious. After the goings-on in the town of Compostela in 1116–17 had subsided, he determined to make another attempt. It was a promising moment, for in January 1118 pope Paschal II died and his successor was none other than Diego's friend and ally John of Gaetà,

pp. 159–62. See also his cautions at pp. 289–92 on the subject of Diego's attempts to realize his ambitions in the period before 1118; on this topic I find him a little over-cautious.

[9] *HC*, pp. 48–50 (= JL 5986).
[10] *HC*, p. 87 (= JL 6252), dated by association with material at *HC*, pp. 84–6.
[11] *HC*, pp. 193–4 (= JL 6397). In the course of an elaborate discussion Dr Vones convincingly adjusts the date from 1114 to the previous year: *Kirchenpolitik*, pp. 289–351.
[12] *HC*, pp. 202–3 (= JL 6466).

who took the name of Gelasius II.[13] The negotiations that
followed were described in great detail by Gerald of Beauvais,
who himself took part in them, in the *Historia*. Diego seems
not to have heard of the change of pope until about July.
He at once dispatched two envoys from the cathedral chapter.
They were intercepted by the Aragonese and one of them
was held in prison. When Diego heard of this he determined
to send two more. They too were unable to get beyond
Castile for fear of the Aragonese, but entrusted their business
to Bernard, prior of the Cluniac house of Carrión. In the
meantime pope Gelasius had sent cardinal Deusdedit to
Spain to summon the higher clergy to the council he proposed to hold at Clermont in March 1119. After the cardinal's
visit to Santiago de Compostela Diego made up his mind to
attend the council so as to put his case to the pope in person.
While waiting on the Tierra de Campos for a safe conduct
to get him through Aragon Diego heard a rumour that
Gelasius had died. He went on to Burgos to attend the royal
court and it was there, probably early in March 1119, that
prior Bernard of Carrión rejoined him. Bernard confirmed
the melancholy news that pope Gelasius, from whom Diego
had hoped so much, had died at Cluny on 29 January. But
there was cheering news of his successor. Only four days
after Gelasius' death there had been chosen to succeed him
Guy, the archbishop of Vienne, who took the name of
Calixtus II. Now Guy was the brother of Diego's old master
Raymond of Burgundy, count of Galicia, queen Urraca's
first husband; the uncle therefore of the young king Alfonso
Raimúndez; and a man known to Diego. (As far as we know
the two men had met only twice, in 1100 and 1107. But it
is difficult to imagine that Guy, who kept an affectionate
watch over his nephew, had had no contact with Diego
between 1107 and 1119.)   `

Diego was elated at the news of Guy's promotion. He was
still more so when he received an encouraging letter—one
of the earliest of Calixtus' surviving letters—brought by no
less a personage than the new pope's brother-in-law. This
time Diego's envoy, Gerald, managed to get through to the
papal court, then at Montpellier, probably at some point

[13] For what follows see *HC*, pp. 255-97.

in June 1119. Discussion of Diego's business was postponed until the council of Toulouse, held early in July. The pope's reply was not as generous as Gerald had hoped. In particular, it was conveyed to Diego that nothing could be done in the matter unless he attended the papal court in person: he was bidden to be present at the council to be held at Rheims in October. On Gerald's return to Compostela, probably in August, Diego started to make preparations for his journey, but was forbidden to go by queen Urraca. Hugo bishop of Porto, a protégé of Diego and formerly a canon of Compostela, offered to go instead. He reached the papal court at Cluny early in January 1120. Over a month was spent in canvassing support. When all preparations had been made Hugo launched his final assault. It was successful. Four papal bulls gave Diego almost all that he could desire. The dignity and metropolitan rights of the see of Mérida were transferred to Santiago de Compostela until such time as the city of Mérida should be reconquered from the Muslims. Diego was appointed papal legate throughout the ecclesiastical provinces of both Mérida and Braga. The bishops of Coimbra and Salamanca were ordered to be obedient to their new metropolitan. The new archbishop himself was urged to be duly grateful to the Roman church and submissive towards her. The papal bulls reached Galicia in the summer. On St. James's day, 25 July 1120, the privileges were solemnly received and read out in a loud voice (*excelsa voce*) to the clergy and people assembled in the cathedral of Compostela. It was the triumphant conclusion to nearly twenty years of striving and the high point of Diego's career.

Such, in briefest outline, is the story of how Compostela became an archbishopric. But the narrative in itself tells us little of how the business was carried through. What strategy and tactics did Diego adopt? Who were his allies and what could they do for him? Fortunately for us, Gerald's narrative in the *Historia Compostellana* is not only detailed but also extremely candid.

Allies were needed both at home and abroad. At home it was desirable and perhaps essential for Diego to have the support of the crown. He consulted Alfonso VI before he went to Rome in 1104 and Paschal II's grant of the pallium was made at the king's request as well as Diego's. Queen Urraca was privy to Diego's negotiations with Gelasius II, and it was to her that he turned for help when he could not pass through Aragon early in 1119. As Gerald observed, 'it was not fitting that such a business should go forward without the queen's being consulted'. She was able to prevent Diego from going to attend the council of Rheims (though it is possible, as was suggested in Chapter VI, that he had no great wish to absent himself from Spain at that juncture). When Gerald was at the curia in the summer of 1119 he was embarrassed by the arrival of letters allegedly from Alfonso Raimúndez which were critical of Diego. (Diego's supporters persuaded themselves, and seem to have persuaded the curia, that the letters had been forged by the archbishop of Toledo.) At all events, the young king supported Diego's ambitions in the end, for the grant of the archbishopric was made 'at the supplication of'—among others—'our nephew king Alfonso'. By contrast, the persistent hostility of the king of Aragon obstructed Diego throughout the negotiations of the years 1118-20.[14]

On his way to Rome in 1104 Diego had called at Cluny and received useful advice from the aged abbot Hugh.[15] You've got to work hard on the papal court, he said in effect; especially on the cardinals. Diego took his words to heart. It was a great stroke for him to have engaged the interest of John of Gaetà, as we have seen that he had done by 1113. The papal chancellor was not simply the head of the pope's secretariat. During this period the holder of the office was increasingly becoming the pope's right-hand man in the daily round of papal government at its highest level; as it were a papal 'prime minister'. There were in addition two cardinals with whom Diego's connections were close. Boso can be traced as cardinal-priest of Sta Anastasia from 1113. In 1116-17 he had undertaken an important legatine journey to Spain in the course of which he held two church councils, the most westerly of them at Burgos in February 1117. This was not attended by Diego, but two of his henchmen were there, Nuño of Mondoñedo and Hugo of Porto.

[14] For the above see *HC*, pp. 42, 48, 262, 266, 269, 276(274), 279(277), 293.　　　　　　　　　　　　　　　　　　　　　　　　[15] *HC*, p. 46.

Deusdedit, cardinal-priest of San Lorenzo in Damaso from 1116, had visited Spain on papal business, as we have seen, in 1118-19. In thé course of this journey he had visited Compostela, where Diego had prudently given him a prebend.[16] Deusdedit was among the electors of Gelasius II in 1118. Both he and Boso were with the papal court at the time of Gelasius' death and the election of Calixtus in 1119. Both men were active in pressing the cause of the Compostelan archbishopric with the pope.[17]

Abbot Pontius of Cluny was another important ally, as Gerald's narrative stressed more than once. Not only could the network of Cluniac houses in Spain provide practical help over the transport of bullion—something that the Spanish Cluniacs had had much practice in: Diego and his advisers believed that abbot Pontius, as head of the whole Cluniac confraternity, was specially well-placed to influence pope Calixtus. They were correct. Pontius' advocacy of Diego's cause was acknowledged in the papal bull which transferred the archbishopric of Mérida to Compostela. It was Pontius who 'leaked' the allegedly forged letters of Alfonso Raimúndez to Gerald, it was he who assisted Gerald at the council of Toulouse, and it was to him that Hugo of Porto presented letters and tokens (*litteras et intersignia*) to establish his credentials in 1120. It was to his great dismay that Hugo found that there was some estrangement between abbot and pope when he reached the curia in January. He could make no headway in his negotiations until the two men had been reconciled.[18]

This does not exhaust the list of allies to whom Diego could look for assistance. Bishop Guy of Lescar, in southwestern France was another.[19] We should like to know more

---

[16] *HC*, p. 268.   [17] *HC*, p. 275(273).

[18] *HC*, pp. 266-7, 274(272), 275-6, 283(281), 284-6, 287(285), 293. For all that concerns abbot Pontius (or Pons) of Cluny, see now H. E. J. Cowdrey, 'Abbot Pontius of Cluny', *Studi Gregoriani* 11 (1978), 177-276, especially pp. 200-3, 219-23. I am most grateful to Dr Cowdrey for sending me a copy of his article. It is possible that Diego and Pontius had met in 1113 when, it has been suggested, Pontius visited Spain and made his way as far as Compostela: see C. J. Bishko, 'The Spanish journey of abbot Ponce of Cluny', *Ricerche di Storia Religiosa* I (1957), 311-19. Like Dr Cowdrey (*art. cit.*, p. 200, n. 76) I find Professor Bishko's suggestion attractive but not quite convincing. See also Reilly, *Urraca*, p. 83, n. 121.   [19] *HC*, pp. 276(274), 278(276).

about the Burgundian noblemen described as *confratres* of the church of Santiago, who in the course of pilgrimages thereto 'had placed themselves beneath the yoke of the apostle' (*seipsos ipsi apostolo subjugaverant*)—whatever this may mean. They included important people such as duke Hugh II of Burgundy, who had twice visited Compostela as a pilgrim and was related to pope Calixtus, and the count of Albon, who had made the pilgrimage in 1102.[20]

Diego had three possible strategies to follow in his negotiations. He could seek the creation of an entirely new metropolitanate; or the transfer of the metropolitan rank of Braga to Compostela; or the transfer of that of Mérida.[21] He seems never to have contemplated the first option. It may have been that recent precedents were not encouraging —for instance in the tangled affair of the archbishopric of Dol in Brittany; or simply that it was well-known that the popes were reluctant to sanction such entirely new departures in the geography of ecclesiastical administration (save in crusading or missionary contexts). As things turned out it was the 'way of Mérida' that prevailed in the end. But it appears that it was only at a late date in the negotiations that Diego—or his envoy bishop Hugo of Porto—finally committed himself to it. The attraction of the 'way of Braga' was that in papal eyes the existing archbishop of Braga had disgraced himself so completely that some signal example should be made of his church by way of punishment. We encounter here one of the most bizarre clerical careers of the early twelfth century.

Archbishop Maurice had been promoted to Braga from the bishopric of Coimbra early in 1109.[22] In the course of

---

[20] *HC*, pp. 289. Hugh II's grandmother Sybilla was sister to Calixtus II's father count William of Burgundy (d. 1087): see J. Richard, *Les Ducs de Bourgogne et la formation du duché* (Paris, 1954). On the count of Albon see Vones, *Kirchenpolitik*, p. 374, n. 31, and pp. 378-80.

[21] Abbot Pontius' words quoted at *HC*, p. 288 suggest that yet a fourth option might have been considered, that of 'reviving' the archbishopric believed once to have existed at Lugo. In actual fact it never had existed, though it may well have been that for much of the eighth and ninth centuries the metropolitans of Braga had resided at Lugo.

[22] For all that concerns archbishop Maurice see P. David, 'L'énigme de Maurice Bourdin', in his *Études historiques sur la Galice et le Portugal du VIᵉ au XIIᵉ siècle* (Lisbon-Paris, 1947), pp. 441-501.

a visit to the papal curia in 1116–17 he was chosen by Paschal II—we do not know why—to act as an intermediary between the papal court and the emperor Henry V. During the course of his embassy Maurice crowned Henry (March 1117). This was not a coronation but a crown-wearing: none the less it gave deep offence at Rome. Maurice was excommunicated shortly afterwards at the council of Benevento. Meanwhile, he remained in the imperial entourage. After Paschal II's death in January 1118, Gelasius II was chosen pope against the wishes of the powerful Frangipani faction. These men, followed by most of the Romans and supported by the imperial court, declared the recent papal election invalid. Once again, as in the days of Gregory VII and Henry IV, a rival imperial pope was chosen. Maurice of Braga was the man selected (March 1118). A vigorous propaganda campaign was conducted against him by Gelasius II and later by Calixtus II, and by some of the cardinals, notably Cuno, cardinal-bishop of Praeneste. Maurice seems to have received hardly any ecclesiastical support, even in his own church of Braga, to whose clergy he wrote very soon after his election.[23] The skilful diplomacy of Calixtus II, ably seconded by the abbot of Cluny, succeeded in detaching the German emperor from his pope. Even Roman opinion finally turned against Maurice and in 1119, isolated, he retired to Sutri. There in 1121 he was besieged by the troops of Calixtus II, captured, subjected to various humiliations and finally confined in the abbey of La Cava where he ended his days many years later. It was a sad end to an extraordinary and in some ways brilliant career. As far as Diego Gelmírez was concerned it meant that during the crucial period between 1118 and 1121 the most dangerous enemy of the pope was the renegade archbishop of Braga. Diego might well have hoped to capitalize on this. Whether a pope would ever have seriously contemplated so sweeping a change in the structure of the Iberian church simply in retribution for the sins of an errant archbishop may be doubted. But in the heady days of 1118 anything seemed possible.[24]

---

[23] *PUP*, no. 20 (22 March 1118).   [24] *HC*, pp. 258–9.

The 'way of Mérida' was different again. The point urged by abbot Pontius was that an organized Christian church had ceased to exist there, at what had undoubtedly once been the seat of a metropolitan.[25] Had he got his facts right? We cannot be sure, but it seems likely. It was certainly the case that the 'Mozarabic' Christian communities of al-Andalus were experiencing intermittent persecution. at Almoravide hands. Numbers of them were decamping to seek new homes in the north; in the exodus from Granada in 1125, very large numbers. We cannot assume that the church leaders of western Christendom were ignorant about such ecclesiastical life as still survived in the formerly Christian lands now under Islamic rule. Gregory VII had corresponded with Christians in north Africa, the Norman conquerors had discovered numerous Christian communities in Sicily, Paschal II had been in touch with the church of Malaga, a bishop of Granada had attended queen Urraca's court in 1116, and the Christian community of Lisbon had a bishop at the time of the crusaders' siege of the city in 1147. Of the church of Mérida we know nothing. At any rate, Calixtus II was evidently persuaded that the see of Mérida was not only vacant but had in some sense lapsed; for so he stated in his bull.[26]

Diego's strategy, therefore, demanded a good deal of hard talking about Spanish ecclesiastical organization past and present, and an awareness of current developments in high politics.[27] His tactics had to be more earthy, but they still demanded a certain flair. Bribes can so easily misfire if offered at the wrong moment, or to the wrong person. However, the engaging frankness of the *Historia Compostellana* shows that Diego was rarely left in any doubt about whose palm to grease and when. It provides ample confirmation of contemporary satire about the venality of the papal curia, such as the poem whose title is quoted at the head of this chapter. Both Gelasius II and Calixtus II made it plain that Diego must be prepared to spend heavily if his cause were to prosper.[28] The message very soon got through to

[25] *HC*, p. 288.   [26] *HC*, p. 293.

[27] Dr Vones observes that Diego's desire for an archbishopric fitted in well with Calixtus II's policy of weakening the authority claimed by *primatial* sees (in this instance Toledo) over metropolitans: *Kirchenpolitik*, pp. 371, 375-6.

[28] *HC*, pp. 259, 277(275).

Compostela. Cardinal Deusdedit may have asked for his prebend; he certainly asked for a costly chasuble a few years later. The cardinals expected to receive 'many big presents' (*magna et innumera munera*), and grumbled when their expectations were disappointed—temporarily, for Hugo of Porto stayed on at the curia to arrange for the distribution of what were tactfully referred to as 'blessings' (*benedictiones*). Keen embarrassment was caused when an allegedly gold reliquary was found to be only of silver plated in gold.[29] We can reconstruct in some detail what Diego had to spend. The first pair of envoys (summer 1118) took with them 120 ounces (*unciae*) of gold; this was captured by the Aragonese and apparently never recovered. The second took 100 ounces (half of which was entrusted to Bernard of Carrión). In 1119 Gerald carried with him the 'gold' reliquary which was to cause so much trouble, 100 *maravedis*, 211 Poitevin shillings, 60 Milanese, 20 Toulousain and more besides (the words—*et cetera*—are his own). In 1120 the sum of 260 silver marks was urgently requested by Hugo of Porto for the final hand-outs. It was made up from a silver dish formerly in the possession of al-Musta'in the *taifa* king of Zaragoza (40 marks); a golden cross and crown, and a chasuble worked in gold thread (*casula aurea*), all formerly given to the church of Santiago by one of the kings named Ordoño (180 marks);[30] and 40 marks contributed by Diego Gelmírez himself. The silver vessel—it is referred to as an *intremissa*, which usually means a big shallow dish—is particularly interesting. Al-Musta'in was the last *taifa* king of Zaragoza, killed in battle in 1110. His son gave hostages to Alfonso I of Aragon, who placed them in the custody of queen Urraca, who freed them on receipt of a large ransom in gold and silver. This is a plausible context for the passage of such a treasure into the hands of the Castilian royal family. There were several occasions between 1110 and 1120 when the *intremissa* might have been passed on from Urraca to Diego. It was acutely observed by López

[29] *HC*, pp. 287(285), 290-1, 300.
[30] In 911 Ordoño II had given to the church of Santiago a gold cross, no less than three golden crowns, and a chasuble: R. 20 April 911. Presumably the crowns were votive, hanging crowns like those found at Guarrazar, not crowns for wearing such as Alfonso III had wished to acquire from the clergy of Tours.

Ferreiro that the king of Aragon probably still regarded it as his property; hence his attempts to despoil successive Compostelan envoys of their bullion.[31]

Thus, by a prodigious expenditure of effort and treasure, Diego became an archbishop. But, as he must have foreseen even amid all the rejoicing on 25 July 1120, the papal bulls which he had just heard read out were to prove dragons' teeth. From them sprang into being a crop of formidable problems which were to dog him for the rest of his career. They occasioned Diego so much vexation and illustrate so well the nature of the relationship between the popes and the western Iberian churches that we must dwell a little on them.

A metropolitan must have suffragans. Calixtus II had allotted two to Diego, those of Coimbra and Salamanca. Diego's problem was how to enforce his authority over them. Both were a long way from Compostela, and Coimbra was in the county of Portugal which was fast emancipating itself from political subjection to the crown of León-Castile.[32] In the recent past Coimbra had moved much in the orbit of Braga; Toledo too had claims upon her. In 1103 Paschal II had ordered bishop Maurice of Coimbra to be obedient to the archbishop of Braga, as his suffragan. The letter probably originated in a complaint emanating from Braga. It is not difficult to guess that his loyalty was being sought by Toledo. Not only was bishop Maurice a protégé of archbishop Bernardo of Toledo, but in addition pope Urban II had in 1088 granted the archbishop of Toledo metropolitan powers over any restored bishopric in Christian Spanish territory whose metropolitan church remained in Islamic hands. It was widely accepted—though not at Braga— that in the Visigothic period the see of Coimbra had been subject to the metropolitan of Mérida: *ergo*, its bishop should now be subject to Toledo. However, the position taken up by the pope in 1103 was maintained. Bishop Gonzalo of Coimbra (1109-28) seems to have been a loyal suffragan

[31] *LFH* III, p. 525, n. 2.

[32] For the conflict over Coimbra see *HC*, pp. 294-5, 308, 336, 359, 395, 404, 409-10, 441, 491-3, 510; *PUP*, nos. 7, 11, 12, 18, 21, 30; JL 6474; AD Braga, Gaveta dos Arcebispos, no. 4; AD Braga, Liber Fidei, nos. 371 (fo. 106ʳ), 548 (fo. 146ᵛ), 573 (fo. 151ᵛ), 713 (fol. 191ᵛ).

of Braga. The archbishop of Toledo was rebuked by the pope for unjustly seeking a profession of obedience from him. In 1115 a papal ruling confirmed Coimbra's subjection to Braga. Early in 1117, however, the question was re-opened. At the council of Burgos the papal legate cardinal Boso— Diego's friend and ally (could he have acted on Compostelan prompting?)[33]—conducted a thorough examination of all the evidence he could assemble and ruled that Coimbra should be subject not to Braga but to Mérida. This was the state of affairs when Diego became archbishop in 1120. Gonzalo was far from being a dutiful suffragan. He failed to attend Diego's first council of Compostela in 1121, leading Diego to complain to the pope. Calixtus was sympathetic in his reply which was dated 21 June 1121. What he failed to tell Diego was that on the day before, his chancery had issued a privilege for the church of Braga stating unequivocally that the bishopric of Coimbra was a suffragan of Braga, i.e. going back to the situation as it had been before Boso's ruling of 1117. Yet three years later, in June 1124, the same pope roundly told Gonzalo of Coimbra that his see was in the province of Mérida-Compostela. Bernardo succeeded Gonzalo as bishop of Coimbra in 1128. Previously a canon and archdeacon of Braga he was elected at the royal vill of Guimarães 'with the consent of the lord king and on the advice of the archbishop of Braga' (i.e. Afonso Henriques and archbishop Paio Mendes), and consecrated at Braga by the archbishop. The text of his profession of obedience on that occasion was copied no less than four times into the cathedral cartulary of Braga. As seen from Compostela, the task of getting him to acknowledge subjection to Diego must have looked daunting. And so it proved, despite fulminations from both Honorius II in 1128 and Innocent II in 1130. Yet it was Innocent II again who some years later, in 1139, ruled that Coimbra was in the province of Braga. And so the tussle went on. It was still going on fifty years later.

At Salamanca the bishop who was ordered by the pope in 1120 to be obedient to Diego Gelmírez was Jerónimo,

---

[33] It is possible that Boso had visited Compostela and Braga before holding the council at Burgos.

now at the end of an exotic career. From his native Périgord
he had gone as a monk to Moissac, and thence under the
patronage of archbishop Bernardo to a canonry at Toledo.
In about 1097 he had entered the service of the Cid and was
promoted to the bishopric of Valencia which he held from
1098 until the abandonment of the city in 1102. He had
been immediately translated to the bishopric of Salamanca.
From Diego's point of view Jerónimo was a man of the
Toledan connection. It is probable that he was also courted
by the Portuguese; in ecclesiastical terms, that the archbishop of Braga had designs over Salamanca.[34] But documents that were regarded as authoritative stipulated that
the bishopric of Salamanca should be subject to Mérida.
This was the situation when Jerónimo died in June 1120.
His successor, evidently appointed before the end of the
year, was named Geraldo.[35] He was summoned to and apparently attended Diego's council of Compostela in January
1121. He was consecrated in Rome by pope Calixtus. He
made a profession of obedience to Diego Gelmírez. We sense,
though cannot prove, a prior connection with the church of
Compostela. But Geraldo did not last long. Expelled from
his diocese by the Aragonese in the winter of 1121-2, he
retired to Compostela and later, with Diego's permission,
attached himself to the royal court of queen Urraca. Whether
he subsequently died, or was held to have resigned his see,
we do not know. What we do know is that in 1123 the
Toledo party tried to make a come-back: for Nuño, Geraldo's
successor, was consecrated by the archbishop of Toledo.
Diego protested vigorously, and got the pope to do likewise.
Nuño submitted and made a profession of obedience to
Compostela. But Diego clearly regarded him as unsatisfactory,
and six years later managed to have him deposed, on what
grounds we do not know, by a papal legate at the council of
Carrión. His successor was almost certainly nominated by
Diego. Alfonso Pérez was a canon of Compostela whom

---

[34] AD Braga, Liber Fidei, no. 582 (fo. 152ᵛ); *DMP*, nos. 31, 35.

[35] The Salamanca business is even harder to sort out than the Coimbra story.
It has to be reconstructed from *HC*, pp. 308, 341, 359, 379, 407-10, 498-500;
PUP, no. 22; R. 11 November 1123; B. Dorado, *Historia de Salamanca* (Sala-
manca, 1776), p. 114.

Diego had employed on at least two occasions as an envoy to the papal curia. But he too did not last long. He died at Cluny in November 1131 after attending the council of Rheims. The following three years saw three different con-tenders wrangling over the bishopric of Salamanca; and there for the moment we may leave its troubled history.

What we cannot yet do is to leave the tangled story of Diego's dealings with his suffragans. As we have seen, the pope had allotted him two only. But he thought that he had two more, Avila and Zamora. The bishopric of Avila was an ancient one—Priscillian had been its bishop—and belonged to the province of Mérida. The see of Zamora, however, had not existed in the Roman or Visigothic periods. It was a creation of the ninth century, though it had been in abeyance from the early part of the eleventh. Its metro-politan allegiance was not clear. When the two sees were re-established they were held in plurality by Jerónimo of Salamanca. Diego was determined that Avila at least should be his. He did not shrink from interpolating the text of the papal privilege which gave him his archbishopric to gain his point.[36] There is some mystery about the succession to Jerónimo in the see of Avila.[37] We hear of a bishop-elect, P., who was summoned to attend the Compostela council of January 1121. But shortly afterwards we hear of another bishop-elect named Sancho. Some irregularity was alleged about his election. The business was examined at Compostela by Diego's old friend cardinal Boso—another friend, bishop Guy of Lescar, was also present—and the election declared satisfactory. Sancho was consecrated by Diego and made profession of obedience. Not all were satisfied, notably the archbishop of Toledo, who was still complaining about it three years later. We know nothing of Sancho's background but it does look as though he were Diego's candidate. He held the see of Avila until 1133.

At Zamora Diego was less fortunate. Jerónimo's successor there was a man of the Toledan connection. Bernardo, who

---

[36] The authentic text of JL 6823 is to be found in AC Santiago de Compostela, Tumbo B, fo. 261ᵛ–262ʳ (pd. *LFH* IV, ap. i, pp. 3–5); the interpolated text is in *HC*, pp. 292–4.

[37] For what follows see *HC*, pp. 308, 322–3, 406, 408.

became bishop of Zamora in 1121, had previously been a canon and archdeacon of Toledo. The *Historia Compostellana*, significantly, hardly ever mentions him. He outlived Diego to die after a long and distinguished episcopate in 1149. Zamora did eventually become a suffragan of Compostela; but that was much later on and in very different circumstances.

Diego therefore had in Coimbra a suffragan whom he could not discipline, in Salamanca and Avila suffragans whom he could control only with a struggle, and in Zamora a suffragan over whom he had only shadowy claims. It was a familiar predicament for a twelfth-century archbishop. An instructive parallel is provided by the dealings of Diego's contemporary, archbishop Thurstan of York, with his Scottish suffragans: like Diego he found the exercise of metropolitan authority practically impossible.[38] Both archbishops fell back on papal authority. But it will by now be plain that there was little that papal authority could do to help them. Rulings were contradictory, as in the extraordinary case of Coimbra in 1121.[39] Mandates were disregarded, and sanctions ineffectual. The evidence on which decisions might be based was rarely unambiguous. And money talked —doubtless the money of Diego's opponents as vocally as his own.

Such practical power as Diego could exercise as a metropolitan over his suffragan bishops would depend on local initiatives that he himself could take. Systematic metropolitan administration such as we find later on—provincial councils, metropolitical visitation, archiepiscopal jurisdiction —did not exist in early twelfth-century Spain; nor indeed in any part of Latin Christendom. What mattered was patronage; to put it more bluntly, jobbing your own candidates into bishoprics—any bishoprics, not just those of your own province. It was correctly regarded as a triumph for Diego to have got his own men into the sees of Mondoñedo and Porto in 1112. Given that in Spain, as elsewhere, kings and

---

[38] D. Nicholl, *Thurstan, archbishop of York (1114–1140)* (York, 1964), ch. IV.

[39] I should be tempted to regard the privilege of 20 June 1121 as a forgery, did the original not survive at Braga.

queens had a large say in episcopal elections, Diego's ability to get his way would depend to a great extent upon his relations with the royal court: we shall see further examples of this in Chapter X. There was not much that a pope could do to give force to an archbishop's pretensions. However, it was quite a different matter where *legatine* authority was concerned.

In April 1093 archbishop Bernardo of Toledo was appointed papal legate throughout all the ecclesiastical provinces of 'the Spains', including that of Narbonne. He held this position for an astonishingly long time. It was not until November 1114 that he was deprived of his legatine powers over the province of Braga.[40] The concession to Diego of legatine authority over the provinces of Mérida-Compostela and Braga in 1120 was an important one. It enabled him to override the authority of the archbishop of Braga and to summon the higher clergy of that province to legatine councils held at Compostela in 1121, 1122, 1123 and 1124. It gave him a handle for disciplining recalcitrants. Gonzalo of Coimbra might claim that he was not bound to attend a council summoned by an archbishop of Compostela; he could not claim exemption from attendance at a council convened by a papal legate. He was suspended for failing to attend the councils of 1121 and 1124. This does not mean that all was plain sailing for Diego. In 1123 he sought confirmation of his legatine powers from Calixtus II (a sure sign of trouble),[41] and in 1124 the archbishop of Toledo forbade him to hold the council at all.

Diego knew that he could rely on the help of pope Calixtus. For nearly seven years Diego had enjoyed the consistent friendship and active benevolence of two successive popes. In 1120 he had got nearly everything he wanted. Four years later, in June 1124, he finally got what he had most anxiously waited for: the temporary transfer of the metropolitanate of

[40] There are important discussions of the legatine question in J. F. Rivera Recio, *La iglesia de Toledo en el siglo XII* (Rome, 1966), ch. III, and Vones, *Kirchenpolitik*, ch. IV.

[41] *HC*, p. 394 (= JL 7085). Dr Vones, *Kirchenpolitik*, pp. 445-51 has argued convincingly that *HC*, pp. 385-6 (= JL 7020) is a forgery. Yet the temptation to resort to forgery over this issue is in itself of some significance.

Mérida to Compostela was made permanent.[42] He was only just in time.

Popes are as mortal as other men. Calixtus II died on 13 December 1124. His successor was Lambert, the cardinal-bishop of Ostia, who took the name of Honorius II and was to occupy the papal throne until 1130. Diego was to find it far more difficult to get his own way with the new pope. This was not simply because he had had—so far as we know—no contact with Honorius before 1124. Nor was it just that he could no longer rely on friends at the curia: Boso had left to become bishop of Turin in 1122, and though Deusdedit remained in the curia until his death in 1129 he seems to have exerted little influence on affairs.[43] It is rather the case that changes were afoot in Rome which were to alter the character of papal action over the next generation or so. Once more it must be emphasized that Diego's career cannot be interpreted without some reference to that wider stage on which he aspired to play a part.

In September 1122 the concordat of Worms had brought to an end the long struggle over investitures between successive popes and emperors. (Lambert of Ostia had been one of the principal negotiators on the papal side.) In March 1123 Calixtus presided over the first Lateran council. It was the biggest and most imposing assembly of its kind ever seen in western Christendom, and its decrees established a standard of disciplinary excellence the realization of which was to be the aim of reforming churchmen for the rest of the century. Shortly afterwards the office of papal chancellor was granted to Aimeric, a Frenchman like the pope, an Augustinian canon, a friend of Bernard of Clairvaux, and a man committed to the ideas of the reformers. He was to hold this vitally important office for eighteen years.[44] During the same period

---

[42] *HC*, pp. 396–402 for the negotiations, 402–3 for the bull (= JL 7160). A draft of the bull was sent unsealed to Diego so that he might emend it: the whole passage (*HC*, pp. 398–400), if credible, is of exceptional interest for the *modus operandi* of the papal chancery.

[43] A letter he sent to Diego early in 1125 spoke of the new pope in rather guarded terms: *HC*, p. 425.

[44] Aimeric's career is charted in F.-J. Schmale, *Studien zum Schisma des Jahres 1130* (Cologne, 1961), part II, pp. 93–191: for what follows on the cardinals see *idem*, part I, ch. 2, pp. 29–90.

in 1122 and 1123 the pope created a considerable number of new cardinals. For the most part they were not of Roman origin; many were natives of northern Italy or France. Several were connected in some way or another with the order of canons regular, and some with the Cistercians. All were men of reforming temper. It was this group, ably led by Aimeric, who managed—one might even say rigged— the election of Lambert of Ostia in 1124. Lambert's choice of pontifical name deliberately recalled Honorius I (625-38), the devoted follower of Gregory the Great, who more than any other pope of the seventh century tried to put his master's ideals into practice: he might also have had in mind a more recent pope Gregory. The years 1122-4 marked a turning-point in the history of the twelfth-century papacy. The dreary and latterly futile conflict with the emperor was over. A new generation of younger men came to the fore. They included men of outstanding talents and energies who were associated with others who were striking out new directions in the spiritual life of Christendom such as Bernard of Clairvaux, Peter the Venerable of Cluny and Norbert of Xanten. Attracted by new departures within the church, the new men were dedicated to the inward renewal of the clergy as a means for the transformation of Christian society in a fashion pleasing to God. So they saw themselves. Others found them shrill, abrasive, intolerant and sanctimonious. Their most determined domestic enemies were the men they had displaced at the curia, the 'old guard' of cardinals surviving from the pontificates of Urban II and Paschal II. The hostilities generated by this conflict between generations and—in a sense—ideals were to erupt in the papal schism of 1130. During the pontificate of Honorius II there were signs, all over Europe, of the trouble that was brewing.

The new pope's attitude to Diego Gelmírez was distinctly chilly. The tone was set in his first communication, a letter dated 1 May 1125.[45] It was the practice of the papal chancery to address bishops as 'venerable brother' (*venerabilis frater*) in courteous acknowledgement of their equality of rank with the bishop of Rome, all other clergy and laymen being addressed as 'beloved son' (*dilectus filius*). In an

[45] *HC*, p. 430 (= JL 7208).

extraordinary departure from diplomatic practice Honorius pointedly addressed Diego as 'son'—not even a 'beloved' to soften the blow!—and did it not once but twice in the course of the letter. This was tantamount to an insult. Diego must have experienced keen anxiety about his prospects. His office of papal legate had automatically lapsed at the death of Calixtus II and he wanted to have it renewed. His messengers to the curia later in the year encountered strong opposition there:[46] this they attributed to the machinations of the new archbishop of Toledo, Raimundo, who was in Rome in November 1125, and Diego's unruly suffragan Gonzalo of Coimbra. The distribution of a *benedictio* and the application to friendly interests— perhaps cardinal Deusdedit—availed them little. In a letter to Diego dated 10 January 1126 Honorius curtly told him that his request, presumably for the legation, could not for the moment be considered, and darkly warned him that he should 'study to use, not to abuse, the dignity of the pallium, which is a symbol of humility granted to you by the clemency of your mother the holy Roman church'.[47] A later communication, in July, was positively menacing. The pope referred to ugly rumours about Diego and with scarcely veiled hostility expressed the hope that he need lend no credence to them: let Diego so conduct himself that he lose not 'the goodwill (*gratiam*) of St. Peter and ourselves'.[48] With his usual political good sense Diego had also identified and addressed himself to the man who mattered, perhaps, even more than the pope himself. But chancellor Aimeric's letter was of an icy formality. He thanked Diego for his presents—note Diego's usual tactics —and announced as briefly as was consistent with courtesy that he would continue to work 'towards the end which you have indicated'.[49] This was the coldest sort of comfort. Diego persevered: but the pope's next letter was as discouraging as the last.[50]

How had Diego given offence? The pope's allusion to the

[46] *HC*, pp. 441-2: two embassies were sent.
[47] *HC*, p. 442 (= JL 7236).
[48] *HC*, p. 442 (= JL 7237): the correct date is 13 July 1126.
[49] *HC*, pp. 442-3; undated, but evidently of January or July 1126.
[50] *HC*, p. 445 (= JL 7274): undated, apparently of 1126-7.

abuse of the pallium might suggest that Diego had worn it on feasts other than those laid down in the bull by which the distinction had been granted to him twenty years earlier. This was in itself a fairly trivial offence, though it is only too easy to see how it could have served as the handle for a Toledan faction eager to find fault with Diego. Very much more seriously, though oddly never mentioned by the pope, Diego had continued to claim the office of papal legate. So he styled himself in three documents that we know of from the year 1126.[51] The latest of them (21 July) must have been drawn up after Diego had received the pope's letter of 10 January refusing him the legation (and possibly the earlier ones as well). But we are still left wondering why the pope's earliest letter to Diego (1 May 1125) was so cold. Perhaps it simply was that the churchmanship of Diego—who was now about sixty years of age and had been a bishop for a quarter of a century—was not of a sort to appeal to the faction which had seized control of the curia in the years 1122-4.

There was no improvement during the remainder of the pontificate of Honorius II. If anything, indeed, relations deteriorated. Diego complained to Aimeric about the pope's attitude, but got a reply almost as formal as the earlier letter. He believed that Honorius had sent a secret agent to spy on him. Though he enlisted the help of Alfonso VII in the matter of the legation, it was to no avail.[52] Honorius for his part put off Diego's requests by saying that he would send a legate *a latere*, but delayed doing so until 1129. In the letter that finally announced the coming of this legate —Humbert, cardinal-priest of San Clemente—the pope expressed his thanks for Diego's recent 'visit', through his envoys, to the papal curia; a heavily ironical allusion, we may suspect, to Diego's oath sworn many years earlier to visit the curia once every three years.[53] In all the five years and more of Honorius II's pontificate the only crumb of consolation that Diego got was the pope's summons of

[51] R. 13 April 1126, 21 July 1126; AHN 894/19 of 3 May 1126.

[52] *HC*, pp. 490, 491-2 (= JL 7383).

[53] *HC*, p. 50. The oath had specified a visit *aut per me, aut per meum nuntium*, which implies that at least some of the journeys should have been made by Diego in person. He never again visited the curia in person after 1104.

archbishop Paio of Braga to answer for his wrongful consecration of the new bishop of Coimbra.[54]

Cardinal Humbert, whose legatine journey to Spain
occupied the early months of 1130, was typical of the new
generation of cardinals. He was a northern Italian, a native
of either Pisa or Bologna; had been a regular canon at Pisa;
was promoted to the college of cardinals by Honorius II
in 1126; and was entrusted with responsibility for the
first general legatine visitation of Spain since cardinal
Deusdedit's in 1123, and which was also the first of the reign
of Alfonso VII of León-Castile. A few years later he was
advanced by Innocent II to the archbishopric of Pisa.[55] He
was, in short, a very distinguished churchman. A fair amount
of information about his legation of 1130 has survived, and
we shall have to return to it later on. What matters for the
present is that Diego seems to have made a good impression
on him. Humbert spent a week in Compostela, doubtless to
investigate the charges made against its archbishop before
the pope and to carry out a narrow scrutiny of the ecclesiastical arrangements there. There is no indication that he was
dissatisfied with what he found. The *Historia* implies—
but this is hardly surprising—that Humbert was deferential
towards Diego. Certainly the tone of the letter which he
wrote to Diego in the following year was friendly.[56] Humbert's visit may have done something to ease the strained
relations between Diego and the papal curia. But another
series of events did far more to this end; events which were
quite beyond Diego's or Humbert's control.

Only a few days after the council of Carrión which was the
high point of Humbert's visit (4-7 February 1130), pope
Honorius died (13 February). The process of choosing his
successor brought to the surface the divisive issues which had
been simmering within the curia for the last seven years or
so. Two rival popes were elected by different factions within
the curia, Anacletus II and Innocent II. This schism in the

---

[54] *HC*, p. 492 (= JL 7381).

[55] For all that concerns the careers of the cardinals during this period the
essential works of reference are R. Hüls, *Kardinäle, Klerus und Kirchen Roms
1049-1130* (Tübingen, 1977) and B. Zenker, *Die Mitglieder des Kardinal-
kollegiums von 1130 bis 1159* (Würzburg, 1964).

[56] *HC*, pp. 495-8, 526.

papacy was to last for the next eight years. The more one looks at the papal schism of 1130-8 the harder it is to persuade oneself—or allow oneself to be persuaded by the frothy rhetoric of St. Bernard—that any very profound issues of principle were at stake. The most acute of modern investigators, Klewitz, brilliantly highlighted the fact that it was first and foremost a conflict between different generations.[57] The Anacletans were generally the older among the cardinals, the Innocentians the younger men who had come to the fore under Calixtus II and Honorius II. The two groups held, as different generations tend to do, subtly different ideals. The older men had grown up in the heroic days of struggle with the Salian emperors: that conflict had ended in 1122, it was no time to stir up further strife. But the younger men saw the settlement of 1122 only as a prelude to what they interpreted as the true task of church reform adumbrated by the great forerunners of the previous century such as Peter Damian, Humbert of Silva Candida, and Gregory VII: the transformation first of the clergy and then, through them, of lay society as a whole. The Anacletans stood for old-fashioned Benedictine monachism. The Innocentians championed a far stricter monasticism such as the Cistercian or Carthusian, but were also keen supporters of new orders which were active within the secular church such as the Augustinians and Premonstratensians.

Sooner or later Diego would be forced to take a decision. Which way would he be likely to jump? It is a little unwary to assume too readily that Diego was a natural Innocentian.[58] On the contrary, there were several factors which might have inclined him to the Anacletan side. In the first place, his relations with Honorius II had been conspicuously bad. Second, like many of the Anacletans he was now an old man. Third, he could hardly be said to be in the forefront of the most up-to-date reform: the new religious orders, for instance, had made no impact as yet upon his diocese. Fourth, the Portuguese were notably loyal Innocentians: but the archbishop of Braga was Diego's rival (and the count of Portugal his king's). Anacletus certainly thought Diego worth courting

[57] H. W. Klewitz, 'Das Ende des Reformpapsttums', *Deutsches Archiv* 3 (1939), 371–412.   [58] As does Schmale, op. cit., pp. 215–19.

—he was doing so as late as 1134—and it is significant that Diego had the letters preserved in his *registrum*, the *Historia Compostellana*.[59]

This is precisely the point. Diego was courted by both parties. This is always agreeable, and it must have been distinctly so after the cold-shouldering that Diego had had from Honorius II. In the end, church and state in León-Castile came out for Innocent II. (We do not know precisely when, nor in what circumstances.) It was this, far more than cardinal Humbert's visit, which helped to restore Diego to papal favour. The signs of this restoration are writ large in the surviving communications which passed between the papal curia and Compostela. The batch of letters dispatched from Genoa on 2 August 1130 are the first evidence of it: their tone was notably friendly.[60] Innocent's attitude continued warm, but also circumspect. Diego's unwavering loyalty could not be taken for granted. The pope's letter of 16 February 1131 was in these respects a masterpiece.[61] He opened with honeyed words of flattery, even deference, towards his correspondent; then continued with an elaborate bulletin of his recent doings—the interviews with Louis VI and Henry I, the coming meeting with the emperor Lothar (surely in part at least intended to suggest to Diego's mind that he was on the same sort of footing as these great men); went on to report action in the case of the still-contumacious archbishop of Braga; and wound up by praising Diego's two envoys. The tone thus set in 1130-1 was maintained. Diego was thanked in 1133 for his devotion to the rightful pope, and favoured in 1134 with a further bulletin on papal progress. Even the begging letter which Innocent sent him at about this time was cast in such courtly circumlocutions that its drift is not immediately clear.[62] Diego's other contacts at the curia caught their tone from

[59] *HC*, pp. 512-13, 550-1 (= JL 8374, 8426). The wording of the second of these letters implies that Anacletus had sent more letters to Diego than now survive, and that Diego had replied to one or more of them.

[60] *HC*, pp. 509-11 (= JL 7415-7419).

[61] *HC*, pp. 521-2 (= JL 7449).

[62] *HC*, pp. 529, 549-50, 561-2 (= JL 7610, 7653, 7665). The last of these, sent from Pisa, is undated: it could have been dispatched at any time between the autumn of 1133 and the spring of 1137.

the pope. Aimeric's letters to Diego during the schism were much warmer than the curt missives he had fired off in the time of pope Honorius.[63] And it was with one of the most devoted of the Innocentians, Guido, cardinal-deacon of SS. Cosmas and Damian, that Diego struck up a friendship during the latter part of the 1130s.[64] Thus harmony had been restored. It is fitting, if accidental, that our last record of Diego's relations with the papal court should be the invitation sent to him in 1138 to attend the second Lateran council which the pope intended to hold in 1139. The summons was conveyed by a loyal papal servant who was also an old friend of Diego's, bishop Guy of Lescar.[65]

Relations between the papacy and Galicia underwent a transformation during the forty years of Diego's tenure of the see of Santiago de Compostela. Historians are prone to mistake increased evidence for increased activity. In this instance, however, there can be no doubt that the essence of this transformation lay in the vastly greater amount of traffic that passed between the two by the end of Diego's lifetime. Cresconio, bishop of Compostela in Diego's infancy, in all probability never in his life so much as set eyes on a papal letter. Consider, by contrast, the trafficking that took place during the eighteen months that succeeded the formal reception in July 1120 of the papal privileges exalting the see of Compostela to archiepiscopal rank.

At some point in the second half of the year cardinal Boso set out for another legatine visit to Spain, his second (if we exclude participation in the Pisan expedition against the Balearic Islands in 1114): he travelled in the company of bishop Hugo of Porto as far as Oloron Ste-Marie in the western Pyrenees.[66] Diego, meanwhile, was reporting to the pope on the alarming political developments of the summer in the kingdom of León-Castile: we know of Diego's communication only through the pope's reply, dated 19 December.[67] At the very end of the year a letter giving Diego

[63] *HC*, pp. 526, 584-5.
[64] See Zenker, op. cit., pp. 146-8 for a sketch of Guido's career. We shall hear more of him in ch. X.
[65] *HC*, pp. 597-8; AHN 526/7. [66] *HC*, p. 298.
[67] AC Toledo, cod.42/21 fo. 66^v; cod.42/22 fo. 48^r. For the context, see ch. VI.

news of pope Calixtus' recent doings—it will be recalled that the antipope Gregory VIII was still at large—was dispatched to Compostela by the hands of 'abbot D.', who cannot now be identified.[68] Among other things, this letter asked Diego to 'aid and sustain' the Roman church—a polite request for money. (The flow of bullion from Compostela had evidently dried up since Diego had been given his arch-bishopric in the summer.) It was perhaps in response to this request that a canon of Compostela who is probably to be identified with Pedro Fulco was sent off to the curia, where he can be traced towards the end of June 1121.[69] He was probably accompanied by the bishop-elect of Salamanca, Geraldo, Diego's suffragan, himself the recipient of a papal letter in the course of the year.[70] Geraldo was consecrated by the pope at some point in the early summer of 1121. Pedro Fulco was certainly accompanied by another Geraldo who had been sent to the pope by Diego on account of his marital entanglements.[71] At very much the same time, representatives from the church of Braga may be traced at the curia.[72] Meanwhile cardinal Boso had paid a visit to Compostela, perhaps in about May or June. It cannot have been long afterwards that Boso heard of the capture of the antipope at Sutri on 23 April: he communicated the news to Diego in the letter he sent to summon him to the legatine council he proposed to hold.[73] The council met at Sahagún on 25 August 1121. It may have been at about the same time that a *fidelis* of the Roman church named Guido arrived as a pilgrim in Compostela: Calixtus suggested that Diego might like to make use of him as a trustworthy messenger.[74] But Diego failed to attend the council of Sahagún, and may not have been present when Guido reached Compostela. A quarrel between himself and queen Urraca had occurred in July in the course of which she had had him arrested.[75] One of Diego's reactions was to get word to the pope, which he did by way of his nephew who was studying in France,

---

[68] *HC*, p. 309 (= JL 6877).   [69] *HC*, p. 336 (= JL 6911).
[70] L. Serrano, *El obispado de Burgos y Castilla primitiva* (Madrid, 1935), III, no. 82, p. 153.   [71] *HC*, p. 381 (= JL 6912).
[72] *PUP*, no. 21.   [73] *HC*, pp. 322-3, 326-7.
[74] *HC*, p. 339 (= JL 6920).   [75] See ch. VI.

who turned for help to abbot Pontius of Cluny. The pope's reaction came in letters dated from Melfi early in October (by which time Diego had long been once more at liberty).[76] The year 1121 ended with a Toledan party at the curia in November,[77] and the return of cardinal Boso (late 1121 or early 1122) which would have enabled Calixtus to get up-to-date reports on the ecclesiastical situation in north-western Spain.

The sheer quantity of traffic, at first sight rather startling, becomes less so when set in the context of contemporary papal relations with other areas of Christendom.[78] Two points are worth making about it. First, the envoys whom Diego employed to transact his business must have become very skilful at it. Of all the men who made the long journey on his behalf, the most frequently employed was Pedro Fulco. He visited the papal curia in the winter of 1119-20 and again in 1121; twice or possibly thrice in 1123-4; thrice he undertook the thankless task of journeying to the curia during the pontificate of Honorius II; in 1130 he was entrusted with the delicate job of investigating for Diego which of the rival papal elections was canonical; and he almost certainly paid a last recorded visit to the curia in 1135—a total of nine or possibly ten visits in sixteen years.[79] These embassies—which incidentally proved materially advantageous to him—not only marked out Pedro Fulco as a talented diplomat. They must also have contributed to a stock of expertise about how to deal with the papal curia which became the common possession of the archbishop and chapter of Compostela. There was no longer any need to rely, as in 1104, on friendly counsel from the abbot of Cluny. In a church which was becoming ever more bureaucratic and 'professional' this was a capital of skills which would prove indispensable. It was not the least of Diego's contributions to the church of Compostela to have nurtured its growth.

---

[76] *HC*, p. 346.   [77] JL 6931-4.

[78] See for example the appendix 'Anglo-Papal contact 1100-35' in M. Brett, *The English Church under Henry I* (Oxford, 1975), pp. 234-46.

[79] *HC*, pp. 290, 336, 394, 397, 400-1, 441-2, 444-5, 490, 509, 567. My earlier estimate (*Episcopate*, pp. 90-1) was too low.

The second point arises from the marital career of the otherwise unknown Geraldo. After living for a long time (*diu*) with a certain woman he subsequently married another who was related to the first in the third degree of consanguinity (*consanguinea in gradu tertio*). Was this marriage a lawful one in the eyes of the church? Diego did not know, we presume, and sent Geraldo to the pope, who ruled that it was not.[80] This is an example of the kind of thing that was happening all over western Christendom during this period. Bishops were sending difficult cases to the curia, were encouraging litigants to seek justice in the highest Christian court. The lawyers at the curia were becoming very busy. Soon new collections of canon law—Gratian, and a whole succession of decretists and decretalists—would appear, building upon and refining the existing ones (such as the *Polycarpus*), and a new and more comprehensive corpus of ecclesiastical law would gradually become current.

Geraldo's love-life is glimpsed only in one short papal mandate. It focuses our attention upon Diego's relations with the curia. But it also directs our gaze back to Compostela. It is one of the rare glimpses that we have, albeit indirectly, of Diego's activities as a judge. The exercise of ecclesiastical jurisdiction is part of the business of being a bishop. What do we know of Diego's running of his diocese?

[80] *HC*, p. 381 (= JL 6912).

IX

The bishop in his diocese

'I am the servant and herald of almighty God, empowered to protect the rights of holy church.' Bishops have been instituted 'to lead their subject people, to instruct them in the Lord's teachings . . . we pontiffs are the most exalted servants among the ministers of God . . . to us kings, dukes, princes, all the people reborn in Christ, are subject; we exercise responsibility for all men.' So Diego lectured queen Urraca in 1113.[1] This is heady rhetoric, but it gives us some clues as to how he viewed his role. Such claims on behalf of bishops were neither new nor unusual, and Diego was supported in them by his ecclesiastical superiors. When Urraca imprisoned him in 1121 pope Calixtus II reminded her sharply that Diego was God's and Christ's vicar (*Dei et Christi eius vicarium*).[2] However, we should never forget that Diego exercised temporal as well as spiritual lordship, was charged with secular as well as ecclesiastical responsibilities. His biographers referred to him as 'the shield of his fatherland' (*clypeus patriae*), 'the head and mirror of Galicia' (*caput et speculum Gallaeciae*), and the like.[3] These two roles, the ecclesiastical and the secular, overlapped and interpenetrated at every stage of his career. It is impossible for the historian to distinguish them, and he may take comfort from the likelihood that it rarely occurred to Diego himself so to distinguish. 'Just as princes exercising secular power reward those who serve them faithfully, so I Diego . . . (make a grant of privileges) . . . to you abbot Pedro and the monastery of Anteáltares.'[4] Precisely so. Or, more pithily, in the memorable phrase of his panegyrists,

---

[1] *HC*, pp. 165-6.

[2] *HC*, p. 344 (= JL 6929).

[3] *HC*, pp. 133, 204.

[4] AHRG, Documentos Particulares, Monasterio de San Payo de Anteáltares, no. 27: from the *arenga* of one of Diego's charters dated 11 October 1113.

Diego was at once both the crozier and the catapult of St. James.[5]

Unlike some of his contemporaries in other parts of the Iberian peninsula—notably the archbishops of Toledo—Diego presided over an ecclesiastical structure which was already very old when he became bishop of Compostela. The great achievement of the previous five hundred years in the ecclesiastical history of Galicia had been the slow diffusion of Christianity in the countryside. Even in those parts of Europe where the surviving sources are reasonably abundant this process remains mysterious. In Galicia the sources are extremely sparse: in particular, we have no early hagiography apart from the *Vita Fructuosi*, and the archaeology of early medieval Galicia is still in its infancy; there is little conciliar material, and few charters before *c*.850. We do know, however, that a large number of rural churches had been founded. Our starting-point is that precious document known as the Suevic *Parochiale* of *c*.580.[6] It lists the principal churches of each see, diocese by diocese. While it is emphatically not a complete census of churches then in existence, there is some reason for supposing that few other churches did then exist, beyond those named. With this we may contrast the evidence provided by a number of surveys from the late eleventh and early twelfth centuries. The most revealing of these is the so-called *Censual* compiled in the diocese of Braga probably between 1085 and 1089.[7] It lists the parish churches and the dues they owed every year to the bishop (as he then was) for the area between the rivers Lima and Ave, a region corresponding to only about a tenth of the diocesan territory, but that the most densely-settled and the richest. Comparison of the sixth-century *Parochiale* and the eleventh-century *Censual* yields startling results. In the late sixth century there were

[5] *HC*, p. 253. Little attention has been paid by modern historians of the medieval Spanish church to the matters touched on in this chapter; in an earlier book I treated some of them very briefly: see *Episcopate*, ch. 4.

[6] Edited and discussed by P. David, 'L'organisation ecclésiastique du royaume suève au temps de saint Martin de Braga', in his *Études historiques sur la Galice et le Portugal du VIᵉ au XIIᵉ siècle* (Lisbon-Paris, 1947), pp. 1-82.

[7] An elaborate edition of and commentary on this important text forms the core of the work of David's pupil, A. de J. da Costa, *O bispo D. Pedro e a organização da diocese de Braga* (Coimbra, 1959).

thirty principal churches (including the cathedral church of Braga) *in the whole diocese*; in the late eleventh there were 573 parish churches between the Lima and the Ave *alone*. From the diocese of Compostela we have comparable lists for certain areas whose ecclesiastical allegiance was a matter of dispute between the bishoprics of Mondoñedo and Compostela in the early years of the twelfth century.[8] Here too the results are startling. The Suevic *Parochiale* listed eight churches in the diocese of Iria; not one of them lay to the north of the river Tambre, in the extreme north-westerly corner of Galicia. We possess a list of churches in the district known as Bezoucos—the peninsula between the Ría de El Ferrol and the Ría de Ares—compiled in 1110. The Bezoucos peninsula is only about eight miles long and at its widest point no more than four miles wide. There were eleven parish churches there in the early twelfth century. In the only slightly larger neighbouring district of Trasancos, to the north of the modern town of El Ferrol, there were fifteen.

How had these churches come into existence? Some owed their foundation to ecclesiastical initiative. The church at Cela in the diocese of Tuy had been constructed, so it was believed in the early twelfth century, by St. Fructuosus of Braga.[9] We have already seen that Odoario, bishop of Lugo, was active in the foundation of rural churches in the middle years of the eighth century.[10] It is likely, however, that the great majority were built on the initiative of prominent local laymen. We learn from a document possibly of the ninth century of the church at Vilariño in Nendos 'which Romanus founded with his dependants' (*fecit cum suis gasalianis*); or of the church of Folgoso founded in the tenth century by Aloitus, Zendon and Segeredus and their wives on their own land.[11] While the motives that led men and women to establish these churches were doubtless diverse—and some were certainly envisaged as straightforward investments[12]—we can be sure that nearly

---

[8] *HC*, pp. 80-4.   [9] *HC*, p. 40: quam beatus Fructuosus fabricaverat.
[10] See above, ch. III.
[11] *LFH* II, ap. ii, p. 8; *Sobrado Cart.* I, no. 48 (also pd. *LFH* II, ap. lxxx, pp. 194-5). Many other examples could be cited.
[12] See the very revealing c. 6 of the second council of Braga held in 572: early conciliar material is most easily accessible in J. Vives, *Concilios visigóticos e hispano-romanos* (Barcelona–Madrid, 1963).

all these foundations remained 'proprietary churches'. That is to say, the church with its endowments and profits remained the possession of the founder's kin, and like any other possession was subject to partition among co-heirs and co-heiresses in successive generations. This is the reason for the extraordinary fragmentation of rights in churches, just as of rights over land, serfs, livestock, etc., which we en-counter in the Galician charters of the tenth, eleventh and twelfth centuries. Scores of examples could be cited: let two suffice, both from Diego's day, and both from areas already mentioned in this chapter.

The village of Franza was probably the largest settlement in Bezoucos. Its church, dedicated to Santiago, was some-times referred to as a *monasterium*. In the early years of the twelfth century the church was shared among various mem-bers of the Traba family. Between the years 1114 and 1148 it passed bit by bit into the control of the monks of Jubia, after a series of transactions (four gifts, two sales) between six separate individuals and the monastery.[13] In neighbouring Trasancos, the church of St. Mary at Val was similarly divided, as we learn from an undated document of c.1150:[14]

These are the partitions of Sta. Maria Mayor (= Val) in Trasancos. Suero Peláez was the husband of Ermesenda and they had three children —Gonzalo, Fernanda and Elvira Suárez. On the death of their parents they divided that church between them in three parts. Gonzalo Suárez had six children—Oveco, Azenda, Froila, Guntroda, Ermesenda and Jimena González. When Oveco González was born his aunt Elvira Suárez and her husband Osorio gave him the whole of their third share of the church to celebrate his birth (? *in afiliatione*). Oveco himself had a sixth of the other third which had belonged to his father. He also acquired the sixth belonging to (his sister) Azenda González by judge-ment of Pedro González before count Fernando ...

At this point the story peters out, though we know that Oveco's daughter Guntroda gave her share of the church, inherited from her father, to the canons of Caabeiro in 1165.

Diego Gelmírez almost certainly owned churches, though his biographers—perhaps significantly—never tell us so. His brother Munio, as we have already seen, gave his shares in five

---

[13] *Jubia Cart.* nos. xxiii, xxx, xxxvi, xxxvii, xlv, xlvii.
[14] AHN 491/15.

churches to the cathedral of Santiago, and Munio's children inherited shares in other churches from their father.[15] But Diego knew that ecclesiastical reformers frowned on the proprietary church system. Their disapproval was voiced in successive church councils. The legislation issued at every major council of Diego's adult life, from Clermont in 1095 to II Lateran in 1139, contained canons forbidding laymen to exploit churches and their endowments and tithes. This legislation was received and diffused in western Spain. In 1114, for example, Diego's council of Compostela prohibited the buying and selling of churches or their granting by charter to laymen (*seu alicui laico incartet*).[16] In 1117 cardinal Boso's council of Burgos, which was attended by at least one Galician bishop though not by Diego himself, prohibited the partition of churches and their endowments in accordance with the norms of secular law, and forbade the alienation of church property to kinsfolk, except—a revealing saving-clause—'in cases of need' (*pro paupertate*).[17]

The passage of proprietary churches from lay into ecclesiastical hands was the most considerable and lasting achievement of the reforming churchmen of western Christendom between *c.*1050 and *c.*1200. (Whether or not its results were beneficial is quite another matter.) The process was certainly going forward in the diocese of Compostela during Diego's tenure of the see. Our sources rarely permit us to glimpse the motives that lay behind the recorded surrenders of churches. Thus the *Historia Compostellana*, which records many such transactions, usually notes them in the bleak form 'X gave the church at Y to St. James'. For instance, early in Diego's episcopate count Sancho gave the church at *Maurim* (unidentified, probably near Mellid) to Santiago.[18] Some of the gifts of churches of which we hear may have been concealed sales. Given queen Urraca's insolvency, we might suspect that the surrenders of churches which she made to Diego, for instance in 1115 and 1116, were made

---

[15] See above, ch. VII; *Galicia Histórica. Colección Diplomática* (Santiago de Compostela, 1901), no. xxix (and cf. *Episcopate*, pp. 164-5).
[16] *HC*, p. 192 (c. 7).
[17] F. Fita, 'Concilio nacional de Burgos (18 febrero 1117)', *BRAH* 48 (1906), 387-407: see cc. 11, 16.   [18] *HC*, pp. 69-70.

in return for some kind of payment.[19] Some grants of churches were made by way of compensation, or in ecclesiastical terms penance, for wrongdoing. At some point in the early 1120s count Pedro Froílaz struck Alfonso, count of Limia, inside the cathedral of Santiago; for this act of sacrilege Diego 'imposed a fitting penance in accordance with the precepts of canon law'; the offender was compelled to surrender the church of Cospindo to St. James.[20] Other acquisitions of churches were recoveries of foundations previously held which had been alienated. We hear of churches 'justly liberated', or 'freed from the thirsty covetousness of knights'.[21] Some light on what such phrases might mean is cast by the sources relating to the church of Piadela in Nendos.[22] The church there had been founded probably towards the middle of the tenth century. Shortly before 1020 it had been restored by the descendants of the founders, Fronosilde and her brother Vimara Gundemáriz, evidently as some sort of monastic community. But it was to pass to Santiago after their deaths. We next hear of it in 1101, in the earliest surviving of Diego Gelmírez's episcopal *acta*. The estate and church had been granted by an earlier bishop of Compostela to certain knights (*milites*) as a benefice (*in atonito*). They held it for some time. Bishop Diego Peláez recovered the church and entrusted it to the archdeacon of Nendos, Juan Rodríguez, who completely rebuilt it. Diego Gelmírez consecrated the new church for the use of 'the clergy leading the religious life there'—they are not described as monks—and laid down that henceforward no lay person was to have any power (*imperium*) over it.

Matters did not always proceed smoothly. The acquisition of a church by an ecclesiastical corporation could be a protracted business, as we saw in the case of Franza, and it could be a contentious one. The case of the church of Sabugueira furnishes a good example.[23] This was a well-endowed church

---

[19] R. 3 January 1115, 26 November 1115, 18 May 1116, and cf. *HC*, p. 189.
[20] *HC*, p. 414, and cf. the case of Sancho Sánchez in *Episcopate*, pp. 160-1.
[21] *HC*, p. 59.
[22] For what follows see R. 30 December 1020; *HC*, p. 73; *LFH* III, ap. xvi, pp. 52-3.
[23] *HC*, pp. 72, 185, 464, 468-70. For Bermudo Suárez see also *HC*, pp. 313, 329, 335; R. 3 January 1115, 13 June 1120, 31 May 1124.

lying a few miles to the east of Compostela. Diego initially acquired a quarter-share of it, and later the remainder. But his possession of it was contested by the family of Bermudo Suárez who claimed it as his property (*pro hereditate*). Eventually the parties agreed to compromise, dividing the church and its endowment equally between them. However, a third party represented by Sabugueira's priest, another Bermudo, lodged claims against both the contenders, took his case to the royal court of Alfonso VII, and won it. It was not until after this Bermudo's death that the church of Compostela received its due share.

Diego's dealings with proprietary churches demonstrate to perfection the intermingling of pastoral care and lordly stewardship already referred to. It was Diego's job to care for his saintly patron's material interests in lands, rights and churches. At the same time, as a bishop charged with guiding the spiritual life of a Christian community, Diego was in duty bound to swim with the reforming currents in the church at large and to encourage the drift of pro- prietary churches from lay to ecclesiastical control. Happily for him the crozier and the catapult were one and the same. The encouragement of this drift was perhaps the most important of Diego's pastoral endeavours. To it he could bring those talents and qualities of character which had served him so well in the pursuit of his other ambitions: his intimate knowledge of local aristocratic and gentry families; his legal expertise; his flair for fixing, for wheeling and dealing; his tact, patience and tenacity; his opportunism, ruthlessness and lack of scruple. In his pastoral activities he had also at his disposal a workable machinery of diocesan administration and in his entourage a team of servants both able and dedicated.

It was assumed that every settlement (*locus*) in the diocese was subject to the ministrations of an archdeacon and/or (*sive*) an archpriest (or rural dean).[24] This information allows us to infer the existence of territorial circumscriptions whose clergy and people were under the direction of ecclesias- tical officials who were themselves answerable in the last

[24] *HC*, pp. 178-9.

resort to the diocesan. But we can do better than resort to inference. A succession of documents ranging in purported date from the early ninth to the early twelfth century hints at the existence of such territorial administrative divisions from an early period. Furthermore, the names of some of the regions thus revealed may be identified with most of the names furnished by the Suevic *Parochiale* of the late sixth century in its listing of what were then the principal local churches of the diocese of Iria. An example will serve both to introduce the evidence and to tantalize the reader with the perspectives it opens up.

Pestemarcos is the name of one of the principal churches listed in the Suevic *Parochiale*. (It should not escape notice that this Celtic name-form is obviously many years older than the Suevic period.) *Pistomarcos* is named as one of the divisions of the diocese of Iria in a document ostensibly of the year 830 and perhaps most conveniently labelled the *Ordinatio Tructini.*[25] In the same form, and with the same signification, the name occurs again in what purports to be a charter of Alfonso V of 1019 recording the results of a 'great inquisition' (*exquisitio magna*) into the rights and privileges of the church of Iria.[26] *Pistomarcos* is listed among the districts (*dioceses*) of the bishopric of Iria in a schedule preserved by the *Chronicon Iriense*, a work which took on its final shape in Compostela in about 1080-90.[27] *Pistomarcus* features in Paschal II's solemn privilege of 1110 as one of the divisions of the diocese of Santiago de Compostela.[28] Finally, *Pistomarchis* was one of the archipresbyterates, or rural deaneries, of the archdiocese in the time of archbishop Pedro Suárez in 1177.[29] Postmarcos is the name of the pensinula to the west of Padrón between the Ría de Muros and the Ría de Arosa; the village of Postmarcos is on the southern side of that pensinsula. An early ecclesiastical foundation, perhaps originally serving the needs of what had once been a pre-Roman Celtic tribal group, may thus

[25] *LFH* II, ap. ii, pp. 6-8.   [26] R. 30 March 1019.

[27] See the edition by M. R. García Alvarez in *Memorial Histórico Español* 50 (1963), 1-240.

[28] *HC*, pp. 85-6 (= JL 6264): cf. also *HC*, pp. 59, 72, 125, 186, 504, 558; AHRG, Documentos Particulares, Monasterio de San Payo de Antealtares, no. 27.

[29] *LFH* IV, ap. 1, pp. 122-4.

be traced from the sixth century to the twelfth, after which its history is that of a minor cog in the vast and intricate machinery of Latin Catholic bureaucracy. It is an imposing genealogy, and one that can only rarely be matched among the multitudinous rural deaneries of the western church.

But the chain of institutional, as of human, genealogy is only as strong as its individual links. And the documents that form the links in this chain are woefully lacking in credibility. They have taken a punishing from the bruisers who have operated to such sparkling effect in the ring of early Spanish diplomatics—notably from Barrau-Dihigo[30] —and emerged battered. I am inclined to think that these early instruments deserve more credence than the hard men of the École des Chartes allowed them. But the case would take long and intricate argument to present, and the attempt will not be made here. Instead, let us proceed (in a distinguished tradition) 'from the known to the unknown'.

In 1177 archbishop Pedro Suárez carried out a reorganization of the administrative structure of his diocese. The document recording the arrangements, though surviving only in a corrupt copy of the fourteenth century, is agreed to be reliable.[31] The archdiocese was divided into five administrative areas, the jurisdiction of the dean (*decania*) and the four archdeaconries of Salnés, Cornado, Nendos and Trastámara. Each of these five regions was subdivided into archipresbyterates; so that, for example, Bezoucos was in the archdeaconry of Nendos, and Postmarcos subject to the dean. Of the thirty-one subdivisions listed in the 1177 document, at least twenty-four can be identified in evidence surviving from the period of Diego Gelmírez's tenure of the see; of the seven remaining districts, four had been created by the splitting-up of the old district of Deza, itself well-attested in documents of Diego's day: only three districts remain unaccounted for. In this evidence from Diego's pontificate, each district was usually referred to as a *territorium* or a *terra*, occasionally as a *pagus*.[32] The district

---

[30] L. Barrau-Dihigo, 'Étude sur les actes des rois asturiens (718–910)', *Revue Hispanique* 46 (1919), 1-192.   [31] *LFH* IV, ap. 1, pp. 122-4.
[32] For example, Salnés: *HC*, p. 441 (*terra*); R. 1 April 1101, AHN 512/5, *HC*, p. 70 (*territorium*); *HC*, pp. 59, 347, 476 (*pagus*).

names were used for the identification of places in legal
documents: in conveyances of land, for instance, the scribe
would identify a place by describing it as situated *in terra/
territorio de X*.[33] The assumption was that the district
and its bounds were well known; that this state of affairs
had persisted since a distant antiquity. The same impression
is conveyed by the evidence relating to the long-drawn-out
dispute between the dioceses of Mondoñedo and Santiago
de Compostela over their common boundary.[34] Were certain
archipresbyterates in the diocese of Mondoñedo or in that
of Compostela? The existence of these administrative divisions with their evidently well-known territorial bounds was
taken for granted; they had been there time out of mind;
they were a given factor in the dispute. Yet again, the same
impression is conveyed by the few pieces of evidence we
possess which bear upon the careers of some of the archdeacons. Juan Rodríguez, who received the church of Piadela
in Nendos from bishop Diego Peláez, may be traced as archdeacon of Nendos between 1087 and 1110. He was active
in building churches there and assisted in the foundation
of a Benedictine monastery at Callobre. The latter place
is in the district of Pruzos, which was one of the archipresbyterates in the archdeaconry of Nendos by 1177.[35]
Pedro Crescónez was a slightly later archdeacon of Nendos;
he can be traced as such between 1118 and 1138. Since
Diego entrusted the castle at Faro to his care, it is fair to
assume that it lay within his archdeaconry. Faro was an
archipresbyterate in the archdeaconry of Nendos by 1177.
At one point Pedro was seized and imprisoned by count
Fernando Pérez de Traba: his jurisdiction extended over the
count's estates; indeed it did—the archdeaconry, as defined
in 1177, embraced those areas where the Traba charters
reveal concentrations of the family landholdings.[36]

We do not need, therefore, to resort to controversial
documents such as the *Ordinatio Tructini*, the *Exquisitio*

[33] e.g. R. 18 May 1123, a certain church *habet iacentiam in terra de Barcala*:
by 1177, Barcala was an archipresbyterate in the archdeaconry of Trastámara.

[34] *HC*, pp. 74-84, 374-8. For an elaborate discussion see Vones, *Kirchenpolitik*, pp. 149-218.

[35] *HC*, p. 73; R. 30 May 1087, 24 December 1110; *LFH* III, ap. vi, pp. 34-6.

[36] *Sobrado Cart.* I, no. 135; R. 12 December 1138; *HC*, pp. 357, 547.

magna and the *Chronicon Iriense*. Reliable evidence surviving from the lifetime of Diego Gelmírez suggests that the diocese of Compostela was divided for the purpose of ecclesiastical administration into units which were themselves already old. (Precisely how old must remain a matter for investigation.) It is not unlikely that Pedro Suárez's reorganization of 1177 was simply a clarification of existing practice and custom.

There were five archdeacons in the diocese during the first decade of the twelfth century: Juan Rodríguez, Arias Cipriánez, Odoario, Geoffrey and Hugo. The exercise of archidiaconal authority by the head of the chapter may already have existed, though it is not attested until the year 1113.[37] The number may have fallen slightly in Diego's later years: only four, including the dean, are traceable simultaneously in the 1120s and 1130s. We know little about them, practically nothing about their activities as archdeacons. Hugo, author of a small part of the *Historia Compostellana* and later bishop of Porto, is the best known to us, but we know nothing of him as archdeacon. One thing, however, is clear. These were capable men on whom Diego could rely. With the exception of Arias Cipriánez all visited the papal curia at least once to transact business on their master's behalf. Juan Rodríguez served in the chancery of queen Urraca. Hugo was employed to inspect Compostelan properties in southern France in 1105.[38] Juan Rodríguez, the only one of them of whose archidiaconate we know anything, seems to have been an active man in his archdeaconry. Pedro Crescónez, his successor in Nendos, looks like another man of administrative talent: he was chosen by Diego to accompany him to the papal curia in 1119, he probably represented him at the council of Valladolid in 1123 and he was put in charge of the building of the cloister in 1134.[39] His contemporary Arias Núñez, traceable as archdeacon between 1126 and 1138, is the only other

---

[37] Pedro Díaz subscribed a document of 1113 as *decanus et archidiaconus*.

[38] I owe the last point to Vones, *Kirchenpolitik*, p. 51. The same author has elsewhere (p. 50) convincingly taken me to task for my earlier suggestion (*Episcopate*, p. 90) that Hugo was a native of Compostela.

[39] *HC*, pp. 268, 545; R. 29 November 1123; Vones, *Kirchenpolitik*, pp. 457-8.

man of whose conduct in this office we can form some faint impression. He was so uncompromising an upholder of Christian rectitude that the people of his archdeaconry beat him up and imprisoned him.[40]

If we know little of archdeacons we know even less of arch-priests. We have the occasional name. We can infer that they were men of lowly social status, subordinate to and probably chosen by the local archdeacon. We know that they were re-quired to hold courts at the beginning of each month 'as in the past' (*antecessorum more*).[41] They presided over them in the company of law-worthy men (*discreti viri*) who might be either priests or gentry or farmers (*milites, rustici*). The business that came before these courts is only very vaguely described, but it cannot have been exclusively ecclesiastical in character.

The parish clergy are as silent, in our sources, as the arch-priests. It is in the nature of the evidence, in Spain as else-where, that we should hear most about their shortcomings. Spanish church councils, here again reflecting the drift of reforming legislation in the western church at large, repeatedly passed decrees against clerical concubinage.[42] That abuses of this sort existed, and continued to exist for many years to come, is clear; how widespread they were we cannot tell. But if there were clergy whose conduct provoked disquiet, there were also—and unsurprisingly—some satisfactory figures among them. Theotonio was considered an exemplary parish priest during his years at Viseu (1119-28) and there is no reason to suppose that he was unique in the Galaico-Portuguese church.[43] We even catch a glimpse of a wealthy clergyman of scholarly tastes. Romanus, parish priest of Bandoja in Nendos, lived there with his sister; they rebuilt the church and 'did much good work in copying books from one year's end to another'.[44]

---

[40] *HC*, p. 501, which leaves it unclear as to how he had given offence. His archdeaconry was in the extreme north-west of the diocese, the one known after 1177 as Trastámara.   [41] *HC*, p. 179.

[42] For instance, the councils of Compostela in 1114, of Burgos in 1117 and of Palencia in 1129.

[43] E. A. O'Malley, *Tello and Theotonio, the twelfth-century founders of the monastery of Santa Cruz de Coimbra* (Washington, 1954), ch. 1.

[44] *Sobrado Cart.* I, no. 135 (of 1118). If 'books' is most likely to mean 'liturgical books', this may suggest an answer to the question posed at the end of Appendix D below.

The other sort of clergy whose lot it was to be supervised by Diego were those who lived a monastic or quasi-
monastic life. As he was made to observe in the *arenga* of
one his acts, 'it is the special duty of bishops to make provision for the security and seemliness of monasteries'.[45]
There were certain religious communities with which Diego
and his clergy enjoyed close relations. The foremost among
these were the two black-monk establishments in the town
of Compostela, San Martín Pinario and San Payo de Antealtares. With the monks of San Martín Pinario, beneficiaries
of the act whose *arenga* has just been quoted, Diego's relations were always cordial. Matters went rather less smoothly
with Antealtares. The root of the trouble was that the
monastery, as its name implies, lay immediately to the east
of the cathedral. Friction was bound to occur in the course
of the rebuilding of St. James's church on a larger scale.
Tact could normally overcome any resentments: Diego
called Antealtares the 'special daughter' of his church;
abbot Pedro assisted him in the disturbances of 1116-17;
and Diego rebuilt the monastery church.[46] Yet the relationship can never have been an easy one, and it was made
more awkward by the shortcomings of abbot Pedro revealed,
it is most charitable to suppose, in his declining years. Diego
had to conduct a visitation of the monastery and depose
him in 1129 or 1130.[47] The other religious communities
most closely associated with the church of Santiago were
of course Iria, the former seat of the bishopric, and Padrón,
alleged site of the landfall of the corpse of the apostle on
the Galician coast. At Iria some sort of religious community
seems to have continued to exist after the ecclesiastical
focus of the diocese shifted to Santiago de Compostela.
It was under the patronage of the bishops and apparently
well-endowed. In the middle years of the eleventh century
bishop Cresconio restored it and added to its endowments,

---

[45] *Episcopate*, appendix, no. V, p. 236.
[46] AHRG, Documentos Particulares, Monasterio de San Payo de Antealtares,
no. 27; *HC*, pp. 235-6, 372.
[47] *HC*, pp. 507-8. Even if this account is exaggerated it is clear that serious
scandals existed. The succession of the abbots of Antealtares has not been satisfactorily established, but it is likely that Pedro had been abbot for about thirty
years at the time of his deposition.

buildings and library. Diego Gelmírez carried out another restoration. He established twelve canons there under a prior, but we do not know what rule they observed. He also built himself a palace at Iria.[48] At Padrón likewise he established twelve canons, and built himself another palace; a charter of 1116 refers to the building works there.[49] Finally, among religious closely associated with Santiago, were the hermits dwelling on Picosacro, a mountain about five miles to the south-east of Compostela.

In the absence of 'house histories' of the sort that are reasonably common in other parts of western Europe we know very little about the monasticism of the diocese of Compostela (or of Galicia in general) during Diego's lifetime.[50] By way of example, we hear of a *monasterium* at Moraime in a charter of 1119. It was headed by an abbot named Ordoño, and it contained monks observing a rule (*monachis ibidem vitam sanctam ducentibus*). It was then undergoing restoration after damage inflicted by Saracen raids. One *Hodorius abbas Moriamsisis* subscribed a charter of 1105: this may have been abbot Ordoño of Moraime. In 1134 an abbot Martín subscribed a charter of Fernando Pérez de Traba. This is all we know of Moraime.[51] Or again there is the case of Nemeño. This house was founded and handsomely endowed by Pedro Froílaz de Traba in 1105, with the approbation of Diego Gelmírez. Although its precise status is not clear, it seems likely that it was intended for canons: its inmates were *servis Dei*—not *monachis*— *regulariter viventibus*. The house is mentioned in a Traba family document of 1132; its prior Gonzalo is recorded in

---

[48] For Iria, see *HC*, pp. 59, 362-4, 373, 546; AC Santiago de Compostela, Tumbo de Sta. María de Iria, fo. 2^r-3^r (pd. *Monumentos antiguos de la iglesia compostelana*, ed. F. Fita and A. López Ferreiro (Madrid, 1882), p. 9). The latter document has several suspicious features but the central core of what it records of the community's history seems plausible.

[49] *HC*, pp. 59, 373, 546-7; AHN 512/6.

[50] A further reason for ignorance is that such scanty materials as do exist have received very little modern scholarly attention. Patient work on the charters yields fruitful results, as under the hands of J. Mattoso, *Le Monachisme ibérique et Cluny. Les Monastères du diocèse de Porto de l'an mille à 1200* (Louvain, 1968).

[51] R. 26 September 1119 (not above suspicion); *HC*, p. 559; *LFH* III, ap. xviii, p. 60.

1134. And that is all we know of Nemeño.[52] It follows that there may have been religious houses in the diocese whose names do not feature at all in the records which have come down to us. There were plenty of establishments whose exact character is by no means clear to us, and may not have been to contemporaries. Piadela, already mentioned, is one such house. Another is Caldas de Cuntis.[53] It had an *abbas*, Pedro, who was also a canon of Compostela. The church of St. Julian there was in the possession of queen Urraca, and when she gave it to the church of Santiago in 1116 she threw in with it 'the abbot's house' (*cum casa de abbate*). Was there some sort of religious community there in the early twelfth century? We cannot tell. Had there existed some such community in the past? Quite possibly. Caldas de Cuntis, as *Contenos*, had been one of the principal churches of the diocese of Iria in the late sixth century according to the Suevic *Parochiale*. One of the great difficulties is in knowing what was meant by the word *monasterium*. At one extreme it can indicate a religious community of monks, canons or nuns living according to a rule, as at Moraime. At the other, it can designate simply a proprietary church—usually, it would seem, one of a certain dignity, antiquity and wealth—as at Franza in Bezoucos.

Despite these difficulties and uncertainties a few general observations may be made. In the first place, though the diocese of Santiago de Compostela was touched by the influence of Galicia's tenth-century monastic revival, it did not contain any of the foremost houses which were founded then. The most imposing was Sobrado: but by the time of Diego's episcopate this was in a state of such decline that monastic life there had quite probably ceased. The other foundations of the tenth century within the diocese— Caabeiro, Camanzo, Carboeiro, Lérez, Mezonzo and Poyo— had never been particularly distinguished even in their great days; which were well past by the year 1100. The diocese contained no Celanova, no Lorenzana, no Samos—probably to the profound relief of the diocesan. Second, very few Galician monasteries were royal foundations. Toques was

---

[52] Madrid, IVDJ, C.9/25; *HC*, p. 560; *LFH* III, ap. xviii, pp. 56-60.
[53] *HC*, pp. 57, 108-9; R. 18 May 1116; *LFH* III, ap. xvi, pp. 52-3.

founded by king García at the beginning of Diego's lifetime, and Tojos Outos by Alfonso VII towards its end: there were no other royal foundations in between. Neither of these houses achieved any prominence. Third, and as a corollary, it was the aristocracy who patronized new initiatives in the monastic life during Diego's lifetime. It was the Traba family who granted their house at Jubia to Cluny in 1113, who were active as patrons of the religious life for women, who brought the Cistercians to revive Sobrado in 1142.

Diego Gelmírez's attitude to monasticism is hard to gauge—if indeed he had anything so coherent. As far as we know, no member of his family had connections with any religious house. The monastic life was part of the religious scene to which he was accustomed. If he was on friendly terms with individual Galician abbots that was because they formed part of a Galician social community to which he belonged. If he had some dealings with those very great figures in the monastic world, the abbots of Cluny—Hugh, Pontius and Peter—that was because they might be useful to him. Unlike many of the bishops who were his contemporaries elsewhere in Christendom he showed no interest in the new directions which were being struck out in the monastic life. The canons regular were starting to attract interest in the western parts of the Iberian peninsula from the 1120s onwards, the impulse coming, it seems, from Tello's visit to the famous house of St. Ruf at Avignon in the company of Maurice Bourdin in about 1107. This connection bore fruit in the foundation of the Augustinian house of Sta. Cruz at Coimbra in 1130.[54] It may have been from there that the impulse spread north into Galicia. The first Augustinian foundation in Galicia was indeed made just outside the walls of Compostela at Sta. María la Real del Sar in 1136: the initiative, however, came not from Diego but from the retiring bishop of Mondoñedo, Nuño Alfonso. At Tuy the cathedral chapter adopted the Augustinian rule in 1138, but Diego had no part in that decision. As in other parts of Europe some older, decayed or anomalous communities were 'tidied up' by being reformed on Augustinian

---

[54] O'Malley, op. cit., ch. 2 and 3.

lines. This happened, for example, at Caabeiro, probably during Diego's episcopate (though the date is hard to establish); but there is no sign that he took any of the new initiatives there. The case of Coba may be more revealing.[55] A church there allegedly founded by bishop Sisnando I, and possibly therefore once the site of some kind of religious community, was acquired by Diego early in his episcopate and granted as a fief (*in prestimonio*)—contrary to canon law—to one of the judges of Compostela. It was at this man's prompting that not Diego but his successor archbishop Pedro Helias established a house of Augustinian canons there in 1143.

It was much the same with the Cistercians. A well-known letter from St. Bernard to abbot Artald of Pruilly written *c*.1127 has been construed as indicative of his reluctance to countenance Cistercian foundations in Spain.[56] It may not necessarily have meant this—it could simply have been advice to Artald himself—but, whether it does or not, the tardiness of the Cistercians in settling in the Iberian peninsula is striking. Their earliest foundation was at Fitero in Navarre in 1140. The first certain foundation in the north-west was Sobrado in 1142, followed by Tarouca in northern Portugal in 1143. (One has to say 'certain' since there are other claimants, though their documents will not stand up to critical scrutiny.[57]) The great period for Galaico-Portuguese Cistercian foundations was the early part of the 1150s, with the establishment of Alcobaça, Armenteira, Meira, Melón, Montederramo and Oya—none of them, incidentally, in the diocese of Compostela.[58]

It may be significant that all Diego's recorded benefactions to monasteries went to the older black-monk houses.[59] There may, however, have been one direction in which he made an advance. The *Historia Compostellana* informs us

[55] *HC*, p. 71; *LFH* IV, ap. xii, pp. 32–6.

[56] *Ep.*, no. 75, in *Patrologia Latina* CLXXXII, col. 189.

[57] e.g. Osera, in the diocese of Orense, whose very dubious foundation-charter is subscribed by Diego Gelmírez: R. 2 September 1135.

[58] Two Benedictine houses in the diocese of Compostela, Monfero and Tojos Outos, later adopted the Cistercian rule.

[59] Apart from San Martín Pinario and San Payo de Antealtares, there survives the *notitia* of a lost grant to Carboeiro in *Carboeiro Cart.*, no. 90.

that Diego was distressed by the lack of nunneries in Galicia. He founded a house for women at Conjo, a little to the south of Compostela, where he rebuilt the church and endowed the community with orchards and fish-ponds. Although the work seems to have been undertaken early in his episcopate it was not until 1129 that the first nuns took up residence.[60] There may have been a little more to this venture than meets the eye. The *Historia* tells us that there was no religious house for women in Galicia; it does not say that there were no houses for women and other religious. In a letter to Diego pope Paschal II expressed a sense of shock that double houses for men and women existed and ordered that the sexes should be separated.[61] It was possibly in response to the pope's bidding that Diego took his rather leisurely steps to establish the nunnery at Conjo. The existence of double houses in Galicia may provide the answer to the question posed in chapter II as to where Pedro Froílaz's sisters Viscalavara and Munia exercised their vocation.[62] Perhaps it lay behind the disputes over the status of the community at Cines.[63]

Diego's administrative staff and circle of advisers did not include monks. Indeed, it is hard to see how it could have done. The archdeacons, of course, were seculars. His few surviving charters whose scribes identify themselves were drafted by members of the cathedral chapter: even if two of them do describe themselves as *abbas* they also describe themselves as canons of Santiago and Diego's notaries.[64] To write in these terms—a staff, charters, notaries—is to imply administrative and in particular secretarial routine. But this is anachronistic.[65] It is indeed likely that Diego transacted more business by letter then we shall ever know.

---

[60] *HC*, pp. 57-8, 493.   [61] *HC*, pp. 33-4 (= JL 5881).

[62] It should be noted that two of Pedro Froílaz's children founded nunneries, Bermudo Pérez at Genroso in 1138 and Lupa Pérez at Dormeán in 1152: AHN 526/7; R. 12 December 1138; AHRG, Particulares, nos. 58, 497. Note the characteristic stipulation that the prioress of Genroso should if possible be founder's kin.

[63] *HC*, pp. 91-3 (= JL 5944, 6001, 6027); for further references and a very brief discussion see *Episcopate*, p. 192.

[64] *LFH* III, ap. xvi, p. 53; IV ap. viii, p. 25.

[65] For some general discussion of bishops' secretarial arrangements see *Episcopate*, ch. 3.

It is significant that we hear of his correspondence with archbishop Anselm only from the latter's reply. The authors of the *Historia Compostellana* preserved only such documents as were of more than fugitive interest. But the day-to-day administration of the diocese did not call for much in the way of writing. Apart from surviving correspondence with, for example, the queen or the archbishop of Toledo or the papal chancellor, all Diego's *acta* that have come down to us are beneficial charters cast in the form of the solemn diploma: an ancient form, heavy with ponderous circumlocutions, intended to impress, even to awe. Furthermore, these were personal documents in a way in which the routine products of an office are not. They bore the autograph subscriptions of witnesses, some, the more elderly and conservative, still using the ancient 'Visigothic' script, others the new-fangled 'French' script. Diego wrote a big, leisurely, distinctive Visigothic hand, and his subscription was usually accompanied by a device of two concentric circles containing lettering known as the *rota*, which he had borrowed from the practice of the papal chancery.

Diego's administration of his diocese was personal, too, in that it rested in the last resort upon what he himself did. With his household of clergy, soldiers and servants,[66] he was as peripatetic as the royal court, and for the same reasons—to collect and consume renders in kind, to show himself, to perform important rituals, to act as an arbiter in disputes when called upon, to keep an eye on his subordinates: in short, to make himself available. How big his entourage was at any moment we have no means of telling. If bishop Jorge of Tuy—a small and not a very wealthy see—was accustomed to have an entourage of twenty people in the early 1070s it is reasonable to suppose that Diego's was bigger. Half as big again, perhaps? Doubtless its size fluctuated. However, a mental picture of something between twenty-five and thirty-five people in his company is probably accurate enough. These persons, their mounts and their draught animals needed food. As we have already seen, some at least of the estates that made up the temporalities of Santiago owed renders in kind. Much of this produce

[66] e.g. *HC*, p. 329.

must have been intended for consumption on the spot:
the eggs rendered annually, among much else, by the
inhabitants of Cacabelos cannot have been transported to
Compostela. It was not only the temporalities which paid
such rents. Every church in the diocese, except those to
which a special exemption had been granted, owed an annual
tribute to the diocesan. The evidence of the Braga *Censual*
gives us some idea of what this might bring in every year.
The five hundred and seventy-three churches between the
Lima and the Ave rendered annually about 300,000 dry
litres of corn and 20,700 litres of wine, together with a
certain quantity of fish, ducks, partridges, wax, iron, cloth
and salt.[67] We have no such detailed lists from the diocese
of Compostela, simply the occasional reference to payments
customarily made. These fall into two categories: the *tercias*,
or third part of the tithe;[68] and annual renders simply referred
to as 'tax and due' (*census et debitus*).[69] No doubt the
renders were made in several different forms; the only sure
information we possess is that they were sometimes in wax.[70]
It is surely safe to assume quantities comparable to those
listed in the Braga *Censual*. Some of this produce was brought
to Compostela,[71] but much of it must have been consumed
on the spot. Diego and his household had to go to their
food; it did not always come to them.

What the authors of the *Historia Compostellana* primly
called 'holy visitation'[72] may not often have gone much
further than this—the arrival in your village of a band of
hungry men, some of them armed. But if a bishop in quest
of his *tributa ecclesiarum* could be indistinguishable from
a secular lord, he also had special duties which a secular
lord did not. Only a bishop could consecrate churches,
ordain clergy, confirm the laity; and it may still at this

---

[67] A. de J. da Costa, *O bispo D. Pedro e a organização da diocese de Braga*, I.
209–12.

[68] e.g. *HC*, p. 377: tributa ecclesiarum quae tertias dicimus.

[69] e.g. *HC*, p. 81; *LFH* III, ap. xxxiii at p. 100.

[70] *HC*, p. 377: praeter candelam . . . quam annuatim ecclesiae B. Iacobi
exolvat. Since writing this I have rediscovered a reference which I had over-
looked to a church which rendered fish and wheat: AHN cód. 986B, fo. 117
(quoted but I think misinterpreted in *LFH* II, p. 102, n. 2).

[71] *HC*, p. 181.   [72] *HC*, p. 59.

date have been thought desirable that the sacrament of baptism be administered by the bishop himself. Of Diego's discharge of these pastoral duties, with the exception of the building and consecration of churches, we know nothing. Our sources were not concerned with them. We sometimes glimpse him consecrating churches built by others. We frequently see him consecrating churches built directly or indirectly through his agency: for example, the church at Cacabelos, or the four churches in Postmarcos which he found either in ruins or converted into peasant dwellings (*tuguria*) and rebuilt, or the six churches in Nendos restored by his archdeacon Juan Rodríguez.[73] Diego was an indefatigable builder of churches in his diocese. He built or rebuilt three parish churches in the town of Compostela, a cemetery chapel for the hospital there, two successive chapels at his castle at Oeste, and at least seven rural parish churches in addition to those already mentioned.[74] These building operations are alluded to casually, so we are justified in regarding this total as a minimum. The consecration of a church was an important social occasion. Here, arrayed in full pontificals, the bishop could display the gorgeous image of episcopal might to the assembled clergy and people; perhaps even condescend to be affable. Here he could preach, perhaps conduct those other pastoral rituals of which we know nothing. In the absence of any formal and regular scheme of visitation,[75] such contacts between the diocesan and his flock assumed a special importance.

The meeting of assemblies presided over by the bishop, and the exercise of jurisdiction by him, provided further occasions for contact between the diocesan and his clergy and thus for the carrying out of pastoral duties. Some of these gatherings were not, formally speaking, councils or synods at all. The assembly of clergy for the consecration of a church or of a bishop would have been a gathering of this informal type: for example at the consecration of Hugo as bishop of Porto at Lérez in 1113, or at that of Iñigo as bishop of Avila in 1133; and the particularly imposing

---

[73] *HC*, pp. 59, 69, 73.   [74] *HC*, pp. 54, 186-7, 372, 472.
[75] This begs a question: what little we know of episcopal visitation is brought together in *Episcopate*, pp. 175-8.

witness-list to Diego's charter in favour of San Martín Pinario when he consecrated the new abbey church in 1115 suggests a gathering of this sort.[76] Fourteen years after Diego's death, in 1154, archbishop Pelayo issued a statute requiring the heads of all the religious houses that were subject to him in the diocese to come to attend mass in the cathedral of Santiago on the two principal feast-days of St. James (25 July and 30 December).[77] If, as is likely, this was by way of being a reminder rather than an entirely new stipulation, it provides us with a further occasion, the celebration of patronal festivals, for ecclesiastical gatherings at Compostela. It is at least suggestive that one of Diego's charters in favour of a monastic house in his diocese—Camanzo—was dated 23 July, close to St. James's day.[78] The consecration of Iñigo of Avila, referred to above, occurred on 25 July.

Conciliar gatherings properly so called were held frequently on Diego Gelmírez's initiative. But we have to be careful to distinguish between them. As a papal legate he held annual councils between 1121 and 1124, attended— in theory—by the higher clergy of the provinces subject to his legatine authority. The councils over which he presided in 1114 and 1130 were called to promulgate in Galicia the decrees recently passed at councils held on the *meseta*, at León and Carrión respectively. At the council of 1114 Diego made arrangements for annual Lenten meetings of bishops at Compostela. This was in pursuit of his ecclesiastical ambitions at the expense of the archbishopric of Braga. We do not know how frequently these meetings were held.

These councils were—and were intended to be—imposing affairs. They were attended not only by members of the higher clergy and their entourages—eight bishops and twenty-seven abbots, together with *religiosis personis* and *bonis clericis* in 1124—but also by members of the secular nobility of Galicia. We are asked to believe that so many people attended the legatine council of 1122 that the

[76] *HC*, pp. 147-8, 545; *LFH* III, ap. xxxiii at pp. 102-4. See also the remarks of Professor García in his review of *Episcopate* in *Anuario de Historia del Derecho Español*, 49 (1979), 755-9.

[77] *LFH* IV, ap. xxiv, pp. 67-8.

[78] *Galicia Histórica. Colección Diplomática* (Santiago de Compostela, 1901), no. xxviii: the year is in doubt—perhaps 1125.

cathedral of Santiago could scarcely hold them all.[79] In
addition to these councils we can just glimpse another sort
of assembly referred to in our sources as a synod, which
seems to have been a more humdrum affair. The bishop's
synod was attended by the clergy of the diocese, though
presumably not by all of them. Since one of its functions
was to receive the church tributes it must have met regularly,
and at least once every year.[80] This is all we know of it,
though it must have had other functions too. Ecclesiastical
legislation affecting church life at parish level would presumably have been disseminated by way of the bishop's
synod. For instance, the higher clergy showed repeated
concern for the protection inviolate of the area immediately
round a church within a radius of eighty-four paces: laymen
were to exercise no authority there and knights were not to
use churches as a rendezvous (*militum conventus*). This sort
of requirement must have been publicized to the parish
clergy (or their archdeacons and archpriests) in the first
instance through the synod.[81] (Archdeacons may have held
archidiaconal synods already by this date, though we know
nothing of them. We have already seen that archpriests were
meant to hold some sort of court every month.)

We may also presume that the synod would have been
the occasion for the exercise of episcopal jurisdiction, though
here too we have perforce to resort to conjecture. We know
that Diego held a court every Friday in his palace at Compostela. But its business sounds rather seigneurial than
ecclesiastical: it dealt with what are vaguely described as
'plaints and compensations' (*querelae, injuriae*).[82] We possess
only two glimpses of Diego at work as a judge. On one
occasion when the court was meeting not in the palace but
in the half-built cathedral (*in fabrica ecclesiae*) the platform
on which it met collapsed, leaving Diego with one com-
panion stranded on a beam: coolly he waited above the
groaning mass of injured humanity until he was rescued
with a ladder. He had been hearing the case of a knight
accused of theft, in other words a seigneurial rather than an
ecclesiastical suit (unless the theft were of church property).

---

[79] *HC*, pp. 359-60, 417.   [80] *HC*, p. 181.
[81] *HC*, pp. 176, 181, 191, 485.   [82] *HC*, p. 179.

On another occasion he was presiding over his court at Iria, a little surprisingly on Easter Day. The *Historia* tells us that it had met to hear *causas publicas*, than which nothing could sound more secular; yet the only suit we hear of was a matrimonial one, concerning a knight who had been excommunicated by Diego for marrying within the prohibited degrees (*propter incestam consanguinitatis*).[83] The point was made at the beginning of this chapter that it is impossible to distinguish Diego's ecclesiastical role from his secular one. This was a common feature of church life throughout western Christendom in the early twelfth century. The struggle to delimit a strictly ecclesiastical jurisdiction was to be a long and sometimes a bitter one.

'The shield of the fatherland' had extensive secular responsibilities. Foremost among them was defence. The *honor* of Santiago contained several castles. There was the castle of San Jorge near Cape Finisterre, and Faro at what is now Corunna. Further south there was Cira, at the confluence of the rivers Deza and Ulla—the only one among Diego's fortresses that was not on the coast—and Lanzada near the island (now peninsula) of El Grove. The nearest to Compostela and the most important was at Oeste, on the south side of the estuary of the Ulla where it debouches into the Ría de Arosa.[84] Oeste was in existence before 1024, was rebuilt by bishop Cresconio in the middle of the eleventh century, and then enlarged by bishop Diego Peláez. Diego Gelmírez devoted much attention to it. Early in his episcopate he carried out another rebuilding. (It is of great interest that in addition to exacting forced labour he was able to impose a tax of one *solidus* on every household in the diocese to finance it.) To the walls, towers and barbicans (? *propugnaculis*) then constructed he added at some point a *pons* —perhaps the causeway which crosses the boggy ground

---

[83] *HC*, pp. 361-2.

[84] For what follows see R. 29 October 1024; *HC*, pp. 15, 73-4, 186, 304-7, 372, 393; AHN 1749/21. The site has not changed much since Diego's day. Although I have inspected the buildings carefully in the light of these texts on three occasions (1968, 1972 and 1978) I am still not sure of the exact building sequence. The site deserves the attention of an expert. However, when I was last there it was rumoured that it was about to undergo the terrible fate of 'restoration', so it may already be too late.

on the landward side?—and a chapel. Round about 1120
he built a keep inside the fortified area. At some point he
pulled down and rebuilt the chapel on a larger scale. Torres
del Oeste, as it is now known, served many purposes. It was
an episcopal residence, an administrative centre, a toll-
station and a prison. But it was first and foremost a formidable stronghold. It needed to be.

Saracen and 'Norman' raids on the coast of Galicia have
been mentioned in chapter I. There are several references
to them in our sources. In 1101 a Frisian skipper was taking
a party of pilgrims to the Holy Land by sea. His ship was
intercepted by a Saracen pirate referred to as *Avitus Maimon*.
In the fight that ensued the Frisian was saved after invoking
St. James, who conjured up a tempest which scattered the
aggressors.[85] At least twenty Saracen ships were lurking
in Galician coastal waters in 1118. English, Norman, 'and
other barbarian peoples' were a constant fear. No doubt the
arrival of king Sigurd the Jerusalem-Farer with a fleet of
sixty ships to spend the winter near Compostela was greeted
with mixed feelings.[86] Diego realized that the raiders had to
be tackled on their own element.[87] Although native shipping
was sometimes used in naval operations, the only ships
which the Galicians knew how to construct were cargo
ships (*naves sarcinarias*). In about 1115 Diego engaged
Genoese shipwrights to build him two galleys (*factis duabus
biremibus quas vulgus 'galleas' vocat*). These were big ships,
holding a hundred men apiece, and they successfully carried
out a daring—and brutal—raid against the pirates' bases.
A further naval engagement took place in 1120. Neglected
by the men of Padrón, to whose care they had been entrusted,
the galleys decayed. A replacement was built in 1124 and put
under the command of a Pisan captain named Fuxo who
conducted further successful operations.

Diego's military activities were not confined to repelling
attacks from the sea. As a young man he had had experience of warfare in count Raymond's Portuguese campaigns,

[85] *LSJ*, p. 270: on 'Avitus Maimon' see also *CAI* c. 104.
[86] *HC*, pp. 261 287(285), 305; *Heimskringla*, trans. E. Monsen and A. H.
Smith (Cambridge, 1932), p. 607.
[87] For what follows, see *HC*, pp. 133-5, 198-9, 301-3, 325, 424-5.

and this stood him in good stead later on. As a bishop he was bound to provide troops for the royal army, and to serve with them in person until he secured exemption from this obligation in 1113. The disturbances of Urraca's reign involved him in operations against peace-breakers in Galicia. We find him directing sieges. He besieged Rabinato Núñez in Puente Sampayo in 1112, for example, and his old enemy Arias Pérez at Tabeirós in 1126.[88] Many of Diego's episcopal contemporaries—though by no means all—would have criticized such conduct as unbecoming in a bishop. The question was one which was keenly debated during his lifetime.[89] To such critics Diego would doubtless have replied that the end justified the means. In violent times violent men must be confounded by violent means. Only thus could the defenceless be protected against oppression.

Diego's concern for those whom the *Historia Compostellana* often refers to as *pauperes*—a term which probably indicated anyone not of noble rank—was a continual one, and we need not doubt that it was genuine. (The fact that such concern was often in his own material interests does not make it any the less genuine.) There is no reason to disbelieve his panegyrists when they tell us that Diego was stirred by the plight of Christians in Moorish captivity; or moved by pity to release some captive English pirates; or angered so fiercely by the depredations of a certain Munio Pérez that he razed the latter's castle so completely that not one stone was left upon another.[90] There is plentiful evidence of his concern. He ruled that the goods of those captured by the Moors were to be inviolate for a year so that ransoms might be paid. Merchants and pilgrims were not to be molested. When a powerful man went to law with a poor man, let him be represented by someone of the same rank as his adversary, lest justice by supplanted by might. Poor men were not to be distrained upon so ruthlessly that all their possessions be taken from them. Let only such weights and measures be

---

[88] *HC*, pp. 136, 444: note the reference to siege-engines.
[89] The classic treatment is that of C. Erdmann, *Die Entstehung des Kreuzzugsgedankens* (Stuttgart, 1935).
[90] *HC*, pp. 135, 198, 520.

used as accord with the standards in the market-place at Compostela.[91]

We may suspect that it was the actions of Diego's subordinates as well as those of predatory knights and noblemen which provoked such concern. The town of Compostela was administered on the bishop's behalf by a number of judges (*iudices*), perhaps as many as four at any one time, some of whom at least were members of the chapter. Pedro Daniélez, for example, a member of the chapter by 1102, can be traced as a *iudex* for the better part of fifty years, between 1090 and 1138. The *honor* of Santiago outside the town was in the hands of bailiffs (*villici*) assisted by men who held the office of *saio*, in the vernacular *sayón*. The *sayones* had a bad reputation.[92] As the executive officers of the *villici* their main task seems to have been distraint. They were men of fairly humble social status: they could be flogged for misdemeanours. Clearly they were in a position to abuse their powers and often did so. They were bracketed with rustlers as men from whom livestock should not be bought, and with those of ill-repute (*mali*) whose testimony should not be accepted in lawsuits.

The society over which Diego presided in his diocese was in many ways a harsh and brutal one. (Galician society was to remain so for many centuries to come.) Did he leave it any better than he found it? Can we, in fine, make any assessment of Diego as a pastor? Not with any confidence, certainly: the evidence simply does not permit it. But we can, indeed must, say something, if only to summarize the drift of a rather discursive chapter.

Diego eagerly accepted the reforming legislation of his age and promulgated it in his diocese. He commissioned an up-to-date code of canon law. He maintained and increased communication with the popes. All the major themes of the reformers as enunciated in the church councils of his time were sounded by him in the diocese of Compostela: the

---

[91] All these instances are drawn from Diego's decrees *ad protegendos pauperes* issued in 1113: *HC*, pp. 176-81.

[92] R. 14 May 1112, 13 June 1120; *HC*, pp. 471, 534-5; AC Santiago de Compostela, Tumbo de Sta. María de Iria, fo. 2r-3r. See also A. López Ferreiro, *Fueros municipales de Santiago y de su tierra* (Santiago de Compostela, 1895).

condemnation of lay investiture and simony, the insistence on clerical celibacy, the protection of churches and their endowments from lay depredation, the proclamation of a specially privileged status for the clergy. How successful he was in improving the character of his clergy we have not the remotest idea. He did not—neither did any of his contemporary bishops—command the machinery for disciplining the lower clergy which prelates were to have at their disposal in the following century.

What of the laity? With regard to them we are even more in the dark. We saw that Arias Núñez had a hard time of it trying to get across some rudiments of Christian discipline to the inhabitants of the archdeaconry of Trastámara. Gerald of Beauvais regarded them as a rude and unschooled bunch of people (*idiotae et fere indisciplinati*), and we may well suppose that up there in the wilder corners of the extreme north-west (still today an almost unbelievably remote and backward area) indeed they were. 'The Church's expectations from the laity were realistically minimal.' The words are those of a recent scholar writing on popular religion in Spain in the Visigothic period.[93] The judgement may be applied to the twelfth century as appropriately as to the seventh. Much rustic belief and ritual that is often unhelpfully dismissed as 'superstition' was undoubtedly present. For example, the seeking of auguries in the flight of birds is said to have aroused Diego's displeasure.[94] It had aroused Martin of Braga's over five centuries earlier. It is still there, providing reassurance for the participant and employment for the anthropologist, nine centuries later. (The holy wells which also had distressed Martin of Braga seem still to have been revered in Diego's day. I do not know how else to interpret 'the spring for blessing' (*per fontem benedicenti*) which we encounter among the bounds in the Nemeño foundation-charter of 1105.) Diego could rail as he might, but there was no eradicating these ancient, pre-Christian observances. Churchmen could and did present to the laity the barest requirements of a distinctively Christian discipline.

[93] J. N. Hillgarth, 'Popular Religion in Visigothic Spain', in *Visigothic Spain. New Approaches*, ed. E. James (Oxford, 1980), pp. 3–60; quotation from p. 27.
[94] *HC*, p. 101, and cf. p. 116.

Lent, feast-days and Sundays must be marked by certain abstentions. On Sundays the country people must not come in to Compostela to trade. Divine punishment awaits those who work on feast-days. Even *sayones* must suspend their nefarious activities between Saturday afternoon and Monday morning.[95] The surviving sources tell only of prohibitions, but positive commands—for example, to attend church—must have existed alongside them. The laity were enjoined to respect the persons and property of the clergy, and especially to respect churches.[96] They were told that they must pay their tithes. We find Diego advising count Pedro Froílaz 'that he should more fully pay tithes of all that he possessed to the churches and their clergy': Diego's biographers referred to this as 'the nutriment of spiritual teaching' (*spiritualis doctrinae pabulum*).[97] Some rudimentary rules regarding marriage were laid down. 'A lawful marriage must not be dissolved, but those who are connected by blood or other relationship must be put asunder', ruled the council of Compostela of 1114.[98] The sanction of excommunication and the discipline of penance were at the disposal of churchmen for bringing offenders to heel.[99]

In what light the episcopal biographers of this age chose to present their subjects to their readers is a topic to which as yet curiously little attention has been devoted. The authors of the *Historia Compostellana* did not present Diego as a busy administrator, nor as a spiritual guide, nor as a pastoral teacher, nor as an intellectual force, nor (least of all!) as a troubled soul. He may have been some or all of these things. But his chroniclers chose to lay the emphasis elsewhere. For them he was before all else the guardian of the shrine of St. James. For them, images of majesty and power were more fitting than those of humility and godliness. Vigilant and if necessary forceful defence of St. James's rights was a high and exacting task. The apostle's glory must shine forth, his enemies cringe and his suppliants bow

---

[95] *HC*, pp. 178-80; *Sancti Rudesindi Miracula* III, c. 27, in *Portugalliae Monumenta Historica, Scriptores*, ed. A. Herculano (Lisbon, 1856), pp. 39-46.
[96] *HC*, pp. 181, 191, 501-2, 547-8. [97] *HC*, pp. 174-5.
[98] *HC*, p. 192, and cf. pp. 362-4, 381, 485.
[99] *HC*, pp. 192, 363, 414.

before him. With satisfaction Diego could contemplate the
milling hordes of pilgrims, the shuffling, stinking crowds of
maimed and sick who thronged Santiago's basilica. With
satisfaction he could think on enemies worsted—'that fool',
the archbishop of Braga, and 'that Jezebel', queen Urraca.
But he could never relax his vigilance; not even in his dealings
with Alfonso VII, Urraca's son, whose early boyhood had
been passed under his care.

X

'The undefeated emperor':
Diego and Alfonso VII

Alfonso Raimúndez's boyhood was spent in Galicia. His guardians were bishop Diego Gelmírez and count Pedro Froílaz de Traba. He may have retained some affection for the land of his childhood, troubled though that childhood had been; years later he founded a monastic house, Tojos Outos, in Galicia. But the young Galician prince is scarcely visible in the Leonese-Castilian emperor that Alfonso later became. His panegyrist could say of him, with some exaggeration, that his kingdom stretched from the Atlantic to the Rhône. Christian kings and Muslim princes were his vassals. He was the conqueror of Calatrava and Almería; as one his last charters put it, the *pius, felix, inclitus triumphator ac semper invictus, totius Hispaniae divina clementia famosissimus imperator.*[1] It was a long way from Galicia that Alfonso VII finally met his end, far to the south, in the pass of Despeñaperros in the wastes of the Sierra Morena. And though he had once promised to be buried beside his father beneath the cathedral of Santiago de Compostela, it was in Toledo that he found his final resting-place. That was in 1157, when Diego Gelmírez had himself been dead for seventeen years. But the development of Alfonso VII's career, as hinted at in these contrasts, was a matter of the keenest concern to Diego and the clergy of Compostela.

As the heir apparent to his mother queen Urraca, Alfonso Raimúndez would one day rule the whole of León-Castile. So much was clear at latest from the breakdown of the Aragonese marriage in 1110–12. In other words, a time would come when Alfonso's tutelage could no longer be exclusively Galician. That time seems to have come in the years after 1116, when the young man was serving his apprenticeship as a ruler in Extremadura under the guidance

[1] R. 28 October 1156.

of archbishop Bernardo of Toledo. The indications of his movement into a Castilian 'orbit' are plain to see: the ceremony (a crown-wearing?) at Toledo on 16 November 1117; the confirmation of Toledo's *fueros*, perhaps about the same time; the capture of Alcalá in 1118 and its subsequent grant to the see of Toledo; the grants to Castilian beneficiaries from 1118 onwards; the restoration of the bishoprics of the southern and eastern frontiers, Avila, Segovia, Sigüenza, in the early 1120s. However, a Castilian, or more narrowly Toledan interest was not the only one to be playing about the young prince. In the last few years of Urraca's reign, and especially after the death of the old archbishop of Toledo in 1124, we can detect Leonese and Asturian claimants upon his notice and patronage. When the queen died in the spring of 1126 Alfonso VII succeeded her at the behest of Leonese and Asturian as well as Castilian notables, and their influence on him was to be marked during the first few years of his reign.[2]

The most important official in the royal household was the *mayordomo*. Of the three men who held this office between 1126 and 1130 two were certainly Leonese (Pedro Díaz and Rodrigo Bermúndez) and the third (Pelayo Suárez) very probably Leonese or Asturian. The other principal household officer was the *alférez*. Of Alfonso VII's *alfereces* during the same period, Lope López was a native of Carrión de los Condes on the frontiers of León and Castile, García Garcés was Castilian, count Rodrigo a native of the Asturias, and Pedro Alfonso was Leonese. In the early years of the reign the king's most prominent adviser was probably count Suero Bermúdez, whose landholdings lay in the Asturias and the extreme north of León; he was the uncle of Pedro Alfonso the *alférez* and related (we do not know exactly how) to Rodrigo Bermúdez the *mayordomo*. Another prominent counsellor was count Rodrigo Martínez, also Leonese; a third was Ramiro Froílaz, again Leonese; and a fourth

---

[2] In general I keep references to a minimum in treating the reign of Alfonso VII, even though no satisfactory modern study of it exists. The most important source is the *Chronica Adefonsi Imperatoris* (*CAI*): the notes to the edition by L. Sánchez Belda (Madrid, 1950) are of great value. M. Recuero Astray, *Alfonso VII, emperador: el imperio hispánico en el siglo XII* (León, 1979) is the latest general treatment; but it has many shortcomings.

Rodrigo Vélaz, who as we have already seen was a Galician, but from the east of the region, the mountainous zone where Galicia merged into León. The bishops who figured most prominently in the witness-lists of Alfonso VII's early charters were likewise predominantly Leonese or Castilian: Alo of Astorga and Diego of León; Pedro of Palencia and his name-sake (and uncle) of Segovia; archbishop Raimundo of Toledo. Another official who was prominent among the king's servants was the *merino* of León, Albertino, to whose dealings with Diego Gelmírez we shall have to return shortly.

For the first five years of Alfonso VII's reign, then, his court had a mainly Asturian-Leonese-Castilian complexion. This is hardly surprising. It was the entourage of a ruler whose main concerns were with the *meseta*. As far as the external affairs of the kingdom were concerned, the most pressing need was for a settlement with the king of Aragon. This was achieved at Támara in July 1127, and except for a short campaign round Almazán in the autumn of 1129 it proved definitive until the death of Alfonso *el Batallador* in 1134. Only a little less urgent was the need for some definition of relations between the new king and his aunt Teresa of Portugal. A meeting took place at Ricobayo, west of Zamora, in April 1126, and an accord was made; but as we shall see it proved far from lasting. The southern frontier was peaceful at the time of Alfonso VII's accession under the terms of a treaty made in 1121. Almoravide hostilities were resumed on a small scale in 1128 and 1129, and then far more dangerously in 1130 and 1131. From 1130 onwards the king's energies would be directed ever more vigorously to defensive and, later, offensive operations on the southern frontier.

Within his kingdom, Alfonso busied himself much during these early years with efforts to heal the scars left by the upheavals of his mother's reign. He put down rebellions, made amends to those who had suffered, re-established authority and routine. It was a process which culminated in the holding of a council at Palencia in March 1129 where decrees were enacted 'for the well-being of holy church and the prosperity of the whole kingdom'.[3] His itinerary

[3] *HC*, p. 485.

for these years, in so far as it can be traced, reveals him at Sahagún, Burgos, Palencia, Carrión, Segovia, Zamora, but most frequently of all at the *urbs regia* of León.

It is time to turn to Galicia. Queen Urraca's death on 8 March 1126 was evidently sudden and unexpected. It is a minor point, but one not devoid of interest, that the new king seems to have been in no hurry to tell his Galician subjects of his accession. His messengers, among them bishop Nuño of Mondoñedo, did not reach Compostela until about three weeks later; they cannot have been told to make haste. Archbishop Diego could not believe his ears. But with his usual decision he swung into frenzied activity. Leaving Compostela on Friday 2 April, he was at León by the 10th— effectively within a week, when allowance is made for no travel on Palm Sunday (the 4th) and Good Friday (the 9th) —only to find that the king had already left for Zamora. On the Tuesday in Easter week, 13 April, he left León and hastened to the royal court at Zamora.[4] The *Historia* makes much of the reception and privileged treatment he received from the king, but it is hard to think that Diego was himself so elated. He was being cold-shouldered by Alfonso VII in much the same way as he was simultaneously being cold-shouldered by pope Honorius II. It is likely that Diego felt not a little dismayed.

Alfonso VII did not visit Galicia until the autumn of 1127. What took him there then was a Portuguese invasion of southern Galicia and capture of Tuy—events which signalled the breakdown of the accord reached at Ricobayo in April 1126. After chasing the Portuguese back across the Miño Alfonso spent some time at Compostela in November. Two years later he again visited Galicia for a five-week stay in the winter of 1129–30. After that the king was not seen in Galicia until Portuguese affairs once more brought him back in the summer of 1137. His old guardian Pedro Froílaz de Traba died in 1128: he had subscribed no royal charters for some years before his death, and though loss of influence could have been precipitated by age or illness, it

---

[4] *HC*, pp. 432–4. Alfonso VII's actions as recorded in other sources make it impossible to believe the *Historia*'s story that he wanted Diego to crown him at León.

is quite possible that the Portuguese exploits of his two eldest sons had caused the family to fall from royal favour.[5] Donations by Alfonso VII to Galician beneficiaries are exceedingly rare in the early years of the reign. It is indeed difficult to identify with certainty any native of Galicia who achieved prominence in Alfonso VII's kingdom during these years. The only name which comes readily to mind is that of the famous frontiersman Munio Alfonso, and his celebrity was achieved by his own efforts, unaided by royal patronage.[6]

The *Historia Compostellana* has some harsh words for Alfonso VII during this period. 'He never stopped persecuting the church of Compostela—just like his mother.'[7] (And we know what the authors of the *Historia* thought of her!) As usual, it is fair to suppose that this was Diego's own attitude. What was going wrong? It may simply have been that after the experiences of his boyhood and youth Alfonso Raimúndez no longer trusted Diego. The bishop had been entrusted with at least some degree of responsibility for Alfonso's upbringing; the boy had been encouraged to look towards his guardian as standing in the place of the father who had died when he was only two years old. Diego's actions during the reign of Urraca, whether we characterize them as displaying adroit capacity for survival or ruthless pursuit of self-interest, may not have fostered in his ward that trust and confidence which the relationship had been intended by Alfonso VI to engender. Furthermore, between the age of eleven and nineteen the prince had been subject to the influence of the clergy of Toledo; and he would hardly have learned to love Diego from them.

This is necessarily, perhaps distastefully, speculative. Let us consider instead what occurred on the occasion of Alfonso VII's first visit to Compostela after his accession, in November 1127.[8] Like his mother, Alfonso was short of money during the early years of his reign. We are repeatedly told in the *Historia* that he could not afford to pay his

---

[5] I cannot agree with Reilly, *Urraca*, pp. 175, 191-2, 310, that count Pedro was imprisoned during the last three years of Urraca's reign.

[6] *CAI*, cc. 112, 141, 143-4, 162-74.   [7] *HC*, p. 494.

[8] For what follows , see *HC*, pp. 446-62.

troops, and other evidence bears this out.[9] While he was at
Compostela after the Portuguese campaign he was approached
by Diego's enemies with the proposal that he should arrest
the archbishop and deprive him of his temporalities. This
the king was unwilling to do, but he was prepared to accede
to the more moderate suggestion that he should contrive
to exact a large amount of money from the archbishop.
At an interview between the two men in the cathedral
treasury Alfonso made his demand and Diego offered him
300 silver marks. On the advice of his intimate counsellors
(*secretarii*) the king pressed for 600 marks and the arrest
of three prominent members of the cathedral community,
presumably as hostages or sureties for payment. Diego
refused point blank. At this the king flew into a rage and
demanded 1,000 marks or the surrender of temporalities.
Diego called together his clergy, who urged him to give in to
the lesser of two evils; that is, to find the 1,000 marks
rather than risk the loss of the temporalities. While discussion was going on messengers from the king entered the
meeting, demanding that Diego give an answer to the royal
requests under threat that the king's officers would at once
take over the city. Diego agreed to pay 1,000 marks, on
condition that no arrests were made. The king consented
to this—though Diego's enemies thought that he could have
got a great deal more—and the money was raised (with
some difficulty) and paid over. But this was not the end of
the incident. Before the king departed, Diego delivered
a riposte. Alfonso was invited to attend a chapter meeting
at which Diego upbraided him deferentially but firmly for
his rapacity and suggested pointedly that the insult offered
to St. James could best be offset by some gift or benefit
(*munus aut beneficium*). Would Alfonso promise to be
buried in the church of St. James like his father count
Raymond? At the king's request he ran over the services of
remembrance and prayer offered by his clergy on the count's
behalf. Alfonso was willing. But he made one further stipulation, that he should be enrolled among the number of the
canons; this was done. The king then restored two properties
to the church of Compostela.[10] Finally, Diego reminded

⁹ e.g. R. 2 April 1127.   ¹⁰ R. 13 November 1127.

Alfonso of a conversation they had had shortly before the Portuguese campaign, when the king had promised to expel Diego's enemies from the royal household, particularly from the royal chapel and chancery, and to replace them with Diego's nominees. Alfonso publicly confirmed his undertaking. Diego accordingly chose to keep control of the royal chapel in his own hands, but delegated the chancery to Bernardo, the treasurer of Compostela.

The goings-on of 1127 embody some themes which echo those of Urraca's reign: the penury of the crown, the fragility of Diego's hold over his *honor*, the machinations of domestic enemies, the almost ritual quality of the hard bargaining that took place—all these are familiar. There are some new features, however, But before turning to them it will be useful to glance quickly at the somewhat similar events of 1129.[11] Towards the end of that year Alfonso VII paid another visit to Compostela. Diego was seriously ill at the time, his capacity to resist the royal demands perhaps weakened. These demands were made on the king's behalf by two prominent royal servants, Albertino of León, described as Alfonso's *secretarius*, and the *mayordomo* Rodrigo Bermúdez.[12] Diego started off by offering 70 marks to the king, but this was not enough. He was compelled to agree to make an annual render of 100 marks, the royal envoys promising that when the pacification of the kingdom was complete the king would repay in money or in land all that he had taken. We may think it unlikely that Diego was very sanguine about the prospects of the king's fulfilling this part of the bargain. Albertino was made responsible for the annual collection of the money on the king's behalf.[13] This was not quite all. Alfonso also tried to deprive Diego of his control of the mint of Compostela. Diego managed to head him off by producing Alfonso VI's charter of 1107 which had conceded this to him. Alfonso VII confirmed it—possibly, though we are not told this, for a price.

[11] For what follows, see *HC*, pp. 493–5.
[12] Reading *maiordomum* for *maiorinum*. Rodrigo Bermúdez held the office of *mayordomo* between 1127 and 1130.
[13] Could it have been for the purpose of carrying out this task that he acquired the property in Compostela referred to in a charter of 1149? See *LFH* IV, ap. xix, p. 51.

This chilling of relations between Diego and his king during the early years of the reign made necessary new initiatives by the archbishop and clergy of Compostela to recapture, so to say, their ruler: to re-engage his interest and to re-focus his devotion upon St. James and his church. It is in this light that Diego's activities during these years may most fruitfully be considered. Diego was dutiful towards —if we are to believe his panegyrists, indispensable to— the king during the Portuguese campaign of 1127. At a time when this could not be said of all the higher clergy of Galicia, he was conspicuously, ostentatiously loyal. Alfonso VII had been knighted at Compostela in May 1124;[14] in 1127, as we have seen, he promised to be buried there, and was made a canon of the cathedral: honours and undertakings which were intended to reassert a special relationship between the king and Santiago.[15] When he came to Compostela to extort money in 1127 Alfonso claimed that he came as a pilgrim (*causa orationis*), and the clergy of Compostela prayed 'that he might defeat his enemies and subdue barbarian peoples'.[16] The façade behind which the king's *secretarii* went about their business was reassuringly traditional. Diego held up to the young king the example of earlier rulers, 'your predecessors, devout and God fearing men, who loved this shrine and this church above all others in Spain'.[17]

On the practical level of the day-to-day affairs of the kingdom Diego's most significant initiative was his reassertion of control over the royal chancery and the royal chapel. Despite some excellent scholarly work over the last sixty years or so there is still much that remains mysterious about the secretarial arrangements of the rulers of León-Castile.[18] It is difficult to fix on even an approximate date for the

---

[14] *HC*, p. 396; R. 31 May 1124.

[15] The king's sister Doña Sancha also promised to be buried there, as did his aunt Teresa of Portugal: *HC*, pp. 462-3.

[16] R. 13 November 1127.   [17] *HC*, p. 456.

[18] The most important studies are by P. Rassow, 'Die Urkunden Kaiser Alfons' VII von Spanien', *Archiv für Urkundenforschung* 10 (1928), 328-467 and 11 (1930), 66-137; L. Sánchez Belda, 'La cancillería castellana durante el reinado de Doña Urraca', *Estudios dedicados a Ramón Menéndez Pidal* 4 (1953), 587-99; B. F. Reilly, 'The chancery of Alfonso VII of León-Castile: the period 1116-1135 reconsidered', *Speculum* 51 (1976), 243-61.

emergence of an organized chancery, to say anything with confidence about how it was staffed, to describe with any precision how and even for what purposes official documents were drawn up. One thing, however, is clear, that for at least a generation before 1127 the clergy of Compostela had been closely associated with the writing-office of the Leonese royal house. Diego Gelmírez himself had started his career as notary to count Raymond. Pelayo Bodán had served as one of the notaries of Alfonso VI for at least ten years, between 1097 and 1107. Nearly all the men who served queen Urraca in the same capacity may be connected with the church of Compostela. Some of them, like Martín Peláez and Fernando Pérez, went on to serve her son. Others who worked in Alfonso VII's chancery in the 1120s may also be linked to the church of Compostela, such as Ciprián Pérez, active in the chancery between 1125 and 1130 and a canon of Compostela. If St. James's clergy had so firm a grip on the royal chancery, why was Diego so anxious to reassert his control in 1127? Who were the *adversarii* whom he wanted to see expelled? It would seem sensible to seek them among the Leonese and Castilian advisers of the king whose influence he so much distrusted. One name suggests itself. Two royal charters of 1123 were drawn up by the recently appointed bishop of Sigüenza, Bernardo: in one of them he subscribed himself *regis notarius*, in the other *regis capellanus*.[19] Now Bernardo was a man of the Toledan connection. He had been brought from his native Agenais by archbishop Bernardo of Toledo, been made a canon and then precentor of Toledo, and afterwards promoted to the newly restored bishopric of Sigüenza. His uncle was bishop of Segovia and his brother was bishop of Palencia; both of them loyal suffragans of Toledo and as we have seen closely associated with Alfonso VII during the 1120s. Two charters from four years before the 1127 concession may not seem much to go on, but the paucity of royal charters from the 1120s means that we must grasp at what straws we can. I would suggest that when Diego referred to 'enemies' and 'traitors' the

[19] R. 1123, 30 November 1123. The date of the reconquest of Sigüenza and the restoration of a bishopric there is disputed: see most recently Reilly, *Urraca*, pp. 177-80.

bishop of Sigüenza was one of the men he had in mind. One wonders how he would have reacted could he have known that Bernardo would one day be archbishop of Compostela.

If our knowledge of the royal chancery is less precise than we might wish, we know next to nothing about the royal chapel. Several charters have survived which bear the subscriptions of men who described themselves as royal *capellani*; such as Bernardo of Sigüenza in 1123, or Diego's protégé bishop Nuño Alfonso of Mondoñedo in 1126. It is particularly noteworthy that the church of Soria was 'attached to the royal chapel',[20] for this suggests an established institution provided with endowments. How many royal chaplains there were at any one time and what duties they carried out, we do not know. By analogy—possibly a hazardous one, but it deserves to be explored—with royal chaplains elsewhere, in Germany or in the Anglo-Norman kingdom, we might expect the office to have been a responsible and influential one. Diego's anxiety to retain control of it would therefore be intelligible.

The man whom Diego appointed to the office of royal chancellor, Bernardo, the treasurer of Compostela, we have already encountered. It was he who had designed the fountain outside the north transept of the cathedral and planned the watercourses which fed it. He had held the office of treasurer from at least 1118. He held office as royal chancellor from 1127 until 1133, with a hiatus between January 1129 and March 1131 when the chancellorship was delegated to his brother Pedro. His temporary resignation was occasioned, we are told, by his desire to undertake a pilgrimage to Jerusalem.[21] Diego dissuaded him from this: alms could easily be sent to the Holy Places through intermediaries, he briskly urged, and the money that Bernardo would have spent on the journey could be devoted to Santiago. Bernardo bought a golden chalice from the king and presented it to the cathedral. (The king's broker was the indispensable Albertino. Diego's pleasure in the acquisition must have been sharpened by the thought that the chalice had previously

[20] R. 1127: 'quia regie capallanie usque ad presens tempus fuisse cognoscitur'. This charter, incidentally, was subjecribed by yet another royal chaplain, Arias González, canon of Santiago. [21] *HC*, pp. 487–8.

belonged to the archbishop of Toledo, who had had to sell it to the king because he was so hard up.) What the *Historia* does not tell us is that Diego settled Bernardo on a very important task during these two years: the preparation of the cathedral cartulary.

Bernardo's plan was nothing if not ambitious. He proposed to bring together a comprehensive collection of the muniments of Santiago de Compostela in five volumes. The first would contain royal diplomas, the second grants by the higher nobility (*consularia testamenta*), and the third the charters of archbishops and bishops; the fourth would consist of donations from laymen of lesser rank (*minorum potestatum et aliorum hominum qui potestates non fuerunt*) and the fifth of documents associated with the cathedral community (*ecclesiastica familia*). All that has survived—and I suspect all that was ever completed—is the first volume, now known as Tumbo A.[22] A passage on the first folio attributes it to Bernardo, sketches the plan outlined above, and dates the beginning of the work to 1129. The first forty folios, copied in a single hand, contain copies of very nearly all the early royal charters of the see from the spurious grant of Alfonso II in 829 down to and including Alfonso VII's diploma of 13 November 1127 recording his promise to be buried at Compostela. (The later continuations after fo. 40 do not concern us here.)

Cathedral and monastic cartularies of this period were rarely if ever prepared simply on the promptings of orderly archival instincts. Such instincts are the creation of later and more innocent ages. This is not to imply that Tumbo A is not an orderly production. On the contrary, it is an extremely efficient piece of work, and a handsome example of the scribe's and miniaturist's art. But it is not innocent. We should see it as part and parcel of Diego's design to buttress the rights and pretensions of the church of St. James at a moment when he judged that they needed precisely this kind of buttressing. The documents copied into Tumbo A were the archival counterpart to Diego's lecture to the king in the autumn of 1127. The cartulary was therefore not

[22] In AC Santiago.

simply a muniment; it was also in some sense a manifesto.[23] There, neatly recorded for all who might consult it to see, was the record of royal generosity towards the church of St. James, the grateful recognition by successive kings of their special relationship with their apostolic patron and his servants, the bishops and clergy who were entrusted with his shrine. It was a witness in parchment and ink to an armoury of wealth, privilege and spiritual power; it was also a reminder to kings of where their duty lay. Diego was urging this duty upon Alfonso VII throughout the early years of the reign.

Six months after taking office as royal chancellor Bernardo presided over the drawing-up of a very important diploma in favour of the church of Compostela, at Segovia, on 25 May 1128.[24] It cost Diego a gigantic sum of money (*incomputabilem pecuniam*) and was acquired only after a good deal of lecturing of the king on his special obligations towards the church of Santiago. It is likely that Bernardo had had a hand in the negotiations which led up to it; at the royal court in constant attendance on the king, he would have been well-placed to act as Diego's agent in these preliminaries. We may see it as both further evidence of Alfonso VII's shortage of money and also as an instance of Diego's success in recapturing the king's goodwill. What was granted to the church of Santiago was a privilege of exemption from the exercise of regalian right which had played such havoc with the temporalities of the see during the vacancies of the 1090s. Alfonso VII promised

that when the present archbishop Diego, or any successor of his, should meet his end, neither I, nor any of my successors, nor any secular

[23] Of course, as a muniment the cartulary presents formidable problems to the student of diplomatic; in particular, of the extent to which the forged or interpolated charters (actually a very small proportion of the whole corpus) may be attributed to the agency, direct or indirect, of Diego and Bernardo. My concern here is with the impulse behind the making of the Tumbo and (so to say) with its function, not with the technical problems of its composition and construction (which deserve extended study.) I am inclined to think, however, that the charters of doubtful authenticity had been concocted before Diego's day.

[24] For what follows see *HC*, pp. 464-8, and cf. 510-11 (= JL 7416). For a fuller treatment of regalian right see R. A. Fletcher, 'Regalian right in twelfth-century Spain: the case of archbishop Martin of Santiago de Compostela', *Journal of Ecclestical History* 27 (1977), 337-60.

person, shall exercise any right or any power over the whole church of St. James, or over its castles and the temporalities belonging to it . . . but the church and its temporalities shall remain quit and free of any interference, according to the disposal and judgement of the canons of the same church; until the fitting, holy and religious election of an archbishop shall be made by those canons themselves.

This was a very far-reaching concession. The diploma record-ing it was couched in language of unusual solemnity, at times reminiscent of the phraseology of the papal chancery. Much later, after Diego's death, Alfonso VII was to break his word. But in 1128 that lay far in the future, and at the time Diego must have thought that the concession—prudently fortified by a papal confirmation in 1130—had placed the possessions of his archbishopric safely beyond the reach of needy kings.

It was not the only gain of these years. We have already seen that in the autumn of 1127 Alfonso VII had restored two properties to the church of Compostela. Significantly, they had been lost during the 1090s, when the *honor* of the see had been in the hands of the royal *villicus* Pedro Vimara. One was an estate at Montaos, to the north-east of Com-postela, which had been in the church's possession since 924, and the other was the castle (*castellum*) of San Jorge to the north-west, looking across the Ría de Corcubion towards Cape Finisterre, originally granted in 1028. Each was the hub upon which depended ancillary territories— multiple estates—whose inhabitants owed dues and services to the central place. They were, in short, valuable properties which Diego did well to bring back under the control— though not the undisputed control—of his own church.[25] A further concession was gained, albeit a shadowy one, in 1129, when the king granted Diego possession of the city of Mérida at such time when it should have been conquered.[26] Of course, it is easy for a king to give away what he does not yet possess. But the prospective grant of Mérida usefully

[25] For Montaos see R. 17 September 924, 31 May 1124; *HC*, pp. 18, 72, 200, 212, 396, 461, 504, 588; *LFH* IV, ap. xxix, pp. 76-7. For San Jorge see R. 30 December 1028, 13 November 1127; *HC*, pp. 18, 200, 460.

[26] R. 25 March 1129 (whose wording implies that the king was planning an attempt on Mérida in the near future).

matched Diego's ecclesiastical ambitions in the Extremaduran region.

The diploma of 25 May 1128 was granted jointly by Alfonso VII and his queen Berengaria. The marriage had taken place about Christmas 1127, probably at León. From 1128 until her death in 1149 the queen was usually associated with her husband in his beneficial charters. Berengaria was the daughter of Ramón Berenguer III, count of Barcelona (1097-1131). Unfortunately for the royal couple, they were distantly related to one another; their great-great-grandmothers, who had lived in the early part of the eleventh century, had been sisters. This remote consanguinity was to cause the king the gravest anxiety when, two years after the marriage, a papal legate visited his kingdom. Diego, characteristically, was not slow to turn these circumstances to his advantage.

Cardinal Humbert reached the kingdom of León-Castile towards the end of the year 1129. We have already seen that part of his brief was to acquaint himself with the doings of the archbishop of Compostela, then labouring under ill-concealed papal displeasure. He had also been charged to look into the business of Alfonso VII's consanguineous marriage. The marriage had been diplomatically advantageous, for an alliance with the house of Barcelona was a counterweight to his old enemies the Aragonese. It may also— though this is guesswork—have been financially advantageous too: the count of Barcelona ruled one of the most prosperous areas of the Mediterranean seaboard, and Berengaria's dowry is likely to have been a handsome one. It is likely that Berengaria had already given birth to a son, later Sancho III of Castile (1157-8), before Humbert's arrival, so that the succession was assured—a matter on which Alfonso VII is likely to have been even more sensitive than other twelfth-century rulers. The possibility that a papal legate might attempt to annul the marriage was alarming.

The cardinal's visit culminated in the ecclesiastical council held in the Cluniac priory of San Zoil de Carrión early in February 1130. Diego attended the council, despite his recent illness, at the pressing insistence of both cardinal and king. After crossing the mountains which separate

Galicia from the Spanish *meseta* he was met at León by Alfonso VII. The two men held secret discussions and 'talked of many things' as the author of the *Historia Compostellana* darkly puts it. Happily he tells us that one of them was the question of the royal marriage. The king enlisted Diego's help in the event that the matter should be brought up at the council. It undoubtedly was.[27] Whatever the arguments employed by the king's friends, they evidently impressed the cardinal. The marriage survived Humbert's scrutiny and Berengaria remained Alfonso's queen. Diego's reward was ample. The king granted privileges of immunity to two estates of the church of Santiago, at Cacabelos between Villafranca del Bierzo and León, and at Lédigos between Sahagún and Carrión. He also made a grant of olive groves near Talavera: Diego wanted oil for lighting his cathedral in winter.[28]

These were not the only benefits which Diego managed to reap from his advocacy of the king's case at the council of Carrión. At the same meeting there were deposed the abbot of Samos and the three bishops of León, Oviedo and Salamanca. These depositions have always puzzled historians. They have never been satisfactorily explained, and unless new evidence should come to light further speculation is fruitless. But if the causes are obscure the results are clear, and of the greatest interest to us. The new bishop of Sala-manca, Alfonso Pérez, was (as we have already seen) a canon of Compostela; so too the new bishop of León, Arias.[29] (The antecedents of the new bishop of Oviedo, another Alfonso, are unknown.) These appointments were a triumph for Diego. Not only had he contrived to reassert control over his distant and troublesome suffragan see of Salamanca, but he had also managed to insert his own candidate into the important bishopric of León.

[27] It is noteworthy that the queen was not associated with her husband in a diploma drawn up while the council was in session: R. 7 February 1130.

[28] *HC*, pp. 498-9 and R. 22 February 1130. Lédigos had been in the possession of Santiago since 1028: see R. 26 September 1028. For Cacabelos see also *HC*, p. 69.

[29] Arias is referred to as canon and cardinal of Compostela at *HC*, p. 498, a point which I overlooked in *Episcopate*, p. 70. It has been suggested that he is to be identified with Arias González the king's chaplain: this is possible though not certain.

In April 1130 Diego consecrated the bishop-elect of Salamanca and held a council at Compostela for the dissemination of the decrees of Carrión—of which no text survives—in Galicia. He could probably congratulate himself on a successful climb back into royal favour. It had been achieved at no little cost in anxiety, effort and hard cash. Yet the prospect for the future was rosy. Diego had helped and instructed his king, taken steps to strengthen the claims of his church, recovered old properties and gained new ones, acquired important privileges, inserted his dependants into positions of influence at the royal court and into vacant bishoprics, and patched up his relations with the papal curia. Could he maintain himself in this advantageous position? He was now in his mid-sixties; the answer would depend partly on his state of health. It would depend also on the continued smooth functioning of his network of friendship and patronage. It would depend most of all on the actions and attitudes of the king.

During the decade which began in 1130—the last of Diego's life—the scope of Alfonso VII's ambitions and the theatre of his actions grew wider. In the first place, the affairs of the southern frontier and of Andalusia generally came to bulk ever larger in his vision.[30] In 1121 the city of Córdoba had risen against Almoravide rule. The Almoravide caliph Ali ben Yusuf returned from Morocco to suppress this rebellion, at the same time sending ambassadors to queen Urraca; peace with the kingdom of León-Castile would give him a free hand for putting his own house in order. The envoys were in Galicia in July,[31] and it is to be presumed that a truce for several years was agreed since no further fighting apart from sporadic frontier 'incidents' is recorded until 1128. In that year the governor of Córdoba raided the Toledo region, and in 1129 (probably) there was a raid on Talavera, a little further down the valley of the Tagus. In December 1129 the caliph's son Teshufin ben Ali became

---

[30] Operations on the southern frontier have not yet been treated as amply as they deserve. What follows is only a sketch. In addition to the books cited at the beginning of this chapter I have found J. González, *Repoblación de Castilla la Nueva* (Madrid, 1975) useful: see especially vol. I, ch. 2.

[31] *HC*, pp. 350-2.

governor of Granada, in itself an indication that some new offensive was being planned. The first blow was delivered in 1130. Teshufin led an army towards Toledo, veered off up the Tagus to sack the fortress of Aceca, raided Bargas, and attacked the monastery of San Servando just outside the walls of Toledo before escaping back to the south. Aceca was utterly destroyed. Its castellan Tello Fernández was captured and spent the rest of his life imprisoned in Morocco. At least 250 Christians were killed; they could ill be spared from the sparsely-populated frontier territories where manpower was in such short supply. In 1131 another Almoravide army, commanded this time by the governor of Calatrava, was sent to the Tagus valley. The governor of Toledo, Gutierre Armíldez, was absent near Escalona; he was captured by a ruse and killed. The castellan of Mora, the Galician Munio Alfonso, was captured and carried off to Córdoba; he was ransomed later and returned to his command. Later in the year there seem to have been further operations, this time at Oreja, where the Christian forces were defeated and their leader killed.

Vigorous countermeasures were called for. Towards the end of 1131 Alfonso VII entered into alliance with the Muslim prince usually referred to in the Christian sources as Zafadola. His true name was Ibn Hud al-Mustansir Sayf-al-Dawla and he was a member of the family who had ruled Zaragoza as *taifa* kings between 1039 and 1110. (He was the son of al-Musta'in whose silver *intremissa* came into the possession of Diego Gelmírez and was used by him in 1120 for bribing cardinals.) At this time Zafadola was governing a small principality, the rump of his ancestors' kingdom, based at Rueda del Jalón to the west of Zaragoza. By the terms of the alliance he became Alfonso's vassal and was entrusted with a string of castles along the exposed southern frontier of León-Castile.[32] Also before the end of 1131 the king appointed a new *alcaide* of Toledo to take the place of Gutierre Armíldez. Rodrigo González de Lara was a member of the greatest of Castilian noble families and a man of proven military skill. His task was to re-animate the flagging spirits of the frontiersmen.

[32] *CAI*, cc. 27-9.

The year 1132 started auspiciously. In the early spring the towns of Avila and Segovia sent a raid to Lucena, south of Córdoba, where Teshufin had concentrated his army prior to the summer campaign. In a daring surprise attack Teshufin himself was wounded and much booty taken. No serious harm had been inflicted on the Almoravide forces but Castilian morale had received a much-needed fillip. In June Rodrigo González de Lara led a larger army on an even more ambitious expedition down the valley of the Guadalquivir as far south as Seville: the land was devastated, captives and plunder taken, and the governor of Seville defeated and killed. Teshufin dared not counter-attack. Instead he turned upon a raiding-party from Salamanca which was operating near Badajoz and defeated that. A little later in the summer he intercepted another Toledan contingent near Calatrava and defeated it too. So in 1132 the honours were about equal.

Alfonso VII had as yet taken no hand in the fighting on the southern frontier. In 1131 he had been occupied throughout the campaigning season with the siege of one of the last Aragonese strongholds in Castile, at Castrogeriz. In 1132 he had been engaged in suppressing the rebellion in the Asturias of count Gonzalo Peláez. But in 1133 he took the field himself. Accompanied by Zafadola he set out from Toledo at the end of May. The route followed was that pioneered by Rodrigo González in the preceding year. The country about Seville was laid waste and the army pushed on even further south down the Guadalquivir valley. Jerez was sacked and the area round Cadiz devastated. A vast horde of livestock—camels, horses, cattle, sheep and goats —accompanied the triumphant royal army back to the safety of the Tagus valley later in the summer. The reverses of 1130 and 1131 had been avenged.

In the year 1134 the king's attention was diverted eastwards by a series of events of the first importance in the kingdom of Aragon.[33] On 17 July the Almoravide forces

[33] The Aragonese succession crisis has provoked an extensive scholarly literature. The most valuable recent contributions are: F. Balaguer, 'La *Chronica Adefonsi Imperatoris* y la elevación de Ramiro II al trono aragonés', *Estudios de Edad Media de la Corona de Aragón* 6 (1956), 7-40; A. Ubieto Arteta,

inflicted a shattering defeat on the Aragonese army at Fraga, in the valley of the Ebro to the east of Zaragoza. It was Alfonso *el Batallador*'s last battle: old, wounded, humiliated, he died near Huesca on 8 September 1134. His death precipitated a political crisis. Apart from the disastrous marriage to Urraca, the king of Aragon had never taken a wife and left no children legitimate or illegitimate. But he had taken steps to make provision for the succession. In 1131 he had made a will which he confirmed just before his death leaving all his dominions to the Orders of the Temple, the Hospital and the Holy Sepulchre. This extraordinary decision has never satisfactorily been explained. All that matters for our purposes is that the will was set aside. The younger brother of the dead king, Ramiro, was proclaimed king of Aragon; in Navarre, which had formed a part of the kingdom of Aragon since 1076, a member of the old Navarrese dynasty, García Ramírez, was proclaimed king. Ramiro's elevation occurred very soon after *El Batallador*'s death and by the end of September he had established himself in Zaragoza. It was in all probability in the same month that García Ramírez was proclaimed king of Navarre.

Alfonso VII's decision to intervene was prompted by straightforward territorial ambition. For many years the rulers of León-Castile had harboured designs upon southern Navarre and the Aragonese territories in the valley of the Ebro—especially the city of Zaragoza, which had nearly fallen to Alfonso VI in 1086. Presented with this opportunity in the summer of 1134, his grandson was not slow to act. Alfonso VII was in the Rioja by the middle of November, by Christmas he was in control of Zaragoza. He had been formally welcomed into the city by clergy and people led by the bishop, García; his lordship had been recognized

'Navarra-Aragón y la idea imperial de Alfonso VII de Castilla', ibid., pp. 41–82; H. Grassotti, 'Homenaje de Garcia Ramírez a Alfonso VII. Dos documentos inéditos', *Cuadernos de Historia de España* 38 (1963), 318-29; S. de Vajay, 'Ramire II le Moine, roi d'Aragon, et Agnès de Poitou dans l'histoire et dans la légende', *Mélanges offerts à René Crozet*, ed. P. Gallais and Y.-J. Riou (Poitiers, 1966) II. 727-50; A. J. Forey, *The Templars in the Corona de Aragón* (London, 1973), pp. 17-20; E. Lourie, 'The will of Alfonso I *el Batallador*, king of Aragon and Navarre: a reassessment', *Speculum* 50 (1975), 635-51. Here again I confine myself to a summary treatment.

by Ramiro II and the leading men of Aragon; and he had performed royal acts there, confirming by charter the customs (*fueros et usaticos*) of the Aragonese and the privileges of the church of Zaragoza.

But the crisis had only just begun. The fortunes of Navarre are the easiest to follow. In January 1135 García Ramírez was recognized as king in return for doing homage to Ramiro II of Aragon. Alfonso VII was quick to move against this combination and by May had managed to detach Navarre from Aragon. García Ramírez did homage to the king of Castile, whose imperial coronation in León at the end of May he dutifully attended. Later in the same year Alfonso VII granted him Zaragoza and its territory—the *regnum Caesar-augustanum*—as a fief. But García of Navarre proved a restive vassal. In 1136 he attacked his overlord, and for the next four years sporadic warfare between the kingdoms of Navarre and León-Castile dragged on until peace was made in 1140.

García's rebellion against Alfonso VII in 1136 led to his forfeiture of the *regnum Caesaraugustanum*. In the summer of that year Alfonso VII gave the *regnum* back to Ramiro II, presumably to win him over from possible alliance with the Navarrese against León-Castile. The treaty that was made between the two rulers at this time is likely to have contained further provisions. Pope Innocent II had been pressing for a settlement of the Aragonese succession for over a year. Before the end of 1135 the elderly Ramiro II had been hastily married off to Agnes of Poitou, the daughter of William IX of Aquitaine and a widow of proven fecundity. She bore him a daughter in July 1136 and then, her duty done, returned to France to live out the remaining twenty-four years of her life in the congenial surroundings of the impeccably aristocratic nunnery of Fontevrault. The baby girl, Petronilla, was the heiress to the kingdom of Aragon. It is possible, though not demonstrable, that decisions about her future were taken at the time of the settlement between Alfonso VII and Ramiro II soon after her birth. What is certain is that a year later, in August 1137, Petronilla was married to Ramón Berenguer IV, count of Barcelona. Ramiro II ceded his kingdom to his daughter and new son-in-law, though retaining the title of king during his long retirement at Huesca until his death in 1157. The union of Aragon and Catalonia in 1137 was one of the most important stages in the formation of the federation of territories later to be known as the *Corona de Aragón.*

This was not quite the end of the Aragonese succession crisis. Compensation for the military orders in respect of their claims under the terms of Alfonso I's will was not finally arranged until 1140 (for the Hospital and the Holy Sepulchre) and 1143 (for the Temple). As for the *regnum* of Zaragoza, we have seen that Alfonso VII gave it back to Ramiro II in 1136, though it was agreed that he was to hold it for life from the Aragonese king. After the cession of the kingdom of Aragon to the count of Barcelona in 1137, Alfonso VII became Ramón Berenguer's vassal for Zaragoza. But the count was already *his* vassal. This awkwardness was resolved, probably towards the end of 1137, by a further deal involving a reversal of roles. Ramón Berenguer IV consented to hold the *regnum* of Zaragoza as Alfonso VII's vassal. As events turned out, Alfonso VII's actual power over the *regnum* was almost non-existent. In the last resort the Aragonese adventure of 1134–7 profited him little or nothing.

Alfonso VII turned his attention towards his southern frontier again in 1138. In May he led a raid to the Guadalquivir valley and laid waste the country round Andújar, Ubeda, Baeza and Jaén; in July he laid abortive siege to Coria, south of Salamanca. In the following year he took the important strong point of Oreja, on the Tagus some miles upstream of Toledo, after a siege that lasted from April to October. These two directions of assault upon Muslim Andalusia—south-westward into Extremadura, and south beyond the Tagus towards Calatrava and the Guadalquivir—were to be the guiding principles of the emperor's strategy during the following decade of the 1140s.

Of the intense and complicated diplomatic and military manœuvres on the eastern and southern frontiers of the kingdom of León-Castile during the 1130s the *Historia Compostellana* tells us nothing, beyond a stray reference to Alfonso VII's Andalusian foray of 1133. There is no word of the Aragonese succession crisis; no mention of the imperial coronation in 1135; no interest shown in the southern campaigns. This silence is instructive. Diego Gelmírez had no part in the high politics of these years.[34] There remained one area of the kingdom which occasioned anxiety and trouble for Alfonso VII, and of this the *Historia* does tell us something; small wonder, for it is not far from Compostela to the Portuguese frontier in the basin of the river Miño.

In the summer of 1128 there had been a revolution in Portugal.[35] On 24 June, at São Mamede near Guimarães, the army of the young Afonso Henriques had defeated the forces of his mother the countess Teresa and her paramour Fernando Pérez de Traba. Afonso was thenceforth count of Portugal until he assumed the title of king eleven years later. Teresa retired to France, to end her days as a nun in the Cluniac priory of Marcigny. Fernando Pérez returned to his estates in Galicia, to assume the headship of the Traba family on his father's death. Afonso Henriques was in effect an independent ruler, and probably looked upon himself in that light. Alfonso VII, in his more optimistic moments, is likely to have regarded him as simply a contumacious vassal. There was, in short, a grumbling hostility between these cousins. The river Miño, at least in its lower reaches, had long been recognized as the frontier between Galicia and Portugal. It was as little satisfactory as, at the same period, the rivers Esk and Tweed as frontiers between England and Scotland. The diocese of Tuy extended south of the river. Galician monastic houses owned estates in northern Portugal; their Portuguese counterparts, lands in southern Galicia. The

---

[34] It has been suggested that Diego attended the imperial coronation, on the basis of the occurrence of his name in the subscription-lists of two royal diplomas issued at León just afterwards: R. 29 May 1135, 2 June 1135. The latter is probably a forgery. The former is not without suspicious features, but even if it is genuine Diego's subscription does not serve to establish his presence at the coronation. It is inconceivable that the *Historia Compostellana* could have failed to mention the ceremony had Diego attended it. The silence of our text is the best argument for Diego's absence. However, representatives of the clergy of Compostela certainly were there. The only name we can be sure about is that of Ciprián Pérez, *iudex* of Compostela: see R. 25 May 1135.

[35] The most recent survey of the history of Portugal during this period, with full references to earlier literature, is that of P. Feige, 'Die Anfänge des portugiesischen Königtums und seiner Landeskirche', *Spanische Forschungen der Görresgesellschaft* 29 (1978), 85–436.

prominent families of the Minhotan flood plain on both banks of the river were connected by marriage, by regional ecclesiastical loyalties, by dialect, by shared economic concerns, by common social arrangements; and by less tangible bonds such as a mutual fear of intrusion (whether from north or south) by hostile seafarers along the Atlantic coastline. It was much the same in the hinterland, up the valley of the Limia for example, or in the mountainous country east of Chaves towards Bragança, and beyond in the basin of the Duero.

During the years that followed the revolution of 1128 this frontier region was greatly disturbed. In 1130, probably, Afonso Henriques raided southern Galicia for the first time.[36] These forays were to be repeated often in the next few years. They evidently disrupted the day-to-day life of the region. Monks of Celanova travelling to the coast to get fish were glad to do so under armed escort. We hear of the murder of an archdeacon in the diocese of Orense. A prominent rebel against Alfonso VII, Gonzalo Peláez, when exiled in about 1134, sought asylum at the court of Afonso Henriques.[37] Subscriptions to charters tell us something of Teresa's and then Afonso's attempts to find friends among the leading clergy of southern Galicia.[38] Teresa had founded a monthly market at Orense in 1122; in 1125 she had granted churches and privileges to the bishopric of Tuy. The 1122 charter was subscribed by the abbots of Celanova and Ribas del Sil; in one of the 1125 charters bishop Alfonso of Tuy referred to Teresa as his *domina ac regina*. A grant to the see of Coimbra in 1122 was subscribed by the bishops of Tuy and Orense and by the abbot of Celanova. In 1130 bishop Diego of Orense and abbot Pelayo of Celanova subscribed Afonso's charter issued at Villaza referred to above, and in 1134 bishop Pelayo of Tuy subscribed another such charter.

For Alfonso VII a new stage of danger was reached in

[36] *HC*, pp. 517-18; *CAI*, cc. 75, 115; *DMP*, no. 113 shows him at Villaza in September 1130.

[37] *Sancti Rudesindi Miracula* III, c. 30, in *Portugalliae Monumenta Historica, Scriptores*, ed. A. Herculano (Lisbon, 1856), pp. 39-46; AC Orense, Obispo y Dignidades, no. 17; *CAI*, c. 46.

[38] For what follows see *DMP*, nos. 60, 64, 70, 71, 113, 142.

1136 when Portugal and Navarre came together in an alliance directed against him. We have already seen that the king of Navarre attacked Alfonso VII's eastern frontier in 1136. His ally in Portugal invaded southern Galicia in the early summer of 1137. Several castles were taken and, more seriously, the town of Tuy.[39] Alfonso VII was in eastern Castile at the time. He at once hastened over to Galicia. Peace was made between the cousins at Tuy early in July.[40] After the negotiations were over Alfonso VII spent about two weeks at Santiago de Compostela.[41] The peace made at Tuy endured for some years. Alfonso VII made one more visit to Galicia during archbishop Diego's lifetime—he can be traced at Compostela in December 1138—but it was probably not Portuguese business that brought him there.[42] Renewed diplomatic strain between Portugal and León-Castile did not develop until after Afonso Henriques's great victory over the Moors at *Aulic* on 25 July—St. James's day—1139, for it was as a result of this battle that he assumed the title of king.[43] The first surviving charter which bears this title is dated 10 April 1140 (four days after the death of Diego Gelmírez).[44] The friction to which this gave rise endured until the legation of cardinal Guido in 1143, when Alfonso VII was brought to recognize the independent Portuguese monarchy.

Diego's loyalty to his monarch had never wavered through-out the period of strained relations with Portugal between 1128 and 1137. We may imagine that Alfonso VII was duly grateful for this. But loyalty in itself did not do much to enhance Diego's influence with the king. The two men rarely met. In the last decade of Diego's life Alfonso VII was at Compostela only thrice (December 1129-January 1130, July 1137, December 1138). Diego's visits to the royal court were equally rare. He attended the ecclesiastical councils of Carrión in February 1130 and Burgos in October 1136, at both of which the king was present. He can be traced at the

[39] *HC*, pp. 585–6; *CAI*, cc. 73–5; *DMP*, no. 164.
[40] *DMP*, no. 160.
[41] R. 17 July 1137, 20 July 1137, 28 July 1137.
[42] R. 11 December 1138, 12 December 1138.
[43] *Aulic* has never been identified with certainty.
[44] *DMP*, no. 176.

royal court in the spring of 1133 (as we shall see shortly), and he probably paid it another visit in May 1138. And that is all.

The court itself was one in which the elderly Diego would have found few intimates in the 1130s. Peripatetic and thereby unstable in composition though it was, it displayed nevertheless a certain consistency of character, as it had in the late 1120s, which reflected the king's will. It was cosmopolitan. The queen will have brought some Catalans in her household. There were troubadours from Aquitaine and from Galicia. The king's cousin Alphonse Jourdain, count of Toulouse, was a frequent visitor. The alliance with Zafadola in 1131 injected a Moorish presence. The king had a Jewish astronomer, and some other Jews rose very high in his service, like Judah ibn-Ezra to whom the town of Calatrava was entrusted after its conquest in 1147. But the nucleus of the royal court, the inner circle of the king's advisers, is to be sought in his household and among the witness-lists of surviving royal charters. The office of *mayordomo* was held during these years successively by Lope López (1131-5), Gutierre Fernández (1135-8) and Diego Múñoz (1138-44). Lope López, as we have seen, came from Carrión. Gutierre Fernández belonged to the Castro family whose landholdings were concentrated in eastern Castile. Diego Múñoz's family originated from Saldaña, to the north of Carrión. During the same period the office of *alférez* was held by Pedro Garcés (1131), Gonzalo Peláez (1131-2), Ramiro Froílaz (1132-3), Manrique de Lara (1134-7) and Diego Froílaz (1137-40). The connections of the first of these men are unknown. Gonzalo Peláez belonged to one of the leading families of the Asturias. Ramiro Froílaz came from the region of Astorga and León; Diego Froílaz was his brother. The Lara family to which Manrique belonged was the greatest noble family of north-eastern Castile. During the 1130s the household of Alfonso VII continued to have a distinctly Leonese and Castilian flavour. So did the witness-lists of his diplomas, though the point needs no detailed demonstration here. Not surprisingly, it was to a Castilian environment that Alfonso VII entrusted his eldest son for his upbringing. This flavour of the *meseta* is explained by and

and in turn helps to explain the king's central preoccupations during these years.

Diego Gelmírez could have made little headway among a group of king's friends so constituted. His trump card was of course his control of the royal chancery, publicly confirmed by Alfonso VII in 1127. But here matters went badly wrong for Diego. Between February 1130 and March 1133 he had had no contact that we know of with the royal court. Following Bernardo's resumption of his duties as chancellor in March 1131 we may think it probable that he and Diego saw little of each other for the next two years. Diego seems to have been afraid that Bernardo and the department of state which he controlled were slipping away from his influence. This is the background to the quarrel which broke out when Diego next visited the royal court at Carrión in March 1133.[45] Diego demanded that Bernardo surrender the office of chancellor to him, presumably with a view to replacing him with a more pliant nominee. Bernardo refused to do so, claiming that he held the chancery from the king and not from Diego. Alfonso VII supported him, sending his agents—who included Albertino of León—to intercede with Diego on Bernardo's behalf. A meeting was held at the Cluniac priory of San Zoil de Carrión, its prior presumably acting as a neutral intermediary, and matters were for the moment resolved. As the *Historia* tells it, Bernardo was brought to admit his dependence on the archbishop and surrendered the chancellorship to him. Diego granted the office back to him for a time (*ad tempus*). On 15 March Alfonso VII confirmed Diego's control of both chapel and chancery. But Bernardo's reinstatement was short. The last royal diploma drawn up under his aegis is dated 29 March 1133.[46] He accompanied Diego back to Compostela. By 11 April the chancery was headed by Martín Peláez, a canon of Compostela and presumably a nominee of Diego's. The king then departed on his Andalusian

[45] For what follows see *HC*, pp. 531-2, 551-8, 561, and the discussion in B. F. Reilly, 'The chancery of Alfonso VII of León-Castilla: the period 1116-1135 reconsidered', *Speculum* 51 (1976), 243-61.

[46] R. 20 December 1133 is subscribed by Bernardo, but as Reilly art. cit. p. 254 note 68, has shown the correct date is between 1127 and 1130.

campaign. So far the story reads as a triumphant vindication by Diego of the rights granted to him by the king in 1127.

But there was a sequel, and one that is by no means easy to understand. During or after (*deinde*) the Andalusian campaign the king decided to imprison Bernardo and strip him of his possessions. He sent messengers—on no less than five different occasions according to the *Historia*—to Compostela ordering Diego to place Bernardo in custody. This Diego consistently refused to do until the king's menaces became serious. Then, reluctantly, he imprisoned Bernardo. Shortly after this—and we have probably reached the winter of 1133-4—a papal legate, cardinal Guido, visited Compostela in the course of a legatine journey to Spain and upbraided Diego for holding Bernardo a prisoner. Diego exculpated himself by showing that he was doing so only on the express orders of the king. When Alfonso was approached with a request for Bernardo's release, he angrily transferred him from Diego's custody to that of bishop Nuño of Mondoñedo. Soon afterwards (*non longe post*) cardinal Guido held a council at León at which Diego, who apparently did not attend it, was ordered to restore to Bernardo all he had lost during his captivity and to reinstate him as a canon of Compostela. Diego complied.[47] There the controversy appeared to end. However, after his release Bernardo went off to the Tierra de Campos and once more began to intrigue against Diego. But as the *Historia* puts it 'God's judgement took a hand' (*divino interveniente iudicio*) and Bernardo died before he could do any further damage, at Burgos, at some point in 1134.

What are we to make of this strange story? As always we must beware of accepting the testimony of the *Historia Compostellana* uncritically. Where much will forever remain obscure, some things are tolerably clear. In the first place, it is obvious that Diego and Bernardo were divided by bitter hostility, which their long previous association can have served only to sharpen. Whatever the rights and wrongs of the

---

[47] This is our only reference to the León council. We cannot date it precisely. Given the developments sparked off by the death of the king of Aragon early in September, it is most unlikely to have met later than August 1134. See below, Appendix E.

matter, Diego was wounded and enraged by betrayal at the hands of a trusted protégé.[48] Second—and this is of great importance—it is clear that cardinal Guido, an outsider and a churchman of the highest repute, considered that Diego and not the king was the guilty party in the hounding of Bernardo. Third, although the *Historia* insists—perhaps protesting a little *too* much (the king's *five* messages)—that Alfonso forced Diego to imprison Bernardo, it is hard to believe that a ruler who wanted to ensure the custody of the latter should entrust him to the bishop of Mondoñedo. But an archbishop of Compostela so desirous well might, for if Nuño of Mondoñedo was anyone's man he was Diego's. Fourth, the doings at the council of León reveal that Bernardo had been deprived of his canonry at Compostela: but this was a degradation which could be inflicted only by the archbishop and chapter, not by the king. Fifth, the council of León witnessed a striking rebuff to Diego in the matter of the controversial election to the see of Salamanca (of which more presently): it is very hard to believe that in the case of Bernardo he won there what the *Historia* presents as a qualified victory. Finally, if Bernardo had indeed been persecuted by the king, why was it that he went straight back to the royal court after his release?

In the light of these considerations, perhaps it is permissible to make out a train of events somewhat different. Diego succeeded in depriving Bernardo of the chancellorship and escorted him back to Galicia. There it was on Diego's orders that he was imprisoned and at Diego's instance that he was transferred to Mondoñedo—away from his *consanguinei* in Compostela. Cardinal Guido identified Diego as Bernado's persecutor, and at León insisted that Diego should set him free.

Be this as it may, by far the most significant result of this quarrel was the loss of Diego's undisputed control of the royal chancery. Martín Peláez cannot be traced as a royal notary later than May 1133.[49] For over a year thenceforward

---

[48] See especially *HC*, pp. 551-2. It is of great interest to discover that Bernardo was a relative (*consanguineus*) of Pedro Helias the dean of Compostela, another man whom Diego no longer trusted. The quarrel had a local dimension whose precise contours cannot now be delineated.

[49] His last subscription is of R. 13 May 1133.

very few royal charters survive, and those few diplomatically suspect. (This paucity may in itself be an indication of the struggle for power within the chancery.) But then, on 1 June 1134, a diploma was drawn up for the king by one Berengar. In two other charters of the same year Berengar identifies himself as *archidiaconus*. He accompanied Alfonso VII to Zaragoza at the end of the year and there, at the foot of the confirmation charter for the church of Zaragoza referred to above, he further identifies himself as archdeacon of Toledo (*archidiaconus Toletanus*).[50] If the course of the struggle is obscure, its outcome is clear. The archbishop of Toledo had managed to insert his own candidate into the chancery and supplant the influence of his rival at Santiago de Compostela.

Berengar remained in control of the royal chancery until July or possibly August 1135. He was succeeded by a partnership which was to direct Alfonso VII's chancery for the next sixteen years—master Hugo the chancellor and the scribe Geraldo. Nothing is known of Hugo's antecedents, but we may be sure that he had no connections with the church of Compostela. The *Historia* has nothing whatsoever to say about the chancery after the death of Bernardo in 1134, and in the abundant documentation of the church of Compostela no Hugo is mentioned who might be identified with master Hugo the royal chancellor.[51] Hugo had a French name. It is reasonable to guess that like his predecessor Berengar he came from the circle of the French archbishop of Toledo, Raimundo. Geraldo is more problematical. His name, like Hugo's, was French but it was not all that uncommon in mid-twelfth-century Spain. It is just possible that he is to be identified with Gerald of Beauvais, canon of Compostela and the author of much of the *Historia Compostellana*.[52] If this were so, Compostelan influence might have been maintained in the chancery during the period 1135-51—but in a subordinate position. In short,

[50] R. 1134, 1 June 1134, 10 November 1134, 26 December 1134. Reilly, art. cit., p. 258, note 90, voices some doubts as to the authenticity of R. 1 June 1134.

[51] The only Hugo who is at all prominent in the *HC* is Diego's protégé bishop Hugo of Porto who died in 1136.

[52] This is a guess, though it has (I think) more plausibility than might immediately appear. But the case is too long a one to be argued here.

never again after 1133 could Diego Gelmírez feel confident in unrivalled domination of the most important office, beneath the monarchy itself, in the kingdom of León-Castile.

There was another sector of public life in which Diego would have expected to continue to exert influence, as he had done successfully in the past—episcopal elections. But here too the appointments made in the 1130s bear witness to a waning of Compostelan influence.[53] The episcopal elections of this period, in Spain as elsewhere, were the outcome of the interplay of diverse forces. The king, the archbishops, the cathedral chapter, the local monastic or aristocratic or urban élites, and very occasionally the popes or other prominent ecclesiastical outsiders all jostled for influence. Only rarely do our sources permit us to see something of the conflicts which lay behind the promotion of any one candidate to the bench of bishops. But we may be reasonably certain that most elections were complicated and hard-fought affairs.

One area was now closed to Diego's influence. The nascent state of Portugal would prove impervious to Compostelan pressure. Appointments to Braga he could have had no hope of ever influencing. At Coimbra Bernardo was promoted in 1128 as the choice of Afonso Henriques and the archbishop of Braga. He survived Diego to die in 1146. At Porto, Diego had managed to slip his candidate in back in 1112. Bishop Hugo died in 1136. His successor João Peculiar had previously been a canon and *magister scolarum* of Coimbra. In 1138 he was translated to the metropolitan see of Braga where he was to enjoy a long and distinguished tenure, notable for the closeness of relations between archbishop and king. He was succeeded at Porto by his nephew Pedro Rabaldis.

Diego had tried consistently and by no means unsuccessfully to influence the appointments to the Galician suffragans of Braga. In the 1130s these bishoprics tended to fall to local men of no discernible connections either with Santiago de Compostela or with Braga. Roberto of Astorga (1131-8)

---

[53] The best recent treatment is B. F. Reilly, 'On getting to be a bishop in León-Castilla: the emperor Alfonso VII and the post-Gregorian church', *Studies in Medieval and Renaissance History* 1 (1978), 37-68.

had previously been archdeacon there; so too his successor Jimeno Eriz (1138-41), a member of a prominent local family. Pelayo Menéndez of Tuy (1131-55) was likewise drawn from the local nobility. Guido of Lugo (1134?-52) was an outsider in that he was French by birth, but he had previously been prior (i.e. dean) of the cathedral chapter of Lugo. At Mondoñedo Diego's faithful protégé Nuño Alfonso resigned his see in 1136. His successor was very much a local man, Pelayo, abbot of the monastery of Lorenzana. We may suspect some royal influence at Astorga and Lugo. Tuy and Mondoñedo seem to have gone their own way. Compostelan influence is conspicuously lacking; and so too, of course, is that of Braga.

The see of Orense might at first sight seem untypical. Bishop Martín (1133-56) had very probably been previously connected with the church of Compostela—if it is correct to identify him with the canon and cardinal Martín Pérez who visited the papal curia on Diego's behalf in 1129 and 1130.[54] But the significant thing about Martín of Orense was his connection not with Diego but with the king. Four royal charters refer to him as a king's chaplain, and we know that he visited the papal curia on the king's business in 1135-6.[55] Given the state of relations between Alfonso VII and his cousin of Portugal, given too the disturbed conditions in the diocese of Orense in the early 1130s, it is plausible to suppose that Alfonso VII took steps to insert a strong loyalist at Orense in 1133. To judge only by the frequency of his subscriptions to royal charters, Martín was certainly that.

Diego's achievement in getting his candidate into the see of León in 1130 was, as we have seen, a triumph. When Arias died towards the end of 1135 he was succeeded by Pedro Anáyaz, who held the bishopric of León until 1139. Pedro

---

[54] *HC*, pp. 490, 509. *HC*, p. 511 (= JL 7415) shows that he also held an archdeaconry.

[55] R. 15 May 1131, 18 January 1133, 3 February 1133 and 18 August 1136: on the last of these see Reilly, art. cit., p. 54, note 64. The visit to the papal curia is referred to in R. October 1136: Martín travelled in the company of another ex-royal chaplain, bishop Bernardo of Sigüenza. I know of no evidence that Martín was the brother of his predecessor at Orense, Diego, as asserted by Reilly, p. 46. It is surely unlikely on chronological grounds, since Diego became bishop in 1100 and Martín died in 1156.

was another man from the circle of clergy at Compostela—
and a most distinguished one, successively canon, treasurer
and dean of the cathedral chapter. It is most surprising that
the *Historia Compostellana* says nothing whatsoever of
his promotion to León, nor of his episcopate there. Given
the compilers' habit of saying nothing about what displeased
them or their master the archbishop, it is fair to suppose that
the promotion of Pedro Anáyaz gave no pleasure at Compostela. Why this should have been so we cannot tell. At any
rate, it would seem that Diego's personal influence at the
see of León was not maintained after 1135. The successor
of Pedro Anáyaz, bishop Juan (1139-81) was without doubt
a king's man. He was the son of Albertino, the faithful
servant of Alfonso VII with whom Diego had crossed swords
several times in the 1120s.

The suffragans of Compostela in the kingdom of León-
Castile were Avila and Salamanca (if we leave aside the
insubstantial claims over Zamora). During the 1130s, two
appointments occurred about which we are rather well-
informed owing to the survival of correspondence relating to
them which was copied into the *Historia Compostellana*.
Bishop Sancho of Avila died in the early months of 1133. He
was succeeded by his brother Iñigo, previously the archdeacon
of Avila. The letters make it clear that Diego Gelmírez, as
metropolitan, had no say in the matter. Iñigo seems to have
been chosen by the clergy and people of Avila, and then presented to the king for his approval.[56] Alfonso VII—at that
time, we should remember, embroiled in conflict with Diego
over the control of the chancery—confined himself to notify-
ing the archbishop of Compostela of the election in a curt
letter and requesting that the bishop-elect be consecrated without delay. Diego complied. Iñigo was consecrated at Compostela on 25 July 1133. He held the see of Avila until 1158.

The most controversial episcopal election of the last
decade of Diego's life was that of Berengar to the see of
Salamanca. It proved a signal defeat for Diego.[57] We saw

[56] *HC*, pp. 536-42. R. 11 April 1133 shows that the king was at Avila at the
time. It is noteworthy that the staunchly royalist bishop Pedro of Segovia attended
bishop Sancho's funeral.

[57] The principal sources for what follows are the letters preserved in *HC*,

that bishop Nuño of Salamanca was deposed at Carrión in 1130, and that his successor Alfonso Pérez was a canon of Compostela and almost certainly Diego's nominee. But the new bishop was short-lived: he died at Cluny in November 1131 after attending Innocent II's council of Rheims. Nuño had retired to Idanha in Portugal after his deposition and returned to Salamanca in an attempt to regain the bishopric after Alfonso Pérez's death. (This was a surprising course of action but it can be paralleled: Pelayo of Oviedo, deposed like Nuño at Carrión in 1130, had a second spell as bishop of Oviedo in 1142-3, after his successor Alfonso's death.) His return precipitated a schism at Salamanca. Nuño's strategy seems to have been to ingratiate himself with Diego Gelmírez. To this end he went to Compostela and came back to Salamanca claiming—with what justice we do not know—that Diego had recognized him as the rightful bishop. Some among the clergy of Salamanca were content with this: in a charter of 21 January 1133 issued by an archdeacon of Salamanca, Hugo, (and subscribed by another archdeacon, the prior of the chapter and at least three of the canons) Nuño is referred to in the dating-clause as bishop. However, Nuño evidently considered that he needed the sanction of an even higher authority to regularize his position, for he took his case to the papal curia. When he returned he boasted that the pope had confirmed him in his episcopal title. But this was very far from the truth, as one of St. Bernard's letters makes clear. Innocent II, a man of unbending canonical rectitude and one, moreover, likely to be acutely sensitive on the subject of irregular episcopal elections, had disallowed Nuño's claims and imposed a sentence (of excommunication?) upon him. Nuño had enlisted the interest of St. Bernard, and also it seems that of Peter the Venerable of Cluny, in an attempt to have the sentence lifted (but not, be it noted, the principal judgement reversed). Whether or not he was successful we do not know. What we do know is that

pp. 542-3, 562-6; St. Bernard, *ep.* 212, in *PL* CLXXXII, col. 377; *Documentos de los archivos catedralicio y diocesano de Salamanca (siglos XII–XIII)*, ed. J. L. Martín Martín (Salamanca, 1977), no. 7; and royal charters as cited below. The sequence of events is not easy to establish and I claim no more than plausibility for what follows. Others, notably Professor Reilly, have interpreted these materials rather differently.

on his return to Salamanca he not only claimed to be the rightful bishop but also started to reward his supporters with the endowments of the bishopric.[58] When his opponents there protested at his action he flew into a rage and continued yet more recklessly in his alienations not only of lands but of churches too.

At this point—perhaps somewhere in 1133—the enterprising Nuño disappears from the surviving records. But it is obvious that Diego had been placed in a highly embarrassing situation. A man whose deposition from episcopal office he had been instrumental in securing had managed to impose upon him in such a way as to make it seem that Diego was prepared to countenance proceedings utterly at variance with the canon law of the church. Diego had, unwittingly perhaps, furnished his opponents with a handle which they could not fail to grasp.

Diego's arch-enemy was Raimundo of Toledo; and Raimundo, abetted by a powerful team of allies—the king, the papal legate Guido, and the loyal 'Toledan' bishops of Segovia and Zamora—succeeded in inserting his candidate into the see of Salamanca. This candidate was Berengar, to whom we must now turn. Berengar had been a member of the Toledan ecclesiastical circle since, at latest, 1121.[59] By 1133 he had become archdeacon of Toledo.[60] As we have seen, he was in control of the royal chancery probably by the summer, certainly by the autumn of 1134. It was at the mysterious council of León in 1134, at which Diego's faction suffered such serious reverses, that Berengar was appointed to the bishopric of Salamanca. He did not, however, style himself bishop elect until the summer of 1135; and the earliest time by which we can be sure that he had been consecrated (by his metropolitan, Diego) does not occur until

[58] We should bear in mind that alienations of this kind, a matter of perennial concern to churchmen, had recently been attracting an unusual degree of attention: see for example the conciliar legislation of Rheims (1119) c. 4, Lateran I (1123) c. 4, Rheims (1131) c. 10, and in Spain Burgos (1117) cc. 8 and 11, Sahagún (1121) c. 6, Palencia (1129) c. 5. Nuño's earlier failure to halt depredations should be remembered: *HC*, pp. 430–1 (= JL 7208) of 1 May 1125.

[59] Assuming that he may be identified with the Berengar who features in a witness-list made up of Toledan clergy in a charter of that year, published by F. Fita in *BRAH* 14 (1889), 456–9.

[60] R. 3 May 1133.

March 1136.[61] This is as firm a chronology as we can get and it instantly prompts one to ask why there was so long a delay between Berengar's appointment and his consecration. It must have been because there was opposition to his appointment, partly at Salamanca, partly at Compostela: we can be sure of the former, but have to guess at the latter. But the guess is a plausible one; and if we care to make it we may further care to consider whether these two sources of hostility to Berengar might not have been in collusion.

Berengar's own attitude to Diego was gratuitously provocative. After his election he wrote to Diego reporting it, dwelling on the fact that he had been chosen in the presence of the archbishop of Toledo and the bishops of Segovia and Zamora. It only remains, he went on, for me to come to you for consecration—there was no question of *requesting* it!—unless you should happen to be coming in this direction, in which case let me know. Berengar's letter was an extraordinarily, and surely deliberately, tactless document. He had just broken Diego's control of the royal chancery. We might think that a more gracious approach would have been appropriate. Instead, Berengar chose to display the most arrogant disregard for Compostelan sensibilities.

The other three letters in the dossier on the Salamanca election reveal far more than does Berengar's about the state of affairs in the diocese. They were addressed to Diego by the clergy and people of Salamanca, by the archbishop of Toledo, and by the king. These letters make clear, what Berengar's contrives to conceal, that his election took place at León; and they make it pretty plain that the electors were given a strong directive from the king and archbishop as to whom they should choose. They also reveal that Berengar could not take up his new appointment at once because there was another candidate for the office, a certain Pedro, the nominee of count Pedro López. The count was a leading figure in the early years of Alfonso VII's reign. He was a brother of Lope López (the king's *alférez* in 1126-7 and his *mayordomo* between 1131 and 1135), one of the earliest adherents of the king at his accession in 1126, and

[61] R. 18 August 1135, 9 March 1136.

prominent in the subscription-lists of royal diplomas between 1126 and 1135.[62] Between 1131 and 1135 he held office as count, on three occasions during these years he headed the subscription-lists,[63] and Salamanca was the centre of his operations.[64] Of his nominee to the bishopric, Pedro, we know only the following: first, that he had for a time enjoyed the support of a group of influential people in Salamanca who could describe themselves as the 'clergy and people' (*clerici Salmanticenses et populus*), that is, the electoral body—in short that he had actually been elected bishop; second, that he was unacceptable to the archbishop of Toledo who described him as 'altogether unsuitable' (*absolute simplex*); third, that (like Nuño) he had—or was accused of having—rewarded his supporters with ecclesiastical endowments; fourth, that he was so strongly entrenched at Salamanca that not only could he exclude Berengar but also—and very significantly—he had to be removed by negotiation and compromise, not by force; and finally, that it was hinted that he enjoyed the support of Diego Gelmírez.

There are several points of interest here, but only the last is of special concern to us. Much depends on how we choose to interpret the longest letter in our dossier, that of the archbishop of Toledo—both its general tone and one phrase in particular. The letter as a whole is a masterpiece of sarcasm and controlled invective. You will want to know, wrote Raimundo, what has been going on in *your* church of Salamanca; you will rejoice to hear that *your own* suffragan see has a pastor after her long and unhappy widowhood; words cannot express the shocking state of affairs which we found in *your* church when we went there. The reiterations pointed an accusing finger. It was all somehow Diego's fault. Archbishop Raimundo went on to say something of count Pedro López's nominee (whom he did not deign to name):

the electors and the municipality of Salamanca (*totum Salmanticense concilium*) received Berengar with honour and conducted him to the

---

[62] *CAI*, c. 4.

[63] R. 1 February 1132, 18 August 1132, 2 January 1133.

[64] 'mandante Salamancha': *Documentos de los archivos catedralicio y diocesano de Salamanca (siglos XII–XIII)*, ed. J. L. Martín Martín (Salamanca, 1977), no. 7.

altar—except for a certain man of utter unsuitability whom we need not now describe to you, and a few of his hangers-on who had enthroned him as bishop under the shadow and illusion of an invasive and sacrilegious election.

The phrase that concerns us is that translated 'whom we need not now describe to you' (*qualem modo vobis exponere non quaerimus*). The repeated emphasis on the word *you*, taken in conjunction with the taunting use of the second person both earlier and later in the letter, suggests that what the archbishop was really saying was this: 'I've no need to describe the schismatic bishop Pedro to *you*, because *you* know all about him already'.

The king's letter administered further twists of the knife in the wound. (It was drafted of course in the chancery controlled by Berengar.) The reference to Martha and Mary in the opening protocol implied criticism of Diego for neglecting his pastorial duties, and the king wound up with a sentence which must have cut Diego to the quick: 'When you consider who Berengar is and by whom he is sent you will receive him in charity and with honour, and send him back yet more honourably [i.e. after consecration]; you should rejoice not a little to welcome him as a colleague.' Alfonso VII's interests were deeply engaged in the business for reasons not confined to the cut-throat world of ecclesiastical politics. Salamanca was a booming frontier town.[65] It was a bastion in a network of defences against the Muslims of Extremadura and the Portuguese. It is important to remember that Salamanca's troops had suffered reverses at the hands of the Almoravides in the years 1132-4.[66] These troops had presumably been led by—or at least under the responsibility of—the local count, Pedro López. In view of the fact that the count's nominee to the bishopric was prepared to squander ecclesiastical endowments to reward his supporters, it is of interest to find that opinion at the royal court, as represented by the author of the *Chronica Adefonsi Imperatoris*, regarded these reverses as a result of the Salamancans' reluctance to pay tithes and first-fruits

---

[65] J. González, 'Repoblación de la extremadura leonesa', *Hispania* 3 (1943), 195-273.
[66] *CAI*, c. 122-4.

to their clergy. There is a fair amount of material in the *Fuero de Salamanca*, parts of which date from this period, to suggest that relations between clergy and laity were, in Salamanca as elsewhere on the frontier, a focus for conflict.[67] It would have been a matter of concern to the archbishop of Toledo that the schismatic bishop-elect Pedro and his patron the count were capricious in their attitude to ecclesiastical privilege. It would have been a matter of concern to Alfonso VII that count Pedro López was not satisfactorily fulfilling his military duties. (It is interesting to find that the count disappears from our records just about the time that Berengar got his hands on the bishopric; interesting too that his brother Lope lost the office of royal *mayordomo* at the same time.) It would have been a matter of the utmost concern to Diego Gelmírez that he had been manœuvred into a position where he appeared to be the patron of a dubious ecclesiastical adventurer and the associate of a man who had lost the favour of the king.

The Salamanca election has been treated at great length because it reveals so vividly the weaknesses in Diego's position in the mid-1130s. By 1133-4 he had lost control of the royal chancery. He could no longer influence episcopal elections; the attempt to do so at Salamanca in 1134-5 had proved a humiliating defeat. He was far from the counsels of a ruler who was surrounded by advisers much younger than Diego, unfamiliar and, some of them, actively hostile to him. The network of friendship and patronage on which he had relied in getting his way had dissolved. The world which Diego had known so intimately, bestridden so confidently, manipulated so deftly, was no longer there. He was old and isolated. The shadows were lengthening.

This is not to say that Diego had fallen from favour. It was rather that he and his Galicia had been relegated to the fringes of the Leonese-Castilian orbit whose hub was the peripatetic imperial court ceaselessly traversing the central Spanish *meseta*. Diego still attended it from time to time. In

---

[67] 'Fuero de Salamanca' in *Fueros Leoneses*, ed. A. Castro and F. de Onís (Madrid, 1916), pp. 77-207: c. 295-8 concern tithes, and c. 295 itself is attributed to count Raymond at the time of the settlement of Salamanca a generation before the events examined here.

October 1136 he took part in the council held at Burgos by cardinal Guido which was concerned among much else with the punishment to be meted out to the leaders of the insurrection at Compostela which had occurred in the summer.[68] In July 1137 the Portuguese war brought the court to Galicia, and Alfonso VII spent some time at Compostela after peace had been made at Tuy. In the spring of 1138 Diego jolted over the mountains for the last time, to attend the court at Carrión in May.[69] Each of these encounters was attended by unseemly wrangling over money between emperor and archbishop. At Burgos Diego was compelled to pay him 400 marks. At the time of the Portuguese campaign Diego's recorded payments to Alfonso amounted to 2,160 marks. At some point in 1138, possibly though not necessarily at Carrión in May, Diego was forced to make a further payment of 500 marks.[70] In the autumn of 1138 Alfonso excused him from attendance at the court at Palencia 'having regard to the coming cold of winter and the great labour of a long journey'. Instead, the emperor himself visited Compostela in December 1138.[71] It was the last occasion on which the two men met. It is also our last glimpse of Diego. The *Historia Compostellana* breaks off at this point. We know nothing of his doings in 1139, and may guess that there were few of them. Bishop Guy of Lescar, visiting Compostela in October 1138 to summon Diego to the Lateran council in the following year, had evidently thought that there was little prospect that his state of health would permit him to attend. There could have been no question of his making his way to Rome in 1139.

Palm Sunday fell on 31 March in 1140. In the new cathedral, its bells muffled for Lent, its ornaments shrouded and its candles unlit, the laborious round of the Holy Week liturgy would have gone ahead as usual. The canons, haggard after their Lenten fast, would have gone about their offices in unaccustomed quiet, for work would have been suspended on the buildings, the scaffolding unpeopled, the carts and

---

[68] *HC*, pp. 578-82; R. 2 October 1136, 4 October 1136.
[69] R. 10 May 1138.
[70] *HC*, pp. 579-81, 586-7, 595; R. 17 July 1137.
[71] *HC*, p. 597; R. 11 December 1138, 12 December 1138.

pulleys silent. In the dimness of the apostle's church the servants would have been making discreet preparations for the vast congregation, the processions, the explosion of people, of noise and of light, that would occur on the following Sunday. There was a further reason for the unnatural calm. In his palace near by the old archbishop lay dying. Would he last until Easter Day? Would he be able to preside with dignity, would he be able to preside at all, for the fortieth time, at the central festival of the Christian year? So his physician, perhaps still that Robert of Salerno, *medicus*, whom we glimpse in his entourage at an earlier date,[72] must have anxiously worried. Diego kept his attendants in suspense until the last possible moment. Then, with that flair for timing and publicity which had stood by him all his life, he ensured that even the Risen Christ would take second place in the minds of those who celebrated Easter at Compostela that year. He died on Easter Eve, Saturday 6 April 1140.

[72] *HC*, pp. 269, 318.

Epilogue: Santiago Matamoros

Diego Gelmírez's death ushered in a long period of turmoil in the history of the church of Santiago de Compostela. Between 1140 and 1173 six archbishops succeeded one another in a series of short pontificates—two of them lasted less than six months apiece—punctuated by vacancies— one of them as long as two and a half years. The enmities which Diego had striven hard to contain burst out into open conflict. There were divisions within the chapter, quarrels with the king, troubles with the local nobility, hostility from ecclesiastical rivals, disharmony in relations with the papal curia. One consequence of these difficulties is clear: this was a time of financial straits for the see of Compostela. It is significant that building operations at the cathedral— as in the 1090s a sensitive indicator—ceased between Diego's death and the advent of archbishop Pedro Suárez in 1173. It was to be during his long pontificate that the west front was completed by the addition of the famous Pórtico de la Gloria.

It was probably in response to financial stringency that, about the middle of the century, a canon of Compostela named Pedro Marcio concocted a celebrated forgery known as the 'Diploma of Ramiro I'.[1] It purports to be a charter granted by king Ramiro I (842-50) after a battle at Clavijo in 844. In gratitude for St. James's assistance in the defeat of the Moors the king was made to decree that every part of Spain under Christian rule should render annually a certain quantity of corn and wine to the cathedral community of Compostela; and further, that a share of all booty taken in campaigns against the Moors should likewise be made over to Santiago. This was the render which later generations were to know as the *votos de Santiago*. Though the diploma has

---

[1] Printed in *LFH* II, pp. 132-7. As Vones, *Kirchenpolitik*, p. 206, n. 171, points out, no critical edition yet exists.

found impassioned defenders in the past, all scholars are now agreed that it is a forgery. The text convicts itself by chronological inaccuracy and glaring anachronism. There are plenty of other suspicious features about it: to name but one, its absence from the cathedral cartulary Tumbo A, copied (as we have seen) in 1129-31. That said, the question whether the clergy of Compostela were claiming the *votos* before *c.*1150 remains an exceedingly difficult one, on which the last word has not yet been said. (I am fairly confident that they were not, but the matter is too complicated to be debated here.)

The 'Diploma of Ramiro I', however, does have a special kind of interest for us. Little, if anything, as it has to tell us of the ninth century, it does shed light on what Pedro Marcio and his circle believed and wanted others to believe about Santiago in the twelfth. In their minds there was a conviction that St. James was the saintly champion of the Christians of Spain in their armed struggle against the hosts of Islam.

The notion that 'St. James the Moor-Slayer'—Santiago Matamoros—was the patron saint of a crusading *Reconquista* has traditionally been accepted without question by a long line of historians of medieval Spain. But the assumption needs to be examined critically. There is a cluster of related problems here. The character of the *Reconquista* is currently undergoing re-assessment at the hands of a new generation of Spanish medievalists.[2] It may be premature to attempt to summarize the results of this timely and salutary activity, but the present position may be stated in general terms as follows. Two old orthodoxies are being weighed in the balance and found wanting: first, the belief in the distinctiveness of the Christian Spanish medieval experience,

---

[2] See the articles of A. Barbero and M. Vigil collected in their *Sobre los orígenes sociales de la Reconquista* (Barcelona, 1974); the same authors' *La formación del feudalismo en la Península Ibérica* (Barcelona, 1978); S. de Moxó, *Repoblación y sociedad en la España cristiana medieval* (Madrid, 1979); J. A. García de Cortazar and C. Díez Herrera, *La formación de la sociedad hispano-cristiana del Cantábrico al Ebro en los siglos VIII al XI* (Santander, 1982); and the contribution of J. Faci Lacasta to *Historia de la Iglesia en España*, vol. II, part i, 'La Iglesia en la España de los siglos VIII al XIV', ed. J. Fernández Conde (Madrid, 1982), pp. 99-139.

and second—and closely connected—the interpretation of that experience in Catholic and nationalist terms. In place of these, scholars are displaying a willingness to seek analogies for the history of Spain in the experience of other parts of medieval Europe, notably France, and to lay a new stress on the force exerted by economic and social pressures in the development of the *Reconquista*. Thus, attention has been drawn to evidence of slow but steady demographic growth in the Asturo-Pyrenean mountain zone of the northern strip of the peninsula during the eighth, ninth and tenth centuries; archaeology and the historical study of climate will surely have more to tell us of this process. Attention has also—and most interestingly—been directed to certain archaic, aboriginal features of the social institutions and cultural life of this region in the period before *c.*800; for example, the tribal organization of society, the almost complete absence of Romanization and the very slow spread of Christianity. From about 750 or so onward, these aboriginal communities began to expand towards the plains, obedient to a Malthusian imperative. In doing so they encountered a Mediterranean culture entirely different from their own in its settlement patterns, economic concerns, legal arrangements, political organization, religious belief, and so forth. From this encounter there gradually emerged between *c.*900 and *c.*1100 in the central band of the Spanish peninsula a new form of society and a new culture which the revisionists have chosen—not very happily —to label 'feudal'. This expansion, encounter and emergence *was*, it is urged, the *Reconquista*.

The challenge of the new thesis is lost in a crude summary of this kind. Certainly, it is being very ably argued and defended, and bids fair to become a new orthodoxy as potent as the old ones it has displaced. This prospect may be viewed not altogether without a degree of disquiet. Some of the emphases—but only some—of the traditional school were valuable; for instance, the stress laid by Menéndez Pidal and Sánchez Albornoz on the 'neo-Gothic' ideal of kingship at the court of Alfonso III is one which we should be unwise to displace. There is also the risk that some of the new concepts will be embraced too eagerly; that the importation of an over-rigid schema first worked out and applied to their own country by French medieval historians might have as constricting an effect on our understanding of Spanish medieval history as it has had on that of French. One feature in particular of the revisionist school, which may owe something to French intellectual fashion, is a little disturbing: its devotees singularly lack interest in the church —except as a landowning corporation—or religion. This results in the curious paradox that, because they have not been subjected to critical scrutiny, completely traditional ideas about Santiago's patronage of a crusading *Reconquista* continue to find expression even in the writings of those who are among the most strident of the revisionists.[3]

Insistent questions remain. Can we any longer be sure that the military operations of the Asturian and Leonese kings were sustained by the moral imperative—whatever its social roots—of 'reconquest'? How closely was St. James associated with this impulse in the minds of kings, clergy, nobility? Did these wars always have a 'crusading' character? If not always, when and how did they acquire it? Simply to ask these questions is to be reminded how little we yet know about the 'thought-world' of the Christians of Spain in the early middle ages. To attempt to answer them would demand another book at least as long as this one. A very few observations, however, may be put forward here by way of an epilogue to the career of Diego Gelmírez.

We have already seen in chapter III that Alfonso III in the later part of the ninth century could regard St. James as his patron and the giver of victory over his enemies. So did several of his tenth- and eleventh-century successors. What is noteworthy, however, is that it is not until the twelfth that widespread evidence exists to testify to any real intimacy of relationship between St. James and aggressive warfare waged by kings against Muslims. In 1140 Alfonso VII put it on record that he owed the conquest of Coria to the intercession of St. James. His son Fernando II referred to himself in 1158 as 'the standard-bearer' (*vexillifer*) of St. James.[4] It was in the

---

[3] See, for example, Faci Lacasta, op. cit., pp. 112-13.
[4] R. 1 July 1140, 30 September 1158; cf. also R. 24 August 1165, 18 March 1169.

1130s that the militias of Avila, Segovia and Toledo were to be found invoking St. James during campaigns against the Almoravides.[5] Significance was discovered in the fact that the great Portuguese victory at *Aulic* was won on St. James's day, 25 July, in 1139.[6] Two of the miracles of St. James associate the apostle with warfare against Islam.[7] Given this climate of opinion it is not surprising that when a Spanish military order was founded in the 1170s it was placed under the patronage of Santiago.

When did the Spanish wars become 'crusades'? To those who would claim that they had never been anything else it is refutation enough to point out that the term 'crusade' is being employed too loosely. Warfare that has a vaguely Christian character is not crusading warfare. Historians today insist that 'crusade' is a technical term. (Possibly they insist on its technicality a little too much.) To qualify as a 'crusade' a campaign must be sponsored or blessed by the pope or his representative and underpinned by the notion of warfare as spiritually meritorious. Those who participate in it must be shown to have enjoyed a special type of ecclesiastical privilege, the crusading indulgence, and to have fortified their intention with a vow. Not a single one of these characteristics may be encountered among the records relating to warfare in Spain before the very end of the eleventh century.[8] Certain pronouncements of Urban II and Paschal II show that the popes were slowly coming to see the wars against the Muslims of Spain as sharing in the distinctiveness of those waged against the Muslims of Palestine and Syria. But it was not until 1123 that pope Calixtus II made it unambiguously plain that he

---

[5] *CAI*, cc. 117, 121.

[6] M. Blöcker-Walter, *Alfons I von Portugal* (Zurich, 1966), pp. 33–5; P. Feige, 'Die Anfänge des portugiesischen Königtums und seiner Landeskirche', *Spanische Forschungen der Görresgesellschaft* 29 (1978), 85–436, at pp. 244–6.

[7] *LSJ*, pp. 271–2, 283–5. It is true that the setting of the latter is Fernando I's siege and conquest of Coimbra in 1064. But the story is an elaboration of that to be found in the anonymous *Historia Silense* (ed. J. Pérez de Urbel and A. González Ruiz-Zorrilla (Madrid, 1959), c. 89, pp. 191–2) composed at León c.1120. The earliest references to the campaign have nothing to say of St. James: see P. David, 'Annales Portugalenses veteres' in his *Études historiques*, pp. 257–340.

[8] The view that the Barbastro expedition of 1064 was a 'pre-Crusade crusade', as Erdmann argued, is not tenable.

regarded the wars in Spain as crusades.[9] Whether the Spaniards themselves thought of their wars as crusades must remain uncertain until we reach the campaigns of 1147-8 which brought about the conquests of Almería, Lisbon, Lérida and Tortosa.[10] These were certainly perceived as crusades by the contemporaries who recorded them.

Though the argument cannot be developed here, I would suggest that the 'crusade-idea' was an alien importation which took root in Spain only in the second quarter of the twelfth century. It further seems to me of significance that the notion of St. James as a patron saint of warfare against Islam emerges clearly for the first time at the same period. The implications may be far-reaching.

We must return for the last time to Diego Gelmírez. It is a striking fact—and some have found it an awkward one—that the *Historia Compostellana* has so very little to say of warfare against the Moors, of the *Reconquista*, of crusading, of Santiago Matamoros. Two passages, however, deserve some attention. In 1113, at Burgos, Diego was called on by queen Urraca to address an assembly at a time when the Almoravides were pressing hard upon the southern frontier.[11] His speech was a call to stand firm against enemies. We have our backs to the wall, he said in effect. We must avenge the wrongs done to us just as the Israelites slaughtered the people of Gibeah (Judges: 19-20). Our cause is just; God is on our side. Now the elements which would permit us to call this a crusading sermon are conspicuous by their absence. Diego was preaching what Erdmann called a *Verteidigungskrieg* or defensive war, a well-known genre of the pre-crusading era.[12] Far different was it eleven years later when in 1124 Diego addressed one of his legatine councils at Compostela.[13] As

---

[9] JL 7116. For a recent translation see J. and L. Riley-Smith, *The Crusades. Idea and reality, 1095-1274* (London, 1981), no. 12, pp. 73-4.

[10] G. Constable, 'The Second Crusade as seen by contemporaries', *Traditio* 9 (1953), 213-79. The attitudes of the authors of the *Chronica Adefonsi Imperatoris* and the *De Expugnatione Lyxbonensi* seem to me distinctive and (in a Spanish context) novel. The author of the latter work was of course an Englishman but I am prepared to trust his report of the crusading sermon preached by Pedro Pitoës, bishop of Porto.

[11] *HC*, pp. 158-61.

[12] C. Erdmann, *Die Entstehung des Kreuzzugsgedankens* (Stuttgart, 1935), pp. 22-4.   [13] *HC*, pp. 427-30.

the pope's legate he preached an aggressive military campaign (*expeditio*) against the Moors, to the confusion of
paganism and the exaltation of Christianity. To all those
taking part in it he promised full absolution and remission
of sins. A document was drawn up for circulation giving
details of the spiritual and other benefits which would
accrue to those soldiers of Christ (*milites Christi*) who
heeded the call: remission of sins, and protection of their
property, enforceable by the sanction of excommunication, during their absence. All of which, we are told, was
done in accordance with papal decree (*iuxta domini papae
edictum*); it is surely reasonable to detect in this a reference
to the bull of Calixtus II of 1123 to which reference has
aleady been made. The contrast between these two pronouncements is marked. The call to arms of 1113 was not the
preaching of a crusade; that of 1124 was. It would be unwise
to press the implications of this contrast too far. But it is
worth bearing in mind that between these two dates Diego's
contacts with the papal curia had been extremely close.
If the different content of the two speeches does indeed
witness to development in his thoughts on the subject of
Christian warfare in Spain, this evolution was suggestively
parallel to that which papal thinking seems to have undergone during the same period.

Does this make Diego Gelmírez a 'crusader'? Does it place
him among the architects of the idea of St. James's patronage of a reconquest of Spain? I doubt it. The notions we
have glanced at here, hazy as yet, seem to run together and
'set' in a new mould only after he was dead and gone. Diego's
mind had been shaped long before, back in the 1070s and
1080s. His native Galicia was an enormous distance—and
not just geographically—from the southern frontier. He did
not face that way. The reticence of the *Historia* is eloquent.

That work, as we have had occasion to stress more than
once, is not a window into Diego's soul. We know so much
of what he did, so little of what he was like. Back in 1102,
when he had stolen the relics of St. Fructuosus but before
he had made his escape with them from Braga, he was so
beset with anxiety that he had a sleepless night.[14] There,

[14] *HC*, p. 39.

suddenly, in the twinkling of an eye, we can glimpse the man behind the bishop; and then he is gone. To end this study of him on so many questioning and uncertain notes is to confess the honest perplexities of the twentieth-century historian as he stalks his quarry along the cunning passages, contrived corridors and issues, of history. But to end this book thus hesitantly is hardly just to its subject. Diego Gelmírez always knew where he was going and how to get there. He was nothing if not sure of himself.

Appendix A

The sources for the life and times of Diego Gelmírez

1. *The* Historia Compostellana

Our principal authority is the work known since its publication in the eighteenth century as the *Historia Compostellana*. The work was commissioned by Diego Gelmírez as a record of his pontificate and has therefore the authority of a contemporary witness. Its authorship, mode and date of composition, purposes and trustworthiness are all matters that have generated scholarly debate. On none of these questions, in my view, has a definitive conclusion yet been reached: much work remains to be done. That said, certain things are tolerably clear. The work was conceived as a collection (*registrum*) of documents loosely threaded together by stretches of narrative. It was the work of several successive authors—at least four—of whom the most prolific was Gerald, a native of Beauvais, canon of Compostela from perhaps 1112 and *magister scolarum* from c.1118 to c.1134. The internal evidence of the text confirms that composition was intermittent: parts of the *Historia* may have been written as early as about 1106, it is unlikely that any of it was composed later than 1139. Since the authors' aim was to record and to glorify the deeds of Diego Gelmírez it is inevitably a tendentious work, for instance in their attitude to queen Urraca or to Diego's ecclesiastical rivals; but it is not difficult to make allowance for strident partisanship of this sort. The authors were men who wore their hearts and their prejudices on their sleeves. The *Historia* is not a work of subtle complexity but a plain and at times almost embarrassingly candid record of a great prelate's *gesta*.

The *Historia* was first printed by Enrique Flórez in 1765 as volume XX of his *España Sagrada* under the title *Historia Compostellana, sive de rebus gestis D. Didaci Gelmirez primi*

Compostellani archiepiscopi. This edition was reproduced under the auspices of the Real Academia de la Historia in 1965. In my footnotes I have abbreviated the title to *HC* and given references to pages of this edition, not to book or chapter numbers. The pagination of Flórez's edition is bedevilled by misprints between pages 273 and 287: references to these pages are given in the form 278(276), where (276) is the page number printed and 278 is the correct one.

Flórez's text of the *Historia* was reprinted in Migne's *Patrologia Latina*, vol. CLXX (Paris, 1854), cols. 889–1236. In 1950 a translation into Spanish was published at Santiago de Compostela by M. Suárez, with notes by J. Campelo: the annotation is particularly useful in its bearing on Galician topography.

Flórez worked from the earliest surviving manuscript, now Salamanca, Biblioteca de la Universidad, MS 2658. This is a copy of the mid- or late-thirteenth century, probably more than one remove from the original manuscript, the work of a careless scribe whose Latin was poor. Flórez made the best of a bad job and by recourse to liberal and intelligent emendation produced a usable text. But it cannot be said that the *Historia Compostellana* has ever been critically edited. (It is rumoured that a new edition is in preparation in Spain.) Not without considerable difficulty, Professor Antonio García y García procured a microfilm of Salamanca MS 2658 for me; for which I am profoundly grateful to him. With the aid of this, and some readings from the later, fourteenth- and fifteenth-century manuscripts in the cathedral archive of Santiago de Compostela, I have ventured to depart from Flórez's text here and there. My changes have been for the most part of minor significance and I have not drawn attention to them. Where they seemed of more importance, for example in their bearing on chronology, they have been documented in a footnote.

The most recent discussion of the *Historia Compostellana*, with full references to earlier literature, is to be found in Vones, *Kirchenpolitik*, pp. 4–74.

2. *Royal charters*

All royal charters granted to the church of Santiago de Compostela down to the year 1127 were copied into the cathedral cartulary now known as Tumbo A between 1129 and 1131; subsequent charters of Alfonso VII and his successors were added to this manuscript later in the century. The originals do not survive. On the circumstances in which this cartulary was compiled, see chapter X. Very nearly all these documents have been printed either by Flórez in the appendices to *España Sagrada* vol. XIX or by López Ferreiro in the appendices to his *Historia de la Santa A. M. Iglesia de Santiago de Compostela.* Judged by modern standards, the editing leaves something to be desired. Through the good offices of Professor Antonio García I was enabled by the kindness of D. Salvador Domato Bua, Director del Archivo Histórico Diocesano de Santiago de Compostela, and D. José-María Díaz, Canónigo-Archivero de la Catedral de Santiago de Compostela, to secure photographs of the relevant folios (1-46^r) of Tumbo A in 1978, so that I have been able to check the printed versions against the manuscript copies. This photographic record was executed under difficult conditions (there was then no electric light in the cathedral archive) by Sr. Nóvoa, whose skill I acknowledge with admiration and gratitude.

On the mode of reference in this book to these and other royal charters of the rulers of León-Castile, see below, Appendix B.

3. *Other charters*

Some hundreds of private (i.e. non-royal) charters of the tenth, eleventh and twelfth centuries from Galicia and northern Portugal have survived either as originals or as cartulary copies. They constitute invaluable materials for the reconstruction of the economic, social and ecclesiastical history of the region. Only a proportion—perhaps, in rough terms, between a third and a half—of this corpus of evidence has found its way into print in some form or another. The printed collections which I have found the most useful are those of the charters of the monasteries of Carboeiro, Jubia and Sobrado: bibliographical details may be found in the list of abbreviations. I have also made use of large numbers of unpublished documents from the following archives: the Archivo Histórico Nacional (AHN) in Madrid, the Archivo Histórico del Reino de Galicia (AHRG) in Corunna, the Instituto de Valencia de Don Juan (IVDJ) and the Biblioteca Nacional (BN), both in Madrid, and the Archivo de la Catedral (AC) of the several cathedrals of Galicia.

4. *Papal letters*

Nearly all the papal letters which I have cited are preserved in the *Historia Compostellana*. In addition to the page references I have provided cross-references to Jaffé's *Regesta Pontificum Romanorum* in the revised (1885) edition by Löwenfeld and others. References are given in the standard form used by medievalists, i.e. JL followed by the number of the letter. A few unpublished papal letters have also been cited.

5. *The* Liber Sancti Jacobi

This is the title conventionally, if incorrectly, given to the bizarre compilation put together in France about the middle years of the twelfth century containing in its five books (i) lessons, sermons, prayers and hymns for the feasts of St. James; (ii) a collection of the miracles of St. James; (iii) materials relating to the translation of the body of St. James from Palestine to Galicia; (iv) a fabulous account of Charlemagne's campaigns in Spain attributed to archbishop Turpin of Rheims; and (v) a guidebook for the use of pilgrims from France to the shrine of St. James at Compostela.

Historians of medieval Compostela, particularly those concerned with pilgrimages thereto, have traditionally made somewhat incautious, at times reckless, use of materials contained in the first, second and fifth books. My acquaintance with these puzzling texts had left me somewhat baffled, but at any rate convinced that greater circumspection was needed in using them for historical purposes than had usually been shown in the past. It was then that I encountered Mr Christopher Hohler's 'A note on *Jacobus*', *Journal of the Warburg and Courtauld Institutes* 35 (1972), 31-80. Mr Hohler's learned, vigorous and richly entertaining polemic, which contains references to recent contributions to the voluminous literature on the *Jacobus*, is now the best introduction to this desperately problematical group of texts. His work convinced me that I must needs be even more circumspect in my employment of them than I had allowed. Certain references which had found their way into earlier drafts of this book have accordingly been excised. But not all. Some materials in *Jacobus*, it seems to me, *may* be used for certain limited ends by the historian of twelfth-century Compostela; and I have permitted myself this liberty here and there, notably in chapter VII, though not without a degree of trepidation.

The only (and far from satisfactory) edition of the whole text is that of W. M. Whitehill, *Liber Sancti Jacobi, Codex Calixtinus* (Santiago de Compostela, 1944), vol. I. In my notes I have given page references to this edition under the abbreviation *LSJ*.

6. *Modern work*

The above is not an exhaustive list of the original sources which I have used, but it should serve to indicate the main categories of those which have proved the most useful. Since, as will be apparent to the reader, the modern or secondary literature devoted to my subject is not extensive, I decided after some consideration that to provide a formal bibliography would serve little useful purpose. Accordingly, the bibliography is to be found in the footnotes. However, it might be helpful to comment briefly here on those secondary works to which I have repeatedly turned, invariably to the profit of my understanding, and to whose authors I owe a debt of gratitude not readily to be appreciated from my references to them in the footnotes; references too often occasioned (as is the way with footnotes) by a wish merely to record dissent; but this (I trust) in no carping spirit.

Pride of place must go to Antonio López Ferreiro, *Historia de la Santa Apostólica Metropolitana Iglesia de Santiago de Compostela* (Santiago de Compostela, 1898-1911), of which volumes II, III, and IV have been, after the *Historia Compostellana* itself, my prop and stay. This is a noble work, learned and stately, pious and humane; a monument of devout historical scholarship. An English historian, approaching in the 1980s that period of Compostelan history treated in those three majestic volumes, will necessarily view it in a somewhat different perspective; moreover, he will or should have access to techniques of historical scholarship not indeed unavailable to López Ferreiro but which have undergone refinement since the time at which he did his work. Which is only to say, as discreetly as may be, that López Ferreiro has, inevitably, dated. He was a Catholic priest of the nineteenth century who wrote to celebrate the traditions of the church of St. James. Minute and painstaking, loving but also critical, though his attention was to the early history of his native Galicia, his vision did not stray far beyond her confines. Acutely conscious of being but 'a pygmy on the shoulders of a giant', I have sought here only to hint at additional ways of interpreting the materials which he knew so much better than anyone before or since; to afforce his scholarship, not to attempt (which would be presumptuous) to supplant it. A word of gratitude must finally be said, before we leave him, for the documentary appendices which so stoutly buttress his text. In the three volumes in question they amount to over five hundred pages of documents for the most part previously unpublished, some of which have been lost since his day. My debt to this great store of information is apparent in the footnotes to this book.

My first acquaintance with Diego Gelmírez was made through the work of A. G. Biggs, *Diego Gelmírez, first archbishop of Compostela* (Washington, 1949), which remains the only full treatment of Diego's career in English. It has to be said that this is a somewhat pedestrian work; furthermore, the author relied only on sources available in print. For all these limitations, however, this is a very careful work which brings together conveniently much information not otherwise easy of access. The only other work in the

English language which deserves mention is both more recent and of very much higher quality: B. F. Reilly, *The kingdom of León-Castilla under queen Urraca 1109–1126* (Princeton, 1982), is the first adequate study in any language of the reign of queen Urraca and deserves to lead the field for many years to come. I have elsewhere in this book, at the beginning of chapter VI, acknowledged my indebtedness to this work and to certain kindnesses shown me by its author in connection with it.

Of works in languages other than English, easily the most stimulating is the collection of essays by Pierre David, *Études historiques sur la Galice et le Portugal du VIe au XIIe siècle* (Lisbon–Paris, 1947). David was a most remarkable scholar who single-handedly transformed the study of the medieval history first of Poland and then of Portugal. His *Études historiques* are distinguished not only by the breadth of their range in time and by the depth of their erudition, but also and above all by the alert and sparkling intelligence which informs them and all other of his writings on Iberian history (and, so I am told, on early Polish history too). Whether assessing the evidence of annals or charters, church-dedications, place-names or liturgy; whether investigating the ecclesiastical organization of the Suevic kingdom in the sixth century or the strange and tragic career of archbishop Maurice of Braga in the early twelfth; he invariably had something to convey that was fresh, clever and arresting. A gifted teacher, he imparted something of his distinctive style and tone and approach to his pupil Avelino de Jesus da Costa, whose book *O bispo D. Pedro e a organização da diocese de Braga* (Coimbra, 1959: first published in the journal *Biblos*) is the most acute as well as the most exhaustive study of any Iberian churchman in the eleventh and twelfth centuries.

Of works devoted to Galicia proper in the early middle ages, I have learnt much from the writings of Manuel Ruben García Alvarez. To a large number of articles published over the last twenty years or so, for the most part in the periodicals *Compostellanum* and *Cuadernos de Estudios Gallegos*, he has recently added the first instalment of a book, *Galicia y los gallegos en la alta edad media* (Santiago de Compostela, 1975). Dr García Alvarez's work has attracted a good deal of *odium academicum* (possibly, I suspect, because he is an 'amateur'); to my mind, unjustly. Most of his work has been sober, careful and thorough. To one series of studies in particular I am deeply indebted, his very useful catalogue of royal charters relating to Galicia: on this see further below, Appendix B.

German scholarly interest in the ecclesiastical history of the western parts of the Iberian peninsula during the eleventh and twelfth centuries first manifested itself in a series of characteristically distinguished studies by Carl Erdmann; notably his fine edition of the surviving *Papsturkunden in Portugal* published in 1927. After lying dormant for many years it has recently flowered again in the exceptionally thorough and penetrating study of Dr Ludwig Vones, *Die* Historia Compostellana *und die Kirchenpolitik des nordwestspanischen Raumes 1070-1130* (Cologne, 1980); a work to which I have already paid tribute in this book, at the beginning of chapter VIII. Dr Vones's book is provided (pp. 564-603) with a full bibliography: readers who are distressed by the absence of such an apparatus in this book may turn with confidence to Dr Vones.

Appendix B

Royal charters referred to in the text

About 170 charters issued by the rulers of León, for the most part beneficial diplomas, have been cited in the course of this book. They range in time from the early ninth century to the late twelfth. In order to avoid cumbersome footnotes I have referred to them simply by the form 'R. + date', where 'R.' indicates 'royal charter': e.g. R. 22 July 1109. Nearly all Leonese royal charters of this period are dated by day, month and year. A few bear only month-and-year dates, or year-only dates; very occasionally royal charters are undated, and internal textual evidence has to be used to provide an approximate date: such charters are referred to by the appropriate forms, e.g. R. December 1075, R. 1127 or R. 866 × 910.

All the charters cited are listed in chronological order in this appendix, with references. My aim has been to furnish references in the shortest and simplest possible form: for lack of space I have deliberately, if reluctantly, eschewed any discussion of individual documents—of questions of provenance, manuscript tradition, modern publication, authenticity, and so forth. It need hardly be pointed out that many of the documents cited do raise insistent and difficult questions of this order. All I have sought to do, however, is to direct the reader as briefly as possible to modern discussion of them or, in the case of unpublished documents, to the texts themselves.

Wherever possible I have provided a reference to one of four principal catalogues, namely:

(a) M. R. García Alvarez, 'Catálogo de documentos reales de la alta edad media referentes a Galicia (714-1109)', *Compostellanum* 8 (1963), 301-75; 9 (1964), 639-77; 10 (1965), 257-328; 11 (1966), 257-340; 12 (1967), 255-68, 581-636. This will be referred to as García, *DRG*, followed by the number of the document. This is the only comprehensive catalogue of royal charters relating to Galicia issued before 1109, and though it is not absolutely without blemish it is an invaluable work of reference. It should be noted that it includes instruments issued on the authority of members of the royal family other than the reigning monarch, e.g. Raymond of Burgundy, count of Galicia, the son-in-law of Alfonso VI: no attempt has been made to differentiate these in the lists which follow.

(b)   Bernard F. Reilly, *The kingdom of León-Castilla under queen Urraca, 1109-1126* (Princeton, 1982). The footnotes to this work provide what is now the best guide to the charters not only of queen Urraca but also of her son Alfonso Raimúndez before his accession to the throne of León-Castile on his mother's death in 1126. It will be referred to, as elsewhere in this book, as Reilly, *Urraca*, and page references will be given to the first occurrence of each charter cited in the narrative section of the book, that is chapters 1-6.

(c)   P. Rassow, 'Die Urkunden Kaiser Alfons' VII.von Spanien', *Archiv für Urkundenforschung* 10 (1928), 327-467; 11 (1930), 66-137. The first part of this study includes at pp. 415-67 a catalogue of all Alfonso VII's charters known to the author. Although the quality of Rassow's work is of the highest, many charters which were inaccessible to him when he conducted his researches some sixty years ago have since then become available. Where possible I give page references to Rassow's catalogue; elsewhere to printed or manuscript sources.

(d)   J. González, *Regesta de Fernando II* (Madrid, 1943), is the essential guide to the charters of Fernando II (1157-88), of which a few have been cited in this work. I have abbreviated the title to *GRF* and given page references to the royal charters catalogued at pp. 345-517.

4 September	829	García, *DRG* no. 12
	858	″ no. 41

20 January	867	García *DRG*	no. 48
30 June	880	"	no. 65
17 August	883	"	no. 67
25 September	883	"	no. 68
	885	"	no. 70
24 June	886	"	no. 72
25 July	893	"	no. 73
11 July	895	"	no. 75
25 November	895	"	no. 76
6 May	899	"	no. 85
30 December	899	"	no. 88
30 November	904	A. C. Floriano, *Diplomática española del período astur* (Oviedo, 1949–51), II, no. 174.	
	906	García, *DRG* no. 99 (and see also below, Appendix C)	
866 × 910		García, *DRG* no. 102	
7 June	910	"	no. 125
20 April	911	"	no. 127
6 December	914	"	no. 140
29 January	915	"	no. 141
30 January	915	"	no. 142
8 January	918	"	no. 160
18 May	920	"	no. 171
28 June	924	"	no. 210
17 September	924	"	no. 211
21 November	927	"	no. 226
8 August	929	"	no. 240
5 March	951	"	no. 296
2 March	958	"	no. 323
21 May	958	"	no. 324
28 March	959	"	no. 327
29 September	985	"	no. 378
1 June	986	"	no. 382
24 May	991	"	no. 388
5 March	1011	"	no. 455
30 March	1019	"	no. 467
30 December	1020	"	no. 468
29 October	1024	"	no. 471

26 September	1028	García, *DRG*	no. 483
15 November	1028	"	no. 484
30 December	1028	"	no. 485
25 August	1032	"	no. 489
9 June	1037	"	no. 493
8 January	1061	"	no. 508
19 August	1061	"	no. 510
17 February	1066	"	no. 525
25 June	1066	"	no. 527
23 February	1067	"	no. 529
1 February	1071	"	no. 535
13 June	1071	"	no. 539
31 July	1071	"	no. 541
10 November	1073	"	no. 542
December	1075	"	no. 544
17 October	1077	"	no. 550
25 April	1087	"	no. 557
30 May	1087	"	no. 558
18 June	1088	"	no. 560
21 July	1088	"	no. 562
17 June	1089	"	no. 564
28 January	1090	"	no. 567
13 November	1094	*Portugalliae Monumenta Historica, Diplomata et Chartae,* vol. I (Lisbon, 1867), no. 813	
11 February	1095	García, *DRG*	no. 569
25 February	1095	*LFH* III, pp. 183–4	
24 September	1095	García, *DRG*	no. 571
11 January	1096	"	no. 573
1 May	1096	Reilly, *Urraca*, p. 23	
21 August	1096	García, *DRG*	no. 575
19 May	1097	"	no. 579
28 March	1098	"	no. 582
23 January	1099	"	no. 583
16 January	1100	"	no. 585
13 November	1100	"	no. 586
1 April	1101	"	no. 587
24 October	1102	"	no. 590
17 March	1107	"	no. 599
14 May	1107	"	no. 600

13 December	1107	García, *DRG* no. 607
21 January	1108	" no. 608
22 February	1109	Reilly, *Urraca*, p. 54
1088 × 1109		García, *DRG* no. 610
22 July	1109	Reilly, *Urraca*, p. 56
10 September	1109	" p. 58
24 December	1110	León, Archivo de San Isidoro, no. 135
14 April	1111	Reilly, *Urraca*, p. 72
19 September	1111	" p. 73
8 December	1111	" p. 74
2 March	1112	" p. 79
May	1112	" p. 81
14 May	1112	" p. 81
17 June	1113	" p. 92
12 October	1113	" p. 94
8 December	1113	" p. 96
3 January	1115	" p. 103
26 November	1115	" p. 108
29 February	1116	" p. 109
31 March	1116	" p. 109
18 May	1116	" p. 110
15 October	1116	" p. 115
27 November	1116	" p. 116
5 July	1118	" p. 129
29 July	1118	" p. 129
26 September	1119	" p. 140
13 June	1120	" p. 144
6 August	1120	" p. 147
21 August	1120	" p. 148
	1123	" p. 178
18 May	1123	" p. 175
11 November	1123	" p. 177
29 November	1123	" p. 178
30 November	1123	" p. 178
6 April	1124	" p. 186
8 April	1124	L. Sánchez Belda, *Documentos reales de la edad media referentes a Galicia* (Madrid, 1953), no. 201

31 May	1124	Reilly, *Urraca*, p. 188
10 May	1125	" p. 196
1 June	1125	" p. 198
21 July	1125	" p. 199
13 April	1126	Rassow, p. 417
21 July	1126	" p. 417
	1127	" p. 418
2 April	1127	" p. 418
13 November	1127	" p. 418
25 May	1128	" p. 419
25 March	1129	" p. 419
7 February	1130	" p. 420
22 February	1130	" p. 420
18 March	1131	" p. 421
15 May	1131	" p. 421
1 February	1132	" p. 422
18 August	1132	*Colección de documentos de la catedral de Oviedo*, ed. S. García Larragueta (Oviedo, 1962), no. 149
2 January	1133	*Colección diplomática de San Salvador de Oña*, ed. J. del Alamo (Madrid, 1950), no. 164
18 January	1133	AC Orense, Privilegios, I/22
3 February	1133	Rassow, p. 422
11 April	1133	AC Orense, Privilegios, I/21
3 May	1133	*Colección de Fueros municipales y cartas pueblas*, ed. T. Múñoz y Romero (Madrid, 1847), pp. 507-11
13 May	1133	AC Orense, Privilegios, I/20
20 December	1133	Rassow, p. 423
	1134	" p. 423
1 June	1134	León, Archivo de San Isidoro, no. 143
10 November	1134	Madrid, Biblioteca Nacional, MS 712, fo. 41^v
26 December	1134	Rassow, p. 423
25 May	1135	Madrid, AHN 518/7

29 May	1135	Rassow, p. 424
2 June	1135	" p. 425
18 August	1135	AC Orense, Privilegios, III/16
2 September	1135	Madrid, AHN 1509/5
9 March	1136	Rassow, p. 426
18 August	1136	" p. 428
October	1136	" p. 428
2 October	1136	" p. 428
4 October	1136	" p. 428
17 July	1137	" p. 430
20 July	1137	" p. 430
28 July	1137	Corunna, AHRG, Documentos Reales, no. 3
10 May	1138	Madrid, AHN cód. 1002B, fo. 7^v-8^r
11 December	1138	Madrid, AHN 556/3
12 December	1138	Rassow, p. 432
1 July	1140	" p. 434
13 February	1147	" p. 444
11 July	1147	*LFH* IV, ap. xvii, pp. 46-8
29 October	1156	Rassow, p. 466
19 February	1158	*GRF* p. 347
30 September	1158	" p. 350
24 August	1165	" p. 388
18 March	1169	" p. 406

Few royal documents from peninsular kingdoms other than León have been cited in this work. Two Aragonese royal charters have been mentioned: Pedro I's grant of urban property in Huesca to the church of Santiago in March 1098 is to be found in A. Ubieto Arteta, *Colección diplomática de Pedro I de Aragon y Navarra* (Zaragoza, 1951), no. 48; Alfonso I's grant to the monastery of Samos of 13 July 1110 is printed as an appendix to R. A. Fletcher, 'Obispos olvidados del siglo XII de las diócesis de Mondoñedo y Lugo', *Cuadernos de Estudios Gallegos* 28 (1973), 318-25 (and I may permit myself to say that the inaccuracies of this edition are owing to the circumstance that the author was afforded no opportunity of correcting the proofs before publication).

Several royal charters from Portugal have been cited. All such documents have been published in *Documentos Medievais Portugueses: Documentos Régios*, vol. I (Lisbon, 1958): the quality of the editing and critical apparatus in this magnificent work cannot be too highly praised. In my footnotes I have referred to it under the abbreviation *DMP*.

Appendix C

Alfonso III's letter to
the clergy of Tours

The text of this letter was preserved in a cartulary of St. Martin's at Tours copied between 1132 and 1137, which was destroyed in 1793. All modern printed editions descend from a copy of the letter made for the seventeenth-century antiquary André Duchesne. The text contains some obvious corruptions, but we cannot tell whether these originated in the seventeenth century, or in the twelfth, or at some earlier stage of the manuscript tradition.[1] The techniques of palaeography, in short, are of no assistance to us. Neither are those of diplomatic. For the letter is unique among early Spanish royal documents; there is nothing with which we may compare it. All other of Alfonso III's surviving documents are charters which are in some way beneficial—diplomas granting lands or privileges, precepts relating to title, records of lawsuits, confirmations of rights or properties. No correspondence of any Leonese-Castilian king has survived from before the twelfth century, with the single exception of the letter under consideration here. Lacking a sample of similar documents for comparative purposes, we can undertake no diplomatic tests. The enquirer who wishes to establish whether or not the letter is authentic can do no more than look hard at what it says and ask himself whether it seems plausible. Very well: so what does it say?

King Alfonso, styling himself 'king of Spain' (*rex Hispaniae*), addresses and greets the clergy of St. Martin of Tours. He has received their letter (*literas*), carried by Mansio and Datus to archbishop (*sic*) Sisnando, and delivered by Sisnando to him. He is grieved to learn of the recent Viking attack in the course of which St. Martin's church was burnt. But he rejoices to hear of the work going ahead at Tours

---

[1] For a guide to editions and modern discussion see García, *DRG*, no. 99. I have worked from the text in *LFH* II, ap. xxvii, pp. 57–60.

to restore and fortify the church; is comforted, too, by the news of the miracles worked at St. Martin's shrine. Concerning the imperial crown made of gold and precious stones, fitting to his dignity, which they have again (*rursum*) referred to, urging Sisnando to persuade the king to buy it, he is willing and grateful to do so. He will arrange for a journey by sea (*navalis remigatio*) to be undertaken between us (reading *nos* instead of *vos*) and our friend Amalvinus duke (*sic*) of Bordeaux. In May of this present year, 906 AD (*sic*), his ships with members of his household will make their way to Bordeaux. Would the clergy of Tours please send the crown in the care of their own envoys so that it will reach Amalvinus count (*sic*) of Bordeaux by the middle of May. Then let two or three of their own people return with the king's messengers, and the crown, by sea from Bordeaux to Spain. He tactfully intimates that the church of Tours will be well rewarded. Would they also be so good as to send any written accounts of the posthumous miracles of St. Martin; for as yet he possesses only an account of the miracles worked by Martin during his lifetime. He can offer in return a work devoted to the lives of the holy fathers of Mérida, which he believes (reading *rememoror* for *remoror*) may not be known at Tours. They have asked which apostle's tomb it is that exists in Spain. Let them know that it is the tomb of St. James the son of Zebedee. His body was borne to Galicia after his death and buried there, as many trustworthy authorities (*multae veridicae historiae*) attest. Miracles are worked at his shrine. Should they wish to know how he was martyred, and how and when brought here for burial, the letters (*epistolae*) of our archbishops (*sic*) and the accounts (*historiae*) of our church fathers will tell. There is not time to include these writings in his letter; but when their representatives come here they will hear and see for themselves. They have asked how far from the sea the tomb is, and exactly where. Sail to the confluence of the rivers *Volia* (*sic*: presumably the Ulla) and Sar at *Bisria*.[2] From there to the old (reading *veteris* for *vestrae*) see of Iria in the church of Sta. Eulalia it is ten miles; and thence another twelve to the tomb of St. James.

---

[2] The last passage is very corrupt; only the general sense is intelligible.

Four arguments have been adduced against the authenticity of this document. First, it has been held that the king's title is anachronistic. Alfonso III normally styled himself, in his charters, simply *Adefonsus rex*. To some enquirers it has seemed that the more elaborate title used in the letter—which runs, in full, *Adefonsus pro Christi nutu atque potentia Hispaniae rex*—is in itself enough to brand the document as spurious. On the other hand the emergence of wide territorial claims and of imperial pretensions at the Asturian court can be dated to the latter part of Alfonso III's reign; and a fundamental feature of the Leonese *imperium* of the tenth and eleventh centuries was precisely the claim that the king of León was emperor of all Spain (*imperator Hispaniae*).[3] Alfonso III himself had already been heralded in 883 as the ruler predestined with God's help to unite all Spain under his rule: *gloriosus Adefonsus in omni Spanie regnaturus*.[4] With notions of this sort gaining currency in court circles, the elaborate royal title of the Tours letter seems more acceptable.

Second, some scholars have found it difficult to accept as authentic a document which refers to Sisnando as an archbishop. But here too the difficulty may plausibly be explained away. One possibility is that the original text spelt the word *episcopus* with a dipthong—*æpiscopus*, a usage which can be found in original Spanish documents of this period[5] —and that the earliest scribe to copy the text at Tours incorrectly expanded what he took to be an abbreviation. Another possibility is that there occurred a different kind of error. The copyist of the Tours cartulary was working after the see of Compostela had been raised to metropolitan status in 1120: a slip of the pen, conscious or unconscious, by which the document was brought to reflect the ecclesiastical realities of his own day is not to be ruled out. It would be foolish to reject the letter on such a ground as this.

[3] For the *imperium* of the Leonese kings see R. Menéndez Pidal, *El imperio hispánico y los cinco reinos* (Madrid, 1950); A. Sánchez Candeira, *El 'regnum-imperium' leonés hasta 1037* (Madrid, 1951).

[4] *Crónica Profética*, ed. M. Gómez Moreno, 'Las primeras crónicas de la Reconquista: el ciclo de Alfonso III', *BRAH* 100 (1932), 562-628, at p. 623.

[5] For example, in an original royal charter of 7 March 918: L. Barrau-Dihigo, 'Chartes royales léonaises 912-1037', *Révue Hispanique* 10 (1903), 350-454, no. ii.

Thirdly, the dating of the letter by the year of the Incarnation has aroused suspicions; for Spanish documents of this period were normally dated by the Spanish Era. But need it? The Spaniards were not ignorant of Anno Domini dating. It was used, for example, in the document recording the conscration of the new church at Compostela in 899. The clergy of Tours, however, may well have been ignorant of the Spanish Era. (The greatest computist of the early middle ages, Bede, seems not to have known of it.) Surely it is intelligible that the king should have used a system of dating to which his correspondents were accustomed.

The fourth objection to the authenticity of the Tours letter is more formidable. The passage in it relating to St. James, it has been argued, is dependent on a version of a document known as the *Epistola Leonis Papae*. The letter attributed to one of the popes named Leo gives an account of the translation of the body of St. James from Jerusalem to Galicia. It survives in three different, apparently successive, redactions which were first satisfactorily distinguished by Duchesne.[6] The earliest of them, redaction A, survives in a single copy, inserted by a writer who was trying to imitate the contemporary Visigothic script of Spain into a manuscript of the abbey of St. Martial at Limoges, probably at some point in the latter half of the tenth century.[7] There is reason to suppose that the letter was originally composed in Spain, presumably by someone connected with the cult of St. James. But we do not know who he was nor, more importantly, when he did his work. The second redaction, B, survives in a single twelfth-century copy.[8] It purges A of its grosser legendary matter, improves its barbarous grammar and works into its text the entry relating to St. James in the ninth-century martyrologies. The third redaction, C, does not here concern us. Duchesne argued that the letter of Alfonso III to the clergy of Tours was dependent on redaction B; and that redaction B was composed after—perhaps long after—the year 906: *ergo*, the Tours letter (or at

[6] L. Duchesne, 'Saint Jacques en Galice', *Annales du Midi* 12 (1900), 145-79.

[7] A. Mundó, 'El códice Parisinus lat.2036 y sus añadiduras hispánicas', *Hispania Sacra* 5 (1952), 67-78.

[8] Escorial L. iii. 9, fo. 40; best edition in Z. García Villada, *Historia eclesiástica de España* (Madrid, 1929-36), I. pp. 369-70.

least that part of it relating to St. James) cannot be what it purports to be, a letter composed at the bidding of Alfonso III and sent to the clergy of Tours in 906.

Attentive scrutiny of the texts, however, fails to yield results so clear-cut as Duchesne maintained. The passage concerning St. James in the Tours letter is dependent on material which is *common* to redactions A and B, with the exception of certain turns of phrase in redaction B which are lifted from the ninth-century martyrologies; and there is no way of showing that the Tours letter's dependence is not rather on redaction A-plus-martyrologies than (as Duchesne argued) on redaction B. It is true that we cannot establish with certainty that the martyrologies were known in the Asturian kingdom in the time of Alfonso III. However, as we saw in chapter III, the editor of one of the most important of them, Usuard of Saint-Germain-des-Prés, had himself travelled in Spain before the publication of his work in about 865, where he had been in touch with the adherents of the cult of St. James. It may be that martyrologies lurk behind the *Passiones* mentioned in ninth- and tenth-century inventories of books in Galician libraries.[9] Conceivably they were the *veridicae historiae* referred to by king Alfonso III. It would be a little surprising if such works were not known in his kingdom. As for the date of the composition of redaction A of the *Epistola Leonis*, we have absolutely no means of establishing it. The text could have been composed a century or more before the unique surviving copy was committed to writing at Limoges. Duchesne's argument cannot be decisively refuted: but we may justifiably return a verdict of not proven.

So much for the arguments against the authenticity of Alfonso III's letter to the clergy of Tours. They turn out upon inspection to be far from conclusive. Those in its favour, to which we must now turn our attention, seem to me strong; though here too, it must be confessed at the outset, they are not decisive. We are invited to suppose that the letter was concocted by person or persons unknown, somewhere (it is to be presumed) in France or Spain (perhaps

[9] M. R. García Alvarez, 'Los libros en la documentación gallega de la alta edad media', *Cuadernos de Estudios Gallegos* 20 (1965), 292-329.

more probably the former), at some point before the compilation of the Tours cartulary in the 1130s. What can we say in
answer to this case?

First, and most fundamentally, there could be no con-
ceivable motive for forgery. Second, the historical detail,
where we can check it, is correct. Tours was attacked by the
Vikings in 903 and St. Martin's church burnt. In the years
immediately following, archbishop Hebernus rebuilt the
church and the city. It is very likely, though it cannot actually
be proved, that the clergy of Tours would have had an
object in their treasury which could be described as a *corona
imperialis*, and that they might seek to dispose of it to a royal
purchaser at a time when they needed funds. The most convincing piece of detail concerns Amalvinus, duke (or count)
of Bordeaux. He is a very shadowy figure indeed. Only
a single other reference to him has survived to attest his
existence. A charter passed at Bourges in 887, a sale of land
in the Limousin by Eudes count of Toulouse to archbishop
Frotaire of Bordeaux, was witnessed by Amalvinus *comes*.[10]
His was hardly a name which would have readily occurred
to our hypothetical (and motiveless) forger. Third, although
the author of the letter describes with some precision—and
in so doing displays a familiarity with the coastal topography
of Galicia which might be considered surprising if he worked
in France—the site of Santiago de Compostela, he does not
refer to it *eo nomine*. The name, in this form, became widely
current from the second quarter of the eleventh century. It
did not exist in the time of Alfonso III. Fourth, some of the
Latin terms used seem (to my inexpert eye) to have rather an
early tenth-century 'look' than an eleventh or twelfth: for
instance, *apex, gerulus, ratis* or *virtutes*.

There is finally—and for me most convincingly—a ring
of authenticity about much of the text, hard to pin down,
but which is such as to inspire confidence. The degree of
fuss about the journey, the strong implication that such
a journey, with so precious a cargo, would be both difficult
and dangerous—this seems plausible at a time when the
Vikings dominated the western seaways. Or again, consider
the books mentioned in the letter. The king's reference to

[10] C. Higounet, *Bordeaux pendant le haut moyen âge* (Bordeaux, 1963), p. 43.

a work containing accounts of miracles worked by St. Martin during his lifetime is presumably to the *Vita* by Sulpicius Severus. We can show that this work was known in the Asturian kingdom at this time—hardly surprisingly, for it was the most famous piece of hagiography in western Christendom. Alfonso III himself possessed a copy, which he gave to the church of Oviedo in 908.[11] The other work to which the king referred was the seventh-century *Vitas sanctorum patrum Emeretensium*. Now this was a work which never circulated widely even within Spain. Indeed, its latest editor knows of only one reference to it in any medieval text—and that reference the very one we are discussing, in Alfonso III's letter.[12] Its citation there strikes a strong, clear note in favour of the letter's authenticity.

Alfonso III's letter to the clergy of Tours is certainly a very odd document. Odd enough to be credible? yes— though this, on its own, is a hazardous argument. There seem to me to be powerful reasons for accepting it for what it purports to be. Naturally, one's impressions are subjective. They can be nothing else, given the impossibility of applying to it the usual tests. At any rate, I am prepared to trust it.[13]

[11] A. C. Floriano, *Diplomática española del período astur* (Oviedo, 1949-51), II, no. 192: the text of the charter has been tampered with but the list of books seems genuine.

[12] *Vitas sanctorum patrum Emeretensium*, ed. and trans. J. N. Garvin (Washington, 1946), p. 1, and cf. also p. 448.

[13] So was Carl Erdmann, though I did not discover this until long after I had independently formed my own conclusions: see his *Forschungen zur politischen Ideenwelt des Frühmittelalters*, ed. F. Baethgen (Berlin, 1951), pp. 31-3. I am comforted to find myself in such distinguished company.

Appendix D

Notes on the intellectual life of the cathedral community of Santiago de Compostela under Diego Gelmírez

Not a single manuscript other than those texts concerned with the material interests of the see which may be securely associated with the *scriptorium* of Compostela during this period has yet been identified; possibly none has survived. Given this absence of materials which are rightly regarded as fundamental to an enquiry into this topic, there is very little that may be said.

Diego himself was not an 'intellectual'. He possessed the skills that a man in his position needed: familiarity with Visigothic law and with canon law.[1] He was aware of certain needs: for up-to-date canon law texts; for a reasonably well-educated cathedral chapter. He appointed foreign teachers to the office of *magister scolarum* in his cathedral church. The first of these was Gerald, who held office between *c*.1118 and *c*.1134. He was almost certainly a native of Beauvais, whose school was by no means undistinguished in the years about 1100. The second was a more shadowy figure, master Rainerio of Pistoia, who had studied in England, at Winchester (*Quintonia in Anglia*), and who seems to have succeeded Gerald during Diego's later years.[2] Diego encouraged promising young men to go to France to study.

---

[1] Visigothic law: Diego's remarks on sanctuary at *HC*, p. 228 seem to recall *Lex Visigothorum*, IX.3.1–2 (ed. Zeumer, p. 379). Canon law: *HC*, p. 166, from *Polycarpus*, VI.10.24 (*ex* Burchard, *ex* Isidore); *HC*, p. 178, from *Polycarpus*, VII.11.4 (*ex* Burchard); cf. also the citation of canon law in the episode of the Traba inheritance, *HC*, p. 477. Cardinal Gregory's work had not been wasted.

[2] *Acta Sanctorum, Iulii*, VI, pp. 26–7. This is the earliest reference to a school at Winchester in the twelfth century which we possess. Rainerio's studies at Winchester must have preceded by at least twenty years the tenure there as master of Jordan Fantosme attested in a letter of John of Salisbury of 1154–8,

It is significant that in Diego's day and later on higher education was something that was not available in Compostela.[3]

Diego presented the cathedral library with a few books.[4] Apart from liturgical books these included a *librum pastoralem* (Gregory the Great's *Cura Pastoralis?*), a book of *canones* (the *Polycarpus?*), a *librum de fide trinitatis et de aliis sententiis* (Augustine?), a *librum de vita episcoporum* (another candidate for the *Cura Pastoralis?* or perhaps some historical or hagiographical compilation?), and a theological compendium of some kind described as a *librum ex diversis sententiis*.

The *Historia Compostellana* is the only literary monument to the learning of Compostela in Diego's day. It can hardly be called a striking one. At its best its Latin is unadorned; at its worst, swollen and repetitive. But this is to judge it by twentieth-century canons of taste: it deserves the attention of a good Latinist.[5] Apart from the Bible there are occasional citations or reminiscences of Augustine (pp. 391, 579), Boethius (213), Cicero (587), Gregory the Great (205, 568), Horace (368) and Virgil (198, 334). In other words, there are no surprises. It is noteworthy that all these citations occur in those sections of the work which were composed by immigrants. It is also worthy of note that the author who was a native of Galicia twice took pride in the fact that on one occasion his bishop and on another occasion one of his colleagues were able to address assemblies in Latin.[6]

Such intellectual activity as there was at Compostela seems to have been directed almost exclusively to the

hitherto regarded as the earliest mention of the school: see N. Orme, *English schools in the middle ages* (London, 1973), p. 320. I owe this point to Dr P. P. A. Biller.

[3] *HC*, pp. 238, 346; *LFH* IV, ap. xl, pp. 99-101 (of 1169).

[4] *HC*, pp. 379-80.

[5] For the authors' use of the *cursus* see A. G. Biggs, *Diego Gelmírez, first archbishop of Compostela* (Washington, 1949), pp. xxxvi-xl.

[6] *HC*, pp. 79, 87. See also the important study of R. Wright, *Late Latin and Early Romance in Spain and Carolingian France* (Liverpool, 1982), chs. 4 and 5, especially pp. 220-7. Dr Wright convincingly argues that what is being referred to here is not knowledge of the Latin language as such but knowledge of 'Medieval Latin', that is, a new way of spelling and pronouncing the Latin language introduced from France into Spain after 1080.

consolidation and defence of rights claimed or exercised by bishop and chapter. This preoccupation contrasts markedly with the state of affairs in other churches which were undergoing intellectual modernization at this period; for example, the Canterbury of Lanfranc and Anselm.[7]

Lastly, it is only fair to point out that Galician *scriptoria* during the late eleventh and early twelfth centuries must have been kept so busy churning out the new liturgical books required by the change from the Visigothic to the Roman liturgy that their scribes would have had little if any time for copying other manuscripts. The change had officially occurred in 1080. But if even so important a monastic house as Samos had not equipped itself with the new texts by 1098,[8] one wonders when—and how—the parishes of the remoter parts of the diocese of Compostela acquired their new mass-books.

[7] See R. W. Southern, *Saint Anselm and his biographer* (Cambridge, 1963) and M. Gibson, *Lanfranc of Bec* (Oxford, 1978).

[8] AHN 1240/1 (forcing the sense a little, I must confess).

Appendix E

Cardinal Guido's first visit to Spain and the council of León, 1134

Guido, cardinal-deacon of SS. Cosmas and Damian, was promoted to the college of cardinals by Innocent II early in 1132 and was nominated papal chancellor by Eugenius III at the end of 1146. Between these dates he undertook three legatine journeys to Spain. The second of these occurred in 1136–7 and the third in 1143. The date of the first has never been satisfactorily established. It is known that during this first visit Guido held an ecclesiastical council, or attended a royal *curia*—and for our purposes it does not matter which —at the city of León. At this meeting the case of Bernardo of Compostela was discussed and Berengar, archdeacon of Toledo, was elected to the bishopric of Salamanca: these matters have been treated above, in chapter X. This assembly at León is referred to only in the *Historia Compostellana*, where it is not dated, though it seems to fall in 1134. Some historians have wished to place it in 1135 and to identify it with the *curia* held at León in the last week of May at which Alfonso VII was crowned emperor. But the *Chronica Adefonsi Imperatoris*, whose account of the imperial coronation and its associated gatherings is very full, says nothing of the cardinal's presence. This is an argument *e silentio*, but it seems to me to be a strong one. However, there is another, perhaps stronger. It has not been noticed by historians of Spanish affairs that cardinal Guido was sent on a mission to Milan in 1135 to win the city over from the antipope Anacletus to the Innocentian side in the papal schism that then divided western Christendom. It is just possible, but very unlikely, that he should have undertaken a legation to León-Castile as well in the same year. I maintain the contention advanced in chapter X that Guido's first legatine visit to Spain and the council of León belong to 1134, and that the council was probably held not later than August of that year.

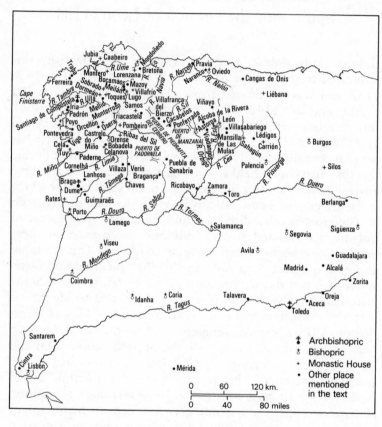

Map I. Western Spain and Portugal in the lifetime of Diego Gelmírez

Map II. The diocese of Santiago de Compostela in the lifetime of Diego Gelmírez

Index

Persons are entered under their given names rather than their patronymics, e.g. Pedro Froílaz de Traba under 'Pedro' rather than 'Froílaz'. Bishops of Iberian sees are normally entered under the name of the see, e.g. Nuño Alfonso, bishop of Mondoñedo is to be found under 'Mondoñedo': cross-references are provided for prominent and frequently-mentioned bishops, e.g. Bernardo, archbishop of Toledo; Diego Gelmírez gets an entry of his own. Popes and antipopes are entered under 'popes', and ecclesiastical councils under 'councils, ecclesiastical'.